A HISTORY OF
Emery County

A HISTORY OF
Emery County

Edward A. Geary

1996
Utah State Historical Society
Emery County Commission

ISBN 0-913738-050-0
Library of Congress Catalog Card Number 96-60167
Map by Automated Geographic Reference Center—State of Utah
Printed in the United States of America

Utah State Historical Society
300 Rio Grande
Salt Lake City, Utah 84101-1182

Contents

Acknowledgments

This project could not have been completed without the assistance of many people. The officers and members of the Emery County Historical Society have been most helpful in providing materials, correcting errors and omissions, and offering suggestions and support. I have tried to acknowledge specific obligations in chapter notes. I am especially grateful to Sylvia H. Nelson, coordinator of the county history project for the ECHS, who has gone far beyond the call of duty. County officers and courthouse employees have been unfailingly cooperative. Allan Kent Powell and Craig Fuller of the Division of State History were extremely helpful in ferreting out sources of information and in offering editorial advice.

This study would not have been possible without the work of those who have gone before. It will be apparent that I owe a large debt to the compilers of the Daughters of Utah Pioneers history, *Castle Valley* (cited in the notes as *CV*), and the Emery County Historical Society's *Emery County, 1880–1980* (cited as *EC 1880–1980*). I also express gratitude to the editors and correspondents of the *Emery County Progress* (cited as *ECP* or, from 1968 to

1977, as *ECPL*). I hope this newspaper's ninety-five years of service to the county will continue long into the future.

My grandparents Edward G. Geary, Huntington pioneer of 1884, and Grace Wakefield Geary, who belonged to the first generation born in Emery County, first awakened my interest in history by their talk of early times. That interest was further stimulated by the research of my father, Elmo G. Geary, into early theater and by the stories told by my mother, Estella Ungerman Geary Guymon. I am grateful for them and for all of the "old folks" whose lives have touched mine. I am grateful also for the support of my wife, Janet, and my children, who have endured with good grace my fascination with a place that must in the nature of things be for them another country.

In the course of my research, I have often indulged a lifelong habit of visiting the county's cemeteries and have come to feel something like a personal acquaintance with many of those memorialized there. They have kept me aware that the history of Emery County is the story of people working individually and in family and community groups. It is not possible in a work of this scope to do justice to all of those who have contributed to the making of the county. For every person included in this book, there are others equally worthy of mention. I hope my omissions will motivate readers to record and preserve their own personal and family histories, both as an intrinsically valuable legacy and as a resource for future work on the county's history.

General Introduction

When Utah was granted statehood on 4 January 1896, twenty-seven counties composed the nation's new forty-fifth state. Subsequently two counties, Duchesne in 1914 and Daggett in 1917, were created. These twenty-nine counties have been the stage on which much of the history of Utah has been played.

Recognizing the importance of Utah's counties, the Utah State Legislature established in 1991 a Centennial History Project to write and publish county histories as part of Utah's statehood centennial commemoration. The Division of State History was given the assignment to administer the project. The county commissioners or their designees were responsible for selecting the author or authors for their individual histories, and funds were provided by the state legislature to cover most research and writing costs as well as to provide each public school and library with a copy of each history. Writers worked under general guidelines provided by the Division of State History and in cooperation with county history committees. The counties also established a Utah Centennial County History Council to help develop policies for distribution of state-appropriated funds and plans for publication.

Each volume in the series reflects the scholarship and interpretation of the individual author. The general guidelines provided by the Utah State Legislature included coverage of five broad themes encompassing the economic, religious, educational, social, and political history of the county. Authors were encouraged to cover a vast period of time stretching from geologic and prehistoric times to the present. Since Utah's statehood centennial celebration falls just four years before the arrival of the twenty-first century, authors were encouraged to give particular attention to the history of their respective counties during the twentieth century.

Still, each history is at best a brief synopsis of what has transpired within the political boundaries of each county. No history can do justice to every theme or event or individual that is part of an area's past. Readers are asked to consider these volumes as an introduction to the history of the county, for it is expected that other researchers and writers will extend beyond the limits of time, space, and detail imposed on this volume to add to the wealth of knowledge about the county and its people. In understanding the history of our counties, we come to understand better the history of our state, our nation, our world, and ourselves.

In addition to the authors, local history committee members, and county commissioners, who deserve praise for their outstanding efforts and important contributions, special recognition is given to Joseph Francis, chairman of the Morgan County Historical Society, for his role in conceiving the idea of the centennial county history project and for his energetic efforts in working with the Utah State Legislature and State of Utah officials to make the project a reality. Mr. Francis is proof that one person does make a difference.

ALLAN KENT POWELL
CRAIG FULLER
GENERAL EDITORS

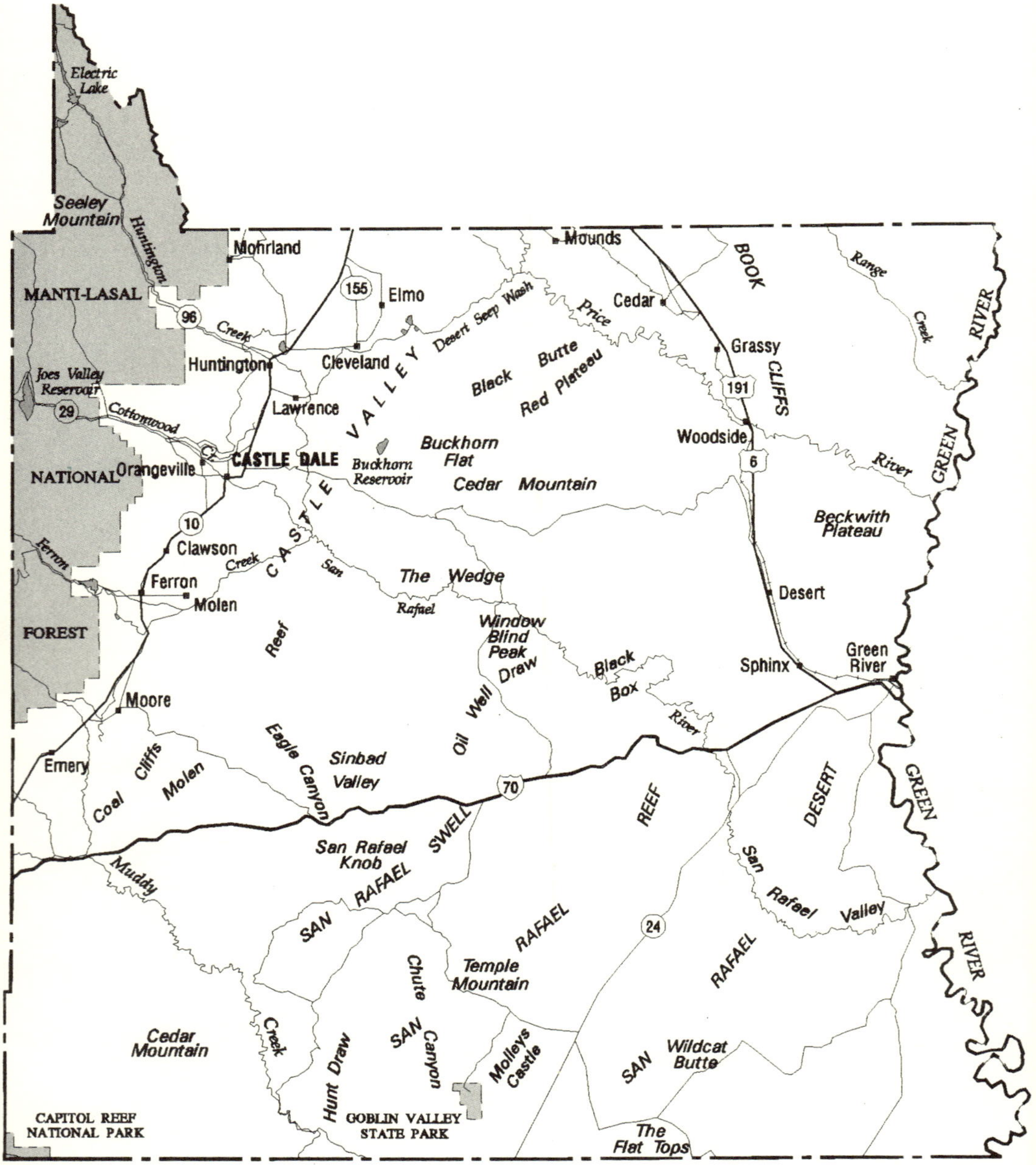

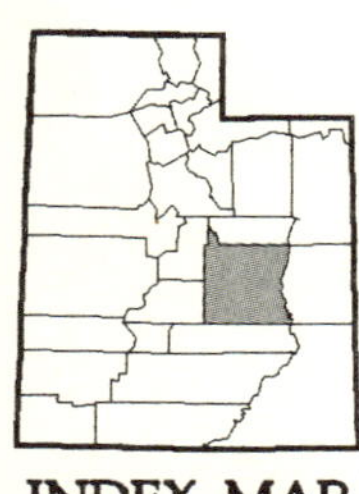

INDEX MAP

EMERY COUNTY

1

Where the Desert Meets the Mountains

Emery County is located in the southeastern quadrant of the state of Utah. It covers an area of 4,439 square miles in a roughly square outline and is bounded on the west by Sanpete and Sevier counties, on the north by Carbon County, on the east by Grand County, and on the south by Wayne County. The elevation ranges from under 4,000 feet at Saddlehorse Bottoms on the Green River to 10,728 feet at the summit of East Mountain. With only two exceptions, the county's borders are arbitrarily drawn political lines. The Green River forms a natural boundary on the east (although a shift in the streambed since the boundary was established has put a portion of the west bank in Grand County). The other natural border forms one side of a narrow "panhandle" at the county's northwest corner. This boundary line follows the ridge that divides the Huntington Creek watershed from that of the Price River.

The population of Emery County in 1990 was 10,332, most of whom resided in the county's nine incorporated cities and towns: Huntington (1,875), Castle Dale (1,704), Ferron (1,606), Orangeville (1,459), Green River (744 plus an additional 122 in Grand County),

Cleveland (498), Emery (300), Elmo (267), and Clawson (151). The most important industries are mining, electrical power generation, farming, livestock raising, and recreation and tourism. The county has been an important transportation corridor since prehistoric times when the Green River crossing provided a link between the Ute people in central Utah and those in western Colorado. The Green River crossing and Wasatch (Salina) Pass were key points on the Spanish Trail, a nineteenth-century trade route between the Hispanic settlements in New Mexico and those in California. Major transportation arteries today include the Denver-Salt Lake City main line of the Southern Pacific Railroad, which passes through Green River; Interstate 70, which crosses the entire width of the county; U.S. Highway 6, which connects Green River with Price, Carbon County; Utah Highway 10, which links the communities in the western part of the county with Price to the north and Interstate 70 to the south; Utah Highway 31, which crosses the Wasatch Plateau from Huntington to Fairview, Sanpete County; and Utah Highway 24, which provides access to the eastern portion of the San Rafael Swell with connections south to Wayne, Garfield, and San Juan counties.

The Lay of the Land

Emery County is situated at the western edge of the Colorado Plateau and exhibits the characteristic landscape elements of that large province, including massive uplifts, buttes, mesas, badland hills, deep canyons, and long lines of sheer erosional cliffs where thousands of feet of geologic strata are exposed with textbook clarity. There are five distinct physiographic regions in the county, including the Wasatch Plateau, the lowlands area commonly known as Castle Valley, the San Rafael Swell, the Green River Desert, and the West Tavaputs Plateau.

Wasatch Plateau. The Wasatch Plateau is the largest of the elevated tablelands that trend north and south through central and southern Utah and are known collectively as the High Plateaus of Utah. The High Plateaus form a transition zone between the Colorado Plateau province to the east and the Basin and Range province to the west. The transitional character of the Wasatch Plateau is evident in its drainage, with the western slopes belonging to the Sevier Lake and Utah Lake watersheds of the Great Basin and the eastern slopes draining into the Green and Colorado rivers.

The Wasatch Plateau is composed entirely of sedimentary deposits. It extends north and south for seventy miles and varies in width from about fifteen to twenty-five miles. The plateau's western wall is a monoclinal fold that rises at a steep angle from beneath the floor of Sanpete Valley to a continuous summit ridge reaching elevations above 11,000 feet. At the summit, the geologic strata become almost horizontal in a broad platform that extends to the eastern escarpment, which is a wall of erosion. This distinctive front of alternating sandstone cliffs and shale talus slopes forms an imposing skyline for the residents of Castle Valley.

The geology of the Wasatch Plateau is complicated by numerous north-south trending faults that have displaced the strata up and down. In some instances, these faults have formed "grabens," or rift valleys, created when a block of earth sinks below the adjacent terrain. The largest graben on the Wasatch Plateau is Joe's Valley, where the vertical displacement ranges from 1,500 to 3,000 feet. The Joe's Valley fault zone slices through the plateau from southeast to northwest, intersecting the drainage basins of the Ferron, Cottonwood, and Huntington creeks, and including Black Dragon Canyon, Scad Valley, and Miller Flat in addition to Upper and Lower Joe's valleys. Within the rift are two prominent "horsts," blocks that did not sink with the graben: Middle Mountain, which divides Upper from Lower Joe's Valley, and Bald Mountain, which divides Scad Valley from Miller Flat.[1]

The Wasatch Plateau has had a profound influence on the history, economy, and even the climate of Emery County. It formed a barrier to travel that deflected the early trails to the north and south and delayed the colonization of Castle Valley for more than two decades after Anglo-European settlements were established in Sanpete Valley. Its grazing lands and timber and coal deposits have been vital props to the Emery County economy from the beginning, and its deer and elk herds, its trout streams and lakes constitute important recreational resources. Most importantly, the plateau's abrupt uplift milks the moisture from Pacific storms during the winters, storing it in the form of snow on the broad uplands to be released gradually through the spring and summer to the streams that flow from the plateau and supply water to the otherwise arid lowlands.

John Wesley Powell, who led the first exploring parties through the canyons of the Green and Colorado rivers and whose ideas about the arid West were to have an important influence on national policy, proposed that political boundaries in the West should conform to watershed boundaries. If this advice had been heeded in the creation of Emery County, the western border would have followed the skyline ridge of the Wasatch Plateau. But political considerations intervened with the result that most of the high country, including the headwaters of Emery County streams, falls within the borders of Sanpete and Sevier counties. Because of the vital importance of these watersheds to Emery County, however, they will be treated throughout this book as if they were part of the county's territory—as they are certainly part of the county's history.

Four major creeks have their headwaters on the Wasatch Plateau and flow into Emery County. The northernmost of these, Huntington Creek, runs through a long, narrow canyon that slices diagonally into the Wasatch Plateau for more than thirty miles on a northwest-southeast axis. The main canyon and the Right Fork, which forms a continuation of the main canyon, drain portions of the Gentry, East, and Candland Mountain segments of the high plateau through numerous side canyons. Electric Lake, the largest impoundment on Huntington Creek, was created by damming the Right Fork some twenty miles above the canyon mouth. The Left Fork drains the northern portion of the Joe's Valley graben and its feeder canyons that descend from the skyline ridge. Cleveland, Huntington, Rolfson, and Miller Flat reservoirs are human-made impoundments occupying natural reservoir sites in the graben zone. In addition to these high-elevation reservoirs, some Huntington Creek water is stored in the Huntington North Reservoir, a low-elevation impoundment in Castle Valley.

Cottonwood Creek, the largest stream flowing from the Wasatch Plateau, was named for the numerous cottonwood trees on its valley bottomlands. It shares this name with a minor tributary that drains East and Trail mountains and joins the main creek at the mouth of

Straight Canyon. The major tributaries are Seely Creek and Lowry Water. The Lowry Water drainage basin is similar to the Left Fork of Huntington Creek. Several relatively short, steep canyons head in glacial cirques under the skyline ridge and drain into the Joe's Valley graben where their outflow is gathered into Lowry Water. Seely Creek also has its headwaters in glacial cirques near the skyline ridge but flows through a longer canyon and gathers tributaries from several side canyons before it reaches Lower Joe's Valley. Seely Creek and Lowry Water merge with the smaller Indian and North Dragon creeks in Lower Joe's Valley before entering Straight Canyon. Glacial moraines in the canyons above Joe's Valley provide natural reservoir sites that have been developed into small impoundments including Blue Lake, Grassy Lake, Academy Mill Reservoir, and Grass Flat Reservoir. The best reservoir site, however, recognized as such from early times, was the narrow passage from Joe's Valley into Straight Canyon. The Joe's Valley Reservoir was completed in 1966, the keystone of the Emery County Reclamation Project and the largest impoundment on the Wasatch Plateau except for Scofield Reservoir, which is similarly situated in another graben in Carbon County.

Ferron Creek drains a wide amphitheater with tributary canyons like the fingers of a spread hand. From north to south, the major canyons include Black Dragon (a southern extension of the Joe's Valley graben), Big Bear, Little Bear, Cove, Indian, Singleton, Wrigley, and Stevens. Here too small reservoirs have been built on glacial moraines, including Ferron, Duck Fork, and Wrigley Creek reservoirs. These lakes are currently maintained at a stable level for recreational purposes. The major impoundment for irrigation, industrial, and culinary water is Mill Site Reservoir, completed at the mouth of the canyon in 1971.

Muddy Creek is similar to Ferron Creek in that its drainage basin is an amphitheater with finger canyons. The chief tributaries are Horse Creek, North Fork, Beaver Creek, South Fork, and Cowboy Creek. Storage impoundments include Emery, Spinner's, Henningson, and Julius Flat reservoirs.

Most of the water from these creeks is consumed for irrigation, industrial, and domestic purposes in Castle Valley. The remaining flow of Huntington, Cottonwood, and Ferron creeks passes through "breaks" in the western reefs of the San Rafael Swell. These three streams then merge to form the San Rafael River, which cuts through the Swell and joins the Green River about twenty miles below Green River City. Muddy Creek flows through the southern part of the San Rafael Swell and joins the Fremont River near Hanksville, Wayne County, to form the Dirty Devil, which runs into the Colorado River in the upper reaches of Lake Powell.

In addition to these major creeks, several smaller streams, Cedar Creek, Rock Creek, and Quitchupah Creek, also emerge from canyons in the Wasatch Plateau and join the larger streams in Castle Valley. The southern third of Emery County has the Fish Lake Plateau as a natural western boundary. Except for Ivie Creek, a perennial Muddy Creek tributary, the major Fish Lake Plateau drainage runs in other directions, and only intermittent streams, Last Chance, Solomon, and Salvation creeks, sometimes reach Emery County before they sink into the desert soil. The Price River, which heads in the northern Wasatch Plateau, passes through northeastern Emery County on its course to its confluence with the Green.

The landscape characteristics and flora and fauna of the Wasatch Plateau vary according to the elevation and precipitation pattern. The skyline ridge is tundralike, with low shrubs and grasses, scattered groves of stunted aspens and subalpine fir, and some bristlecone pines. The canyons descending from the skyline typically have dense climax forests of Englemann spruce and Douglas fir on the north-facing slopes and groves of quaking aspen on the bottomlands and the south-facing slopes. The Wasatch Plateau is host to one of the largest aspen forests in North America, and in favored locations the trees attain to great size. In the lower canyons, the aspens give way to narrowleaf cottonwoods. The Colorado blue spruce is a prominent stream-side tree, as are water birch, chokecherry, and bigtooth maple. An immense variety of wildflowers grow at every elevation of the plateau, blooming in a colorful sequence from early spring until late fall. East of the Joe's Valley graben are the tablelike platforms of North and South Horn and Nelson Mountain. A similar wide shelf extends from Muddy Creek Canyon south to Old Woman Plateau, overlooking Ivie Creek. These tablelands, at elevations ranging from 8,000 to 9,000 feet, lie in the rain shadow of the higher ridges and resemble broad plains with mixed bunch-grass and sagebrush and scattered groves of Ponderosa pine.

Wildlife on the Wasatch Plateau is typical of the High Plateau region, with abundant mule deer, one of the largest elk herds in Utah, and a few moose transplanted by wildlife agencies in an attempt to establish a breeding population. At one time the plateau supported a population of mountain bighorn sheep and perhaps mountain goats, but these species are no longer found here. Bears were reportedly numerous on the plateau in the nineteenth century, and a population remains though reduced in numbers. Mountain lions inhabit the rocky ledges. Coyotes and bobcats are at home in the high country as well as in the lower valleys. There are numerous beaver, porcupines, yellow-bellied marmots, squirrels, chipmunks, and the all-pervasive little rodents best known as "potbellies." Golden eagles and several species of hawks can be seen on summer days soaring on the thermals above the plateau. Other birdlife includes sage grouse, mountain bluebirds, crested woodpeckers, and several kinds of waterfowl. The reservoirs and streams of the Wasatch Plateau are popular trout fisheries, with a naturalized population of native cutthroat in remote streams and planted rainbow trout in more heavily fished areas.

Coal has been mined from the Wasatch Plateau since before 1875. Numerous small "wagon mines" have operated in the plateau canyons over the years. One major coal camp, Mohrland, was established in Emery County. Most of the coal produced by the Hiawatha mines came from Emery County, but the mine portals and the town were in Carbon County. The extensive deposits in the southern part of the Wasatch Plateau were not fully exploited until recent years, when the construction of coal-burning electrical generating plants led to the development of large mines in East and Trail mountains. Natural gas has also been produced on the Wasatch Plateau.

Castle Valley. Castle Valley is not a true valley by the usual definition but rather a lowland plain eroded into the Mancos shale between the uplifts of the Wasatch Plateau and the San Rafael Swell. It is narrow at the south end, where Molen Reef comes near to the high plateau escarpment, and widens toward the north, continuing into Carbon County, where it follows the base of the Tavaputs Plateau back into Emery County and on through Grand County to western Colorado. While the lowlands are continuous, they are known by several different names: Castle Valley in the western portion, Clark Valley east of Price, and Grand Valley east of the Green River. Several river valleys cross the lowland plain. These valleys and the adjacent benchlands, at elevations ranging from 5,700 to 6,300 feet, are the site of agricultural lands and towns and villages: Huntington and Lawrence on Huntington Creek, and Cleveland and Elmo on irrigable benchlands to the east; Orangeville and Castle Dale on Cottonwood Creek; Ferron and Molen on Ferron Creek, and Clawson on a bench between Ferron Creek and Rock Canyon Wash; Emery on a bench south of Muddy Creek and Moore on a bench to the north.

Lying in the rain shadow of the Wasatch Plateau, Castle Valley is a region of little precipitation, averaging less than ten inches per year. The predominant Mancos shale soil is lacking in fertility, almost devoid of organic matter, and permeated with alkaline salts. In the arid climate, this soil yields little except greasewood (which predominates in the most alkaline locations), mat saltbush (known locally as "Castle Valley clover"), and shadscale, plus a thin growth of annual forbs. The benchlands typically have a layer of gravelly material on top of the Mancos shale. This is a more fertile soil that supports native bunchgrasses, sagebrush, prickly pear cactus, and on the higher benches pinyon-juniper woodlands. The best agricultural land in the valley is the alluvial loam of the river valleys, but the gravel benches are also productive where water can be brought to them. Native wildlife includes some mule deer that winter in the valley, coyotes, foxes, rabbits and hares, grounddogs, badgers, skunks, and a native birdlife including magpies, swallows, meadowlarks, crows, blackbirds, and several species of hawks and owls.

Castle Valley has a distinct four-season climate. Winters are typically cold but sunny with little accumulation of snow. Normal maximum temperatures in January are in the midthirties and minimums near ten degrees Fahrenheit. It is not uncommon, however, to have daytime highs near fifty and nighttime lows below zero. Spring tends to be a harsh, blustery season with brief periods of pleasant weather. Except in a few favored microclimates, late frosts are an almost annual threat to farmers and gardeners. Summers are characterized by hot, sunny days with normal July temperatures in the nineties. Nights, however, are almost always pleasant because the Wasatch Plateau canyons serve as a natural air-conditioning system, discharging a flow of cool mountain air shortly after sunset. July and August are the monsoon months when tropical moisture drifts in from the south to produce scattered thunderstorms with attendant flash flooding. Fall is perhaps the most pleasant season in Castle Valley, typically dry and mild well into November.

San Rafael Swell. The San Rafael Swell is a massive anticlinal uplift some seventy-five miles long and thirty miles wide, located entirely within the boundaries of Emery County and occupying about half the county's area. When originally formed during the mountain-building period known as the Laramide Orogeny, the Swell might have resembled a kidney-shaped, inverted bowl. However, subsequent erosion has cut through the various geologic strata until the Swell now comprises a series of concentric rocky ridges or "reefs" separated by racetrack valleys surrounding a relatively level interior area known as Sinbad. The eastern and southern boundaries are formed by a steep monoclinal fold known as the San Rafael Reef. The western boundary is buried beneath the Mancos shale of Castle Valley. Cedar Mountain is a northern extension of the main uplift. Once difficult of access, the region has been opened to visitors by Interstate 70, which cuts directly through the middle of the Swell.

The erosional formations of the San Rafael Swell are the main source of the name Castle Valley. The "castles" form a dramatic southeastern skyline extending from Windowblind Butte (7,030 feet) to the San Rafael Knob (7,921), especially striking at sunrise and sunset. The San Rafael Reef gives Green River City a similarly castellated western skyline. Numerous other reefs, buttes, pinnacles, and cliffs are to be found within the Swell.

The Swell's canyons are as remarkable as its castles. The San Rafael River has carved a gorge popularly known as the Little Grand Canyon between the Wedge and Sid's Mountain. The river passes through the San Rafael Reef by way of the Black Box. The most dramatic portion of Muddy Creek's thirty-mile-long canyon is the Chute, where the stream passes through the San Rafael Reef.

Numerous desert canyons—Cane Wash, Saddle Horse Canyon, Coal Wash, Eagle Canyon, North Salt Wash, Devil's Canyon, Red's Canyon—begin near the Head of Sinbad and cut several hundred feet into the Wingate and Navajo sandstones as they drain their rare floodwaters north to the San Rafael or south to the Muddy. Other canyons drain into the San Rafael River from the north, including Pine Canyon, Spring Canyon, and Buckhorn Draw with its tributaries Calf and Cow canyons. Numerous short canyons cut into the San Rafael Reef bearing such names as Wild Horse, Spotted Wolf, and Black Dragon. The major canyons in Cedar Mountain are Bull Hollow and Humbug.

Though often referred to by Emery County residents as "the desert," the San Rafael Swell is by no means barren. Indeed, the Swell's potential as grazing land was among the chief attractions that brought settlers into the region. The higher portions of Sinbad, reaching elevations above 7,000 feet, and extensive mesas such as Sid's Mountain support a good growth of native bunch grasses. Cedar Mountain has extensive pinyon-juniper woodlands. Ponderosa pines and oakbrush are found in several sheltered elevated locations. Scattered springs and seeps create oases with birches, chokecherries, and other water-loving shrubs. The three rivers, Price, San Rafael, and Muddy, that cut through the Swell in apparent obliviousness to routes of less resistance, have floodplains lined with Fremont cottonwoods, willows, and tamarisk. Wildlife includes the species found in Castle Valley plus antelope, desert bighorn sheep, and wild horses and burros.

The vast expanse of exposed rock in the San Rafael Swell has intrigued prospectors for more than a century. Efforts to locate commercially viable deposits of copper, lead, marble, gypsum, and other minerals have brought recurrent excitement but no substantial production. Oil seeps and asphaltic rocks have periodically attracted drillers, but no commercial oil fields have thus far been found. Uranium was mined at Temple Mountain and Tidwell Draw from the early years of the twentieth century. The uranium rush of the 1950s brought renewed production from those areas as well as the Delta–Hidden Splendor deposit and several smaller deposits. Despite this history of exploration and hopeful development, however, the

San Rafael Swell remains essentially unpeopled. While stockmen, rockhounds, hikers, and off-road vehicle riders flock to the region each year, and many thousands pass through the heart of the Swell on Interstate 70, there are no permanent, year-round human habitations in the San Rafael Swell. The 110 miles from Green River to Salina represent the longest stretch without services on the entire Interstate Highway System.

Green River Desert. Between the San Rafael Reef and the Green River lies the Green River Desert, a region of sandy plains, isolated buttes, and sparse vegetation. The San Rafael River has carved a broad valley across the desert, with a flood plain covered with Fremont cottonwoods, the site over the years of several ranching operations. Near the southeastern corner of Emery County, the ground rises toward the Robbers Roost country in adjacent Wayne County. Horseshoe or Barrier Canyon, heading in the Robbers Roost and running north into Emery County is a striking desert gorge and site of some of the most important examples of prehistoric rock art.

The Green River Valley is a pleasant oasis in this desert landscape.[2] The river emerges from Gray Canyon and flows between low banks for several miles before rising ground confines it within the walls of Labyrinth Canyon. Water diverted from the river irrigates several thousand acres of farmland on both banks. The valley's 4,100-foot elevation gives it a significantly longer growing season than other parts of Emery County and makes possible the widely known Green River melons.

The Green River crossing, the only easily accessible point on the river in several hundred miles of canyonlands, has played a long and vital role in the history of Western exploration and transportation. This role continues as both Interstate 70 and the main Denver-to-Salt Lake line of the Southern Pacific Railroad cross the river at this point. In addition, Green River State Park serves as the ending point for recreational river trips through Desolation and Gray canyons, and the starting point for trips through Labyrinth and Stillwater canyons. Fertile bottomlands extending both upstream and down from Green River Valley have been the site of ranching operations in earlier years, remnants of which remain in the form of fruit trees and historic names such as Bull Canyon, Range Creek, and Saddle Horse Bottom.

Tavaputs Plateau. The Tavaputs Plateau is an elevated table occupying the northern and eastern portions of Carbon County, cutting through the northeastern corner of Emery County, and continuing eastward through Grand County into Colorado. This plateau is popularly known as the Book Cliffs, but strictly speaking that name should apply only to the sandstone escarpment at the base of the plateau. The Roan or Brown Cliffs form another escarpment at a higher elevation on the Tavaputs Plateau. The plateau itself is far more extensive than these two cliff lines, however. It is a wide tableland about 1,000 feet lower than the Wasatch Plateau in average elevation and therefore a less productive watershed but perhaps a more productive range, since it does not include the subalpine tundra.

Only a small wedge of the Tavaputs Plateau extends into Emery County. The Book Cliffs form an almost continuous cliff face along the plateau front, broken only by Horse Canyon, just inside the county line, and by the canyon cut through the plateau by the Price River on its way to join the Green. The triangle of plateau south of this canyon is known as the Beckwith Plateau, named for Lieutenant E. G. Beckwith, a member of the 1853 Gunnison expedition and the compiler of the expedition's report. Several canyons descend from the plateau uplands to join the Green River in Gray Canyon. The largest of these is Range Creek, which heads near the highest point on the plateau in Carbon County and flows southeast into Emery County through a narrow valley. Several historic ranching operations have been associated with the Tavaputs Plateau and particularly with Range Creek. The flora and fauna of the Tavaputs Plateau are similar to those found at comparable elevations on the Wasatch Plateau.

The Tavaputs Plateau has been a major coal producer. Its largest mine was at Horse Canyon, just inside Emery County's borders. However, the town built to house the miners (originally known as Dragerton, more recently as East Carbon City) is located in Carbon County.

Geology

The oldest exposed rock in Emery County is the Coconino sandstone that forms the lower walls of the Black Box on the San Rafael River and the Chute on Muddy Creek. Older strata dating to the

Cambrian period have been penetrated by drill holes. The Coconino formation belongs to the Permian period, dated by geologists at more than 250 million years ago, and was evidently deposited during a dry climate. The Kaibab limestone that sits atop the Coconino and forms wide benches in the eastern and southern parts of the Swell was deposited on the bottom of a warm sea described as extending west from the Gulf of Mexico and covering much of what is now the southwestern United States.

Rocks from the Triassic period (about 245 to 208 million years ago) are exposed over large parts of the Swell. The Moenkopi formation has three fairly distinct layers, including the Black Dragon member, a blue-gray or yellow-gray siltstone; the Sinbad limestone that forms benches surrounding Sinbad Valley; and an upper member of red-brown or gray siltstone. These formations had their origins in a time when an arm of the Pacific Ocean extended eastward into Utah, leaving deposits of various kinds as it periodically retreated or advanced. Sometime in the middle of the Triassic period, the Pacific was shifted westward by the rising ground of the Mesocordilleran High in what is now eastern Nevada. The area that is now Emery County then became part of a large interior basin with a climate ranging from semihumid to arid. Under these conditions, the rocks of the Chinle group were deposited, including the Moss Back sandstone that has been the most productive source of uranium ore in the San Rafael Swell, including the deposits at Temple Mountain and Hidden Splendor.

Toward the end of the Triassic period and in the early Jurassic (208 to 144 million years ago), the climate grew more arid, and massive dunes of windblown sand spread across the land. These dunes eventually became the cliff-forming Wingate and Navajo sandstones, separated by the river-deposited Kayenta formation. Wingate cliffs surround the Head of Sinbad. Wingate, Kayenta, and Navajo formations are all apparent in Buckhorn Draw. In the mid-Jurassic period, a sea extended south from Canada into central and eastern Utah. The marine waters deposited immense quantities of salt in a deep trough located under the present Wasatch Plateau and Sanpete and Sevier valleys. The shallower water that covered the present San Rafael Swell deposited the gypsum-laden San Rafael Group, including the Carmel formation, the Entrada sandstone, and the Curtis and Summerville formations. The Carmel formation covers wide expanses of Buckhorn Flat, North Salt Wash, and the area east of Cedar Mountain. The grotesque sculptures of Goblin Valley are carved from Entrada sandstone. The greenish-gray Curtis formation and the thin-bedded Summerville are found along the western and northern edges of the Swell.

During the latter part of the Jurassic period, the sea retreated and Emery County was on a wide plain fed by rivers flowing from the west and south. The Brushy Basin and Salt Wash members of the Morrison formation that make a broad band across the western edge of the San Rafael Swell are products of this period. The abundant fossil record indicates that the landscape included forests of Sequoia and other large trees, and shallow lakes filled with freshwater mollusks. Dinosaurs roamed the plain, including the Allosaurus found in large numbers at the Cleveland-Lloyd quarry.[3]

The Cretaceous period (144 to 66 million years ago) began with several million years of erosion, rather than deposition, in what is now Emery County. About 110 million years ago, deposits gradually started to accumulate, once again carried by rivers from higher country in what is now western Utah. The Cedar Mountain formation laid down during this period resembles the Morrison so closely that it was not identified as a distinct formation until 1944, by Cleveland native William Lee Stokes. The most conspicuous member of the Cedar Mountain formation is the Buckhorn conglomerate that predominates in the area around Buckhorn Reservoir and on the western slopes of Cedar Mountain. The fossil record from the early Cretaceous period has been rather scanty, especially for dinosaurs. Hence the great paleontological significance of the Long Walk Quarry, opened in 1986 in the Cedar Mountain formation southeast of Castle Dale. While excavations are still in a relatively early stage, specimens already discovered do much to fill in the fossil gap between dinosaurs of the late Jurassic period and those of the late Cretaceous.[4] Above the Cedar Mountain formation is the Dakota sandstone, a thin, hard formation found around the western and northern edges of the San Rafael Swell.

The Sevier Orogeny, or mountain-building episode, dated by

geologists between 80 and 100 million years ago, brought a massive uplifting of what is now western Utah, accompanied by the subsidence of eastern Utah to elevations below sea level. Seas swept into the region from the east, with the shoreline successively advancing and retreating through Emery County. These conditions persisted for some 60 million years, during which time marine deposits more than a mile deep were laid down over the region. When the sea was shallow, sandy deposits were washed down from the western mountains. When the sea advanced, muddy sediments accumulated, eventually becoming shale. When Emery County was a low-lying coastal plain, great forests and swamps grew in the river deltas. Advancing waters then buried the organic material under fresh deposits of sand or mud, and the pressure of the growing overburden changed the organic deposits to coal.

This entire series of deposits is known as the Mancos shale group. Its oldest member, the Tununk shale, forms the hills and flats east of Desert Lake and in the valley where the Castle Dale-Buckhorn road crosses Huntington Creek. Next comes the Ferron sandstone that caps Molen Reef and contains the coal fields southeast of Emery. The Blue Gate shale is the notorious "blue clay" of Castle Valley. It continues around the base of the Tavaputs Plateau to Green River and beyond. The lower cliffs in the Wasatch Plateau escarpment are made up of Emery sandstone. The thick talus slope between the Emery and Star Point sandstones is Masuk shale. The Star Point sandstone can be traced as a distinct cliff line all along the Wasatch Plateau. It became an important marker for economic geologists because it was early recognized that the lower part of the Black Hawk formation above the Star Point was the most likely place to find commercially valuable seams of coal. Above the Black Hawk is the cliff-making Price River formation, whose most conspicuous member is the Castle Gate sandstone. The Book Cliffs are composed of the Price River and adjacent formations.

Near the beginning of the Tertiary period, some 65 million years ago, the San Rafael Swell was uplifted as part of a more extensive mountain-building episode known as the Laramide Orogeny. The area that is now the Wasatch Plateau was then a basin between higher regions to the east and west. This basin was filled by a long, relatively narrow body of fresh water known as Flagstaff Lake. Rivers draining into the lake deposited the sediments that became the North Horn formation that covers most of the Wasatch Plateau today. The skeletons of mollusks and other animals settled to the lake bottom and became the Flagstaff limestone that caps many high peaks and ridges and forms the massive cliffs of White Mountain, west of Emery. The river-deposited Colton formation is found little if at all on the portion of the Wasatch Plateau in Emery County but appears farther north in Carbon County and forms part of the Roan Cliffs that cap the Tavaputs Plateau. Later deposits of the Green River formation are also found on the Tavaputs.

The disappearance of the early Tertiary lakes was followed by a 25-million-year period of volcanic activity that largely missed Emery County except for some intrusive dikes in the southwestern corner. During this period, the entire Intermountain region rose from near sea level to its present elevation of a mile or more. The greater elevation increased the energy of the streams. The Colorado River captured the Green River (which had previously flowed east from Wyoming into the Missouri River drainage) and consolidated the drainage of eastern Utah, including the Price, San Rafael, and Muddy rivers. To the west, the Great Basin subsided, and the Wasatch Plateau was uplifted. What we now recognize as the Emery County landscape was taking shape.[5]

During the last several million years, the great escarpments of the Wasatch and Tavaputs plateaus have retreated and deposited some of their rock on the gravel pediment benches that extend into the shale lowlands. The San Rafael Swell acquired its dramatic architecture from the differential erosion of its harder and softer strata. The Green River cut its canyons. Faulting on the Wasatch Plateau produced the Joe's Valley graben. During the ice ages that ended only some ten thousand years ago, glaciers carved cirques into the higher ridges of the Wasatch Plateau and left moraine deposits on what would later become reservoir sites. Huge mammals roamed the region, including the mastodons whose skeletal remains have been discovered in several locations and the Columbian mammoth unearthed near Huntington Reservoir in 1988, almost unique in its state of preservation and in the high elevation at which it was found. By the time the ice-age mammals disappeared (and perhaps contributing to their disappearance), humans had taken up residence in what is now Emery County.

Prehistory

Paleo-Indian Culture. Anthropologists use the term Paleo-Indian to designate the period from about 12,000 to 8,500 years before the present. Only scattered artifacts from this period have been discovered in the Emery County region, most notably fluted projectile points of a size to suggest that the Paleo-Indian people hunted big game, including mammoths, camels, bison, and giant sloths. The earliest Paleo-Indian cultural complex clearly identified in Utah is the Llano, dating to around 11,000 years before the present.[6] What has been described as "the first unequivocal specimen" of a Clovis point from the Llano culture was discovered in 1964 on the ridge between Acord Lake and the head of Convulsion Canyon.[7]

After the Llano complex came the Folsom complex, dating from about 11,000 to 10,000 years before the present. Folsom projectile points resemble Clovis points but are somewhat smaller and more finely chipped.[8] A possible Folsom point was discovered by Homer Behunin in the wall of Horn Silver Wash, about twelve miles east of Ferron.[9] Most Clovis and Folsom artifacts have been found at elevations between 5,000 and 6,000 feet, suggesting that the Paleo-Indian people occupied the Castle Valley lowlands. As the climate became warmer, however, the game may have retreated to the higher elevations on the Wasatch Plateau.[10] This may explain why the Huntington Mammoth was found at an elevation of 9,000 feet, and why a projectile point identified as a possible "Pryor stemmed point" dating to approximately 9,500 years ago was found near the recovery site.[11] Stemmed projectile points were characteristic of the later stages of the Paleo-Indian era.

Archaic Culture. As the large ice-age mammals disappeared, the Paleo-Indians were compelled to rely on a wider variety of animal and plant resources. Over the period from about 8,300 to 7,500 years before the present, the Paleo-Indian culture in the Colorado Plateau region evolved into the Archaic culture, characterized by side-notched projectile points and migratory hunting and gathering practices. Populations and lifestyles varied in keeping with changing climatic conditions, but Emery County was occupied during all four identified phases of the Archaic era. Components from the Black Knoll phase (8,300 to 6,200 years before the present) have been found in the Joe's Valley Alcove and in Sudden Shelter in Ivie Creek Canyon. The Castle Valley phase (6,200 to 4,500 years before the present) experienced a drought period and a population decline, with an increased dietary reliance on grasses and forbs. Sudden Shelter is among the few sites containing remains from this phase. The Green River phase (4,500 to 3,300 years before the present) brought a resurgence of hunting, especially for mountain sheep. Remains have been found at Sudden Shelter, Joe's Valley Alcove, and Pint Size Shelter east of Ferron. The final Archaic phase, the Dirty Devil, brought a more sedentary lifestyle and the introduction of the bow and arrow and of corn. The period from about 1,800 to 1,500 years before the present (A.D. 200–500) was a transition period from the Archaic culture to the Fremont culture.[12]

Fremont Culture. Emery County was an important center for the Fremont culture and home to what is known as the San Rafael variant. Judging from archaeological sites, the Fremont people were probably most numerous in the region from Ferron Creek to Ivie Creek, but remains of their dwellings and storage structures have been found in Joe's Valley and the lower canyons of the Wasatch Plateau, throughout Castle Valley, the San Rafael Swell, Range Creek, and the Green River canyons.

Most Fremont sites in Emery County appear to date to the Muddy Creek phase from about A.D. 700 to 1000. During this period a largely sedentary, agricultural lifestyle developed, though much of the diet still depended on seasonal migration and hunting and gathering practices. Rabbits, prairie dogs, ground squirrels, and deer provided most of the animal protein in the Fremont diet.[13] The period was characterized by plain Emery Gray pottery, a variety of dwelling structure styles, and corner-notched arrow heads.[14] The later Bull Creek phase (A.D. 1000–1200) seems to have developed during a wet cycle that allowed for more extensive agriculture and larger dwelling groups. The Emery Gray pottery became more decorated, and the Ivie Creek Black-on-White style appeared, as did a larger number of

Anasazi trade wares, coursed masonry dwelling and storage structures, and the intriguing clay figurines found at Range Creek and the Ferron area. The Fremont people evidently practiced ditch irrigation as well as flood irrigation. Remains of irrigation ditches were reportedly found near the mouth of Ferron Canyon when the Anglo settlers first arrived.[15] Some scholars have suggested on the basis of a study of Clyde's Cavern, east of Ferron, that the Fremont Dent variety of corn that became a Fremont staple may have been developed in the Emery County area.[16]

Excavations at several sites, including Innocents Ridge, east of Ferron, Old Woman, south of Emery, and three sites near Cedar Creek, north of Huntington, have indicated a pattern of small village sites, typically made up of fewer than a dozen dwellings. Fremont architecture in the Emery County area was "the most varied and elaborate of the five Fremont regions." It included three basic types of dwelling structures: semisubterranean pit dwellings, ranging from circular to rectangular, lined with large slabs of stone; coursed masonry and adobe dwellings with wall heights from four to six feet; and boulder-lined dwellings using tightly spaced basaltic rocks one to two feet in diameter. In general, stone was used more extensively by the San Rafael Fremonts than by other Fremont groups. Slab-lined storage cists are found only in Emery County. The predominant pottery type is called Emery Gray.[17]

The Homer Behunin collection of Fremont artifacts provides striking insights into the culture's craftsmanship, even though individual items were not fully documented in their cultural context. In the collection are several unbaked clay figurines recovered from a sealed storage cist three miles east of Ferron. These figurines resemble the Pilling figurines from Range Creek, with appliqued clay facial features and ornaments. The collection also includes a small female figurine of fired clay, remarkable for its detail and its modeling in the round; a figurine carved from red stone, found near Fremont Junction; and three wooden figurines from Ferron Canyon, two of which resemble Hopi Kachina figurines. There are also several animal-like figurines carved from bone, decorative items, and awls and needles also made from bone; a pipe made from deer antlers; and numerous pottery items and a wide variety of chipped stone points and blades. One of the most intriguing items is a clay disk with radiating wooden spokes, which may resemble the legendary Hopi "water plant," intended to create springs of water.[18]

The Fremont culture disappeared around A.D. 1200, at about the same time as Shoshonean peoples, ancestors of the Utes and Paiutes, migrated to Utah from the southwestern Great Basin.[19] It is an unsolved mystery whether the Fremont people were absorbed into the hunting and gathering culture of the Shoshoneans or whether they migrated south, perhaps joining the agricultural Hopi or Pueblo peoples.

Rock Art. Emery County is a virtual museum of prehistoric rock art, with many fine examples of both petroglyphs (etched into the rock) and pictographs (drawn or painted on the rock surface). Most of these are thought to be products of the Fremont culture. There was a distinctive San Rafael art style just as there were distinctive architectural styles. Fremont rock art panels typically incorporate anthropomorphs (human-like figures), sometimes wearing what appears to be ceremonial costume; zoomorphs (animal-like figures), most commonly what appear to be representations of sheep and snakes; and abstract figures, including circles, concentric circles, rainbow arcs, and wavy lines. Sometimes the anthropomorphs are depicted with exaggerated genitalia, suggesting that they might be fertility icons. Occasionally a humped-back flute player appears, resembling the Kokopeli figure of the Hopi.

Compared with the Fremont rock art of the Uinta Basin, the San Rafael style tends to have more crowded panels with numerous small figures, anthropomorphs that are smaller and less elaborately decorated—sometimes merely stick figures—and a higher proportion of abstract elements. There are excellent examples of this style at the high point overlooking the junction of Rochester Wash with Muddy Creek, at Dry Wash east of Moore, at the Indian War Camp site on Molen Reef, near Buckhorn Reservoir, and in Buckhorn Draw. Less typical panels are to be found in Ferron Canyon, in the Ferron Box below Molen, and at the Sid and Charley site near Sand Wash.[20] There are also numerous Fremont petroglyphs in Range Creek Canyon and along the Green River in Gray Canyon.

Another style of rock art found in Emery County is the Barrier

Restored Buckhorn Draw Pictograph Panel. (Courtesy Reed E. Martin)

Canyon style, thought by some scholars to predate the Fremont era. This style takes its name from the Great Gallery in Barrier or Horseshoe Canyon, an immense panel located in Wayne County a short distance south of the Emery County border. This style is characterized by highly abstract, elongated anthropomorphs, sometimes heroic in size, with small extremities or none at all, sometimes wearing headdresses, and often with large staring eyes producing a ghostlike effect. Zoomorphs are also highly abstract.[21] Fine Barrier Canyon panels are located at the Head of Sinbad. There are red Barrier Canyon style paintings as well as Fremont petroglyphs in Buckhorn Draw, in Quitchupah Canyon, and at Temple Mountain Wash. The so-called "dragon" and "praying dog" in Black Dragon Canyon are probably Barrier Canyon work. In addition to the better known panels, there are dozens of Fremont and Barrier Canyon sites known only to a few stockmen and rock hounds. Lee M. Swasey of Ferron has recorded some 226 rock art sites in Emery County.[22]

Utes. When the first Europeans entered eastern Utah, what is now Emery County was part of the Ute domain. The Ute people were composed of several fairly distinct bands that occupied homelands in central and eastern Utah and western Colorado. Although the bands sometimes raided one another, they shared a common language and culture, and trade and ceremonial interchange were carried on from band to band. Maps of Ute homelands do not locate any particular band in what is now Emery County. Yet the accounts of early travelers indicate that there were Utes in the area. The San Pitch band, headquartered in the Sanpete and Sevier valleys, probably also made extensive use of western Emery County, as they continued to do on a seasonal basis well into the settlement era. Early explorers found established trails across the Wasatch Plateau, including trails through Rock Canyon and Convulsion Canyon that provided routes between Castle Valley and the high country without the impediment of the stream meanders in the larger canyons.

The Green River Valley, with its riverine plant life and access to the hunting grounds on the Tavaputs Plateau, was a permanent or semipermanent dwelling site, perhaps for members of the Sheberetch band that also occupied the Dirty Devil region and the area at the base of the LaSal Mountains. It is likely that the Green River crossing was also used in the commerce between the large Tumpanawach band of Utah Valley and the Utes of western Colorado.

ENDNOTES

1. Stokes and Cohenour, *Geological Atlas of Utah,* 46.

2. This valley appears on some maps as Gunnison Valley. However, there are several other Gunnison valleys in Utah and Colorado. To avoid possible confusion, and in deference to local usage, the designation Green River Valley will be used in this book.

3. Stokes, *Geology of Utah,* 98, 115–19.

4. DeCourten, "Long Walk Quarry," 15–22.

5. Stokes, *Geology of Utah,* 131–34, 148–51, 167–69, 189, 194–95.

6. Black and Metcalf, "Castle Valley Archaeological Project," 7.

7. George W. Tripp, "A Clovis Point from Central Utah," *American Antiquity* 31 (January 1966): 435.

8. Black and Metcalf, "Castle Valley Archaeological Project," 7.

9. James H. Gunnerson, "A Fluted Point Site in Utah," *American Antiquity* 21 (1955–56): 412–14.

10. Alan R. Schroedl, "Paleo-Indian Occupation in the Eastern Great Basin and Northern Colorado Plateau," *Utah Archaeology 1991,* 8–9.

11. Newsletter of College of Eastern Utah Prehistoric Museum, 1989.

12. Black and Metcalf, "Castle Valley Archaeological Project," 9–12.

13. Madsen, "Fremont Sites," 15.

14. Black and Metcalf, "Castle Valley Archaeological Project," 13.

15. Gunnerson, "Fremont Culture," 137–38.

16. Joseph C. Winter and Henry G. Wylie, "Paleoecology and Diet at Clyde's Cavern," *American Antiquity: Journal of the Society of American Archaeology* 39 (April 1974): 310–13.

17. Madsen, "Fremont Sites," 23–25; Schroedl and Hogan, "Innocents Ridge," 54.

18. Gunnerson, "Unusual Artifacts," 70–74.

19. Black and Metcalf, "Castle Valley Archaeological Project," 17.

20. Castleton, *Petroglyphs and Pictographs,* 5–6, 112–29.

21. Ibid., 7.

22. Lee M. Swasey, "Emery County Indian Writing Site Study," unpublished manuscript.

2

The Hinterland: Explorers and Adventurers

It is impossible to determine exactly when Europeans first visited the Emery County region. The earliest recorded entry into what is now Utah was the exploring expedition of Juan Maria Antonio Rivera in 1765. Rivera, however, proceeded no farther than Spanish Valley (the present site of Moab). The Dominguez-Escalante expedition in 1776 bypassed the Emery County region. It is likely that an active trade was carried on between the Spanish settlements in New Mexico and the Utes of central Utah after (and perhaps even before) the Dominguez-Escalante visit. Since Rivera had charted a route as far as the Colorado River, it is also likely that the Green River crossing became part of this trade route as it was more direct than the Dominguez-Escalante route.

In 1813 Mauricio Arze and Lagos Garcia traveled from New Mexico to central Utah to trade for furs. No detailed account of their route has been found, so it is not clear whether they came by way of the Green River crossing. They encountered hostility from the Indians on the Sevier River but escaped to Spanish Valley where Chief Guasache (Wasatch) was waiting to trade with them, "as was his custom." This seems to be the first recorded reference to the name *Wasatch.* The most direct route from the Sevier to Spanish Valley would probably have taken the Arze-Garcia party through what is now Emery County.[1]

Mountain Men. A book published in 1847 purported to recount the experiences of two "lost trappers," James Workman and William Spencer, who supposedly became separated from their companions on the Arkansas River in 1809 and wandered into eastern Utah, where they met and joined a Spanish trading caravan bound for Los Angeles.[2] If this account is authentic, then Workman and Spencer would have been the first Anglo-Americans on record as visiting the Emery County region. However, the story is considered spurious by some historians of the fur trade. In any event, there is no independent evidence for the episode or for Santa Fe to Los Angeles trade as early as 1809.

The earliest authenticated literary record of an Anglo-American visitor to the Emery County region occurs in the account of Jedediah S. Smith's southwestern expedition of 1826. This expedition, the first recorded overland journey to California by an American, has long been regarded as one of the most important exploring journeys in the West, but it was assumed that Smith had followed the general route of the Dominguez-Escalante expedition from Utah Lake to the Sevier River. However, in 1967 a detailed narrative of the expedition was discovered in St. Louis, prepared from Smith's notes by his scribe Samuel Parkman. This account indicates that the Smith party did not proceed directly to the Sevier from Utah Valley. Instead they went into the mountains, probably by way of Spanish Fork Canyon, and reached the Colorado River drainage. The account, containing the first written description of what is now Emery County, reads:

> I then moved on South having a high range of mountains on the West and crossing a good many small streams running east into a large valley the valley of the Colorado. But having learned that the valley was verry barren and Rocky I did not venture into it. The country is here extremely rough little appearance of Indians and game quite scarce a few Mt. Sheep and Antelope. after traveling in this direction 2 days the country looked so unpromising that I

> determined to strike westward to a low place in the Mountain and cross over.[3]

It is not possible from this brief account to identify Smith's exact route. The statement that he traveled south with "a high range of mountains on the West" suggests that he passed through Castle Valley. If so, the "low place in the Mountain" might well have been Rock Canyon with its established Ute trail. On the other hand, the statement that he "did not venture into" the large valley could mean that the Smith party traveled south through the graben valleys of the Wasatch Plateau. The report of "crossing a good many small streams" fits well with this route, though the scarcity of game does not. In any case, Smith's description of Castle Valley as "barren" and "unpromising" strikes a note that would be repeated again and again by other early travelers.

Other trappers probably entered the Emery County region by way of the Green River. The mountain men knew the upper Green very well, and trading posts were established in the Uinta Basin as early as the 1830s. Evidence of their presence on the lower stretches of the river is somewhat sketchy, mainly consisting of the name "D. Julien" and the date 1836 written on the canyon walls.

The Spanish Trail. The main travel route through the Emery County region during the first half of the nineteenth century was the Spanish Trail, which has been called "the longest, crookedest, most arduous pack mule route in the history of America."[4] Extending from Santa Fe to Los Angeles, this trail entered what is now Emery County by way of a ford about three miles north of Green River City. While the route was fairly definite at key points such as the Green River crossing and in narrow passes, in more open country it was highly variable. This was especially true when large herds of horses and mules were being driven to New Mexico, requiring feed along the way. From the Green River crossing, the trail went west to a camp at what was known as Green River Spring. This could have been Trail Spring in Cottonwood Wash, or Smith Cabin Spring at the base of the San Rafael Reef in Tidwell Draw, or a spring about two miles farther north in Cottonwood Wash. From Green River Spring the trail skirted the San Rafael Reef by continuing north in Cottonwood Wash, turning to the west at or near Big Hole Wash (using the Big Holes as a watering place) and continuing across Big Flat to another watering place at the Little Holes. The route through Cottonwood Wash later adopted by the unfinished Denver and Rio Grande Western Railroad grade (and later still used as the corridor for a high-voltage electrical transmission line) approximates the course of least resistance that was most likely followed by caravans on the Spanish Trail.

From Little Holes the trail crossed Buckhorn Flat to the Red Seeps. It forded Huntington Creek a short distance downstream from the bridge on the present Castle Dale-Buckhorn road, then passed east of Oil Well Dome, crossed Cottonwood Creek at Wilsonville, followed Rock Canyon Wash through the Molen Reef, then went south across the benches and crossed Ferron Creek at a point near Molen. The route continued southwest, crossing Muddy Creek about two miles east of Emery and continuing over Oak Spring Bench to Ivie Creek Canyon and Wasatch Pass. Near the summit, the trail divided with one branch going to Fish Lake and on through Grass Valley and the other crossing the northwest shoulder of the Fish Lake Plateau and entering Sevier Valley near the present site of Sigurd.

The first recorded journey over the entire Spanish Trail began in September 1830, when a party of trappers led by William Wolfskill set out for California from Taos, New Mexico. Except for Wolfskill's ledger, the surviving accounts of this expedition were all written several years after the event. The most detailed narrative is that of George C. Yount, dictated to an Episcopal clergyman named Orange Clark sometime around 1855. According to the Yount-Clark account, after crossing the Green River the travelers

> shaped their course in a South-west direction, to a place known then by the name of "St-Joseph's Valley"—Which they found to be the most desolate & forlorn dell in the world—Every thing about it was repulsive & supremely awful—Unanimously they resolved to abandon so dreary a region, & rather than sojourn there, forego the acquisition of any benefit in the world.[5]

The reference to St. Joseph's Valley as an established name suggests that there must have been travel on the Spanish Trail before the Wolfskill expedition. The characterization of Castle Valley as "the most desolate and forlorn dell in the world" is not very flattering, but it must be borne in mind that the expedition passed through the region in November or December, and that to a mountain man a place without beaver was a place without value.

For the next two decades, the Spanish Trail was an important commercial route, with one major caravan each year travelling from "the land of sheep" to "the land of horses" and back. A French visitor writing from Los Angeles in 1841 reported:

> Caravans travel once a year from New Mexico to Los Angeles. These consist of 200 men on horseback, accompanied by mules laden with fabrics and large woolen covers called *serapes, jerzas,* and *cobertones,* which are valued at 3 to 5 piasters each. This merchandise is exchanged for horses and mules, on a basis, usually, of two blankets for one animal. Caravans leave Santa Fe, New Mexico, in October, before the snows set in, travel west, . . . and finally reach the outlying ranchos of California from where the trail leads into El Pueblo de los Angeles. This trip consumes two and one-half months. Returning caravans leave California in April in order to cross the rivers before the snow melts, taking with them about 2,000 horses.[6]

By the 1840s there were herds of stolen animals in addition to the official caravans, as the Utes under Chief Wakara and mountain men such as Pegleg Smith discovered that raiding was more profitable than trading. California mules, larger and stronger than those bred in the States, commanded high prices on the Santa Fe Trail. And of course there was always the traffic in Indian slaves for sale in New Mexico, where a Paiute girl could bring $200.

Kit Carson, 1848. The last major caravan traveled the Spanish Trail during 1847 and 1848. Not long after its departure from Los Angeles in April 1848, a small party led by frontier scout Kit Carson also set out from California carrying government dispatches for delivery to Washington, D.C. In Carson's party was a young army lieutenant named George D. Brewerton, who later published an account of the journey. They overtook the New Mexico caravan in the Mojave Desert, and when they reached Utah chose the Fish Lake branch of the trail. Brewerton reported catching large numbers of trout in the streams feeding the lake, indicating that they probably were there during the spawning run. Brewerton gave no details about travel through Castle Valley, but he did describe the party's difficult crossing of the Green River on 3 June. (In his account he calls it the Grand River, but it must have been the Green as it was the first of the two major rivers they crossed.) Most of the party's arms and supplies were lost, along with Brewerton's botanical and mineral specimens and his notebook, when a raft capsized.[7]

The party succeeded in saving bags of California mail including a copy of the 1 April 1848 *California Star*, which brought the first news of the discovery of gold in California. The gold rush that ensued over the next several years marked the end of the Emery County portion of the Spanish Trail as a major route to California as more direct routes were developed through Arizona and along the Humboldt River in Nevada. Some travelers, however, continued to follow the Spanish Trail, and indeed the most detailed descriptions of the trail through Emery County date from the years following its decline as an important trade route.

Orville C. Pratt, 1848. Orville C. Pratt left Santa Fe for a War Department assignment in California on 27 August 1848, supplied with an escort of sixteen men and a route log compiled by a mountain man named B. Choteau. Pratt described the Green River, which he reached on 18 September, as "a large mountain stream, full 300 yards wide, but not so rapid as the 'Grand.'" He found the river "greatly swollen from the late heavy rains" and its banks devoid of grass for his animals, so that he was compelled to feed them cottonwood bark and twigs. The men fared somewhat better, catching "mountain trout weighing at least 6 pounds! They resemble greatly the celebrated 'Mackinaw trout' *in looks* but are nothing so good. They are 'flabby' & are little better in taste than the common white fish of lake Ontario." It appears from this description that the "mountain trout" were actually Colorado squawfish.

The party crossed the river on 19 September. They lost the trail and were forced to camp that night without water. On the 20th they retraced their path until they found the trail, nooned at Green River Spring, and camped that night near a pothole, probably in the Big Holes area. On 21 September Pratt reported, "Made a fine march today of 30 m. & camped on the San Rafell. A fine stream, & the best grass we have found since leaving Santa Fe." Pratt's "San Rafell" was probably Huntington Creek, which the Spanish Trail crossed about a mile above its junction with the Cottonwood. Despite the good feed for his animals, Pratt was unimpressed with Castle Valley:

> The country continues as almost all the way heretofore, sandy, hilly & utterly barren. Water is also scarce, & if there is no mineral wealth in these mountains I can hardly conceive of what earthly use a large proportion of this country was designed for!

Pratt's party traveled to "Garambuya" (Ferron) creek on 22 September and the following day continued on through rain and hail to the "Rio Del Puerto," or River of the Pass (probably Ivie Creek). On the 24th they crossed Wasatch Pass, meeting "four Eute Indians" to whom they traded a rifle for "a fine horse."[8] This is the only reference to their meeting Indians in the Emery County area. Evidently they did not find Indians at the Green River crossing—though it is likely that Ute horses were the reason for the scarcity of grass there. B. Choteau's trail log said of the Green River crossing, "There may be some Eutes here. Diff. bands, but friendly. Wak-Kuh-rai is a principal chief."[9] "Wak-Kuh-rai" was probably the leader known to the Mormons as "Chief Walker."

E. F. Beale, 1853. A twelve-man party under the direction of E. F. Beale passed through Emery County in the summer of 1853. Beale was on his way to California to take up an appointment as Indian superintendent. In the party was Gwinn Harris Heap, who the following year published a book about the journey, *Central Route to the Pacific, from the Valley of the Mississippi to California.* Heap gave a more detailed description of the Emery County landscape than any previous traveler.

The party reached the Green River on 25 July. Heap wrote, "The scenery on its banks was grand and solemn." They assembled a boat from bullhides on a wooden frame to ferry their supplies across. The bullhides were full of holes, having been used to cross several other rivers, and required patching with India-rubber blankets. When the crossing was completed, Beale made a present of the boat to a party of twenty-five mounted Utes who met them on the west bank and who promptly tore it apart for moccasin leather. They camped "in the midst of luxuriant grass" a mile upstream from the crossing. The following morning, the Utes, who had seemed friendly the night before,

> showed a disposition to be insolent, but our party kept close together, and they did not dare to commence hostilities. Most of them had rifles, and all had bows and quivers full of arrows with obsidian heads. They accompanied us for some miles, importuning us for presents, and finally left us in a bad humor. Had we been able to conciliate these Indians with a few gifts, such as blankets, beads, tobacco, brass wire, &c., we should not have had the least trouble with them.

This was the period of the "Walker War" (1853–54), which perhaps accounts for the Utes' "insolence."

The party camped at Green River Spring on 26 July. Heap describes the water as "cool, but not abundant; it is, however, constant, and good grass and some cottonwoods and willows are found around it." Heap noted the "rocky ridges worn into fantastic shapes" of the San Rafael Reef and described the trail as passing "through rocky ravines of red sandstone." The next morning,

> We were on the road before daylight, and travelled thirty-eight miles west by south; crossing the east fork of San Rafael Creek [Huntington Creek], we halted at 8 P.M. on the west fork [Cottonwood Creek], a few miles above their junction. . . . At our encampment, the creek was seven yards in breadth and eighteen inches deep. The water was cool and sweet, and good pasturage on its banks.

On 28 July Heap reported,

> Traveled twenty miles south by west, and halted at noon on the Rio del Moro (Castle Creek, so called on account of the buttes near it resembling fortifications). In ten miles from the San Rafael, crossed a broad brook of clear and cool water, running into Green River. Between the streams vegetation was scanty and stunted, and the soil clayey, dry, and barren; to the westward were steep hills, beyond which could be seen the green and wooded slopes of the Wahsatch range.

The "broad brook" ten miles from Cottonwood Creek would have been Ferron Creek. That would make the "Rio del Moro" Muddy Creek. Heap remarked upon the architectural forms into which the Mancos shale had been sculpted near the mouth of Muddy Creek Canyon:

> At times, long lines of battlements presented themselves; at others, immense Gothic cathedrals, with all their quaint pinnacles and turrets, which reminded us of the ruined castles and churches that we had seen in our travels in the old world. The different colors of the clay added to the singularity of the scenery, and strengthened the resemblance.

Along this stretch of the trail, the party crossed cattle tracks going north. Heap surmised that these were livestock stolen by the Utes from the Mormon settlements in Sanpete Valley. The party camped that night on Ivie Creek and crossed Wasatch Pass on 29 July.[10]

John W. Gunnison, 1853. A few weeks after the Beale party, another expedition passed through Emery County, this time with the official charge to explore a route for a proposed transcontinental railroad. While other parties were assigned to explore northern and southern routes, Captain John W. Gunnison of the Topographic Engineers was given responsibility for the central route along the 38th and 39th parallels. The Gunnison expedition was the first on record to bring wagons through Emery County, thereby changing a trail into some semblance of a road. Gunnison did not long survive his journey through Emery County. Together with seven of his men, he was killed by Pahvant Indians on the lower Sevier River on 26 October. The report of the expedition was completed by Gunnison's assistant, Lieutenant E. G. Beckwith.

Beckwith reported that the party reached the Green River on 30 September. "Many Akanaquint or Green river Utahs were on the opposite bank as we encamped, and soon crossed it to beg tobacco, and, if possible, to trade; dressed deer-skins being the only article they offer for this purpose." The Indian crossing enabled the Gunnison party to locate "an excellent ford . . . from a few yards below our camp (on the Spanish trail) to an island opposite, and from its upper end to the shore. The river is 300 yards wide, with a pebbly bottom, as we forded it, but with quicksands on either side of our path." After they had crossed,

> Indians thronged our camp for several hours. They are the merriest of their race I have ever seen, except the Yumas—constantly laughing and talking, and appearing grateful for the trifling presents they received. A wrinkled, hard-faced old savage, with whom I shared my luncheon of bread and bacon, quite laughed aloud with joy at his good fortune. They confirmed the report we had before heard of a war between the Mormons and Wah-ka-ra's (Walker's) band of Utahs, and his absence in New Mexico to dispose of a herd of cattle which he had stolen from them.

Oddly enough, Beckwith greatly underestimated the magnitude of the plateau that now bears his name, describing it as "but a few hundred feet high." His account shows, however, that he was not insensitive to the remarkable landscape:

> Desolate as is the country over which we have just passed, and around us, the view is still one of the most beautiful and pleasing I remember to have seen. As we approached the river yesterday, the ridges on either side of its banks to the west appeared broken into a thousand forms—columns, shafts, temples, buildings, and ruined cities could be seen, or imagined, from the high points along our route.

This is a good description of the San Rafael Reef as viewed from the vicinity of Green River.

On 3 October the Gunnison party left the Spanish Trail where it entered the San Rafael Swell and in search of an easier route traveled up the Price River Valley (known at that time as the White River). On 7 October, probably a few miles east of Wellington, they turned southwest and passed through the area where Victor and Desert Lake were later established. On 8 October they camped on Huntington Creek, which Beckwith called the San Rafael. He wrote,

> There is not a tree at the point where we crossed this stream; a narrow bottom is covered with dry grass and willow bushes, intermixed with the buffalo berry bush thickly covered with fruit. Two miles and a half from the San Rafael we came upon a branch of that river of half its size, with dry grass covering bottomlands a half

> mile in width, with the usual bushes and a few cotton-wood trees on the margin of the creek.

Apparently, the Gunnison route from Huntington Creek to Cottonwood Creek passed to the west of Oil Well Dome.[11] The party rejoined the Spanish Trail about two miles south of their camp on Cottonwood Creek. On 10 October they crossed the "third branch of San Rafael, called Garambulla by the Indians." Beckwith noted,

> The Spanish trail, though but seldom used of late years, is still very distinct where the soil washes but slightly. On some such spaces today we counted from fourteen to twenty parallel trails, of the ordinary size of Indian trails or horse-paths, on a way barely fifty feet in width. Specimens of coal were brought in from the hills near camp, but were inferior in quality.

Their camp at this time was on "Big Rock Creek" (presumably Muddy Creek), so the coal probably came from outcrops in the Ferron sandstone of the Molen Reef.

On 12 October the party continued through a "broken valley" and across two small creeks to a camp at Oak Spring. Here their Indian guide "told us that a circle in red, high up on a sheltered rock on the face of one of the hills, where some rude human figures are seen, also sketched in red lines, was called Akanaquint."[12] This pictograph was also noted two years later by the Elk Mountain expedition.[13]

Beckwith's assessment of the economic promise of the Emery County region was not favorable:

> From Green River to the Wahsatch mountains, the miserable soil maintains the same ash-heap friability. The country is very rocky sandstone, broken, upheaved, and intersected in every direction by ravines, chasms, and beds of creeks. A little bunch grass is scattered over the hills, but they are generally barren or covered, as on the margins of the streams, with sage. . . . The summit of the Wahsatch mountains is a finely-grassed region but entirely unfit for cultivation. . . . It is not too much, therefore, to say, that, unless this interior country possesses undiscovered mineral wealth of great value, it can contribute but the merest trifle towards the maintenance of a railroad through it, after it shall have been constructed.[14]

It is interesting to compare the various descriptions of the streams flowing through Castle Valley. Beckwith describes Huntington Creek as being twice as large as either Price River or Cottonwood Creek. The measured annual flow of Huntington Creek is in fact somewhat smaller than that of the other two streams. However, Beckwith made his observations in the fall, when presumably all mountain snowpack was exhausted and the streams were fed entirely by springflow. Probably a larger share of Huntington Creek water comes from perennial springs, and therefore it would be a larger stream in the late season, while the Price and Cottonwood would be larger during the snowmelt season. Orville Pratt, traveling through Emery County in September, also described Huntington Creek as "a fine stream" and took it for the main branch of the San Rafael River. G. H. Heap, traveling in July, did not explicitly compare the flow of the Huntington and Cottonwood creeks, but his account suggests that he found the Cottonwood a more impressive stream. His description of it as "seven yards in breadth and eighteen inches deep" would still be reasonably accurate for late July in an average year, if there were no storage impoundments. This suggests that precipitation and streamflow have neither increased nor decreased significantly over the last century and a half, contrary to claims sometimes heard that the region used to be wetter than it is today.

John C. Frémont, 1853–1854. John Charles Frémont, who had cultivated a reputation as the western "pathfinder," had hoped to be chosen to lead the central railroad survey. When Gunnison was appointed instead, Frémont, with the support of his influential father-in-law, Senator Thomas Hart Benton of Missouri, organized a private expedition for the same purpose. He started later than Gunnison, partly because of illness but in part because he was determined to prove by a winter crossing that the central route was usable in all seasons. This determination, combined with inadequate preparations and an unusually severe winter, brought the expedition to the brink of disaster.

The most detailed report of the Frémont expedition is a retrospective account published in 1857 by Solomon Nunes Carvalho, the party's artist and daguerreotypist. One of Frémont's goals was apparently to seek a more direct route across Utah than that provided by the Spanish Trail, and one closer to the 38th parallel. A map published with Frémont's memoirs in 1887 indicates that the expedition crossed the Green River near the mouth of the San Rafael, twenty-some miles south of the Spanish Trail crossing. On their arrival at the river, the party saw "several Indians" watching them from "high sand bluffs" on the west bank. The Indians conducted them to

> a fertile spot on the western bank . . . where their village was. We found that they lived on nothing else but grass-seed, which they collected in the fall. Their women parch it, and grind it between stones. In this manner it is very palatable, and tastes very much like roasted peanuts.

Carvalho purchased "about a quart" of this parched seed, which he credited with giving him the strength that enabled him to survive the ordeal that followed.[15]

Carvalho provides no details of the party's route through Emery County, simply recounting terrible suffering from hunger, snow, and cold before they finally reached the Mormon settlement of Parowan. Joseph M. Bauman, Jr., proposes from a study of the maps later prepared by the expedition's cartographer, F. W. Egloffstein, that Frémont attempted to follow the San Rafael River through the San Rafael Reef and got as far as Mexican Mountain. When his progress was blocked by the Upper Black Box, he retraced his path and went south along the eastern base of the Reef until he could find a way to resume a westward course.[16] It has been traditionally assumed that Frémont traveled up the river that now bears his name, but recent studies of Carvalho's photographs make it more likely that they crossed the Last Chance and Cathedral Valley areas.

William Huntington, 1854. Late in 1854 William Huntington, a Mormon frontiersman and explorer then living at Hobble Creek (Springville), was sent by his brother-in-law Brigham Young to visit the Navajos south of the San Juan River. Upon his return, Huntington wrote an account of his trip in the form of a letter to the editor of the *Deseret News.* The letter is chiefly devoted to a report on the Navajos and on the Anasazi ruins the party discovered near the San Juan River. It is clear, however, that Huntington's route took him through Emery County. Starting from Manti, the party "followed

Gunnison's trail to within 25 miles of Grand River. . . . This road, so far, was a tolerably good one, but the country has little or no wood, grass, or water."[17] Huntington provides no further details about the Emery County region. However, it seems likely that Huntington Creek received its present name on this occasion. There is no record of any of the three exploring Huntington brothers, William, Dimick, and Oliver, visiting the region earlier than this, and Oliver the following year referred to Huntington Creek as if it were an established name.[18]

Elk Mountain Mission, 1855. On 21 May 1855 forty-one men with fifteen wagons, under the direction of Alfred N. Billings, left Manti in response to a call from LDS church leaders to establish a settlement near the present site of Moab. Oliver B. Huntington, designated as clerk to the party, kept both an official and a personal journal of the expedition. According to the official journal, they reached Muddy Creek on 29 May, crossed "Sweet Cotton wood creek" on 30 May, and found a "good camping place" on Huntington Creek, described in the personal journal as "a fine creek with plenty of feed."[19] Here they met some Utes who advised them to take the Spanish Trail route to Green River instead of the longer Gunnison route. Thus the Elk Mountain Mission became the first party on record to cross the San Rafael Swell with wagons. They made this journey in two hard days, sustained by water they found in potholes, and reached the Green River crossing on 2 June. Huntington reported that they "had good ground for a road" until they reached the vicinity of the San Rafael Reef. Then "we began to have it somewhat rocky for 5 miles" followed by several miles of "the worst sand I ever have seen."

The Elk Mountain missionaries made a hasty return trip without their wagons a few months later, after a Ute attack on 23 September killed three members of the party and wounded leader Billings. Billings's diary indicates that they crossed the Green River on 25 September and camped on Huntington Creek on the 27th. The next night they "camped in a Kanyon near the foot of the San Pete range of mountains." On the 29th, "At day break we started up the Kanyon, thence up the Mountain." They arrived at Manti late on the 30th.[20] The description of going up the canyon and *then* up the mountain would suggest that they traveled by way of Rock Canyon, which leads to the saddle of Horn Mountain at the edge of the Joe's Valley graben. From this point a still-used trail ascends Wagon Road Ridge to the plateau summit.[21]

William Wing Loring, 1858. In the summer of 1858, during the period of the so-called Utah War, Col. W. W. Loring was sent with a sizeable detachment of men and more than fifty wagons to make a road from Camp Floyd, Utah, to Fort Union, New Mexico. Loring ascended to Wasatch Pass partly following the Gunnison route but making a new road in some places. He then apparently followed the Spanish Trail route through Emery County.

With the party as a guide was a New Mexico mountain man named Antoine Leroux, whose experience in the region went back to Spanish Trail days. One value of the Loring report is that it uses older names for key sites in Castle Valley instead of the Anglo names that were replacing them. After crossing the divide, Loring reports that they traveled down "Shipley Creek," presumably Ivie Creek or one of its branches. Near this stream they found "a bed of very good bituminous coal." They camped on "Media Creek" on 31 July and after a six-and-a-half-mile journey reached "Garamboyer Creek." *Garamboyer* is obviously a corruption of *Garambulla,* a name we have seen attached to what is now Ferron Creek. But the distances given in Loring's account are much too short for the journey from Muddy to Ferron Creek. "Media Creek" must have been Ivie or Quitchupah. Loring obviously mistook the Muddy for the Garambulla, and called Ferron Creek the "St. Raphael." He then called Cottonwood Creek "San Mateo or Sivareech Creek." Here the party was "visited by several Sivareechee Utah Indians." About two-and-a-half miles from San Mateo Creek, the party reached "San Marcus or Taveajo Creek," presumably Huntington Creek.

From his observations of the Castle Valley terrain, Loring wrote, "we are confirmed in the opinion that a road can be made up White [Price] River to Salt Lake Valley, by way of Provo Fork or Hubble Creek, possibly the Spanish Fork."[22] It seems likely that the military road over Soldier Summit was developed shortly after this time to facilitate travel between the army posts in Utah and those in New Mexico.

Warren S. Snow and Reddick N. Allred, 1865. Despite the paucity of records, Emery County probably had many visitors during the late 1850s and the 1860s, including travelers on the Soldier Summit military road. The growth of Mormon settlements in Sanpete Valley brought exploration and exploitation of the Wasatch Plateau for its timber and to a limited extent for its grazing lands. Some of those explorations must have included forays into Castle Valley.

Orange Seely, who was later to become a leader in the settlement of Castle Valley, recounts in his autobiography a visit he made to Manti in the spring of 1858, when he was fifteen years old. (This was a year before the Seely family located in Mount Pleasant.) During his visit, Seely writes, Indians stole 200 head of horses and cattle belonging to the residents of Beaver and took them to Castle Valley. "Manti men went out and intercepted the Indians and went into Convulsion Canyon and into Castle Valley, got the horses and cattle and brought them into Manti."[23] It appears from this and other accounts that Convulsion Canyon, like Rock Canyon, was an established route between Sanpete and Castle valleys.

In 1865 the Ute conflict known as the Black Hawk War erupted from a scuffle between John Lowry and Jake Aropeen at Manti. Over the next three years, Ute raiders captured several hundred head of the white settlers' livestock and brought them to a refuge in Emery County, where they were either consumed by the Ute forces or, as in the Walker War, driven to New Mexico for sale.

Early in the conflict, in July 1865, the Mormon militia sent a two-pronged expeditionary force into what is now Emery County in an effort to recover livestock. One detachment, under the command of General Warren S. Snow, proceeded up Twelve Mile Canyon, around the headwaters of Salina Creek, and down Convulsion Canyon to Castle Valley, where they reportedly struck the trail of the stolen cattle. The other detachment, commanded by Colonel Reddick N. Allred, apparently traveled by way of the military road over Soldier Summit and down Soldier Canyon. Allred reported, "We formed a junction with General Snow's men on Price River and went to Green River without seeing the marauders. Returning we traveled by way of Cottonwood Creek and Huntington Creek and crossed the mountains on the rocky trail to Manti."[24] Orange Seely, who was in General

Snow's company, identified the meeting place as "the prairie between Wellington and Price River." Seely indicates that when the two companies met, their provisions consisted of "three pint cups of flour or cracker dust to the man." On this slim diet, they went to Green River "by way of the grassy trail," and after finding that the Indians had crossed the river commenced a return march, probably by way of the Spanish Trail route. Seely writes, "On the way back we stopped at Cottonwood springs to feed our horses. . . . We got as far as Castle Dale and had no provisions but went on and were soon met with provisions at the head of Rock Canyon."[25]

Although there is no comprehensive list of the members of these militia parties, they probably included several men in addition to Orange Seely who later settled in Emery County. Indeed, the most important long-range impact of the Black Hawk War on the history of Emery County was its making the region better known to the residents of Sanpete Valley. Even though another decade was to pass before the settlement era began, potential settlers were becoming aware of the land and water resources of Castle Valley.

The Powell and Ferron Surveys

John Wesley Powell's River Explorations, 1869, 1871. On 24 May 1869 ten men in four wooden boats set out from Green River, Wyoming, for what has been considered the last major venture into unknown territory within the contiguous United States: a seventy-one day journey through the canyons of the Green and Colorado rivers. While the promise of adventure had attracted most members of the party, the leader, a one-armed Civil War veteran named John Wesley Powell, was determined to make a scientific investigation of the geography and geology of the canyon region.

The Powell party entered what is now Emery County on 13 July and left it on 15 July. They recorded only passing observations on the landscape, noting "the old Spanish Crossing" and describing the Green River Valley as being "of little use to anyone; the upland is burned to death and on the river there are a few cottonwood trees, but not large enough for any purpose but fuel."[26] They stopped "for an hour or two" at the mouth of the San Rafael and discovered a place where stone projectile points had been made. Some members of the party found Labyrinth Canyon oppressive in its loneliness, but Powell remarked on

> an exquisite charm in our ride today down this beautiful canyon. It gradually grows deeper with every mile of travel; the walls are symmetrically curved, and grandly arched; of a beautiful color, and reflected in the quiet waters in many places, so as almost to deceive the eye, and suggest the thought, to the beholder, that he is looking into profound depths.[27]

Many of the place names along the Green River were bestowed by Powell during this expedition, including Desolation Canyon, Labyrinth Canyon, and Bow-Knot Bend.

Powell organized a second expedition down the Green River in 1871. Powell left the party at Island Park, just below Whirlpool Canyon, and did not rejoin it until it reached the Spanish Trail crossing in Green River Valley. In the interim, Powell's brother-in-law and chief geographer, Almon H. Thompson, was in charge. As with the 1869 expedition, the members of the 1871 party were conscious of the historic significance of their adventure. As a result, several kept journals of the voyage that provide a record of their impressions.

The party camped on 25 August on the dry bed of the Price River (which they called the Little White). The next day they set up camp on the east bank of the Green River near the mouth of Gray Canyon and just opposite Gunnison Butte (which they named). Here, while waiting for Powell to rejoin them, they pulled their boats out of the water for repairs. Jack Hilliers dropped a hook and line into the river and caught several squawfish, one of which was three feet long and weighed forty pounds. (Dellenbaugh called them "Colorado River white salmon."[28]) Others did some exploring of the valley. The area was "literally covered with remains of Indian wigwams," but they found no Indians living there at the time. John F. Steward concluded that the region "is more patronized by bands of Indians who cross in the fall and spring than by any living near."[29] Stephen Vandiver Jones described the landscape as follows:

> The Topography of the valley presents some singular features. A low range of hills is near the river, sometimes on one side, sometimes the other. Back of these there are high buttes, some of them

Gunnison Butte, photographed by E. O. Beaman during the 1871 Powell Expedition. (Utah State Historical Society)

> isolated, some in long sweeps, their sides weathered in very peculiar shapes. Without much stretch of the imagination one could see castles, with bastion, tower and angel. Huge blocks of buildings, churches with spire and steeple, and indeed almost anything else.[30]

A. H. Thompson stated his impressions more succinctly: "Poor country."[31]

Powell arrived with fresh supplies on 29 August, and by 3 September the party was again on the river, advancing slowly with numerous stops to explore the surrounding land. As they drifted down the stream, they saw

> Stretching away westward from Gunnison Butte . . . an exquisitely modelled line of cliffs, some portions being a clear azure blue. At first it was proposed to name them Henry Cliffs, but they were finally called from their colour, Azure.[32]

This was one name bestowed by the Powell survey that did not take hold. The "Azure Cliffs" are now known as the Book Cliffs.[33]

They stopped a few miles below Green River Valley for Powell and Jones to hike toward the San Rafael Reef, which Jones described as "a long range of hills that stretched from north to south and seemed to be upheaved." Jones's impression of the Green River Desert was summed up in the remark, "I never understood before the full meaning of the term 'bare ground.'"[34] A short distance above the mouth of the San Rafael, Fred Dellenbaugh, at seventeen the youngest member of the party, was particularly impressed by a symmetrical, banded butte on the opposite bank from their dinner-stop, and Powell named it Dellenbaugh Butte in his honor.[35]

They camped for two days at the mouth of the San Rafael, where they understood themselves to be in Castle Valley, or "the country called by natives Toom-pin-con-to-weep, meaning 'stone house land.'"[36] J. W. Powell and Jones hiked some twenty miles up the San Rafael Valley. John F. Steward and Clem Powell crossed the Green and hiked to some high buttes they saw in the distance to the east. The other members of the party gathered arrowheads for the Smithsonian Institution from the abundant supply scattered over the ground. Thompson remarked,

> Some are so clear and brilliant that they ought to be called gems. Found the place where the arrow-makers worked and their tools of stone with which they pounded out their wares. The material was obtained from a stratum 100 feet above the river.[37]

Continuing into Labyrinth Canyon through heavy rain that sent spectacular waterfalls pouring from the cliffs, they camped at a site they named Trin Alcove (now known as Three Canyon), where they took photographs. The next day they stopped at Bow-Knot Bend, where E. O. Beaman lugged his photographic equipment up to the narrow hogback to capture a view of the river's entrenched meanders.

J. W. Powell had spent the weeks before rejoining the party in an attempt to find a way to deliver supplies to the mouth of the Dirty Devil. When these efforts failed, he returned to Manti to buy flour and other goods and then made his way to the Green River crossing by way of the Spanish Trail. This overland journey combined with his river experience to give him a broad perspective on the region. In his report to Congress, Powell called the Book Cliffs "one of the most wonderful facades of the world" and declared that to describe Castle Valley would "beggar language and pall imagination." At the same time, he characterized the region as "a land of desolation, dedicated forever to the geologist and the artist, where civilization can find no resting place."[38]

Augustus D. Ferron, 1873. On 19 June 1873 A. D. Ferron, a professional surveyor based at Salt Lake City, signed a contract with the federal government to conduct a survey of irrigable lands in Castle Valley, a necessary step toward the opening of the region for settlement under the homestead laws. Ferron and a crew of four began their work north of Huntington Creek on 7 July. They made their way south to the Muddy Creek area marking range and township lines, then moved north again, surveying the square-mile sections within townships. The Ferron survey was accepted by the U.S. Surveyor General's Office in Salt Lake City on 11 October.[39] Tradition has it that Ferron's assistants offered to name what was formerly known as Garambulla Creek in his honor if he would allow them to throw him into the stream.

Montell Seely has characterized A. D. Ferron as Castle Valley's first "Chamber of Commerce." Where previous visitors had found little or no economic promise, Ferron saw a good potential for development, commenting, for example, of the area east of the present site of Huntington, "This township embraces some excellent bottom and bench lands. It is watered by Huntington and Shangint [Cedar] Creeks; fine grazing grounds abound. It is capable of sustaining a thrifty settlement. . . ."[40] Despite this positive assessment, however, the mere opening of the region for settlement did not immediately attract settlers. The first homestead locations were not filed until almost four years after the Ferron survey.

C. E. Dutton, 1875. The Geographical and Geological Survey of the Rocky Mountain Region, under the direction of John Wesley Powell, continued and expanded its work in the years following the 1871 river expedition. Almon H. Thompson directed a crew that mapped much of southern Utah and the Arizona Strip. Grove Karl Gilbert wrote a landmark study of the geology of the Henry Mountains. Clarence E. Dutton published a book on the high plateaus and another on the Grand Canyon. Dutton's *Geology of the High Plateaus of Utah* was published in 1880, but the on-the-ground work had been done during the summers of 1875, 1876, and 1877. Dutton appears to have begun in the north and worked his way south, which would mean that his study of the Wasatch Plateau most likely took place in 1875.

Dutton's base during his study of the Wasatch Plateau was Gunnison, Sanpete County, and he provides a much more detailed description of the southern and western parts of the plateau than he does of the Emery County portion. Still, his was the first scientific examination of the high tableland that has been so important to the history of the county. He demonstrated that the Wasatch Plateau is not part of the Wasatch Range but belongs "to another age" and is "totally different in [its] forms and geological relations." He was the first to recognize the down-faulted graben valleys on the Wasatch Plateau, though he does not specifically refer to Joe's Valley. He viewed Castle Valley and the San Rafael Swell, most likely from the rim of Horn Mountain, and provided the first published description of the Swell that noted its concentric "racetrack" valleys. He described five concentric rings of cliffs surrounding "an elliptical area about 40 miles long and 12 to 20 broad, its major axis lying north and south, and as completely girt about by rocky walls as the valley of Rasselas."[41] The "valley of Rasselas" (which Dutton refers to a few lines later as "the Red Amphitheatre") is now known as Sinbad.

A. H. Thompson, 1876–1877. As the 1870s progressed, J. W. Powell grew more interested in the development of the arid lands of the West, an interest that was to culminate in his landmark *Report on the Lands of the Arid Region of the United States* (1878), which Wallace Stegner called "one of the most important books ever written about the West."[42] Powell wrote the general chapters of this report and assigned three of his associates to prepare chapters on particular drainage systems. The report on "Irrigable Lands of That Portion of Utah Drained by the Colorado River and Its Tributaries" was written by A. H. Thompson.

Thompson or workers under his direction made on-the-ground studies of streamflow and irrigable lands in the Emery County region during the years 1876 and 1877. He estimated there were "200 square miles of arable land, generally of good quality" accessible to irrigation in the region. The San Rafael River was "carefully measured in July 1876" at a flow of 1,676 cubic feet per second. Thompson estimated that this flow would be "maintained with considerable steadiness" during the critical irrigation season, then would drop to about 400 cubic feet per second by October. He estimated further that the waters of the San Rafael and its tributaries would be sufficient to irrigate 112,000 acres. The various branches of Muddy Creek (which Thompson called Curtis Creek) had "an aggregated flow of 47 cubic feet per second" when measured in September 1876. Thompson estimated that the flow would be double that amount during the irrigation season, and found "25 square miles of good arable land" that could be irrigated by the waters.

The year 1876 must have been an exceptional year for runoff in the San Rafael drainage. Thompson estimated the flow of the San Rafael as being more than half as great as that of the Duchesne River (which he called the Uinta) at its confluence with the Green. In fact the average flow of the Duchesne is several times greater than that of the San Rafael. Thompson's estimate of the irrigable acres was almost double the actual acreage that has ever been brought under irrigation.

Thompson's report on the Green River Valley (which he called Gunnison Valley) reflects the continuing reality that the limiting factor for agriculture there is not the availability of water but rather the availability of land to which the water can be economically delivered:

> In Gunnison Valley, below the foot of Gray Canon, are 25 square miles of arable land. The cost of constructing the necessary irriga-

> tion works at this point would be greater than above the mouth of the Uinta, but still not beyond the ability of a colony. Green River flowed in Gunnison Valley in September, 1877, 4,400 cubic feet of water per second, enough to irrigate at the standard adopted 860 square miles. There seems to be no arable land to which it is possible to take this great surplus, and probably for many years to come it will be suffered to flow "unvexed to the sea."[43]

The *Report on the Arid Lands* was published in 1878, a year after the LDS church call for settlers to locate in Castle Valley. Its very positive estimate of the region's land and water resources could not, therefore, have been an influencing factor on the settlement call. However, the report may have influenced the settlers who came during the early 1880s.

The Grazing Frontier

Unlike the ranch system of the Southwest, where the livestock industry was dominated by a few large owners who employed cowboys to work their herds, early Utah developed a community-based livestock industry. Families typically operated small farms and owned a few head of cattle and horses. The animals were driven each morning to the community grazing grounds where they were herded throughout the day, usually by young children, and then returned to the village in the evening.[44] As livestock numbers multiplied, it became necessary to take them farther from the village to find feed, making it impractical to drive them back and forth each day. In time, "pools" of surplus animals were assembled under the care of particular individuals or families, who typically worked for a share of the milk or of the calf crop. Pooled herds of milk cows were taken to high mountain meadows in the summer. At these "mountain dairies," usually operated by women and children, butter and cheese were manufactured for sale. In the winter cattle, horses, and sheep were driven to the Great Basin valleys of western Utah. As livestock numbers continued to grow through natural increase and the importation of animals from other regions, some individual stockmen began to accumulate sizeable herds, on the ranch model, though small livestock holdings and cooperative herding practices have continued on Utah ranges up to the present time.

With the growth in livestock numbers, the Great Basin ranges soon reached or exceeded the limits of their carrying capacity. As early as 1867, Mormon apostle Orson Hyde, a resident of Spring City, Sanpete County, commented,

> I find the longer we live in these valleys that the range is becoming more and more destitute of grass; the grass is not only eaten up by the great amount of stock that feed upon it, but they tramp it out by the very roots; and where grass once grew luxuriantly, there is now nothing but the desert weed, and hardly a spear of grass is to be seen.[45]

In the search for new grazing lands, it was natural that stockmen should be attracted by the Emery County region with its natural drift between the summer range on the high plateaus and the winter range in Castle Valley and on the San Rafael Swell.

The Ferron and Muddy Creek Region, Circa 1875. A revealing account of the movement of livestock into the Emery County area is found in an article by Glynn Bennion describing the experiences of his father, Israel. In the summer of 1875, the Bennion family moved 2,000 head of cattle from overcrowded ranges in western Utah to the Fishlake Plateau. One of the riders in this roundup was Sam Gilson, who a few years later developed the Oak Spring Ranch south of Emery. Gilson would make a name for himself as a polygamist-hunting deputy U.S. marshal and as the discoverer of the gilsonite deposits in the Uinta Basin. Young Israel Bennion saw in Gilson the prototypical rugged cowboy:

> The man scorned hardship and traveled without food or bedroll. At night he pulled his saddle blanket over his shoulders and slept on the ground. If the night was cold and the ground wet, he woke next morning with his hair usually frozen in the mud. When he got hungry he shot a good-looking calf, cut off a sizable part of its anatomy, threw it on a brush fire burned down to coals and ashes, scorched the meat briefly on one side and then the other, and ate it (ashes, etc.), with blood dripping down both sides of his magnificent beard.

The Bennions left their cattle in the care of sixteen-year-old Tom Simper and fifteen-year-old Israel Bennion. In the fall the boys established a winter camp on Ferron Creek, and "the cattle were allowed to drift . . . south-eastward as far as Green River." The boys stayed with the herd for three years with little or no contact from other members of the family. Their summers on the Fish Lake Plateau were "little short of idyllic" as they fished the abundant streams. In the fall they made their annual trip to Salina for a year's supplies "consisting principally of flour, clothing, rope, and ammunition," then moved the cattle down to Castle Valley. Not far from their camp on Ferron Creek were the winter camps of other stockmen, including the Miller, Swasey, and Nethery boys. And *boys* is the right word. "In nearly every case the owners lived elsewhere, and their sons were the caretakers of the livestock."

For the most part, the cattle were left to fend for themselves in the winter, while the young herdsmen enjoyed the limited social life of the cow camps. They would visit from camp to camp, sometimes staying for as long as a week at a stretch, telling stories, racing their horses, shooting their guns, and in general polishing their cowboy skills. In later years Israel Bennion remembered best his association with the Swaseys:

> Of all the residents of Castle Valley, the Swasey boys rated tops with my father. These boys were of a black-haired, blue-eyed strain of Irish; good-natured, happy-go-lucky, superb athletes, expert horsemen; full of the lore of braiding quirts, bridle reins, horsehair ropes; mending saddles and bridles and fixing anything from a hurt human to a broken-down wagon.[46]

This boyhood idyll came to an end in 1878 with the division of family holdings after the death of John Bennion.

Economically, it had been a losing proposition. Although Simper and Bennion had branded about 700 calves each year (not a very good calf crop from 2,000 cows), the final roundup produced 300 *fewer* animals than they had started out with. This herd was sold to Tom Simper for $10 a head, apparently payable in installments, and Israel Bennion returned to his home in Rush Valley by way of Cottonwood Canyon, meeting a party of Castle Valley-bound settlers on the way.[47] Simper remained in Castle Valley for some time, establishing a home in the Quitchupah region. Later he moved to Salina, where he died in 1932.[48]

In trying to account for the economic failure of the Bennion cattle venture, Glynn Bennion remarks that the family failed to take into account the challenges of eastern Utah ranges, with their cliffs and gorges, compared with the open valleys of western Utah. Taking proper care of a large herd in those conditions was simply beyond the capacity of two inexperienced boys. As a further reason for the Bennion withdrawal from Castle Valley, Glynn Bennion notes, "Other outfits were there first."[49]

Who were these "other outfits"? A. H. Thompson remarked in his irrigation survey that Castle Valley was "much used as a winter herding ground for stock owned by the settlers in other portions of Utah." "Much used" suggests that there were more than just a few herds, and that the practice of wintering livestock in Castle Valley was well established by 1876, when Thompson visited the region. Glynn Bennion's account, largely gleaned from stories told by Israel Bennion in his later years, seems to indicate that the Miller, Swasey, and Nethery families were already established in the region of Ferron Creek by the time Simper and Bennion arrived there in the fall of 1875. At that time, Charles Swasey would have been twenty-four, Sid twenty-two, Rod sixteen, and Joe only fourteen.[50] The Swasey family headquarters were at Mona, Juab County, and they had apparently grazed their herds throughout western Utah during the 1860s. (There is a Swasey Peak in the House Range in western Millard County.) It is not clear whether the Millers referred to by Bennion were the Miller brothers who later developed a large ranching operation in northern Castle Valley. The name of Nethery does not appear in other accounts of early Castle Valley stockmen.

Stephen Washburn ("Wash") Chipman claimed to have come to Castle Valley in 1873, at the age of eleven, with his father, William Henry Chipman, and their livestock. The Chipmans of American Fork, Utah County, had been running cattle in Juab Valley but moved their herd to Castle Valley in search of better feed. Evidently they established a camp somewhere south of Ferron Creek. Wash Chipman recalled,

> Their nearest neighbor to the south, a distance of four or five miles, was the Abraham Acord camp, easily accessible, for they

> were not separated by a mountain ravine or steep hill. Their nearest neighbor to the north was Mike Molen. Here a ravine separated them, making contact more difficult.[51]

Other accounts have Mike Molen arriving on Ferron Creek in 1877 or 1878. It is possible, however, that he had been running livestock in the area for some years before he came as a settler. In addition to Acord and Molen, Chipman identified as other early stockmen in Castle Valley the Bennions, the "Millers from Cottonwood," and the Green brothers, Alva, Jesse, and John, from American Fork. He claimed that William Jennings, a wealthy Salt Lake merchant, was the first to introduce the Hereford breed of cattle to Castle Valley.[52] Other sources indicate that Dave Pratt from American Fork and John Duncan from southern Utah ran livestock in the Muddy Creek region before the first settlers arrived, along with several stockmen from Spring City, including Charles Hyde, Edward Graves, and Abram Acord and his sons Fred, Henry, and Oliver.[53]

Livestock were apparently numerous in Castle Valley in the 1870s and early 1880s. Francis Hodgman, who passed through the valley in early 1881 as a surveyor for the Denver and Rio Grande Railway, reported seeing near Muddy Creek "great numbers of cattle apparently feeding along the mountainside, although I could not see what in the world they found to eat."[54] In northern Castle Valley he observed large herds of sheep.

Cottonwood Creek, 1875. In October 1875 Orange Seely, who was in charge of the Mount Pleasant and Fairview United Order livestock herd on the Wasatch Plateau, elected to winter the stock in Castle Valley instead of taking it back to Sanpete Valley. He moved 1,500 head of sheep and 1,400 head of cattle through Upper Joe's Valley and down Cottonwood Canyon. In order to bring their supply wagons to the valley, the Seely party carved out the first road through the canyon. They established their headquarters near Cottonwood Creek about midway between the present sites of Orangeville and Castle Dale, building a large dugout to house the dozen or so herders. Among the party were Orange Seely's younger brother Justus Wellington, Jr. (who later established a homestead claim to the land on which the dugout was situated), John S. Jorgensen, Aaron Oman,

Eagle Roller Mill, Castle Dale, with (l–r) Alonzo Seely, Ray Jensen, Miller Black, and Orange Seely, Sr. (Courtesy Angie Hayward Family)

August Nielsen, Jacob Jensen, Tim Fullmer, and two Utes called Aub and Piggy.[55] The Seely brothers brought the herds to Castle Valley again for the winter of 1876–77.[56]

Huntington Creek, Circa 1875. Reportedly sometime in 1874, James McHadden, Leander Lemmon, and some other stockmen from Skull Valley, Tooele County, visited Castle Valley in search of new rangeland. In the spring of 1875, McHadden and Lemmon returned together with Bill Gentry and Alfred Starr, bringing a herd of horses. Gentry and Starr lived in dugouts near the mouth of Cedar Creek Canyon. McHadden and Lemmon began work on a ditch to irrigate bottom land along Huntington Creek. Reportedly, the first hay grown in Castle Valley was harvested from this land, which remains in the Lemmon family.[57] In 1876 a company composed of Lemmon, Pete Grant, and Reuben Miller trailed a herd of sheep from California to Castle Valley. McHadden and Gentry brought cattle from Salt Lake Valley, and Starr brought another herd of sheep. Warren H. Brady came with sheep from Mount Pleasant. That fall Leander Lemmon erected a log cabin on his irrigated farmland beside Huntington

Creek, probably the first permanent "above-ground" dwelling in Castle Valley.[58]

Most of these early stockmen moved on within a few years in search of new range. But a few, including the Swasey and Seely brothers, Leander Lemmon, John Jorgensen, Aaron Oman, and John Duncan, became permanent residents of Emery County.

Names on the Land

Included with Powell's *Report on the Arid Lands* was a map of Utah reflecting the work of the "U.S. Geographical and Geological Survey of the Rocky Mountain Region, J. W. Powell in Charge." This map, published in 1878 but prepared at least a year earlier, shows what the Emery County region looked like to the mapmakers on the eve of settlement. Most of the major geographical features had the names by which they are still known: the Wasatch Plateau; Castle Valley; the San Rafael River and Swell; the West and East Tavaputs plateaus and the Book Cliffs; Ivie, Ferron, Cottonwood, and Huntington creeks; and the Price River. The mapmaker has transposed Muddy and Quitchupah creeks (the latter is spelled "Kweechupa), and the stream below the confluence of Muddy, Quitchupah, and Ivie creeks is labeled Curtis Creek. Cedar Mountain is called the Red Plateau, a name that still appears on some maps. As we would expect, the names Powell had bestowed along the Green River appear on the map: Gray Canyon, Gunnison Valley, Labyrinth Canyon, Barrier Creek. Range Creek is accurately represented but not named. Cottonwood Springs and "water pockets" corresponding to the Big and Little Holes are identified on the Spanish Trail route. Not many individual features on the Wasatch Plateau are named on the map, but Young's Peak and Joe's Valley do appear, indicating that the names predate the settlement era.

Many of the major landmarks of Emery County bear Anglo names that replaced Spanish names that in their turn replaced Ute names. The older names are recoverable only in part. The mountain men called the upper Green River the Seedskeedee-agie, presumably an Indian name, but it is not clear whether that name was ever applied to the lower part of the river. E. G. Beckwith seemed to think "Akanaquint" was a Ute name for the Green River. W. W. Loring—

probably drawing on the trail knowledge of Antoine Leroux—apparently listed both Indian and Spanish names for Cottonwood (Sivareech, San Mateo) and Huntington (Taveajo, San Marcus) creeks. Garambulla, the name by which Ferron Creek was known before 1873, is probably an Indian name, as is Shangint, the name A. D. Ferron used for Cedar Creek. Indian names that remain in use today include Quitchupah (variously spelled), Wasatch, and Tavaputs. The Powell party evidently understood Castle Valley to be a translation of the Indian "Toom-pin-con-to-weep," or "stone house land," and applied it to the entire region embraced by the Wasatch and Tavaputs plateaus.

The most prominent Spanish name that remains imprinted on the Emery County landscape is of course San Rafael. George Yount's "St. Joseph's Valley" may be a translation of "Valle de San Jose." "Rio del Puerto" for Ivie Creek and "Rio del Morro" for Muddy Creek were likely taken from Spanish trail logs. Even some Anglo place names are of uncertain date or derivation. Beckwith's "Big Rock Creek" for the Muddy may be a rough translation of "Rio del Morro." John L. Ivie and James Ivie were both members of the 1855 Elk Mountain Mission, but there is no definite evidence that Ivie Creek was named at that time or for them. Other names used at various times for Ivie Creek or nearby streams include Shipley Creek, Media Creek, Stewart Creek, and Cab (or Cob) Creek. The names of Muddy, "Sweet Cotton Wood," and Huntington creeks first appear in the journals of the Elk Mountain Mission, but they are used as if they were already established names. As we have seen, the 1878 map portrays Muddy Creek as a tributary of Curtis Creek.

Convulsion Canyon and Rock Canyon (or "Rocky Trail Canyon") had those names at least by 1865 and perhaps as early as 1858. The Price River was still called the Little White in 1871. J. W. Powell evidently believed the Book Cliffs were named by Gunnison, but there is nothing in the report of the Gunnison expedition to indicate this. Gunnison did refer to the Brown Cliffs, a term still used interchangeably with Roan Cliffs to designate the upper cliff line on the Tavaputs Plateau.

The 1878 map shows three roads in what is now Emery County. One is the Spanish Trail route. A second branches off from the

Spanish Trail about four miles west of Green River and follows the Price River Valley to Soldier Canyon and on to Soldier Summit. The third road leaves the second near Mounds and goes southwest through Castle Valley to join the Spanish Trail near the crossing of Huntington Creek. All three of these roads would play a role in the settlement of Emery County, as would a fourth road across the Wasatch Plateau, not shown in the map, but opened in 1875 by Orange Seely and associates to provide a more direct route from Sanpete to Castle Valley.

ENDNOTES

1. Hafen and Hafen, *Old Spanish Trail,* 86.

2. The account, written by David H. Coyner, is quoted in J. Cecil Alter, *Utah, the Storied Domain: A Documentary History of Utah's Eventful Career,* 3 vols. (Chicago and New York: American Historical Society, 1932), 1:10–11.

3. Brooks, *Southwest Expedition,* 11–14, 47.

4. Hafen and Hafen, *Old Spanish Trail,* 19.

5. "The Chronicles of George C. Yount, California Pioneer of 1826," *California Historical Society Quarterly* 2 (1923), 1: 38.

6. Hafen and Hafen, *Old Spanish Trail,* 187.

7. Ibid., 331–35.

8. "The Journal of Orville C. Pratt," in Hafen and Hafen, *Old Spanish Trail,* 349–51.

9. "Choteau's Log and Description of the Trail," in Hafen and Hafen, *Old Spanish Trail,* 369.

10. Heap, *Central Route to the Pacific,* 83–86.

11. Montell Seely found this section of the road sketched in A. D. Ferron's 1873 survey map. Montell Seely, letter, 26 May 1993.

12. Beckwith, *Pacific Railroad,* 66–72.

13. Alfred N. Billings gives a detailed description in his diary entry for 27 May 1855. Alfred N. Billings, Diary 1855, photocopy in Archives and Manuscripts, Harold B. Lee Library, Brigham Young University, Provo, Utah.

14. Beckwith, *Pacific Railroad,* 89–90.

15. Carvalho, *Incidents of Travel,* 167–68.

16. Bauman, *Stone House Lands,* 99–105.

17. William Huntington, Letter to the Editor, *Deseret News,* 21 December 1854.

18. *CV,* 200, reports that LDS church historian Andrew Jenson had evidence that the creek was not named for the Mormon Huntington brothers but for "an old explorer" who had passed through the valley at an earlier date. No corroborating evidence for this claim has been found.

19. Huntington's official diary is in the Library-Archives, Historical Department, Church of Jesus Christ of Latter-day Saints, Salt Lake City, Utah; his personal journal is in Archives and Manuscripts, Lee Library.

20. Alfred N. Billings Diary, 42–43.

21. Montell Seely cites an entry in surveyor A. D. Ferron's notes in 1873 referring to the Rock Canyon trail as "Elk Mountain Mission." *EC 1880–1980,* 16.

22. Hafen, "Colonel Loring's Expedition," 57–59.

23. Orange Seely, Senior, Autobiography, typescript in Archives and Manuscripts, Lee Library.

24. Gottfredson, *Indian Depredations,* 162.

25. Orange Seely, Autobiography.

26. J. C. Sumner, Diary, 13 July 1869, quoted in Cooley, *Great Unknown,* 102.

27. J. W. Powell, Account of 15 July 1869, in Cooley, *Great Unknown,* 103, 105.

28. Dellenbaugh, *Canyon Voyage,* 98.

29. "Journal of John F. Steward, May 22–November 3, 1871," ed. William Culp Darrah, *Utah Historical Quarterly* 16–17 (1948–49): 225.

30. "Journal of Stephen Vandiver Jones, April 21, 1871–December 14, 1872," ed. Herbert E. Gregory, *Utah Historical Quarterly* 16–17 (1848–49): 72.

31. "Diary of Almon Harris Thompson, Geographer, Explorations of the Colorado River of the West and Its Tributaries, 1871–75," *Utah Historical Quarterly* 7 (1939): 41.

32. Dellenbaugh, *Canyon Voyage,* 99.

33. "Book Cliffs" is actually the older name. Writing several years later, J. W. Powell provided this summary: "In 1869, when the writer first saw this great escarpment, he gave it the name of the Azure Cliffs, but an earlier traveler, passing by another route across the country, had seen them in the distance, and, seizing another characteristic feature, had called them the Book Mountains." Powell, *Arid Region,* 112.

34. "Journal of Stephen Vandiver Jones," 72, 73.

35. Dellenbaugh, *Canyon Voyage,* 102.

36. "Journal of Stephen Vandiver Jones," 73.

37. "Diary of Almon Harris Thompson," 44.

38. Powell, *Exploration of the Colorado River,* 75–79.

39. Montell Seely, "Augustus D. Ferron Survey 1873," in *EC 1880–1980,* 15–16. Ida Conklin of Ferron corresponded in 1963 with a daughter-in-law of A. D. Ferron who indicated that he had also platted parts of Salt Lake City. She also confirmed from family traditions the story of his ducking in Ferron Creek. *EC 1880–1980,* 103.

40. *EC 1880–1980,* 15.

41. Dutton, *High Plateaus,* 2, 19–20.

42. Wallace Stegner, "Editor's Introduction," to Powell, *Arid Region,* vii.

43. A. H. Thompson, "Irrigable Lands of That Portion of Utah Drained by the Colorado River and Its Tributaries," in Powell, *Arid Region,* 170, 171, 175–76.

44. For a brief overview of the development of the livestock industry in Utah, see Charles S. Peterson, "Grazing in Utah: A Historical Perspective," *Utah Historical Quarterly* 57 (Fall 1989): 300–319.

45. Quoted in Peterson, "Grazing in Utah," 316–17.

46. Bennion, "Pioneer Cattle Venture," 316, 319–20, 322.

47. Charles S. Peterson, "Cowboys and Cattle Trails: A Centennial View of Emery County," in Powell, *Emery County,* 93–94.

48. LDS church genealogical records.

49. Bennion, "Pioneer Cattle Venture," 325.

50. Swasey birthdates taken from LDS church genealogical records. An inscription in Coal Wash with Joe Swasey's name plus the date 7 February 1875, suggests that the Swaseys were in Castle Valley during the winter of 1874–75. Inscription reproduced in *EC 1880–1980,* 18.

51. Merle S. Chipman, *The Life of Stephen Washburn (Wash) Chipman, Castle Valley Cattleman, 1862–1947* (Privately printed, 1969), 20.

52. Chipman, *Wash Chipman,* 25.

53. *CV,* 137.

54. Francis Hodgman, "In the Mountains of Utah, February 1881–March 1882," in *Dreams, Visions and Visionaries: Colorado Rail Annual, No. 20,* ed. Jackson Thode and James L. Ozment (Golden, Colorado: Colorado Railroad Museum, 1993), 29.

55. *CV,* 70.

56. *EC 1880–1980,* 18.

57. Jones, *Settling of Huntington,* 3–4.

58. *CV,* 200–202.

3

The Last Colony, 1877–1880

On 22 August 1877 there was issued over Brigham Young's signature and addressed to Sanpete LDS Stake president Canute Peterson what may be considered as the founding document of Emery County, or at any rate the Castle Valley region:

> Inasmuch as it is probable that quite a number of the brethren, who have sold out in Thistle Valley to facilitate its occupancy by the Lamanites, will not desire to settle in Castle Valley, though we should like as many as possible to do so, and as we are anxious to see a good, strong settlement of Latter-day Saints established in the last named valley, we should be pleased to have you make inquiry and find out what brethren in the Stake of Zion over which you preside would like to settle there.
>
> There are numbers of the brethren in different portions of Sanpete County, who have not an abundant supply of water for their land, who would, no doubt, be happy to remove to a valley where the water is abundant and the soil good. We should like to have at least fifty families locate in Castle Valley this fall; but if some of the brethren cannot take their families this year, it would

> be well for them to go themselves, secure their locations and commence work. In making your selection, choose good, energetic, God fearing young men, whether single or with families, and others who can be spared without interfering with the interests of the settlements in which they now reside, such ones as will be a strength to the new settlement and an aid to its growth in all that we, as Latter-day Saints, desire to see increase upon the earth.[1]

President Young had issued similar "calls" for settlers on numerous occasions during the thirty years he had led the church in the West. This, however, was to be his last such directive. Just one week later, on 29 August, the Great Colonizer died. To be sure, LDS church-directed colonization did not end with the death of Brigham Young. It continued on a limited basis into the twentieth century. But the Castle Valley settlement marked a significant transition. Not only was it the last colony founded by Brigham Young, it was the first major Mormon colony established in a region that had been surveyed for entry under the homestead laws.

The call to settle Castle Valley was not unexpected. President Young had expressed interest as early as 1875 in "the lands east of Sanpete" as a possible site for colonization.[2] J. W. Seely, Jr., perhaps anticipating the call, had staked a homestead claim to choice river-bottom land on Cottonwood Creek in May 1877.[3] In June a party consisting of Elias Cox, Jehu Cox, Jr., Benjamin Jones, Elam Cheney, Jr., and Jefferson Tidwell had been sent to Castle Valley by Sanpete Stake officials to investigate possible sites for settlement.[4]

Motives for the Colonizing of Castle Valley. It is not surprising that Brigham Young, as president of the LDS church, would wish "to see a good, strong settlement of Latter-day Saints" established in Castle Valley. Under his direction, almost 400 towns and villages had been established during the three decades from 1847 to 1877. Given its location less than 150 miles from church headquarters, a pertinent question might be not "Why did the church call settlers to Castle Valley in 1877?" but rather "Why not sooner?" One reason for the delay was the mountain barrier formed by the Wasatch Range and the high plateaus, which impeded access to eastern Utah. Another was the ruggedness of the country itself, combined with its reputation as a refuge for renegade Indians. W. H. Lever, writing in 1898 and presumably drawing upon information obtained at first-hand from the early settlers, noted that the Sanpete militia "made frequent trips through portions of Castle valley in pursuit of marauding Indians" during the Black Hawk War period, and that the "most observing ones noticed the many beautiful locations and expressed a desire to found new homes in this section." They were deterred, however, by concerns about the quality of the soil, which was obviously unlike the deep alluvium of Sanpete Valley. Lever wrote that they were also concerned that "the water supply did not appear sufficient to justify colonial settlements."[5] The apprehensions about the soil quality are understandable, but the reference to inadequate water supply seems odd in light of the fact that the Castle Valley creeks are substantially larger than those on which most Sanpete towns were located.

By the 1870s, the more fertile and accessible regions in Mormon country had been occupied. Brigham Young's letter begins with a reference to "the brethren, who have sold out in Thistle Valley to facilitate its occupancy by the Lamanites." The Uintah Reservation had been established in 1861, but some Ute bands resisted attempts to remove them from their traditional homelands. The Black Hawk War (1865–68) can be interpreted as the most desperate stage in that resistance. One effect of the Black Hawk conflict was to accelerate the resettlement of Utes on the Uintah Reservation, but it was still a gradual process. Recollections of early colonists indicate that groups of Utes continued to spend at least a part of the year in Castle Valley well into the settlement era.[6] As late as the 1920s, caravans of Utes would pass through Emery County each year going to Fish Lake in the summer and returning to the Uintah Reservation in the fall.[7] In 1872, in an effort to accommodate Sanpitch Utes who wanted to remain in their homeland, the LDS church established an "Indian Farm" in Thistle Valley (now known as Indianola) and pressed some settlers to sell their land there to enable the Utes to take possession.[8] Evidently, church leaders viewed Castle Valley as an alternative settlement site for those colonists displaced from Thistle Valley.

The need to find new lands to replace those lost to the Indian Farm was only one small manifestation of a larger problem. At an elevation of 6,500 feet, Thistle Valley was marginal farming country.

Mail coach arrives at Ferron. George Edward Anderson photograph. (Brigham Young University Photographic Archives)

It was colonized only after the better land and water resources in Sanpete Valley had been appropriated. The population of Sanpete County grew from 3,815 in 1860 to 6,786 in 1870 and 11,557 in 1880. During this same period, Sevier County was colonized, largely by settlers from Sanpete County, reaching a population of 4,457 by 1880. It is apparent that the combination of immigration and natural increase had created a substantial population surplus for the prevailing agrarian economy. The 1870 census counted 14,094 acres of "improved" land in Sanpete County, or slightly more than two acres per resident. There were 605 farms of which 276 were smaller than twenty acres and only thirty-six larger than fifty acres. The census figures depict a subsistence economy, with few resources available to provide for the second generation that was coming of age in the 1870s. As Ferron-native rural sociologist Lowry Nelson summed up the situation, "Castle Valley provided for these communities an economic release of prime importance."[9]

A likely additional motive for the colonization of Castle Valley was the desire of LDS church leaders to prevent its occupation by non-Mormons. An influx of "Gentiles" to the Salt Lake Valley in the 1860s and 1870s had substantially reduced Mormon political influence at the church's very center. Moreover, the commercial development of Salt Lake City had led some of its Mormon residents, in the words of historian Charles S. Peterson, to turn away "from many of the distinctive practices that had characterized their own pioneer years, and the Mormon capital may well have become the least Mormon of all Mormon places." Peterson adds, "Conversely, the hinterland, where the process of the call, the trek, and the establishment of the village repeated itself, became the bulwark of Mormonism in its most distinctive form."[10] It was in the hope of extending and strengthening that bulwark that Brigham Young called settlers to Castle Valley.

And what if the LDS church had not undertaken the colonization of Castle Valley in 1877? Emery County's history would certainly have been different, but it is impossible to say how much different. It is likely that Mormon settlers would soon have been attracted to the land and water of Castle Valley even without being directed by their leaders. (Escalante, Garfield County, was settled as a Mormon village in 1876–77 without a formal "call" from church leaders, and its location was more remote than Castle Valley.) And if Mormons had not come, non-Mormons would have done so, as they in fact came to Green River and to Carbon County. The Emery County region was ripe for development. The area bounded by the main range of the Rocky Mountains on the east, the Wasatch Range and the high plateaus on the west, the Uinta Range on the north, and the central Arizona mountains on the south was the largest remaining unsettled region in the United States by the late 1870s.

The First Settlers

In accordance with Brigham Young's instructions, seventy-five men from various wards in Sanpete Stake were called as colonists during a priesthood meeting held in Mount Pleasant on 22 September 1877. Christian Grice Larsen, former bishop of Spring City and former president of the Scandinavian Mission, was assigned to be the ecclesiastical leader of the new colony. However, this call did not meet with an eager response. Only a few of the men named were willing to move to Castle Valley. Even Bishop Larsen apparently found it inconvenient to relocate at that time. As Larsen's replacement, Orange Seely, recently installed as bishop of the Mount Pleasant North Ward, was designated as bishop of the region east of the Wasatch Plateau.[11] Seely was well acquainted with Castle Valley and presumably a strong supporter of its colonization. In response to the call, three separate parties set out from Sanpete Valley within a few weeks of one another, taking three different routes to three destinations in Castle Valley.

Huntington Creek. One group assembled in Fairview under the leadership of a middle-aged widower named Elias Cox, who had directed the exploring expedition the preceding summer. In the party were Cox's adult son Elias H.; Elias Cox's brother Jehu with his second wife, Edith Jones, and their seven children; Henderson Cox, an unmarried adult son of Jehu Cox and his first wife; Frederick and Martha Elizabeth Cox Fenn (sister of Elias and Jehu) and their four children; Heber Kimball and Rosannah Brady Jones and their three children; Benjamin and Sarah Jane Cheney Jones and their two children; and Elam Cheney, Jr., a half-brother to Sarah Jane. The exact date of their departure from Fairview and arrival at Huntington Creek is in dispute. The 1949 Daughters of Utah Pioneers history states that the migration occurred in November. James Albert Jones, whose grandfather was among the party, gives the departure date as "about the last of September" and the arrival on Huntington Creek as "about October 15." Up through the first decade of the twentieth century, Huntington celebrated "Settlement Day" on 11 October. Because Elias Cox and several other members of the colonizing party were still alive at that time, 11 October would seem to be the correct date.[12]

From Fairview the Cox party traveled north through Thistle Valley and down Thistle Creek to its junction with the Spanish Fork River. They then followed the military road over Soldier Summit and down through the Park and Soldier Canyon to Castle Valley. They apparently made a new road from Price River to Huntington Creek, closer to the mountains than the old Gunnison road. As they approached their destination, they were met by Rosannah Jones's brothers Warren Brady, Jr., and Marion Brady, who were herding sheep near Huntington Creek. The settlers constructed dugouts in the banks of the creek a short distance upstream from the present Highway 10 bridge. Then they drew lots for various homestead locations in the river valley.

Within a few weeks, the ranks of settlers were augmented by the arrival of William H. and Eliza Jane Shepherd Avery, Anthony and Olive Cheney Humble, Elam and Urilda Todd McBride and their young daughter, Charles S. Hollingshead, and David and Thomas Cheney. During the first winter, the colonists began work on two canals, the Avery Ditch to irrigate a hollow east of the present Huntington townsite and the North Ditch to bring water to the wide bottomlands on the left bank of the creek.[13]

In the spring of 1878, Elias Cox and Charles S. Hollingshead set up a sawmill in a side canyon of Huntington Canyon to provide lumber for the new settlement. Urilda McBride operated a summer dairy in the same canyon, which now bears the name Rilda Canyon. The streamflow proved inadequate to operate the sawmill, and the operation was moved to the adjacent canyon, which was named Mill Fork. The prospects of harvesting a crop from the raw valley soil were so poor that virtually all of the settlers returned to Sanpete Valley by midsummer in order to replenish their supplies by working in the harvest there. Several families came back to Huntington Creek in the fall, and the colony's first child, appropriately named Celestia Castle, was born to Benjamin and Sarah Jane Jones on 15 December 1878.[14] William Alma and Hilma Eckberg Staker and their infant son William Helaman located a homestead that summer several miles down the creek in what would become the Lawrence district.[15] Robert and Lucinda Hill and Philander and Lucretia Burch settled in the Lawrence area in October.[16] William Avery completed a log cabin on his homestead in time for a Christmas dance to be held there, attended by forty-two men and seven women.[17]

The winter of 1878–79 was again a mild one, and new settlers began to arrive early in the spring. From the exhausted ranges of Rush Valley came David Henry Leonard with his second wife, Elizabeth Charles, and their family and a herd of sheep.[18] Noah Thomas Guymon brought his wives Elizabeth Ann Jones and Louisa Rowley and their children from Fountain Green by the Cottonwood

Canyon route. Some of Guymon's adult children, including Noah T., Jr., Clarissa (Mrs. Amasa Scovill), and Amelia (Mrs. Alma G. Jewkes) settled in what would become Orangeville. Others, including son William Albert and daughters Margaret and Harriet and their husband Hyrum Oscar Crandall continued on with their father to Huntington Creek. Also from Fountain Green came seventeen-year-old Christian Ottesen and his elder brother Joseph, who took up the homestead that had been abandoned by stockman James McHadden. The Ottesens cleared some ground for cultivation and built a cabin near the creek then went back to Sanpete Valley for the winter. Joseph did not return to Emery County, but Christian brought his bride, Sarah Crowther, to his homestead the following spring.[19]

Among the others who arrived on Huntington Creek in 1879 were William and Sarah (Sally) Curtis Wimmer. Sally Wimmer played the fiddle for dances and was the first midwife and school teacher in the community.[20] John F. Wakefield and his brother-in-law Joseph E. Johnson made a brief visit from Fountain Green in the fall and staked a homestead claim just east of the Huntington townsite. Also from Fountain Green came Albey Lyman Sherman, Charles Brown, Charles Barnes, William Cordingly, and James Woodward, Jr., his sons William and Benjamin, and William's wife, Mary Guymon.[21] Those reportedly settling in the Lawrence area this year included Simeon C. Drollinger, H. S. Loveless, and Rufus Johnson.[22]

By the end of 1879, most of the riverbottom land easily accessible to irrigation had been claimed, and plans were under way for the Huntington Canal to carry water to the benchlands south of the creek. Also during 1879 the first store in the community was opened by Elias Cox in a dugout built for the purpose. Cox and his son Elias H. hauled their entire stock from Salt Lake City in two wagons. The range of goods was limited and adapted to the most basic needs of a pioneer community, including tools and hardware; denim overalls and coats; fabrics such as calico, canvas, and "factory" (muslin), together with other sewing goods such as needles, thread, and yarn; flour, sugar, coffee, salt, soda, and baking powder; and a few patent medicines.[23]

Cottonwood Creek. On 20 October 1877 a colonizing party led by Orange Seely departed from Mount Pleasant. This group was composed of men only, including John S. Jorgensen and Aaron G. Oman, who had previously herded livestock in Castle Valley; Erastus Curtis and his sons William B. and Erastus, Jr.; Niels Peter Miller, Jasper Petersen, James H. Wilcox, George Bruno, Joseph Burnett, and Chris Peel. They chose the more direct route across the Wasatch Plateau, but even that was rather indirect, requiring them to haul their five heavy wagons north to Dry Creek Canyon in order to ascend to the plateau top. Then they made their way south and east through Gooseberry Valley, Miller Flat, Scad Valley, Upper Joe's Valley, Joe's Valley Canyon, and Cottonwood Canyon. They arrived at the herders' dugout on J. W. Seely's homestead on 2 November. Three additional men, Fred Anderson and James and Andrew Jensen, joined the group about a month later.[24]

Within a short time the settlers began selecting riverbottom homesteads. The Curtises staked out an area upstream, about a mile west of the present site of Orangeville, and began construction of a log cabin. James and Andrew Jensen, Jasper Petersen, Fred Anderson, and Neils P. Miller claimed land south and east of the J. W. Seely homestead, while Orange Seely established a homestead farther downstream, just east of what would become the Castle Dale townsite. Several of the men returned to Sanpete Valley before the high passes were closed by snow, and only seven remained in Castle Valley through the winter. They passed the time herding sheep and cattle and trapping, reportedly catching thirteen wolves in a single night. Apparently work also began that winter on the Blue Cut Canal to irrigate bottomland south of the creek.[25]

New additions to the colony on Cottonwood Creek in 1878 included Erastus Curtis's daughter Matilda, her husband, Joseph Boulden, and their son William (another child died during the journey across the Wasatch Plateau); John Y. Jensen, a brother of James and Andrew; and James Petersen, brother of Jasper. John K. Reid, from Manti, homesteaded what later became the southwest part of the Orangeville townsite. Several members of the Samuel Jewkes family, including sons Alma G., Samuel R., and William, came from Fountain Green, together with Orson Miles and James C. Woodward.[26]

Several miles down the creek, near the Spanish Trail crossing,

Sylvester Wilson and his brothers settled in the spring of 1878 at what soon became known as Wilsonville. Charles Swasey took up a homestead near the Wilsons. Washington Caldwell and his wife Almira Chase reportedly also settled there in 1878 then moved to Huntington Creek in 1879.[27] When the Star Mail Route from Salina, Utah, to Ouray, Colorado, was established in 1878, following the Spanish Trail through Emery County, Wilsonville became Castle Valley's first post office, with Sylvester Wilson as postmaster.[28] Other families reportedly settling on Cottonwood Creek in 1878 or 1879 included William and Emma Higbee and their children; Emanuel Bagley, his wives Mary and Huldy, and their children; and George and Mary Biddlecome.[29] George Biddlecome played the fiddle at dances. Mary was a midwife and herbal healer.

John K. Reid moved his family to his homestead in the spring of 1879. Late in her life, Elizabeth Jackson Reid prepared an account of their journey that describes travel conditions on the Wasatch Pass route. She wrote,

> Well do I remember the first day of May 1879, when my husband myself and six children, the eldest only nine years of age started from Manti with all our worldly goods loaded into a wagon, drawn by two yoke of oxen and one of them blind and followed by one bally cow, to give us a little milk for the children on the way to the Castle Valley Desert.

The six-day journey from Salina took them up Salina Canyon to Gooseberry Creek, up Gooseberry Canyon, over a summit and down Nioche Creek to Meadow Gulch, then over Wasatch Pass to Ivie Creek. The steep uphill pulls were very hard on the oxen, and the blind ox gave out, requiring the milk cow to be yoked in its place. At times they had to drive "over fallen timber and stumps" and at other times got stuck "twenty times in the mud and swampy places." At Meadow Gulch, "The wild animals were so bad that they were howling in every direction and we could not sleep for they made such a racket and they came so close we thought they were in our camp." In Castle Valley the road took them all the way down to Wilsonville before they could turn up Cottonwood Creek to their destination at the future site of Orangeville. When they arrived, they found that the dugout John K. Reid had constructed the previous year had been almost obliterated by the numerous cattle and sheep that had wintered in the area.

The conclusion of the journey did not bring much comfort to Elizabeth:

> There were only three other women on Cotton Wood Creek and two of them were Danish and could not speak English and we were all so far apart that we would not see each [other] once a week. . . . Such a barren desert to come to, to endeavor to make a home in. It almost made me heart sick and does to this day to look back and think of what it was then. Six small children and two hundred miles in every direction to get to civilization with an ox team. When the men folks had lifted the stove down into our hole in the ground and made a little bowery over the hole and this was the beginning of our life here, May 10, 1879.[30]

Also in 1879 Cottonwood Creek saw the arrival of Andrew Peter and Annie Catherine Petersen Rasmussen from Moroni. Annie Rasmussen would live to the age of 102 and assist as a midwife at 464 births.[31] From Fountain Green came Andrew and Diantha Christensen Anderson and their family, and Boye and Mette Anderson Petersen. Joseph Curtis and Theodore Housekeeper also arrived during this year. Several men who had come in 1878 brought their families in 1879. Samuel Jewkes and his sons installed the first sawmill on Cottonwood Creek in the fall.[32] It was operated by horse power until a mill race could be constructed.[33] The Jewkes family also brought the first threshing machine to the valley, either in 1879 or in 1880, and the first grist mill in 1882.[34]

Both Orange and Justus Wellington Seely moved their families to Castle Valley in the fall of 1879. Wellington's wife, Anna Eliza Reynolds, was close to term in a pregnancy but did not want to remain in Mount Pleasant through another winter without her husband. He had to return to Castle Valley in order to meet the residence requirements on his homestead. Bringing Mary Young Wilcox with them as a nurse, the family undertook the journey, but the baby arrived before they reached the valley. Clarissa Ellis Seely came into the world at the Willow Bunch in Cottonwood Canyon on 26

October, the first white child born on the Cottonwood Creek drainage. (The first child born in the settlement was Irwin L. Curtis, born to Johanna and Erastus, Sr., on 12 December.[35])

Orange and Hanna Olsson Seely and their children crossed the mountains a short time after J. W. Seely's eventful journey. At the time of his call to Castle Valley, Orange Seely was a prominent and prosperous citizen of Mount Pleasant with a newly built, spacious brick home. Apparently Hanna was not eager to give up the comforts of her home and the social and educational advantages of an established community in order to take up once again the pioneer hardships she had known as a young woman. According to her own later version of a widely retold story, "The first time I ever swore was when we arrived in Emery County and I said 'Damn a man who would bring a woman to such a God Forsaken country!'"[36]

Because Wilsonville and the mail route were situated at an inconvenient distance from the majority of settlers on Cottonwood Creek, a committee consisting of John K. Reid, Orange Seely, Jasper Petersen, David Latimer, and James Petersen petitioned for the establishment of a post office to be called Castle Vale. The petition was granted on 1 June 1879, but under the name Castle Dale. John K. Reid was appointed as postmaster, and the office was operated, together with the community's first store, in his dugout on the present site of Orangeville.[37]

Ferron Creek. On 15 November 1877 a third colonizing party departed from Ephraim bound for Ferron Creek by way of Salina Pass. This was a small group consisting of six people with three wagons: Nicholas and Helena Larsen, who had been married for only one week; Peter F. and Caroline Peterson; and Swen Larsen and his son Neils Christian. They constructed dugouts on a south-facing hillside a short distance east of the Ferron townsite. The mild winter allowed them to plow some land and begin work on what would later be known as the Molen Ditch.[38]

In the spring of 1878, the settlers moved two miles east to the site of Molen where there was more level ground. They constructed the Peterson Ditch and planted wheat, oats, barley, corn, and potatoes. As was typical of the first crops in Castle Valley, however, the yield was poor. That fall a party of settlers arrived from American Fork,

Utah County, including William Taylor, Sr., his wife Mary Ann, and their children James, Esther, and Susannah; William Taylor, Jr., his wife Mary Jane Singleton, and their children Mary Ann and William; Joseph Wrigley, his plural wife Ann Singleton, and their children Mary, Thomas, Clara, and Caroline; Thomas Cunningham, Edson King, J. S. Thornton, Mads Larsen, and Hyrum and Emily Cook. The Cooks' daughter Millie was the first white child born in Castle Valley, 30 November 1878.[39] One source indicates that Mike Molen also came this year, but this may have been when he decided to settle in the region after having run livestock there in earlier years.[40]

The Taylors, Senior and Junior, erected log cabins. The other families evidently lived in dugouts. William Taylor, Jr., had brought lumber for a floor, and his home was therefore chosen for the community's Christmas party and dance, attended by thirteen men and four women. By this time most of the women had gone back to the established communities for the winter. William Wrigley, who had another wife and family in American Fork, left Castle Valley before winter and was unable to return until spring, leaving Ann to fend for herself and her young children throughout the winter.[41]

The population on Ferron Creek was increased in 1879 by the return of the families who had left for the winter and by the arrival of Andrew, Hyrum, and Christian Nelson and their brother-in-law John Lemon from Manti. Also arriving this year were J. D. Killpack, L. M. Beach, Peter Fjelsted, Seth Wareham, the Ralphs brothers, Joseph, Parley, and John, and the Rasmussen brothers, J. M. and Andrew. Most of these, like the earlier settlers, located on the level bottomland near Molen. However, Lemon and the Nelson brothers selected homesteads farther west on rocky ground that would require an additional irrigation canal.[42] A post office was established on 25 June 1879, though the first postmaster of record, William Taylor, Jr., did not receive his commission until 1880.[43] Francis Hodgman, who visited Ferron Creek in 1881, reported, "There are only about a dozen houses at this settlement and those of the most primitive kind." Some were built of cottonwood logs and some of "small saplings set upright and interwoven with willow like a basket." The roofs were "of poles, brush or hay, and earth."[44]

Church Organization. In January 1879 Bishop Orange Seely organized the settlers on Ferron and Huntington creeks into branches of the LDS church. Elias Cox was chosen as branch president at Huntington, and William Taylor, Sr., at Ferron. In October Sanpete Stake president Canute Peterson visited the Castle Valley settlements, released Bishop Seely from his assignment over the entire region, and established wards in each colony. The branch presidents at Huntington and Ferron were made bishops, and Jasper Petersen was installed as bishop at Castle Dale. Prior to this time, Bishop Seely, a huge, barrel-chested man weighing more than 300 pounds, reportedly made his pastoral rounds, which extended as far as Moab, riding one mule and leading another packed with provisions, camp equipment, blacksmith tools, even dental forceps to care for the various needs of his far-flung parishioners.[45]

Green River Beginnings

Historical records of the early Green River settlement are sketchy. The Salina-Ouray mail route, in operation from about 1878 to 1883, used the Green River crossing, and a postal station was reportedly established there under the supervision of a man named Blake. The postal designation remained Blake or Blake City until 1895.[46] No further information on the mysterious Mr. Blake has come to light.

The first permanent settlers were Thomas Farrer and his five sons and three daughters. W. H. Lever reported that they arrived in the spring of 1878 together with Irvin Wilson and sons and Matthew Hartman. The Wilsons, however, soon moved to the Moab area. The Farrers had emigrated from Bedfordshire, England, about 1868 and lived at St. John and Ophir, Tooele County, before moving to Green River. Tradition holds that Thomas Farrer chose Green River because he "wanted to get as far away from civilization as possible."[47] The family initially located on the east bank of the river in a hut made from willows.[48] In 1880 the William Higby family came from Manti and also settled on the east bank but remained for only a few years. These and other settlers cultivated small riverside plots using waterwheels or steam-powered pumps to lift irrigation water from the river. An 1880 survey map shows five water wheels and one pump site in operation between the upper end of Willow Bend and the mouth of Saleratus Wash. It also shows a diversion dam a short distance below

Green River Ferry. (Special Collections, University of Utah Library)

the present diversion point. In 1880 seventeen men organized the Blake City Water Ditch Company, which, according to early resident Herman Dahling, "took over from the early settlers in the area, a brush diversion dam and a crude system of irrigation ditches which the company proceeded to improve."[49] Among the organizers were Thomas, Alfred, and Levi Farrer, George Larson, Henry (Hy) Penny, and Mads Larsen.[50]

The Penny and Mads Larsen families are listed, along with the Farrers, in the 1880 census. There is no mention of George Larson. Henry Penny was a twenty-three-year-old rancher with wife Mary (21) and infant son James. Mads Larsen was listed as a fifty-seven-year-old farmer with a thirty-nine-year-old wife, Jane, sons George (14), Louis (10), and Mads (5), and daughters Jane (16), Elizabeth (12), and Hannah (3). (This is not the same Mads Larsen who settled in Molen.) Elizabeth Larsen later married J. T. Farrer. The 1880 census also lists Samuel Stowe, a forty-eight-year-old farmer with wife Mary (38), sons Hezekiah (18), Noah (16), and John (14), and daughters Harriett (8) and Verdie (5). Mary Penny was a daughter of the Stowes. Yet another resident of the Green River area in early 1880 was James O'Fallin, a thirty-year-old rancher, with wife Hannah (27) and sons James (11), Jacob (8), James C. (5), and Louis (3). Apparently the Larsens, Pennys, and O'Fallins moved to Moab and the Stowes went to Arizona later in 1880.[51]

When LDS apostle Francis M. Lyman visited the Green River settlement in August 1880, he reported that "Green River City" consisted of "a postoffice, store, ferry, and three families." Lyman was favorably impressed by the region, noting "a large tract of land on each side of the river . . . to make homes and farms for one hundred men." He described the climate as "delightful, as fine as can be found in the Territory," and reported, "Many claims have been staked off on the river, and but little more has been done. The few who are now there have worked hard, but too few to make much of a mark in a large country."[52] The Farrers relocated to the west side of the river in 1880 or 1881, with Thomas Farrer homesteading the land now included in the Farrer and Orchard Home subdivisions and sons John Thomas, Alfred A., Fredrick, Levi, and Henry C. taking up much of the remaining land under the Gravity Ditch. In addition to their farming, the family ran cattle on the Tavaputs Plateau. John T. Farrer operated the ferry and also a general store and saloon that was the community's chief business establishment for twenty-five years.[53] Chris Halverson came in 1884 as a trapper. When the beaver grew scarce, he homesteaded a ranch on the San Rafael River a short distance below the Reef, apparently the first of several settlers who tried to tame that stream's erratic flow.[54] Others who came during the 1880s included the Gamage, Brown, Durant, and Mohr families. It was George W. Durant who named the east bank settlement Elgin after his home town of Elgin, Illinois.[55]

1880—The Formative Year

The Hard Winter. In contrast to the mild weather of the two preceding years, the winter of 1879–80 was very severe. The snow came early and stayed late, accompanied by extreme cold. Alice Leonard Westover, who was four years old at the time, remembered awakening to see long strands of hoar frost that had formed on the dugout's earth walls during the night. One morning she discovered a cow frozen to death in a standing position a few yards from their door.

Almost the entire herd of 1,500 sheep that David Henry Leonard had brought to Castle Valley died from cold and starvation.[56] John Duncan reportedly lost 2,000 head of cattle, their carcasses strewn across a thousand acres in the Quitchupah region.[57] The Jewkes family lost some 200 head of cattle and ten of their twelve yokes of oxen.[58]

The early cold and snow put an end to the canal-building that otherwise would have occupied the winter. Left idle, the men whose families were on the other side of the mountains grew homesick. Some resorted to risky measures to get to Sanpete Valley. In December John F. Wakefield and Milas E. Johnson attempted to walk across the Wasatch Plateau but were able to get no farther than Joe's Valley. Returning to the Cottonwood Creek settlement, they found John K. Reid preparing to go to Manti with a team and wagon. The combined party got part way up Convulsion Canyon before they encountered snow too deep for the wagon. They then packed a few supplies on the horses and walked over Wasatch Pass, taking turns breaking trail through the snow.[59] Another group composed of Joseph E. Johnson, William Albert Guymon, William Cordingly, Charles Barnes, Charles Brown, and William Henry Sanderson set out in February for Sanpete Valley by way of Huntington Canyon on crude skis or snowshoes fashioned from boards. It took them three days to reach the coal mine at Connellsville (now covered by Electric Lake) and another long day from there to Fairview.[60]

Food ran very low in Castle Valley before fresh supplies could be brought across the mountains. When flour supplies were exhausted, the settlers resorted to grinding wheat in coffee mills. Josephine Petersen recalled, "By working hard we could grind about two bushels a day." When the wheat was exhausted, Ferron Creek settlers "subsisted on potatoes; they even tried prickly pears. Once they shot a porcupine and cooked the meat but it was pretty strong." Finally, in late April someone managed to get to Manti and bring back 6,500 pounds of flour.[61]

While the winter of 1879–80 tested the scanty resources of the Castle Valley pioneers, it also provided the stimulus for additional settlers to come to the area. After losing most of their livestock in the frigid climate of the Bear River Valley, the Randolph Stewart, William Howard, and John L. Brasher families were "released" from their settlement mission there and came to Emery County in the fall of 1880.[62] The Howard and Brasher families became permanent residents, but Randolph Stewart and his families left Castle Valley when he was called as the first bishop of the Moab LDS ward in 1881.[63]

The Establishment of Emery County. The 1880 Utah Territorial Legislature created three new counties, Emery, San Juan, and Uintah. The act creating Emery County was signed by acting governor Arthur L. Thomas on 12 February.[64] The legislature acted in response to a petition drafted in the fall of 1879 by Elias Cox, Emanuel Bagley, and John K. Reid, requesting that the portion of Sanpete County lying east of the Wasatch Plateau be designated as Castle County.[65] Instead of accepting the proposed name, the legislature chose to name the new county in honor of Governor George W. Emery, who had just completed a five-year term and in fact was in Washington, D.C., trying to secure an appointment for a second term at the time when Emery County was created.[66] The governor had been on good terms with the Mormon-dominated legislature, and it seems likely that the naming of the county for him was intended as a gesture of support in his quest for reappointment. If that was the intent, the gesture was ineffective as Emery was not reappointed. He was, however, the only Utah governor to have a county named in his honor.

The county boundaries as described in the legislative act embraced the area now included in Emery and Carbon counties. The area east of the Green River and south of the Roan Cliffs was originally designated as part of San Juan County, but acting governor Thomas vetoed the San Juan County act on 13 February on the grounds that it took in too large an area. A revised bill was enacted on 18 February creating San Juan County with its present boundaries and extending the eastern border of Emery County to the Colorado line.[67]

There is no detailed record of the negotiations that led to the establishment of Emery County, but some of the considerations the legislature took into account are apparent from the drawing of the boundary lines. Most north-south trending county lines in Utah follow natural watershed boundaries. However, Emery County's western border is an arbitrary line well to the east of the summit ridge that divides the Castle Valley watershed from that of Sanpete and

Sevier valleys. The Wasatch Plateau trends from northeast to southwest, so that not only the high plateau but even a portion of Castle Valley falls within the boundaries of Sevier County south of Muddy Creek. To the north, where a straight north-south line would have placed the entire Huntington Creek drainage in Emery County, the boundary line jogs three miles east in order to keep the upper part of the Huntington Creek and Price River watersheds in Sanpete County. It seems obvious that Sanpete and Sevier counties must have used their political influence to insure that prime mountain land remained within their boundaries, particularly those areas where transbasin water diversions might prove feasible.

The legislative act designated Castle Dale as the Emery County seat and appointed the first county officers: Samuel Jewkes as probate judge, and Elias Cox, Jasper Petersen, and William Taylor as selectmen. It was, of course, no coincidence that the three selectmen were also the bishops of the new county's three LDS wards. Despite the severe weather, these officers met, as instructed by the legislature, on 8 March in the Niels P. Miller cabin on Cottonwood Creek to complete the county organization. They appointed Emanuel Bagley as county clerk, Erastus Curtis, Sr., as sheriff, Hyrum Oscar Crandall as assessor and collector of taxes, John K. Reid as treasurer, James Woodward as coroner, Joseph S. Thornton as superintendent of district schools, and Emanuel Bagley, John E. King, and J. D. McIntosh as school board members. Meeting again on 9 March the probate judge and selectmen divided the county (or at any rate that portion west of the Green River) into the Ferron, Huntington, and Castle Dale precincts. They also appointed a pound keeper (animal control officer) for each precinct and for the county as a whole.[68] Even though there were several dozen people living in the Moab area at the time Emery County was created, no precinct was established east of the Green River. Given the difficulties of communicating with the state capital, it is possible that the county officers did not know at that time that the region had been added to Emery County. Whatever the reason, it appears that the residents east of the Green River had little contact with the county government during the first few years.

The appointed county officers were to serve only until an election was held in August 1880. At that time Elias Cox was elected as probate judge; J. W. Seely, William Taylor, Sr., and H. S. Hollingshead as selectmen; Samuel Jewkes, treasurer; M. J. Shelton, prosecuting attorney and surveyor; and John Leasil Brasher, assessor and collector. Brasher was also appointed as sheriff after the person elected resigned. Emanuel Bagley continued as county clerk.[69]

The 1880 Census. The decennial United States census was conducted in the new county in June 1880. Census enumerator L. D. Ensign found ninety residents in the Ferron precinct, 237 in the Castle Dale precinct (including Green River), and 126 in the Huntington precinct (including the Price River area). Another enumerator, J. W. Ellsworth, counted fifty-five residents in the "eastern portion" of the county, in the Moab area.[70] This would make a total for the county of 508, but the census summary gave a population of 556 and indicated that the precincts were "not separately returned." The summary report indicated that there were eighty-four farms in the county with 1,618 acres of "improved land," 282 horses, thirty-five mules, ninety-one oxen, 384 milk cows, 575 other cattle, 171 sheep, and fifty-one swine.[71]

There is good reason to doubt the accuracy of the 1880 census of Emery County. Not only is there a discrepancy of forty-eight persons between the enumerators' counts and the summary report, but several people known to reside in Emery County in 1880 are missing from the census list, including such prominent citizens as Orange Seely, Elias Cox, and Mike Molen. J. W. Seely (spelled "Ceily") is listed with wife "Analiza" and sons "Justice" W., William, and James, but there is no mention of daughter Clarissa, who had been born the previous October. Of the six original settlers on Ferron Creek only one, Swen Larsen, appears in the census enumeration. Of the Swasey clan, only Charles and his wife Cena are listed.

The count of sheep and beef cattle seems low in light of the numbers of range livestock reported in earlier years. It is conceivable that the hard winter had actually reduced herd numbers to this level. It seems more likely, however, that the livestock had been moved to the summer ranges by late June and were simply missed by the census enumerator. If he missed the livestock, he probably also missed the herdsmen, which could account for the omission of Mike Molen, the Swasey brothers, and Samuel Singleton, among others. Elias Cox and his helpers were probably at the sawmill in Huntington Canyon when the census enumerator visited the settlement. Other men, including the members of the "snowshoe" party, had not yet returned to Castle Valley from their winter sojourn in Sanpete Valley. When the known omissions are taken into account, it seems likely that even the summary figure of 556 significantly understates the actual number of people who regarded Emery County as their home in 1880.

Nevertheless, the census lists provide some interesting insights into population characteristics. Of the fifty-five people counted in the Moab area, thirty-two were single adult males, and there were only five families. This would probably be fairly typical of the early stages of western ranching and mining settlements. By contrast, the Huntington precinct had among its 126 residents twenty-one families with husband, wife, and children and only nine single adult males, two of whom lived with their parents. It is apparent that the colonizing of Castle Valley was a family enterprise. Many were young families, in keeping with Brigham Young's counsel. Of the ninety-seven heads of household in the three Castle Valley precincts, forty-six were under the age of thirty. Another twenty-six were between thirty and thirty-nine. The older settlers, such as Erastus Curtis (53), Samuel Jewkes (57), and William Taylor, Sr. (54), were typically experienced pioneers who had participated in the settlement of several other colonies. Families tended to be large. For example, Erastus Curtis and his wives Mary (57) and Joanna (39) had thirteen children still living at home. John K. (30) and Elizabeth (30) Reid had seven children under the age of eleven.

The male occupations listed in the census were predominantly farming (83) or ranching (16). Other occupations included four herders, two laborers, two trappers, one lawyer (Marion Shelton), one carpenter (John K. Reid), one blacksmith (Joseph Boulden), one stone mason (Andrew Boyle), one harness maker (Alvin Burdick), and one boilermaker (John Talbot). All married women had "keeping house" listed as their occupation. Unmarried daughters over the age of twelve were typically listed as "in house," and unmarried sons of similar ages as "on farm." No one was listed as "in school," a common designation in later census reports. The occupational picture is clearly that of a pioneer subsistence economy with few established social, educational, or commercial institutions.

Emery LDS Stake. On 20 August 1880 apostles Erastus Snow, Brigham Young, Jr., and Francis M. Lyman, and Sanpete Stake president Canute Peterson presided over a conference of LDS church members held in a bowery on the J. W. Seely homestead. Here they organized the Emery Stake of Zion, thereby giving the Emery County settlements ecclesiastical as well as political independence from the Sanpete motherland. Christian Grice Larsen of Spring City was installed as president of the new stake, with Orange Seely as first counselor. The remainder of the stake organization was not completed until 1882.[72] President Larsen was fifty-one years old with four wives and numerous children. Converted to the LDS faith in his native Denmark in 1851, he had quickly established himself as a powerful preacher and capable leader, becoming president of the Bernholm Conference. He immigrated to Utah in 1857 and served as bishop at Spring City for eight years.[73] In 1873 he succeeded Canute Peterson as president of the Scandinavian Mission, serving until 1875.[74] Larsen had initially been designated as the ecclesiastical leader of the Castle Valley colonization in 1877 but apparently had found it impractical to relocate at that time. He moved to Emery County in October 1880 and spent several days snowbound in an early storm on the mountain.[75] Larsen acquired the homestead originally located by Sanford Forbush, an area that now makes up most of the eastern half of Castle Dale.[76]

The visit by LDS church leaders to Castle Valley was part of a longer tour that took them to Moab, Bluff, and on to New Mexico and Arizona. Francis M. Lyman sent periodic reports of the journey to the *Deseret Evening News.* His letter dated 23 August describes the party's route from Mount Pleasant to Castle Dale and includes his impressions of the new settlement. He found the road across the Wasatch Plateau "tolerably good for new mountain roads," though he noted that "it has cost many dollars and hard licks" to make a passable road through Cottonwood Canyon (which he called "Seely Pass"). The mountain scenery reminded him of New Hampshire and Vermont, but his initial impression of Castle Valley was less favorable: "as we moved down the widening canyon into the valley of castles, my first impressions were that the more of such land a man possessed himself of, the poorer he would be." The outlook improved, however, as they approached the settlement, where "we found unfenced fields and gardens that compare favorably with those of our older settled and cultivated valleys of Sanpete, Juab, Utah and Salt Lake."

The visiting church leaders, accustomed to the compact Mormon villages of the older valleys, were not pleased with the "scattered condition" of the Castle Valley settlers. Lyman wrote,

> I have made diligent inquiry for two days to find the County seat of Emery County, known by the name of Castledale, and it is so scattered up and down the Cottonwood, that it is very difficult to tell which is the centre of gravitation. Every man has located upon his quarter section.

At the conference,

> The great amount of work done by the people here in a little over two years was highly commended, but their scattered condition was deprecated and they were counseled to settle as soon as possible in a town, to build school and meeting houses, to establish schools, and to hold their meetings regularly.

In keeping with the church's program to attract settlers to Castle Valley, Lyman gave a cautiously optimistic report of the region's prospects:

> The climate of this valley is said to be very fine, and only experience will sustain that reputation. There have been but three deaths, and they were of children, since the settlement of this valley, as I am told. The soil is composed of the sand and clay washed down from the white bluffs which stand up high on the west of the valley, somewhat mildly mixed with mineral. Lucern is not easily started to grow, but there are some very good pieces of it that I have seen, and I do not doubt but it will prove a successful crop, and it will be much needed, for the grass that once was plentiful has vanished before the flocks and herds that have to be pastured in this region. Good water, good land, and fine climate are inviting the industrious husbandmen to come and make desirable homes for good Latter-day Saints.[77]

Characteristics of the Early Settlers

Why Did They Come? Like the church leaders who called them, the settlers of Castle Valley were influenced by both religious and economic motives. Orangeville pioneer Alma G. Jewkes emphasized the religious motivation in a statement made in his ninety-first year:

> How did I come to settle in Emery County? I was called on a mission by President John Taylor. Brigham Young organized the mission, but he died in 1877. I came here in 1878, not then quite twenty-one years of age, and had a wife and two children. I have done my best to fill that mission call I received seventy-one years ago. That mission is not yet over. Nor will it be until I am called home.[78]

In a similar vein, Mary Ann Rowbury Brown, who arrived on Huntington Creek in 1880, declared, "We endured willingly many hardships and cheerfully made many sacrifices in order to carry on what we sincerely believed to be God's works in subduing a desert and advancing civilization."[79] These statements probably sum up the feelings of many other colonists.

But not all Emery County settlers viewed themselves as fulfilling a Latter-day Saint mission. Green River began and largely remained outside the sphere of Mormon colonization. But the Castle Valley communities also attracted some non-Mormons or lapsed Mormons. There had been considerable disaffection from the LDS church during the 1870s, some of it the result of conflicts arising from plural marriage or church leaders' attempts to establish the United Order. Presbyterian and Methodist missionaries were active in Sanpete County during this period and had established congregations in most of the larger towns.

An example of conversion from Mormonism to another faith can be found in the career of Andrew Nelson, Sr., of Manti. He joined the LDS church in Denmark in 1851, "gathered to Zion" the following year, married four wives, and served a mission to his native land from 1865 to 1867. Yet by 1877 he had become a stalwart Presbyterian. According to his grandson Lowry Nelson, only one of Andrew Nelson's twenty-six children "took any interest in the [LDS] church."[80] Twelve of those twenty-six were among the pioneer settlers of Ferron.

It is not possible from the available evidence to determine the religious views of all members of the family. One son, Hyrum, served for ten years as bishop of the Ferron LDS Ward. Others were apparently nominal but inactive Mormons. Still others took an active part in establishing a Presbyterian church in Ferron after the turn of the century. It seems obvious that economic motives and the presence of other family members figured more prominently than a sense of religious duty in leading the Nelsons to settle in Castle Valley.

Economic motives likely played a role even for those who viewed colonizing as a religious obligation. Mary Ann Rowbury Brown, while affirming that pioneering Castle Valley was a divinely appointed mission, also noted that she and her husband "owned nothing but a small strip of land in Fountain Green," which they traded for an ox.[81] The young families who colonized Castle Valley represented the generation that had grown up in Sanpete Valley and other settled regions of Utah to find the land and water already appropriated. Albert Collard summed up his motives for relocating in these terms: "After living in Fountain Green for some years, and our family was increasing, and not having much for their support, we moved to Castle Valley in the year 1880."[82] Lars Anderson lived in Huntsville, Weber County, on a farm that was "not large enough to support the family." Two men appeared to him in a dream and told him he could get more land in Castle Valley.[83] William and Martha Allen Marshall moved to Castle Valley in 1882 largely because they saw "no prospects for obtaining a home of their own" in Long Valley, Kane County.[84] David Henry Leonard and his two wives were well established in Rush Valley, but "having a large family of boys . . . felt the need to locate in a territory where each son could have farms of their own."[85]

At a time when fewer than a dozen farms in Sanpete Valley had more than 100 acres, the 160 acres available to a homesteader in Castle Valley must have seemed a very large spread. Most of the colonists had grown up under conditions of pioneer hardship, and they did not expect that prosperity would come easily in Castle Valley. Yet surely many of them hoped eventually to achieve a better life for themselves and their children.

Land Occupancy Patterns. Leonard J. Arrington has described the

Mormon colonization process as proceeding by certain typical steps. First came "preliminary exploration by companies appointed, equipped, and supported by the central Church." After a suitable site was chosen, "colonizing companies were appointed to found the settlements." The colonists "were expected to pattern the new community institutions after those of Salt Lake City, which were in turn patterned after those of Nauvoo, Illinois, and Jackson County, Missouri." Upon reaching the chosen site, "the colonists dedicated the land by prayer and cooperatively erected a fort or stockade which would serve as a temporary home and community center, as well as a protection against Indians." They then marked out a permanent village plat modelled after the "Plat of the City of Zion," with wide streets, a central block dedicated to public uses, and large residential lots. "On these lots the colonists built their homes, planted their orchards, raised their vegetables and flowers, and erected their livestock and poultry sheds." Outside the village, "the big field" was brought under cultivation and divided into plots "ranging from five to twenty acres each, depending on the amount of irrigable land and the number of colonists." These farm plots, like the town lots, would be assigned to families by a community drawing.[86]

The colonization of Castle Valley fits this model in some respects but deviates from it in others. The process of selecting sites for colonizing, calling settlers, and providing ecclesiastical leadership generally followed the pattern described by Arrington. Castle Valley did not go through the fort stage, primarily because by 1877 the danger of Indian attack was too slight to be a concern. Nor did the settlers develop the communal Big Field or immediately plat the villages. In earlier Mormon colonies, established before federal land offices were available in the territory, the settlers had been mere squatters, preempting the land and water by use and relying on church authority for their allocation. In some cases, legal titles were not acquired until several years after settlement. But Castle Valley was settled under the homestead laws that required claimants to live on their land for several years, after which they could obtain title by paying a nominal fee.

The homestead laws were designed for the Midwest, where the rectangular grid survey provided an efficient method of allocating land and where 160 acres represented, in the nineteenth century, a good-sized family farm. However, John Wesley Powell had argued in his *Report on the Lands of the Arid Region* that the homestead laws were poorly adapted to an arid region such as Utah. The rectangular grid survey did not take into account the necessity of bringing irrigation water to the land. Drawing upon what he had observed in the developed valleys of Utah, Powell concluded that irrigated agriculture was both more labor-intensive and, at its best, more productive than agriculture that depended on natural rainfall. Therefore he proposed that irrigated farms should be no larger than eighty acres and should be attached to "pasturage farms" of at least four full sections (2,560 acres). This would allow for the mixed farming and stockraising economy that had developed in Utah. Powell believed this was the best way to extend to the arid region the American ideal of the small independent farmer. He proposed further that the survey system should follow natural drainage boundaries, and that the laws should be made to encourage the "colony" system in which settlers would form cooperative irrigation and grazing districts.[87]

The *Report on the Lands of the Arid Region* was published almost simultaneously with the colonization of Castle Valley. Powell's proposals were not incorporated into the homestead laws, but the Castle Valley settlers made their own adaptations of the homestead system. Even the first small irrigation ditches usually required cooperative labor and served several farms. The high-line canals needed to bring water to the benchlands were constructed by organized companies involving up to several dozen landowners. As more land was brought under cultivation, the streamflow proved insufficient during dry periods, requiring formal determination of "water rights"—a process that required several decades to accomplish.

Although in theory a homesteader could claim 160 acres and add another 160 by preemption, only a few Castle Valley farms were as large as 160 acres during the settlement era. The first comers claimed the prime riverbottom land, but in many cases their rectangular homesteads extended onto the dry benches, making only part of the land irrigable. Furthermore, not all colonists desired so large a farm. For example, John F. Wakefield claimed a 160-acre homestead adjacent to the Huntington townsite, but even before he obtained title to the land he had subdivided it with a brother and two brothers-in-law, giving each of them a more manageable forty acres. The 1880 census found eighty-four farms in Emery County totalling 10,660 acres for an average of 127 acres per farm. However, only 1,618 acres were classified as "improved," an average of less than twenty acres per farm.[88] In 1890 there were 266 farms averaging 111 acres, with improved land averaging fifty acres per farm. By 1900 the number of farms had risen to 458 with an average acreage of 118. Slightly less than half of the farm land, or fifty-six acres per farm, was classified as improved. One hundred and thirty-nine farms were smaller than fifty acres, with forty-nine farms being smaller than twenty acres.[89]

Why did some colonists claim less land than they were entitled to? In many instances a 160-acre farm was beyond the capacity of a single farmer to cultivate with the horse- or ox-powered machinery of the pioneer period. Lowry Nelson points out that

> The pioneering process demands an enormous expenditure of human effort, and this is especially true of the initial development where irrigation is required. The new settlers must not only clear the virgin land of existing brush and trees, plow it and prepare it for seeding, they must immediately construct a canal and a diversion dam and direct water to their fields. Moreover, in an area like Ferron, where usable timber for constructing dwellings is nonexistent, a road had to be made to some nearby mountain to obtain such timber. Meantime, supplies to maintain life must be brought from a distance over sometimes impassable mountain barriers.[90]

To add to these difficulties, diversion dams were often destroyed by floods and had to be rebuilt. Ditches filled with mud and had to be cleaned out. In the first years, before the ditchbanks were stabilized with grass and willows, ditches frequently broke, sometimes gullying the fields, and had to be repaired. In some seasons, grasshoppers devoured most of the scanty crops.

Some sense of just how strenuous the pioneering labor was can be gleaned from the detailed personal history dictated by Mary Ann Rowbury Brown in her last years. Her husband, Charles, had taken up a homestead north of Huntington Creek in 1879. While Charles was working on the North Ditch to bring irrigation water to part of the land, Mary Ann labored as a household helper in Fountain Green, earning for her efforts ten bushels of wheat, 300 pounds of flour, and $5 in cash. The $5 were used to enable Charles to obtain his citizenship papers, necessary for gaining title to their land. When Charles brought his wife and baby to Castle Valley in the spring of 1880, they lived on the 300 pounds of flour and planted the ten bushels of wheat as the first crop in their new land. According to Mary Ann's account,

> The following autumn my husband returned to Fountain Green and cradled wheat to earn our bread stuff, and while he was gone I harvested our crop of grain grown from the ten bushels of wheat. This is how I did it. I turned the water down a row at a time on the patch to loosen the soil then pulled up the grain by the roots and stacked it by hand, for it was too short to cut. I placed my baby on a quilt in the field where I could watch her while working. Uncle Samuel Jewkes thrashed with the first thrasher in the country. He said my grain stack looked like a mound of mud. When the grain was thrashed there were nine and a half bushels.[91]

Under such conditions as these, it required extraordinary efforts to bring twenty or forty acres into production, let alone 160 acres.

Another possible motive for the smaller farms was to enable as many other settlers as possible to obtain land and water. Lowry Nelson describes the founding of Escalante, settled at about the same period as Castle Valley, as follows:

> These men laid out the arable land roughly in 160-acre tracts. Since the land was unsurveyed they measured as best they could and established corners to guide them. According to the testimony of James Schow, they all agreed that they would subdivide these holdings into farms of 22 1/2 acres each in order that other settlers might come in and get land. They were primarily interested in establishing a community rather than large individual tracts.[92]

Perhaps the founders of Emery County were also more interested in establishing a community than in acquiring large individual holdings.

While cooperative water development came at the very beginning of Castle Valley settlement, cooperative management of the grazing resources was still several years in the future. Throughout the nineteenth century and into the twentieth, the range was open to the first or most aggressive comer without regulation. The principles of cooperatively managed "pasture farms" that John Wesley Powell had articulated in 1878 were only gradually and incompletely incorporated, partly though government regulation including the establishment of the Manti National Forest early in the twentieth century and the Taylor Grazing Act in the 1930s, and partly through local initiative in the organizing of livestock growers' associations.

The homestead laws, with their requirement of residence on the land, encouraged a dispersed settlement pattern quite different from the village pattern traditionally preferred by the Mormons. If the platting of townsites was not among the first orders of business for the Castle Valley colonists, it was because they could not have resided in the village even if there had been one. But their eye was clearly fixed on a time when they would have proved up on their homesteads and be free to build homes in town. At Huntington it appears that a mile-square plot on the Prickly Pear Flat was reserved for a townsite as early as 1878, even though it was not divided into lots until late 1880.[93] James Marinus Peterson took up his land on the north side of Cottonwood Creek with the understanding that it was to become the Castle Dale townsite.[94]

Eventually, a majority of the colonists did gather in the towns. However, this process was never complete in Emery County. When Lowry Nelson began his research on the Mormon village in the 1920s, he found "practically no people in Manti or Ephraim . . . who lived on their farms." In his native Ferron, by contrast, "there were many families who built on their homesteads."[95] Some Castle Valley communities were more compact than Ferron, but there were some families in every community who elected to remain "on the farm."

Kinship Groups. One benefit of a "colony" approach to settlement was that it provided an established society from the beginning. In Castle Valley that mutual support was further enhanced by the fact that many of the early settlers were related to one another. Probably the largest kinship group in the first generation was the Nelson clan of Ferron, twelve brothers and a sister, Emma, who was married to John Lemon. That kinship chain was interlinked with others. Hyrum Nelson married Artemicia Lowry, whose brother Daniel was also an early settler on Ferron Creek. Another Lowry sister, Clarabell, was

Howard Mine, Cedar Creek. (Utah State Historical Society)

married to Samuel Singleton; yet another, Evalyn, married Nathaniel ("Tan") Crawford; and a half-sister, Eunice, was married to Mike Molen. Mary Jane Singleton Taylor and Ann Singleton Wrigley were sisters, and Samuel Singleton was their half-brother. He was also a half-brother to Earnest Wild.[96] James B. Crawford of Orangeville was a brother to Nathaniel Crawford of Ferron, Quince G. Crawford who later operated a ranch at Rochester (Moore), and Catherine Crawford Fail of Orangeville. A cousin, James Crawford, Jr., also lived in Orangeville during the 1890s and later as a Manti banker was instrumental in organizing the Emery County Bank. Virtually all of the first party of pioneers on Huntington Creek were related by blood or marriage. Other early settlers included the interrelated Sherman-Johnson-Wakefield-Woodward families and the even more intricately linked Pulsipher-Robbins-Burgess-McElprang-Harmon-Allen-Marshall families.[97] Many other examples could be cited.

Migration Patterns. The dating of events from the early years of settlement is often sketchy or inconsistent. In part this may result from faulty memories, but it also reveals the indefiniteness of the settlement process itself. For a particular family, that process might begin when the husband or a grown son made a trip to Castle Valley to "look over the country." In some instances, a homestead claim might be staked during this visit. A second trip might come a few weeks or even a year or more later and might involve several members of the family, who would construct a dugout or cabin on the homestead, dig ditches, and put in the first crops. Some or all of them would then likely return to the more established settlements for the winter. Perhaps the following spring or summer, the entire family would be moved across the mountains and take up a more or less permanent residence in Castle Valley. Even then, however, wives might go back to the settled communities to have their babies. The entire family might leave for several months or longer at a stretch to go to the mountains with range or dairy stock, or to get out timber for a sawmill. In such a scenario, it is difficult to say with certainty just when the family "settled."

Even after a family had taken up more or less permanent residence in Castle Valley, there was much buying and selling and trading of farms. Some families located initially in one settlement and then moved after a few years to another. Many colonists left the area entirely, including the Wilsons of Wilsonville, who followed their livestock to Wyoming during the 1880s where they became the first permanent settlers in the Jackson Hole area. Fully half of the families who came to Huntington Creek in the fall of 1877 had left Emery County by 1883. Mike and Eunice Molen disposed of their substantial holdings in Ferron and moved to Utah County after their young son drowned in the Molen Ditch in 1889.

ENDNOTES

1. A photographic copy of the letter is reproduced in *EC 1880–1980,* 21.

2. Church of Jesus Christ of Latter-day Saints, "Journal History," 24 May 1875, cited in John H. S. Smith, "Census Perspectives: The Sanpete Origins of Emery County Settlement," in Allan Kent Powell, *Emery County,* 46.

3. Montell Seely, "The Settlement Era: Castle Dale," in *EC 1880–1980,* 23.

4. *CV,* 17.

5. Lever, *Sanpete and Emery Counties,* 594.

6. See, for example, *CV,* 79–80.

7. Estella G. Guymon, personal interview, August 1992.

8. Richard H. Jackson, William M. Rieske, and Howard A. Christy, "Indian Farms and Reservations," in *Atlas of Utah,* ed. Wayne L. Wahlquist et al. (Provo, Utah: Weber State College and Brigham Young University Press, 1981), 104–5.

9. Nelson, *In the Direction of His Dreams,* 19.

10. Charles S. Peterson, *Utah: A Bicentennial History* (New York: W. W. Norton, 1977), 41.

11. Montell Seely, "Settlement Era," 21–22.

12. *CV,* 202; Jones, *Settling of Huntington,* 8, 11; *ECP,* 2 October 1909.

13. Jones, *Settling of Huntington,* 8–13.

14. Ibid., 14.

15. "William Alma Staker," in Jones, *Early Pioneers of Huntington,* 272–75.

16. Vina Hill Miller, "Robert Wimmer Hill," typescript copy in Emery County History Archives.

17. *CV,* 202–3. Many of these early dates are in doubt, the product of memories recorded long after the event. It is possible that the Christmas dance in the Avery cabin may have taken place in 1879 rather than 1878. Reportedly among the attendees were newlyweds James and Annie Petersen, who walked from their home on Cottonwood Creek. But the Petersens were married on 16 October 1879. "A Brief History of James and Annie Eliza Rassmussen Petersen," in *EC 1880–1980,* 422.

18. Jones, *Early Pioneers of Huntington,* 177–78.

19. Elma Ottesen Collard, "Christian Ottesen," in Jones, *Early Pioneers of Huntington,* 219–20.

20. Paris, Violet, and Rodney Wimmer, "William and Sarah Curtis Wimmer," in Jones, *Early Pioneers of Huntington,* 299–306.

21. Jones, *Settling of Huntington,* 17–18.

22. LaVora Kofford and Paulette Kelly, "Lawrence," in *EC 1880–1980,* 224.

23. Jones, *Settling of Huntington,* 28.

24. Seely, "Settlement Era," 23.

25. *CV,* 71, 88.

26. Ibid, 72, 73; Seely, "Settlement Era," 26–27.

27. Jones, *Settling of Huntington,* 22.

28. *CV,* 101.

29. Seely, "Settlement Era," 27–28.

30. Elizabeth Jackson Reid, "Incidents in the Life of a Castle Valley Pioneer," typescript copy in Emery County History Archives.

31. *CV,* 76–78.

32. Emery Stake Manuscript History (Library-Archives, Historical Department, Church of Jesus Christ of Latter-day Saints, Salt Lake City), 1.

33. Joseph H. Jewkes, Personal History (typescript copy in Emery County History Archives), 5.

34. *CV,* 302, 304, 314, 316.

35. Seely, "Settlement Era," 29.

36. Emery County Historical Records Survey, quoted in *Utah: A Guide to the State,* ed. Ward J. Roylance (Salt Lake City: Utah a Guide to the State Foundation, 1982), 700.

37. *CV,* 309.

38. Ibid., 151–52.

39. Velma Petersen, "Ferron," in *EC 1880–1980,* 103.

40. *CV,* 153.

41. Petersen, "Ferron," 103–4.

42. *CV,* 153–55.

43. Petersen, "Ferron," 109–10.

44. Hodgman, "In the Mountains of Utah," 32, 34.

45. *CV,* 27; Argene Olsen, "Orange Seely I and Hanna Olsen Seely," in *EC 1880–1980,* 432.

46. *CV,* 182–83.

47. Lever, *History of Sanpete and Emery Counties,* 595, 644.

48. Recollections of Beatrice Elizabeth Farrer Dahling (1956), typescript copy in Emery County History Archives.

49. Lawrence Hastings, "Water Wheels on the Green River," typescript copy in Emery County History Archives.

50. Pearl Baker and Ruth Wilcox, "Greenriver," in *CV,* 183.

51. Tanner, *The Far Country,* 93. LDS church genealogy records indicate that Mary Stowe died in 1880 at Lee's Ferry, Arizona. The O'Fallins were also in Arizona by 1884. Mads Larsen died at Moab in 1882.

52. F. M. Lyman, Letter to the Editor, *Deseret Evening News* (Salt Lake City), 15 September 1880, 4.

53. Montell and Kathryn Seely, "Green River (Blake)," in *EC 1880–1980,* 130; Billy Howland, "The Planting of a Seed and How it Grew" (1935), typescript copy in Emery County History Archives.

54. Una Gillies, "Chris Halverson: Southern Utah Frontiersman," typescript copy in Emery County History Archives.

55. Howland, "Planting of a Seed," 2.

56. Conover, *George Henry Westover and Family,* 92.

57. Petersen, "Ferron," 113.

58. Joseph H. Jewkes, personal history, 6.

59. Milas Edgar Johnson, Autobiography; John Fleming Wakefield, Jr., Autobiography, in Jones, *Early Pioneers of Huntington,* 151–52, 287–88. Johnson wrote that the party "could only go about half way up Quitchupah Canyon" before the horses were unable to pull the wagon through the deep snow. Quitchupah Creek has three main forks, of which only Convulsion Canyon is suitable for a road.

60. Jones, *Settling of Huntington,* 18–21.

61. *CV,* 155–56; Josephine Peterson, "History of Jasper Peterson," typescript copy in Emery County History Archives.

62. "Biography of John Leasil Brasher"; "William Howard, Jr.," in Jones, *Early Pioneers of Huntington,* 17–18, 133.

63. Tanner, *The Far Country,* 94.

64. "An Act Creating Emery County," Chapter IV of *Laws of the Territory of Utah, Passed at the Twenty-fourth Session of the Legislative Assembly* (Salt Lake City: Deseret News Printing and Publishing Establishment, 1880), 4–5.

65. Journals of the Legislative Assembly of the Territory of Utah, Twenty-fourth Session, for the Year 1880.

66. Seely, "Settlement Era," 29.

67. "An Act Providing for the Organization of San Juan County, and Changing the Boundaries of Emery County," Chapter IX of *Laws of the Territory of Utah, Passed at the Twenty-fourth Session of the Legislative Assembly,* 10; see also James B. Allen, "The Evolution of County Boundaries in Utah," *Utah Historical Quarterly* 23 (1955): 273–74.

68. Meeting minutes photoreproduced in *EC 1880–1980,* 30–31.

69. Lever, *History of Sanpete and Emery Counties,* 607.

70. U.S. Department of the Interior, Bureau of the Census, 1880 (Emery County, Utah). Microfilm copy at Harold B. Lee Library, Brigham Young University, Provo, Utah.

71. U.S. Department of the Interior, Bureau of the Census, *Tenth Census of the United States, 1880: Population.*

72. Montell Seely, "Emery Stake (Castle Dale Utah Stake)," in *EC 1880–1980,* 278.

73. Rose Ryan Bingham, "Christian Grice Larsen," in *EC 1880–1980,* 406.

74. Leonard J. Arrington, "Latter-day Saint Settlement of Eastern Utah: A Story of Faith, Courage, and Tolerance," in Philip F. Notarianni, *Carbon County: Eastern Utah's Industrialized Island* (Salt Lake City: Utah State Historical Society, 1981), 113.

75. Seely, "Emery Stake," 278.

76. *CV,* 69.

77. F. M. Lyman, Letter to the Editor, *Deseret Evening News* (Salt Lake City), 28 August 1880, 2.

78. Quoted in *CV,* 306.

79. "A Life Sketch of Mary Ann Rowbury Brown Gordon," typescript in Special Collections, Lee Library.

80. Nelson, *In the Direction of His Dreams,* 44, 122.

81. Brown, Personal History.

82. Jones, *Settling of Huntington,* 32.

83. "Autobiography of Hettie Elizabeth Guymon McArthur Anderson," in Jones, *Early Pioneers of Huntington,* 11.

84. Jones, *Settling of Huntington,* 44.

85. Alice Leonard Westover, "David Henry Leonard," in Jones, *Early Pioneers of Huntington,* 177.

86. Leonard J. Arrington, "Colonizing the Great Basin," *Ensign* (February 1980): 20–21.

87. Powell, *Arid Lands,* 37–57.

88. *Report on the Productions of Agriculture as Returned at the Tenth Census (June 1, 1880)* (Washington, D.C.: Government Printing Office, 1883), 95, 136.

89. *Census Reports: Agriculture, Part I, Farms, Livestock, and Animal Products. Twelfth Census of the United States, 1900* (Washington, D. C.: United States Census Office, 1902), 130–31, 302.

90. Nelson, *In the Direction of His Dreams,* 37.

91. Brown, Personal History.

92. Lowry Nelson, *The Mormon Village: A Pattern and Technique of Land Settlement* (Salt Lake City: University of Utah Press, 1952), 84–85.

93. *EC 1880–1980,* 184.

94. Seely, "Settlement Era," 31–32.

95. Nelson, *In the Direction of His Dreams,* 25.

96. Ibid., 23.

97. Jones, *Settling of Huntington,* A-C, 50, 52–53, 272.

4

From Colony to Community, 1880–1900

The population of Emery County grew from the 556 recorded in the 1880 census to 2,866 in 1890 (not counting the area that later became Carbon County) and 4,657 in 1900. With this growth in population came a corresponding expansion of the economic base, rapid advances in the built environment, and important developments in the county's social, political, religious, educational, and cultural institutions.

Town Development

Castle Dale. When LDS church leaders visited Emery County in August 1880 to organize the Emery Stake, they encouraged development of "the townsite located by Orange Seely and approved by President Peterson on the north side of the stream."[1] Apparently in preparation for its subdivision into residential lots, James Marinus Petersen had filed a cash entry instead of a homestead entry on the land west of what would become Center Street. (A cash entry allowed a claimant to gain legal title to the land in a shorter time than did a homestead entry.) Sometime before the end of 1880, this land and the adjacent property to the east belonging to Christian G. Larsen was platted into four-acre blocks separated by streets ninety-nine feet in width. The north-south-east-west grid typical of Mormon towns was employed as far as possible, but the constraints of the site required the blocks to be laid out like steps descending along the narrow shelf between the creek and the bench from northwest to southeast. Each block was divided into four lots, which were offered to settlers at a nominal price.

The first residents of Castle Dale were compelled to haul water from the creek in barrels for household use and to nurture trees and shrubs. The Jeffs Ditch, diverted from the creek a short distance west of town, brought domestic and irrigation water to the southeastern part of town in 1882. The West Town Ditch, diverted just below Orangeville, made water available to the remainder of the townsite in 1883. Like most other pioneer irrigation projects, these canals were constructed as informal cooperatives by the water users. Water rights in the Jeffs and West Town ditches were later transferred to the highline Mammoth Canal, and the smaller canals were abandoned.[2] A log school and meeting house measuring eighteen by twenty-seven feet was erected at the west end of Main Street in late 1880. By 1884 this structure had been moved to the corner of Main and First East streets, on the present site of the Emery County Court House, and a bowery had been constructed nearby. A cooperative store was established in the southeast section of town by 1881. In 1882 a temporary log structure was built at Third East and Second South to house the county offices. It was replaced in 1883 by an adobe-lined lumber building. The first residence on the townsite was reportedly a log house built by Charles Snelgrove in the southeast corner of town in 1881.[3] In a pattern typical of Castle Valley communities, most families established homes in town after they had proved up on their homesteads. Property abstract records indicate that eighty-two of the 133 available lots in the townsite survey had been sold by 1890. The 1890 census indicated that 303 of the Castle Dale precinct's 409 residents were living in town. By 1900 the precinct population had grown to 718 with 559 in the town.

The homes and other buildings constructed during the 1880s tended to be small. The chief materials were logs, rough-sawn native lumber, and adobes. One of the first two-story residences was built by Bishop Henning Olsen for his newlywed son Abinadi (Nad) and his wife Hannah in 1887 at the corner of Main and Center streets. This lumber and adobe structure was still standing in remodeled form in 1995.[4] The 1890s brought the biggest building boom the community would see in its first century. The first brick residence was erected by J. W. Seely in 1889 at the corner of First South and Center streets.[5] This house, which was still standing in 1995, was built of an orange-toned brick shipped in from northern Utah. Locally manufactured brick became available a short time later, and by 1898 a Price newspaper reported "at least thirty brick buildings in course of construction in Castle Dale."[6] The most noteworthy public buildings were the two-story Emery County courthouse at the corner of First South and Second East streets (1892), a social hall on the site of the present city park (variously dated at 1890 and 1893), and the Emery Stake Academy building, completed in 1899 on the northwest corner of the public square.[7] Also during the 1890s, the frame and adobe Anderson Hotel was erected at the corner of Main and First East; James Jeffs built a large brick house that was also used as a hotel at the east end of town; and two-story brick commercial buildings were erected by Carl Wilberg and H. Peter Otteson on East Main Street, by William P. Winters on the southwest corner of Main and Center streets, and by C. E. Pearson on Second East, north of the courthouse.[8] Of all these structures, only the Wilberg and Pearson buildings remained standing in 1995.

Orangeville. In addition to approving the Castle Dale townsite, the visiting LDS apostles in August 1880 also gave permission for the upstream settlers "to locate on the Reed [sic] townsite and to build a school-house, as two will be needed on the creek."[9] This townsite had reportedly been surveyed in the spring of 1880 on land claimed by John K. Reid, Andrew Anderson, and Alma G. Jewkes.[10] The towns, less than three miles apart, were known as Lower Castle Dale and Upper Castle Dale until 13 August 1882, when Apostle Erastus Snow returned to Emery Stake to divide the Castle Dale Ward. Upon Snow's recommendation, Upper Castle Dale was named Orangeville in honor of Orange Seely. This designation was somewhat anomalous in that Seely was a resident of the lower town, and the post office designated as Castle Dale had originally been established at the upper settlement.

The Orangeville townsite was watered by the Blue Cut and Clipper canals, both of which were in service by the time the town was platted. With water available, there was nothing to prevent the immediate establishment of homes in town apart from the legal requirement for homesteaders to complete a five-year residence on their claims. The Reid and Anderson families were the first residents of the town by virtue of homesteading the land on which it was located. John K. Reid built a lumber structure to house the post office and a store called "The Pioneer."[11] According to an 1898 account, "several families from Manti and other Sanpete towns began the erection of homes" soon after the townsite was surveyed.[12] By 1890, 313 of the Orangeville precinct's 353 residents were living inside the town boundaries. The 1900 precinct population was 623 with no separate listing provided for the town.

The first public building was a log school with dimensions of eighteen by twenty-four feet, completed in time for a community Christmas celebration in 1880. A large bowery was erected near the school to provide a more spacious meeting place during all but the coldest weather.[13] Sometime between 1886 and 1890, the Orangeville Social Hall was built by a private stock company made up of members of the Orangeville Dramatic Association. Constructed of sawed logs with rustic siding on the exterior and a plastered interior, the building had a good sized stage and seating capacity for 160 persons. Built primarily to serve as a theater, the social hall was used as a meetinghouse by the Orangeville LDS Ward and for a variety of community functions in addition to dramatics. It was Orangeville's only large assembly hall for many years and continued in use until 1951.[14]

Though its population at the turn of the century was almost as large as that of Castle Dale, Orangeville had fewer public and commercial buildings. However, the community participated fully in the residential building boom of the 1890s, with eleven homes reported under construction in the spring of 1897.[15] An 1898 observer wrote, "Many new and commodious residences adorn the town and beautiful shade and fruit trees decorate the streets and town lots."[16] The newly completed Co-op store building was described in 1899 as "the finest in several of the southern counties. It is twenty-eight by fifty-two with a beautiful colored glass front and painted brick walls. The dancing hall in the upper story is strictly up to date."[17]

Huntington. The original center of community life on Huntington Creek was a cluster of dugouts near the present Highway 10 bridge. As the first colonists moved from the "dugout community" to their individual homesteads, newcomers occupied the dugouts until they too could locate homesteads. By 1880 settlers were strung along more than eight miles of riverbottom. Apparently by early 1879, a decision had been made to locate a townsite on a bench known as the Prickly Pear Flat, about half a mile southwest of the dugout community, using the surveyor's boundary between Range 8 and Range 9 East as the center line of what would become Main Street.[18]

Elias Cox reportedly conferred with LDS church officials in the spring of 1879, seeking advice on platting a town, and was given as a guide a plat that had been used in laying out Salt Lake City. The Huntington townsite sloped gently from northwest to southeast, a favorable situation for the distribution of water, and was relatively free from humps and hollows except for a hill that intruded into the northern tier of blocks and a wash that sliced diagonally through the townsite. At the northeast and southwest corners, the mile-square grid dropped off from the bench to lower ground. Some levelling of land and clearing of brush took place early in 1880, and the platting of lots was completed before December by a government surveyor named Henry Fitzhugh.[19] Settlers obtained lots by drawing numbered slips of paper from a hat. Plurally married men were entitled to draw a lot for each wife.[20]

Except for a small area on the east side under the Wakefield Ditch, the townsite was waterless at the time of its platting. In order to bring irrigation water to the town and to the extensive flats to the west and south, the Huntington Manufacturing and Agricultural Company had been organized in 1879. The Huntington Canal was diverted from the creek some four miles west of the townsite. The Town Ditch branch of the canal was completed by 1883. The larger Farm Ditch was placed in service in the spring of 1884. The company record book for 1880 to 1885 has survived and provides some

South Main Street, Huntington. (Utah State Historical Society)

insights into the methods of organizing and financing early irrigation projects in Emery County. Labor on the canal was credited toward water rights at $2 a day for men and $1.50 for boys. Stock assessments were rarely paid in cash, more often in commodities including pork, flour, bacon, potatoes, sorghum, lucern seed, lumber, nails, and blasting powder.[21]

Townsite development did not wait for the arrival of the water. The first structure to be erected was a forty-by-sixty-foot meetinghouse located at the corner of Main and Center streets, the largest building constructed of logs in Emery County. The logs were cut during the summer of 1880 in what was thereafter known as Meetinghouse Canyon. Lumber was sawed at the Cox mill and doors and windows brought from Sanpete Valley. The building was erected in November and December under the supervision of William Howard. The goal of completion by Christmas was not met, but the meetinghouse was finished on 31 December 1880, just in time for an all-night New Year's Eve party.[22] The building originally had mud-chinked walls, rough plank floors, and a dirt roof. The benches were made from split logs. The dirt roof was replaced by shingles within two or three years. Sometime around 1890 the building was expanded with a T-wing on the west end; a bell tower was added to the east front; the log walls were plastered on the inside and weatherboarded on the exterior; and a new floor was laid. In this form the structure continued to serve the community as a social hall until it was destroyed by fire in 1918.[23]

The first homes on the townsite were built by brothers Joseph E. and Milas E. Johnson.[24] About ten additional families, including Benjamin Jones, Olaf Jensen, Oscar Crandall, and William Howard, erected homes on their town lots during the first half of 1881.[25] By 1883, according to the recollections of a settler who arrived in late November, there were "about fifty log houses scattered over the prickly-pear townsite."[26] The first two-story houses were frame structures built by William Howard and Hyrum Oscar Crandall in 1882. Oscar Wood built a two-story brick house probably sometime in the late 1880s. J. W. Nixon completed the first two rooms of a brick home in the fall of 1889 and the remainder of the structure in 1890.[27] This house was still standing in 1995 at the corner of First West and First North streets. Milas E. Johnson erected a still existing frame and adobe house on the northeast corner of Main and First South sometime before October 1891, when the editor of the *Eastern Utah Telegram* wrote, "The plan of it is different from any thing we have seen, and we pronounce it an ideal house."[28] By 1890, 513 of the Huntington precinct's 738 residents were living in town. The 1900 figures were 653 in town and 944 in the precinct.

Huntington, with the county's largest population, had as many as eight retail stores in operation during the 1880s and 1890s. All of them, however, were housed in small log, frame, or adobe buildings until 1900 when James W. Nixon built a two-story frame building on the northeast corner of Main and First North streets and the Huntington Cooperative Mercantile Institution erected a two-story brick building on the west side of Main Street between Center and First North.[29]

The major building project of the 1890s was a brick meetinghouse for the Huntington LDS Ward. Work on this structure began as early as 1890, but little progress was made until 1896. A concerted effort was undertaken under the leadership of Bishop Peter Johnson that led to completion of the assembly hall before the turn of the century. A tower and belfry were added between 1902 and 1904.[30] The period of the meetinghouse construction also saw the building of a number of brick homes.

Lawrence. The Huntington townsite was an inconvenient distance from the settlers who had located lower on the creek. Therefore, the Lawrence precinct was established in 1885.[31] Probably in 1883 Philander Burch, a skilled carpenter, built a two-story house for John P. Wimmer. This house, still standing in 1995, attracted others, and a small townsite was surveyed sometime before the organization of the Lawrence LDS Ward in 1889. A meetinghouse was erected in 1888 or 1889, and several homes were built on the townsite. Stores were operated for brief periods by Thomas Fuller, Henry Roper, and others.[32] Many families, however, continued to reside on their farms, particularly those in the southern part of the precinct where an unofficial community known as "Stakerville" developed.[33] The Lawrence precinct had a population of 107 in 1890 and 160 in 1900.

Ferron. The colony on Ferron Creek initially took the form of individual homesteads strung along the eight miles of riverbottom between the mouth of Ferron Canyon and the Box where the creek cuts through Molen Reef. A log meetinghouse situated midway between the present sites of Ferron and Molen served as the community's church, school, and recreation center. William Taylor, Jr., operated the post office and Hyrum Cook a store in their homes.[34] Townsite development apparently began at about the same time as corresponding developments on Cottonwood and Huntington creeks. The first site chosen was a level area near the creek.[35] However, concerns that this land might turn swampy led to the selection of a hilly site north of the river valley. This site rises in a series of terraces, affording sweeping views across the river valley but posing challenges to ditchbuilders and roadbuilders alike. Moreover, the area was "completely covered with greasewood and prickly pears so dense that no dog or horse could be forced to go through them." Abram Conover cleared a space and built the first house, followed by Sy Goff, Joseph Wrigley, and Dan Henrie. Peter Hansen built an adobe house and a few years later one of rock. In 1882 Mike Molen and Hyrum Nelson burned the first brick to be manufactured in Emery County, and Molen erected a brick house and a store.[36]

This provided an impetus for other families to move to the townsite, including some whose farms were in the Molen area. The log meetinghouse was moved from its original site to the northwest corner of what would become the school block. Late in the decade of the 1880s, locally made brick was used to construct the first brick LDS meetinghouse in Emery County, located at the base of the hill on the corner of State Street and Mill Road. This building, expanded by a T-wing on the west during the 1890s, continued in use until it was destroyed by fire in 1920.[37] By 1898 Ferron also boasted "the largest brick schoolhouse in the county."[38]

Samuel Singleton completed the still-existing double-wing frame house on his riverbottom farm in 1896. The *Eastern Utah Advocate* reported in 1897,

> The growth of the town has within the last year been phenomenal. All kinds and conditions of buildings have gone up in the northern portion of town and the growth has been most rapid . . . of any town or settlement since the settling of the valley.

Among those reported to be building "handsome and substantial dwellings" was John C. Lemon, whose "elegant brick residence" would "cost near $3,500. When completed it will be one of the best residences in the valley."[39] The Lemon and Singleton homes are among the finest surviving examples of nineteenth-century Emery County residential architecture. In 1890, 270 of the Ferron precinct's 399 residents lived in town. By 1900 the precinct population had grown to 660. While separate figures were not reported for the town, it is certain that a majority of the population resided there. However, a substantial number of residents, like Singleton and Lemon, built permanent homes on their farms.

Molen. The wide bottomlands around Molen attracted more settlers during the early years than the upstream region near Ferron. The population balance swung toward Ferron in the 1880s as homesteaders proved up on their land and moved into town. Some, however, preferred to remain in Molen. A small townsite was laid out in 1884, and a log building was erected to serve as school and meetinghouse. This structure was replaced in the early 1890s by separate frame buildings, one for school, the other for church.[40] Molen had its own cemetery, its own outdoor recreation center in Fjeldsteds' Grove, and a sense of being a community quite distinct from Ferron, even though they were only three miles apart. The 1890 census showed a population of 134, growing to 164 by 1900.

Muddy Creek Settlement

Despite the fact that Muddy Creek was the first sizeable stream encountered by travelers who reached Castle Valley by way of Wasatch Pass, potential settlers seem to have passed over the region during the 1870s, perhaps because both the creek and the arable riverbottom land were somewhat smaller than those farther north. Casper Christensen, from Spring City, had apparently grazed livestock in the area for several years before he took the first step toward settlement, beginning construction of an irrigation ditch on 15 May 1881. Christensen's land was on the right bank of Muddy Creek about three miles northeast of the present townsite. Also in 1881 Joseph and Marinus Lund and Charles Johnson selected land upstream from Christensen, but Johnson and Joseph Lund soon became discouraged and returned to Spring City. Christensen then installed his family in the cabin built by Joseph Lund. At season's end he harvested seventy bushels of wheat.[41] That same year, Miles and Daniel Miller located several miles downstream in what came to be known as Miller Canyon.

John T. Lewis and his family settled still farther downstream in 1882. Other settlers arriving during that period included Pleasant and Jacob Minchey, George Merrick, Orson Davis, Judiah Knight, Samuel Babbitt, Jack Jones, William Lisonbee, and Ammon Foote. A post office was established in 1882 with Casper Christensen as postmaster, and on 1 September 1883 the Muddy LDS Ward was organized with Christensen as bishop. A log school and meetinghouse was erected near the place where the Highway 10 bridge now spans Muddy Creek. Samuel M. Williams arrived in the settlement in 1885 and opened a store on the Christensen farm.[42]

The Bishop of Muddy Creek. It will be apparent that Casper Christensen played a prominent role in Emery affairs during the settlement era. Born in Denmark in 1837, he emigrated to Minnesota in 1869 and made his way to Utah in 1875.[43] His multiple roles as Latter-day Saint bishop, postmaster, farmer and stockman, and community leader kept him busy. The story is still retold in Emery of the day when a postal inspector arrived without prior notice to audit the books:

> Casper was down in the field irrigating and, when he was sent for, he continued to regulate his water for a few minutes before coming to the house. The postal employee, being short on patience and puffed up with his own importance, scolded Casper for his delay.
>
> He said, "Do you know who I am? I am a United States Postal Inspector." Casper replied, "Do you know who I am? I am the Bishop of Muddy Creek."
>
> Even today, when someone gets to bragging about his own importance, some of the old people in Emery will say, "I am the Bishop of the Muddy Creek."[44]

Quitchupah. As the settlement on Muddy Creek grew, other families were locating in the valley of Quitchupah Creek, six miles to the southwest. The first settlers there were John and Theressa Duncan, who came from Cedar City in 1882. (John Duncan had apparently run cattle in the area some years earlier.) They were joined in subsequent years by Joseph Christensen, Charles and Frank Foote, Merlin and Martin J. Allred, Oscar Beebe, Carl Albrechtsen, and Peter Olsen. The little community erected a frame school house that also served as a center for social activities. Shortly after the turn of the century, a cloudburst on the creek's headwaters sent a massive flood through the valley, destroying the diversion dams and canals and turning the creek bed into a deep wash. Even though an extension of the Emery Canal restored irrigation water to part of the land, most settlers either moved into Emery or left the region.[45]

The Emery Canal. Even before the disastrous washout, Quitchupah Creek was too small to irrigate more than a few farms, and the Muddy Creek Valley had limited land suitable for cultivation. It was natural, therefore, that the settlers' attention should be drawn to the bench dividing the two valleys. Here was sufficient land for a sizeable community. But in order to bring water to the site, it would be necessary to construct a highline canal for four miles along the base of the mountains. Preliminary work on the canal began in 1885, and in 1886 a stock company was incorporated with Heber C. Pettey as president, Casper Christensen, vice-president, Peter V. Bunderson, secretary and treasurer, and William G. Petty, George Collier, and George Whitlock, directors. The greatest barrier in the path of the canal was a large shale hill. To go around it would lengthen the canal by more than two miles and bring it onto the bench at a lower level, thus reducing the amount of irrigable land. After some discussion, the company decided to dig a tunnel through the hill, a project that also required building a dam across a ravine in order to deliver water to the tunnel.

The building of the Emery tunnel required both ingenuity and tenacity. Existing in a subsistence economy, with no capital to speak of, no trained engineers, nothing but the most rudimentary tools, the settlers labored for two years to complete the tunnel, doing most of the work during the winters. They calculated the proper fall with a homemade water level and sighted over lighted candles to keep the tunnel correctly aligned. To expedite the work, they sank a shaft in the center of the hill so they could work from four ends at the same time. When the various segments met, they were almost perfectly aligned.

Water was turned into the tunnel in 1888, but a new set of problems developed almost immediately. The Blue Gate shale through which the tunnel had been dug is hard and tightly compacted in its original state, but once exposed to air and water it softens and sloughs away. Recurring rockfalls blocked the tunnel. In an effort to solve this problem, the entire length of the tunnel was timbered on the sides and top, a project requiring several months to complete. But rocks continued to fall from the roof, breaking the timbers. The timbered sides made clearing the channel more difficult as there was no room to push the rocks to the side and it was therefore necessary to carry them all the way to the end of the tunnel. One large rockfall in the midsection caused the upper half of the tunnel to fill with muddy sediment three feet deep, which required six weeks to remove. After much discussion, the company stockholders decided to take out the timber, as it seemed to be doing more harm than good. They then converted the lower half of the tunnel to an open cut, an undertaking that required almost an additional year. In the midst of a community party to celebrate the completion of this project, a loud roar signalled the collapse of the dam across the ravine, leaving the tunnel high and dry. Still undaunted, the men took up their picks and shovels once again and constructed a new canal segment above the ravine.

The shortened tunnel was easier to keep clear. Over a few years' time, the collapsing shale formed a natural arch eight to ten feet high, and rockfalls became less frequent. In this form the tunnel continued to serve for some three-quarters of a century before being replaced by an open cut excavated by heavy equipment.[46]

Town Development. As was the case with several other Castle Valley communities, townsite development on the bench began before water was available. A plat bearing the name "Emery" was filed on 12 May 1884. However, this was apparently located about half a mile east of the present townsite, which was platted later in the year when it became apparent that the canal could be routed higher on the bench. The first house in town was reportedly built by Samuel M. Williams, who also moved his mercantile establishment to the new site. He was followed by Heber C. Pettey and Ole Olsen. On 21 December 1888 work began on a log meetinghouse.[47] The 1890 census found 240 people in Emery. By 1900 the population had more than doubled to 572.

Emery was the county's wealthiest town on a per capita basis during the 1890s as measured by assessed valuation.[48] This was primarily a reflection of the residents' substantial livestock holdings. It appears, however, that this relative prosperity did not take the form of larger homes and public buildings until late in the decade. "Several brick houses" were built during the fall and winter of 1897–98.[49] Work began on a wood frame LDS meetinghouse in 1898, and the completed building was dedicated in 1902.[50] This beautifully proportioned and well-preserved structure is the only major public building still standing in Emery County that dates to the nineteenth century.

The Coming of the Rio Grande Western Railroad

The Denver and Rio Grande Railroad began extending its narrow-gauge line through the Rockies toward the Utah border in 1880. At the same time D&RG interests organized the Sevier Valley Railway Company with the announced purpose of building south from Ogden as far as the northern boundary of Arizona. From this route another line was to go eastward over Wasatch Pass, across Castle Valley to the Green River, and from there to Colorado's western boundary to connect with the Denver and Rio Grande.[51] By early 1881 a Salt Lake City newspaper reported, "There are now in Salina Pass about 300 men, [engaged] in grading and tieing the track for the Rio Grande narrow gauge railroad." The *Herald* editor speculated that the railroad's ultimate plan was to "turn in a southwesterly direction and run into the southern part of California to the Pacific Ocean."[52] Later in 1881 the Sevier Valley Railway and several small lines in the Salt Lake City area were combined in a new company called the Denver and Rio Grande Western Railway. Emery County residents were understandably excited about these developments. Not only did it appear that their isolation was soon to end, it also seemed possible that the young communities might find themselves on a Denver to Los Angeles main line.

Company records indicate that a route along the Price River and Grassy Trail Creek had been located by April 1881. On 26 April, however, railroad management decided to build on the Buckhorn Flat route, which would provide a shorter route to Wasatch (Salina) Pass and hoped-for future expansion to southern California. The company's chief engineer claimed that this route could be built with a grade of no more than seventy-five feet to the mile. The plan then was to go from Green River through Cottonwood Wash and Buckhorn Flat to Castle Valley Junction, located in the Hadden Flat area. Here the rails would divide, with one branch going south through Castle Valley to Wasatch Pass and the other going north through Price Canyon. The route from Dead Horse Crossing below Price to Castle Valley Junction was located between 26 April and 25 May 1881, and that from Castle Valley Junction to Green River between 15 May and 27 July.

Roadbed construction began in mid-May and continued almost until the end of the year. It turned out, however, that engineers had made a "grave error" in calculating the elevation of the divide east of Buckhorn Flat, underestimating it by some 700 feet. The result was a maximum grade of 2.2 percent instead of the desired maximum of 1.5 percent. Faced with this unanticipated barrier, the railroad abandoned the Buckhorn Flat route on 23 December 1881 and resumed

Rio Grande Western Depot and Palmer House Hotel, Green River. (Courtesy Denise Hoffman)

work on the Grassy Trail route.[53] The Castle Valley-Wasatch Pass branch remained on Rio Grande Western route maps for many years, keeping alive Emery County residents' hopes for further railroad connections.

Green River as a Railroad Town. If the Rio Grande Western proved to be a disappointment to the Castle Valley communities, it was the making of Green River. From a place with only three families in 1880, it became a construction boom town by 1882 with dozens of workers living in tents or dugouts and laboring on the bridge and roadbed. The last spike completing the connection between Denver and Salt Lake City was ceremonially driven near Desert Siding on 30 March 1883. However, a short time after traffic began moving over the new line it was interrupted by spring floods that destroyed the Green River bridge. The bridge was rebuilt within a few months with stronger piers and made wide enough to accommodate the later standardizing of the railroad gauge, which occurred in 1890.[54]

The Farrer family owned most of the land below the Gravity Canal that is now the eastern portion of Green River. Joseph Gamage also had a farm there. On the advice of a railroad surveyor who boarded at his home, Gamage filed on apparently worthless desert land above the canal. He profited handsomely when the railroad purchased forty acres of this property for its station and other facilities. Green River became a major division point on the railroad, with watering and fueling facilities, switching yards, and engine sheds. The railroad also constructed a hotel named the Palmer House. This building burned down in 1885 but was rebuilt the following year.[55] A three-story mansard-roofed structure with wide verandas and landscaped grounds, the Palmer House was for many years the largest and most elegant building in Emery County. The *Utah Gazetteer, 1892–1893,* declared, "The hotel is the finest and best appointed on the road, with all the modern conveniences, including Brush incandescent light and steam heating, and bears the reputation of serving the best meals of any hotel in the West."[56] Rio Grande Western passenger trains did not begin carrying dining cars until near the turn of the century, and the Palmer House was a scheduled meal stop for trains going in both directions during the 1880s and 1890s.

The railroad's entry into Green River was not accomplished without some conflict with the earlier residents. J. T. Farrer complained that the track had been built across Farrer land without compensation. For its part, the railroad viewed Farrer's ferry approach as intruding on its property and attempted to close it off.[57] On the other hand, the Farrers also profited from the coming of the railroad. A portion of Thomas Farrer's homestead was developed into a four-block, forty-eight lot residential subdivision bounded by Long Street (originally Main Street) on the west, Solomon Street on the east, and Farrer Street on the south. This was the first townsite at Green River (known officially as Blake until 1895) and was home to many in the 1890 population of 375, a majority of whom were railroad employees and their families. Other residents lived on farms near the river, and some Chinese and Japanese laborers occupied dugouts on Reservoir Hill, south of the tracks. A saloon located on "the Island" (now the Grand County portion of Green River) was the site of several gunfights during the boom-town period. The community's first school was held in a log house on the east bank of the river. Later a school was conducted by Miss J. C. Miller in the railroad depot until a log building was erected for the purpose. In 1894 a larger frame school was built that served the community for this purpose for sixteen years. Extensively remodeled as a church and later as a senior citizens' center, this building was still standing in 1995.[58] J. T. Farrer's store was the chief mercantile establishment in the community until 1906.

Green River's railroad boom era lasted only one decade. In 1892 the Rio Grande Western transferred most of its divisional operations to the new town of Helper. While the Palmer House and some operations remained in Green River, employment and population declined significantly during the decade of the 1890s. The 1900 census found only 222 people in the Green River precinct, 123 of whom resided in Green River Village.

Woodside Beginnings. The small steam engines used on the narrow-gauge Rio Grande Western required frequent stops for water. Stations for this purpose were established at Desert Siding, northwest of Green River, at Lower Crossing, and at Grassy Trail Creek. (The latter station was known as Sunnyside several years before the mining camp of the same name was developed in nearby Whitmore Canyon.)

Lower Crossing was an oasis with extensive cottonwood groves in an otherwise treeless and waterless landscape. The first person to take up residence at the site was reportedly Henry H. Hutchinson, who made it a base for his prospecting around Cedar Mountain in 1881. In 1882 Scott Miller and Joseph Curtis and their families took up land and began work on an irrigation canal. They were followed by other settlers over the next several years, including the Coleman, Watson, Turner, McPherson, Presset, Romdal, Liddel, Rutt, Seamountain, and Carswell families.[59] They homesteaded the land along the Price River bottoms, built dirt-roofed log cabins from the abundant cottonwoods (which gave the community its permanent name of Woodside), and attempted to control the erratic flow of the river.

Compared to other Castle Valley streams, the Price River has a large drainage basin but a relatively small extent of high elevation watershed. This combination made the streamflow extremely variable before the construction of Scofield Reservoir. Spring high waters began and ended several weeks earlier than on other Castle Valley streams. By late summer the streambed would in some years be entirely dry on its lower stretches. (The Powell expedition found it so in August 1871.) Summer cloudbursts anywhere in the extensive basin could send flood waters rushing down the channel to wash out diversion dams and fill irrigation ditches with mud.

Despite these difficulties, the Woodside settlers managed to bring several hundred acres under cultivation. The railroad station and adjacent hotel and workers' residences formed the core of a small community center that included a frame schoolhouse, a store, and stockyards. Woodside became a shipping and supply point for neighboring ranches. By 1900 the community had a population of 114, including among its adult males twenty-three railroad workers, thirteen farmers, four stock raisers, a cattle dealer, and a miner.

Other Contributions of the Railroad to Emery County. The money expended by the Rio Grande Western on its construction projects in Emery County contributed significantly to the struggling economy of the pioneer settlements. The railroad construction crews not only offered good-paying jobs but also provided a market for agricultural products to supply their men and animals. Railroad construction employment enabled some settlers to obtain the resources needed to develop their homesteads. For example, nineteen-year-old Hyrum Nelson, who possessed virtually no capital apart from his Ferron Creek homestead and a good team of horses, got a job in Salina Canyon that paid $5 a day for a man with team, wages almost unheard of at that period. His son Lowry reported, "His railroad earnings enabled him to buy a scraper, which was an indispensable implement in constructing the canals."[60] Oscar Crandall and William Howard formed a partnership to purchase a sawmill and install it in a side canyon above Castle Gate to produce railroad ties. They made sufficient profits from this venture to build identical two-story frame houses, the first multiroom dwellings on the Huntington townsite.[61] Samuel Grange of Springville took his family to Price Canyon with a contract to cut railroad ties. By the conclusion of the contract, in April 1883, the family had become sufficiently interested in Castle Valley that they settled in Huntington, where Samuel and his sons applied their skilled axe work to the construction of a two-room house of "logs so well hewn that they were a wonder to some and were almost as smooth as sawed logs."[62]

The railroad connected Emery County with the outside world,

even though that connection remained somewhat remote for the communities in southern Castle Valley. No longer was the region isolated by snowbound mountain passes for months at a stretch. Salt Lake City, which had required a week-long journey in the best of conditions by team and wagon, could now be reached within one or two days. Emery County livestock, wool, and grain enjoyed improved access to markets—albeit at rather steep freight rates. The irregular Star Mail Route from Salina to Ouray was abandoned in favor of thrice-weekly and later daily mail service from Price to Emery.

Before the coming of the railroad, Price was a straggling settlement with fewer than two dozen families. However, it soon became the transportation and commercial center of Castle Valley and the shipping point for the Uinta Basin. By 1891, though its population was still smaller than that of several other towns in the area, Price had a newspaper, warehouses, two hotels, and several stores and saloons. The campground south of the tracks was crowded with freighters and their teams. Many Emery County men and boys found employment hauling supplies to Fort Duchesne and bringing gilsonite to the railroad on the return trip.

The coming of the railroad stimulated the development of coal deposits along its route. The Rio Grande Western acquired the Pleasant Valley Coal Company and its Winter Quarters mines in 1882. Through this and another subsidiary, the Utah Fuel Company, organized in 1887, the railroad opened mines at Clear Creek (1887), Castle Gate (1888), and Sunnyside (1899).[63] This industrial development brought an influx of population to the northern part of what was then Emery County and set in motion the political forces that would lead to the establishment of Carbon County in 1894. The Carbon County coal mines provided seasonal employment for many Emery County residents and an economic outlet for the county's surplus population in the second and third generations.

Cleveland Beginnings

In May 1885 Samuel N. and Ruth Pace Alger and Henry and Sally Whitlock Oviatt arrived on the flats seven miles east of Huntington with the intention of establishing homes. The Algers were a young couple who had been married in early 1884 and moved to

Huntington in the fall of that year.[64] The Oviatts were in their fifties with grown children, several of whom followed them to Cleveland. They had lived in Sanpete Valley for thirty years before coming to Castle Valley in 1883.[65]

The site chosen for the new settlement was four miles from the nearest running water and eleven miles from the diversion point of the Cleveland Canal. It was probably unprecedented in Utah history for an agricultural colony to be established at such a distance from its water supply. By 1885, however, most of the land more easily accessible to irrigation had already been claimed. There appeared to be sufficient water in Huntington Creek to supply additional land beyond that already brought under cultivation in the river valley. Moreover, the Cleveland area appeared to have a good potential for agriculture, with wide expanses of relatively level ground. To these factors must be added some personal qualities shared by many Emery County settlers, including a confidence in their ability to achieve their goals, a capacity for hard work and sacrifice, and a willingness to take risks in the hope of obtaining a better life for their children. The new colony's prospects were sufficiently appealing to attract several dozen settlers, including land-hungry coal miners from Scofield and Winter Quarters.

Cleveland Canal. Samuel Alger surveyed the route of the Cleveland Canal in 1885 with the assistance of Tom and John Richards of Scofield, using a carpenter's spirit level attached to a plank to determine the necessary fall. Morten Mortensen provided a team and scraper, and many others contributed pick-and-shovel work to the project.[66] During the four years of construction, a cooperative arrangement was developed whereby some men worked in the mines and contributed to the living expenses of others who worked on the canal. The canal as originally completed was twenty-five miles in length, much of it built through rock ledges and shale hillsides, and cost a reported $30,000.[67] Later extensions added many additional miles, making the Cleveland Canal the most extensive irrigation system in Emery County. It is likely that much of the construction cost was supplied in labor rather than cash, as had been the case with the Huntington Canal built a few years earlier.

Several families remained on their homesteads during much or all of the time the canal was under construction, living in dugouts or tents or wagon boxes and compelled to travel several miles for every drop of water for livestock or domestic use. The years 1886 and 1887 were poor runoff seasons for Huntington Creek, and some prospective settlers became discouraged and withdrew from the project.[68] When water was finally turned into the canal in 1888, the clay and shale banks washed out at frequent intervals, leaving the settlement without water for several days at a time until repairs could be completed. Furthermore, disputes soon arose between Cleveland and Huntington water users. The Cleveland Canal's diversion point was higher on the creek than the other canals, but the users on the other canals claimed a prior right to the water. In an effort to develop additional water rights, the Cleveland Canal and Agricultural Company, incorporated in 1889, undertook another major project in 1890, building a storage reservoir high on the Wasatch Plateau.

Town Development. While these large projects kept many of the men at work far away from their homesteads, community institutions were gradually being developed in the settlement. Timber was brought from Miller Creek Canyon in 1887 for the construction of log homes. A post office was chartered on 23 January 1889 with the designation Cleveland in honor of President Grover Cleveland and with Henry Oviatt as postmaster. Rasmus Rasmussen and Sophus Olsen opened stores in their homes. Latter-day Saint church meetings were held in the cabins of John and William Cowley with Samuel N. Alger serving as branch president. By 1890 a combination church and school had been erected on the South Flat.

The Cleveland LDS Ward was organized on 10 August 1890 with Lars Peter Oveson of Huntington as bishop.[69] Bishop Oveson moved his family to Cleveland and assumed a major leadership role in building the community. In 1892 he helped organize the Cleveland Cooperative Mercantile Association, which he managed until he moved from the community in 1910. He also oversaw the platting of a townsite on land acquired from John Alger in what is now the southeastern part of town. In order to encourage people to move into the village, Oveson acquired two lots, planted trees, and built the first brick home on the townsite. A frame school was erected in 1892 and expanded with a two-story addition later in the decade. In 1899 a meeting house and social hall was erected on the townsite. Many settlers move into town after they had proved up on their homesteads, but many others established permanent residence on their farms, and Cleveland has remained a relatively scattered community. Several families continued to divide their time between their Cleveland farms and the coal camps at Scofield, Castle Gate, and (later) Sunnyside. The population of the Cleveland precinct was 111 in 1890 and grew to 353 by 1900.[70]

Desert Lake. The natural drainage in the Cleveland area runs east to a hollow near the base of Cedar Mountain where it enters Desert Seep Wash, which drains north to the Price River. Members of the Wells, Powell, Thayne, Winder, Marsing, and Pilling families took up land in this hollow between 1885 and 1888 and began work on an earthen dam that would create a 300-acre reservoir.[71] Their intention was capture runoff from the higher fields and also store the winter flow of the Cleveland Canal. The Desert Lake Reservoir and Irrigation Company was incorporated on 13 July 1892, and it is likely that the reservoir was placed in service sometime near this date.[72] In August 1896 the dam broke and flood waters did extensive damage to farms and homes. The dam was rebuilt during the winter of 1896–97 with financial assistance from the LDS church. In 1897 an extension of the Huntington North Ditch brought additional fresh water to the Desert Lake region.[73] It was hoped this would offset the effects of the saline waste water from the Cleveland farms.

Desert Lake was part of the Cleveland precinct until 1898 when a separate precinct and post office were established. Lever's 1898 *History of Sanpete and Emery Counties* described Desert Lake as having "some nice farms, surrounded by beautiful shade trees, and producing an abundance of cereals and alfalfa." Lever indicated that the store and post office were operated by Silas Winder, but postal records list Elvira Marsing as the first postmistress, followed by Caroline Mills and Eliza Draper. Lever wrote that "a good schoolhouse furnishe[d] ample accommodations for forty-five pupils, the present school population." The 1900 census showed a population of 127 in the Desert Lake precinct.[74]

County Government

The governing body of Emery County during the territorial period from 1880 to 1896 was a "county court" consisting of a probate judge and three selectmen. Other officers included a county clerk, sheriff, assessor and collector of taxes, treasurer, coroner, and pound keeper. All county government positions were regarded as part-time jobs, with some officers being paid on the basis of meetings attended and others receiving expenses or a small salary.[75]

Castle Dale continued as the county seat, though not without challenge. The first county courthouse designed for the purpose was a one-room adobe-lined frame structure built in 1883 by J. W. Seely on First South Street between First and Second East. This building contained a steel vault for the protection of county records and funds. In 1892 there was an attempt by residents in the northern portion of the county to move the county seat to Price.[76] Perhaps partly as a defense against a renewal of that threat, a two-story brick courthouse was erected that same year at the corner of First South and First East streets, giving the seat of county government a more substantial presence.

The county's original borders were also subject to encroachments, some successfully resisted, others not. Fifty-nine citizens of Moab petitioned the 1886 territorial legislature to detach the area east of the Grand River from Emery County and attach it to San Juan County. This request was approved by the legislature but rejected by Governor Eli H. Murray "upon representations to me and by letter and petition of citizens of Emery County." The 1890 legislature with the concurrence of Governor Arthur L. Thomas created Grand County from the portion of Emery County east of the Green River.[77] Also in 1890 Sanpete County attempted unsuccessfully to annex the coal-rich Scofield-Winter Quarters area.[78] Residents of the northern portion of Emery County, having failed to move the county seat, turned their attention to obtaining a county of their own. These efforts were rewarded when the 1894 legislature created Carbon County, thereby reducing Emery County to its present size.

Two Emery County men, William Howard of Huntington and Jasper Robertson of Orangeville, were among the 107 delegates to the

Utah Constitutional Convention in April-May 1895. Robertson had also taken part in an earlier effort to draft a state constitution in 1887. Utah statehood brought a change in county government from the county court to the county commission. The first Emery County commissioners, elected in November 1896, were A. O. Wood, R. P. Rasmussen, and Nephi Williams.[79]

Roads and Bridges. Much of the attention and resources of the county government in the first two decades were devoted to improving the roads. In 1880 the roads in Emery County were nothing more than wagon tracks, and apparently there was not a single bridge in the entire county. The same legislative session that created Emery County appropriated $2,000 "to aid Sevier and Emery counties to make a wagon road through Salina Canyon and Meadow Gulch." During his term as probate judge (1882–85), Orange Seely supervised the laying out of a county road from the Price River to Ivie Creek. In large part this is the route still followed by Utah Highway 10. In 1882 the county appropriated $150 toward construction of a road in Ferron Canyon to provide access to timber. This road was completed in 1884 at a total cost of about $3,000, most of it in labor contributed by Ferron residents. A "good substantial bridge" was built over Ferron Creek in 1886 at a cost of $300. After several unsuccessful requests, the 1888 legislature appropriated funds to enable the county to construct bridges over Price, Huntington, and Cottonwood creeks. As late as 1897, Emery residents were still pleading for a bridge over Muddy Creek, complaining that "crossing is attended with much inconvenience and serious danger."[80]

Efforts to achieve better transportation facilities continued through the 1890s. For example, at its December 1891 meeting the county court received the report of a committee assigned to locate a road through Straight Canyon; a petition for funds to build a road from Wellington to Cleveland and Lawrence; and a petition from residents of Orangeville for the building of two bridges across Cottonwood Creek. At its April 1897 meeting, the court received $1,000 in state funds for construction of the Straight Canyon road and $750 for a road in Huntington Canyon. Under the supervision of Orson Robbins, some forty miles of road in Huntington Canyon were improved and a bridge constructed by early September—just in time for two weeks of heavy rain that brought "the greatest flood in the history of the valley," washing out the bridge and much of the road improvements.[81]

Emery LDS Stake

The three original wards of the Emery Stake were augmented in 1881 by the Moab Ward (later transferred to San Juan Stake) and the Price Branch (a smaller and less independent unit than a ward).[82] In 1882 the Orangeville Ward was divided from Castle Dale, with Jasper Robertson as bishop, and the Price branch was made into a ward. By the end of the decade, rapid growth had brought the establishment of wards at Muddy Creek (1883), Molen (1884), Lawrence (1889), Cleveland (1890), and Wellington (1890).[83] The Scofield and Winter Quarters wards belonged to the Utah Stake with headquarters in Provo.

The Relief Society. The Emery Stake Relief Society was established on 13 August 1882, with Anne Ungerman Larsen, a childless plural wife of stake president C. G. Larsen, as president. The organization was completed during the next two years with Josie E. Childs of Orangeville and Ann Beers Pulsipher of Huntington as counselors and Anna Eliza Reynolds Seely of Castle Dale as secretary. These officers supervised the work of Relief Societies in each of the wards for almost two decades. The Relief Society organization formed a spiritual and social center for Latter-day Saint women, but as its name suggests it was also a means of organizing women for service. Nurses and midwives often performed their duties under the auspices of the Relief Society. A sewing committee in each ward made burial clothing for the frequent funerals, and other committees hung white draperies in the meetinghouses. In the Old Testament tradition, Relief Society women followed the harvesters in the grain fields, gleaning the remaining wheat and storing it for occasions of need. Each Relief Society member was asked to donate a chicken or its equivalent in cash toward the construction of the Manti temple. After its completion, the Emery Stake Relief Society provided fifty yards of handmade carpet for the temple. Relief Society chickens also helped build the Emery Stake Academy. In some communities the Relief Societies erected their own buildings separate from the ward meetinghouse.

While officially under the direction of the priesthood leaders of the stake and ward, the Relief Societies enjoyed considerable autonomy. The organization's general leaders in Salt Lake City tended to be women of intellectual accomplishment and independent spirit, qualities they tried to infuse into the local organizations during periodic visits. On one such visit to Emery County in 1887, President Zina D. H. Young

> told the sisters they had the privilege of being washed and anointed and set apart for confinements. Several sisters asked to have this blessing so she went with the stake officers to their homes and officiated, as a pattern for them to follow.

During this same visit President Young accompanied the stake leaders to Muddy Creek to organize a Relief Society at that settlement. William Taylor of Ferron drove the group in his new wagon with two spring seats. When they reached the steep road over the blue hill south of Ferron Creek Valley,

> Sister Zina told Brother Taylor to stop. She said she would get out and walk because she didn't want those poor horses to haul her up that dreadful climb. Of course the rest would not stay in and ride while she walked. So they all got out and walked, with her taking the lead, the other two, Sisters Larsen and Pulsipher following and Sister Childs, only a girl in comparison to the others, in the rear, stopping at intervals to rest while Sister Zina never faltered until she reached the top. When finally Sister Childs reached the top Sister Zina was a great distance ahead. In overtaking her, for the others had climbed into the wagon, she said how she did enjoy physical culture. . . . She said it was a pity to see girls sitting sidewise on a horse when it was more important for her to sit astride than for a man, if there was any difference. Also it was much safer.

Upon reaching Bishop Casper Christensen's farm on Muddy Creek, they found threshing in progress and Sister Christensen confined to her bed.

> We went in and found his wife in a little lean-to, very sick indeed. Sister Zina hurried us out of the room and told us Sister Christensen would not live and she didn't. She died a day or two

> later. We did not stay to supper but drove back to the little meeting house.

The Relief Society also engaged in political activities in support of women's rights. In 1891 the women of Emery Stake contributed a substantial sum to send a delegation from the Relief Society to Washington, D.C., for the convention of the National Council of Women. The Relief Society also spearheaded the establishment of local suffrage associations, with Sarah Ann Fullmer as president and Josie E. Childs as secretary of the Emery County suffrage organization.[84]

Education

The first schools in most Emery County communities were informal gatherings of students with a volunteer teacher in a dugout or log cabin. One of the first structures on the Castle Dale townsite was a log schoolhouse at the west end of Main Street, where students sat on benches made from log slabs and were taught by Emanuel Bagley. Samuel R. Jewkes offered the first instruction in a similar log schoolhouse in Orangeville. In Green River Miss J. C. Miller taught in the railroad depot. On Muddy Creek sixteen-year-old Hannah C. Christensen taught "about 20 students, some older and larger than she was. Her salary was three dollars a week."[85]

Among the officers appointed when Emery County was established in 1880 were a superintendent of schools and a three-member school board. The superintendent's duties included certifying teachers, conducting an annual training session, and distributing funds appropriated by the territorial legislature to the local schools. However, the primary responsibility for the schools rested with a local school district in each precinct. Local school trustees provided the buildings, hired the teachers, and set the calendar. Buildings were typically financed by a combination of local property taxes and volunteer labor. Teachers were paid in part from territorial appropriations, in part from local taxes, and in part from tuition paid by students, often in the form of room and board or fuel. When J. W. Nixon began his teaching career in Price in 1884, he was paid $80 a month for teaching seventy students. Presumably he earned about the same amount when he moved to Huntington four years later.[86]

Women teachers were paid substantially less. The school year tended to be short, beginning in October or November after the harvest was completed, and ending when spring work required the children's labor on the farm—or when the available funds were exhausted. Even during the designated session, students would come and go according to family needs or personal inclinations as there were no laws making school attendance mandatory.

With a growing population of large families, Emery County schools experienced a rapid expansion during the 1880s and 1890s. The 1880 census listed a school-age population of 119. By 1890 this had grown to 1,933, and by 1900 to 2,019 despite the loss of the northern portion of the county in the creation of Carbon County.[87] Ferron progressed from a one-room log structure shared with Molen in 1880 to the "blue frame" school erected in 1889 to "the largest brick school house in the county," built around 1895 and serving an enrollment of 244 students in 1898.[88] The Cleveland school expanded from a single log room in 1890 to four rooms by 1893.[89] Huntington schools were widely dispersed during the 1880s, with classes held at several different locations. The two-room Seventies Hall was acquired for a school in 1892 and expanded to four rooms in 1894. This "Central School" allowed for some consolidation, but separate schools continued in operation north of the creek and in the south fields until near the turn of the century, with a total district enrollment of 392 in 1898.[90] Lawrence had a two-room brick school by about 1890, with an enrollment of eighty.[91] Molen had a well-equipped frame building with "a beautifully toned bell."[92] Because the Rio Grande Western Railroad paid more than half of the property tax collected in the county, school district boundaries were drawn in such a way as to give each district a slice of railroad land. In 1900 school expenditures in the county amounted to $20,683 for 1,706 school-age children, for an average of slightly more than $12 per student.[93]

Emery Stake Academy and Huntington Seminary. The district schools offered only a primary education in the early years, seldom extending beyond the fifth grade level. Efforts at providing a more advanced education took shape in March 1889 when the Emery Stake Board of Education was formed with a charge to establish an LDS church-operated academy. At a meeting of the board on 10 June 1889, representatives from both Castle Dale and Huntington proposed that the academy be located in their community, and Castle Dale was selected by majority vote. At the next meeting, board member Milas E. Johnson requested permission to establish a seminary at Huntington. This request was approved though some members of the board expressed concern as to whether the stake had sufficient resources to support two schools.[94]

The Emery Stake Academy opened in Castle Dale on 12 February 1890 with Alexander Jamesen as principal and an enrollment of twenty-one. Classes were held in the LDS social hall during the first year then moved to the upper floor of a two-story house owned by William Hinken at Main and First West streets. Enrollment grew to eighty-one in 1892, but the academy was experiencing severe financial difficulties by 1893. The nation was in the throes of an economic depression during this period, which doubtless had an effect on the funds available to the academy. The teachers gave their services without pay in order to complete the 1893–94 school year, and the academy then suspended operations.[95]

The Huntington Seminary opened in the fall of 1890 with James E. Brown as the first teacher. For its first six years, the seminary operated in a two-room frame building on the corner of First East and First North streets. It then moved to what had been the Noah T. Guymon store on Center Street. Upon completion of the brick meetinghouse, the seminary was given use of the old log meetinghouse, which was expanded with a T-wing on the west to provide additional classroom space.[96] In 1895 Huntington residents requested that their seminary be designated as the stake academy. LDS church commissioner of education Karl G. Maeser initially supported this proposal, writing to church president Wilford Woodruff,

> as there is no prospect that the Stake Board of Emery ever will do anything in the matter of education, and the local board at Huntington is manifesting much interest and energy, I suggest that the latter school be recognized as the stake academy.

However, Maeser reversed his recommendation in February 1896 following a visit to Emery County and discussions with stake leaders.[97]

New Emery Stake Academy Building, 1910. (Courtesy Carolyn Jorgensen)

The cornerstone for an academy building was laid on 16 March 1896 on the northwest corner of the Castle Dale public square. The two-story brick structure with dimensions of forty-eight by forty-six feet was near enough to completion to open for classwork to some eighty-five students on 23 October 1899. The completed building was dedicated on 11 January 1903, by which time the enrollment had grown to 120.[98]

Both the Emery Stake Academy and the Huntington Seminary offered a standard academic program similar to that of the public schools plus added courses in LDS doctrine and scriptures. At first they provided instruction at primary levels, but the lower grades were gradually eliminated until only intermediate (seventh and eighth grade) and high school (ninth and tenth grade) divisions remained. The Huntington Seminary was offering instruction through the ninth grade by 1897 and in 1899 requested high school status. Stake president Reuben G. Miller chose instead to concentrate the stake's support in the academy. Under increasing pressure to supply both funds and students to the academy, Huntington Ward bishop James W. Nixon closed the seminary on 1 September 1904.[99] However, the bitterness produced by fourteen years of rivalry for status and support would continue for many decades. Bishop Nixon resigned from his ecclesiastical position within a few months of the seminary closing, amid reports of "dissension" in the Huntington Ward. Nixon wrote in his 1937 memoirs that some Huntington residents never forgave him for his support of the Emery Stake Academy.[100]

Law Enforcement and Law-breakers

The chief—and during some periods the only—law officer in the county was the sheriff. The first Emery County sheriff was Erastus Curtis, Sr. He resigned after only a few months and was replaced by John L. Brasher, who was also serving as county assessor and collector of taxes. Brasher resigned as sheriff in 1882, and H. S. (Hyte) Loveless was appointed. Henry G. Mathis, of Price, was elected sheriff in 1893 but resigned a year later upon the creation of Carbon County. P. C. Borreson replaced Mathis. Borreson was succeeded by Azariah Tuttle in 1896 and John Leamaster in 1898. Tuttle was reelected in 1900 and served until 1902. The first county attorney was Marion J. Shelton, elected in August 1880. He was succeeded by John K. Reid in 1882, A. Ballinger in 1888, Reid again in 1892, Chris Johnson in 1893, and William Howard in 1896.[101] The county jail was adjacent to the court house on Second East Street. Some towns had their own jails consisting in most cases of a single room.

During the territorial period, Emery County belonged to the first judicial district, headquartered at Provo and taking in much of central and eastern Utah. The state constitution of 1896 assigned Emery, Sanpete, Carbon, Grand, and San Juan counties to the seventh judicial district. The district judge from 1896 until 1905 was Jacob Johnson of Spring City, Sanpete County. Johnson made the "circuit" of counties in his district several times a year, holding court sessions at each county seat.

Much of the law-breaking in early Emery County consisted of youthful pranks that got out of hand or disturbances of the peace by cowboys or sheepherders who had come to town after weeks of isolation in the desert. On a June evening in 1897, for example, some young Ferron men attempted to gain the attention of several young women in a buggy belonging to A. G. Conover by removing boards from a culvert in the vehicle's path. The prank took an unanticipated turn when the buggy tipped over, injuring the passengers. The boys were fined $2.50 each by justice of the peace Worthen and required to repair the buggy. The same week a group of Emery boys "got hold of a few revolvers" on Sunday night and amused themselves "by terrorizing the town." This escapade ended with a gunshot wound in the arm of one of the boys and the near-runaway of a carriage loaded with young people. The Emery correspondent to the Price newspaper commented, "The fact that the town is without a constable or justice of the peace probably led the boys to believe that any kind of sport could be indulged without being summoned to the bar of justice."[102]

It is unclear whether these pranks were isolated incidents or represented an upsurge of misbehavior among the young people of Emery County. According to newspaper reports of the period, firearm incidents were common. Emery LDS Stake conference talks frequently mentioned problems with the youth, including alcohol consumption and general rowdyism. Dances sometimes required the services of a "manager" to maintain order. In Ferron, Bishop Hyrum Nelson evidently filled this role quite effectively. One patron forcibly ejected from a dance was reported to have said afterwards, "I have been kicked by mules, and I have been kicked by horses, but I have never been knocked out like I was by that white-haired Danishman."[103] Some "pranks" had sobering consequences. For example, a group of Cleveland boys reportedly laid another boy across a stair railing and used his body as a "teeter-totter," inflicting serious injuries. A seventeen-year-old Castle Dale boy was jailed for stabbing another boy with a pocketknife at a birthday party.[104] It must be borne in mind, however, that the proportion of the county's population in their teens and twenties was exceptionally high during this period. If more young people got into trouble, the reason may have simply been that there were more young people. In most instances the names linked to "hoodlumism" in the 1890s turn up a few years later attached to solid, law-abiding citizens. In some cases, however, juvenile delinquency was a prelude to more serious adult crime.

Property crimes included store burglaries (the Ferron Co-op was burglarized six times in a single year) and theft of livestock from the range. The large Ireland Cattle Company, with ranches at Oak Spring and Salina Canyon, was a frequent target of rustlers. The Emery correspondent for the *Eastern Utah Advocate* noted in November 1897, "There seems to be a good deal of cattle and sheep stealing in this region at present." A prominent Castle Dale resident was sentenced in 1897 to five years in prison for stealing livestock but was paroled after three years on the basis of a petition "numerously signed" by his fellow-townsmen.[105] Apparently this was a rather common pattern. Lowry Nelson recounts an incident in which his father, Hyrum, caught another resident of the Ferron Creek area stealing his horses. The offender was convicted and sentenced to the state prison, but Hyrum Nelson himself circulated a petition for the defendant's early release "so he could come home and look after his family."[106]

Some crimes in early Emery County evoke images of the Wild West. In 1891 A. F. Kohler was killed and a bystander named Frank Drake wounded in a gunfight in Green River between Kohler and prospector Cass Hite.[107] In September 1894 Sanpete County sheriff James Burns died in a gunfight at a sheep corral on Reeder Ridge above Joe's Valley. Burns had gone to the mountain to investigate reports that Fred Mickel's sheep herd included animals stolen from the Moroni cooperative herd. Gunfire erupted while Burns was in the corral inspecting the sheep with herders Jim Mickel and Moen Kofford. Sheriff Burns died on the spot. Kofford and Mickel escaped to Castle Valley, and neither man was ever apprehended.[108] Kofford and the Mickel brothers were residents of Spring City but like many other young men from Sanpete County spent most of the time with their herds on the Wasatch Plateau or the San Rafael Swell. Several years later Fred Mickel and another brother, Pete, were involved in an incident at the Court Saloon in Castle Dale in which proprietor Lew Link was stabbed to death. Fred Mickel was charged with murder but was acquitted by a Sanpete County jury after a change of venue from Castle Dale to Manti.[109]

The Robbers Roost Gang. Emery County's reputation as a refuge for outlaws is apparent in newspaper accounts of the Sheriff Burns shooting. The *Manti Messenger* reported in its issue of 26 September 1894,

> A posse of nine men headed by J. T. Henrie, city marshal, left this city Wednesday night for the purpose of trying to head off the assassins in Castle Valley. If not caught before they reach the San Rafael bluffs, there will be but little use of following them.

This reputation was magnified in subsequent years through the activities of the "Wild Bunch" who made the Robbers Roost area one of their hideouts. Robbers Roost is a region of high benches and slickrock canyons in eastern Wayne County, but outlaw trails and activities extended into Emery County. Green River, the closest town to the Roost except for the hamlet of Hanksville, served as a supply point and was on the trail between the Roost and other outlaw havens at Brown's Park and Hole in the Wall. Pearl Baker, whose family later operated a ranch at Robbers Roost, dated the beginning of outlaw activities to the mid-1870s, when Cap Brown pastured stolen horses there before selling them in the Colorado mining camps. The most active period, however, was the 1890s, when the Burh brothers of Denver operated a cattle and horse ranch at the Roost. The Burh foreman, Jack Moore, reputedly kept the welcome mat out for men wanted by the law all the way from Texas to Wyoming.[110]

This single decade provided the stuff of legends, as notorious outlaws such as Butch Cassidy, Matt Warner, Joe Walker, the McCarty brothers, Elzy Lay, and "Flat Nose" George Curry frequented the Roost and the surrounding country. While most of the Wild Bunch's depredations were committed in other places, some episodes occurred in and around Emery County. On 24 March 1897 Emery County sheriff Azariah Tuttle and Sheriff Allred of Carbon County surprised Joe Walker at Mexican Bend on the San Rafael River with a herd of horses stolen from the Whitmore ranch. Sheriff Tuttle was hit in the hip during the exchange of gunfire and lay unattended for thirty-six hours while Sheriff Allred rode to Price for assistance.[111] Tuttle recovered from his wound but walked with a painful limp for the rest of his life. The county commission posted a $250 reward for the arrest and conviction of Walker. Walker met his end the following year when he was shot at Florence Creek on the Green River by a nine-man posse including sheriffs Tuttle and Allred.[112]

The most sensational event of 1897 was the daring payroll robbery at Castle Gate on 21 April. Butch Cassidy and Elzy Lay relieved Pleasant Valley Coal Company paymaster E. L. Carpenter of a satchel full of gold and made their escape by riding up Gordon Creek then across the Washboard Flat to Desert Lake and from there to Buckhorn Flat and Mexican Bend.[113] Joe Walker reportedly assisted them by cutting the telephone line between Castle Gate and Price and by stationing fresh horses at Gordon Creek. Pearl Baker claims that Walker received the loot at Desert Lake and took it to Brown's Park.[114]

Finding the telephone inoperative, Carpenter commandeered a steam engine and traveled at full speed to Price to deliver word of the robbery. A telephone message was then sent from Price to Huntington and Castle Dale but was interrupted in progress when the outlaws cut the line. Sufficient information had got through, however, to lead to the formation of posses in both towns. Traveling by different routes, they arrived at dusk in Buckhorn Draw, where each posse mistook the other for the outlaws. A horse was wounded in an exchange of gunfire before the mistake was discovered. The robbery took on added interest in Emery County when it became known that Cassidy and Lay had spent part of the winter living at the Jens Nielson ranch on Huntington Creek, going by the names of Tom Gillis and Bert Fowler.[115] Joe Walker reportedly worked for the Staker family of Lawrence during the same period.[116]

The Castle Gate robbery provoked a flood of editorial commentary in the newspapers. The *Eastern Utah Advocate* expressed the hope that the crime would "be the means of drawing the attention of state officials to the necessity of concerted action in obliterating these gangs of audacious outlaws who reign supreme in Robbers Roost." The *Deseret Evening News* quoted a report by Seventh District judge Jacob Johnson that during a cattle rustling trial for Jack Moore and Lars Thompson held at Castle Dale "I received word from several citizens warning me that if the men were convicted an effort would be made to rescue them." Moore failed to show up for trial, and Thompson was convicted. Johnson claimed,

> I told Sheriff Tuttle to take Thompson to Price as soon as possible. Thompson was taken the same day on the regular stage to Price. It was a fortunate thing he did, for early the next morning sixteen armed men came into Castle Dale with the full intention of rescuing Thompson at the peril of losing their own lives. They were very much chagrined when they learned Thompson had been spirited away, and threatened dire vengeance on those that had been responsible for it.[117]

There is reason to doubt the accuracy of this report, as well as Judge Johnson's high estimate of "between 225 and 250" men associated with the Robbers Roost gang. Jack Moore did indeed skip bail and take refuge at the Roost, but Lars Thompson, who was a resident of Ferron, appealed his conviction and was permitted to come and go freely for several weeks until the appeal was resolved—hardly a situation that would provoke such desperate measures as the judge related.[118]

Public opinion in Ferron was apparently divided as to Thompson's guilt or innocence. The community was more united in resenting suggestions that they were hospitable toward outlaws. The Ferron correspondent wrote to the *Eastern Utah Advocate,* "Much has been said of late regarding the friendliness of the people of the south part of Emery County to the Robbers Roost gang. It is going abroad that we are in sympathy with them. The report is erroneous and does our people a very great injustice."[119]

Polygamy Prosecutions. Emery County was visited periodically in its early years by deputy United States marshals bent on enforcing the antipolygamy laws. The period known in Utah history as "the Raid" extended from 1884 to 1890 and was characterized by concentrated efforts to arrest polygamists and bring them to trial.[120] Exact figures are not available for the number of polygamous families in early Emery County, but a cursory survey indicates that more than two dozen early settlers had plural wives during the time they lived in Emery County. Of these, apparently only one served prison time, O. J. Anderson of Castle Dale, who had married sisters Kathinka and Nathalia Wilberg. He was sentenced on 19 November 1888 to 120 days imprisonment and a $50 fine.[121]

The Woodruff Manifesto of 4 October 1890, announcing that the church would no longer authorize marriages that were contrary to the law, opened the way for a resolution of the conflict between the LDS church and the federal government. However, polygamy prosecutions continued for some time. In February 1891 Huntington residents Thomas Stolworthy, William Howard, and John L. Brasher were summoned to the district court in Provo on charges of violating the Edmunds-Tucker law. Stolworthy's case was reportedly dismissed for lack of evidence; Brasher was acquitted; Howard pleaded guilty and was fined $100. A few months later Emery Stake president C. G. Larsen and Castle Dale bishop Henning Olsen were similarly charged. Interviewed as they waited for a train at Price, "both gentlemen expressed themselves as being abundantly able to disprove the charges against them."[122] President Larsen was sixty-two years old at the time; Bishop Olsen was sixty, and their wives were beyond the age of child-bearing. Since both men were known to have plural wives living in Castle Dale, their defense would presumably have been that they had ceased to cohabit with any but their legal wives.

Agriculture and Stockraising

The Mormon colonies in Castle Valley were established as agrarian settlements. The first settlers at Green River were also attracted primarily by the region's agricultural promise. For the first few years the emphasis was on subsistence crops to feed the settlers and their domestic livestock. The 1880 census listed a harvest of 2,496 bushels of wheat, 762 oats, 195 corn, and 126 barley, and only twenty tons of hay and fifty bushels of potatoes. Cultivated acreage in the county increased from eighty-four farms and 1,618 acres in 1880 to 266 farms with 13,347 acres in 1890 and 458 farms with 25,918 acres in 1900.[123]

Irrigation Development. This expansion was made possible by the building of highline irrigation canals. On Huntington Creek the Huntington Canal (1880–85) brought water to the flats south of Huntington and to Lawrence. The Cleveland Canal (1885–89) opened up extensive acreage north and east of the river valley. On Cottonwood Creek the Mammoth Canal (circa 1884) made it possible to bring the benchlands north of Castle Dale under cultivation. Eventually the Huntington and Mammoth canals made possible a continuous stretch of farms between Castle Dale and Huntington. The Great Western Canal (begun in 1884) was built at great expense to irrigate the land south and west of Orangeville, eventually reaching as far as the Rock Canyon flats. On Ferron Creek the North Ditch (1879), King Ditch (1879), and Upper South Canal (1881–82) combined with the lower-level Peterson and Molen ditches to bring almost the entire river valley under cultivation. The Emery Canal (1885–89) supplied the benchlands south and west of Muddy Creek eventually extending to Quitchupah Valley. In 1894 the Independent

Canal and Reservoir Company was organized for the purpose of building a canal to carry Muddy Creek water north to what is now the Moore area. Apparently this canal began delivering water shortly before the turn of the century. By 1899 Emery County had 154 miles of irrigation canals, divided among twenty-two ditches and representing an investment of $385,750.[124]

Crops. As more land was brought under cultivation, subsistence farming was succeeded by more commercial operations. Wheat was the most important cereal crop at 1,678 acres and 25,216 bushels in 1890. Oats, a desirable short-season crop that could be harvested before irrigation streamflows declined in late summer, totalled 1,092 acres and 24,974 bushels. Corn (589 acres; 9,113 bushels) and barley (nine acres, 159 bushels) made up a smaller portion of the county's cereal production. By 1900 wheat production had increased to 87,920 bushels from 3,875 acres; oats to 93,510 bushels from 2,751 acres; and barley to 1,000 bushels from 33 acres; while corn had declined to 7,210 bushels from 306 acres.[125] These grains found a ready cash market at Price where they were resold to the freighters whose teams plied between Price and the Uinta Basin, to the army post at Fort Duchesne, and to the coal mines for their horses and mules.

Alfalfa was among the first forage crops to be grown successfully in Emery County. "Lucern" (as it was more commonly known until the midtwentieth century) was still relatively new to the United States and produced far larger yields than the meadow hay the Castle Valley settlers had known in Sanpete Valley. Alfalfa hay was used for domestic horses and milk cows and as a supplemental feed for range livestock. Some hay was also sold at the Price market. In 1890, 3,200 acres of land produced 6,867 tons of hay. This had increased by 1900 to 7,029 acres and 14,470 tons.[126] Fifteen bushels of alfalfa seed were harvested in 1890 and ninety-five bushels in 1900. In later years alfalfa seed would become a highly profitable cash crop for Emery County farmers.

The fields of alfalfa and clover blossoms combined with the wildflowers on the dry hills to give Castle Valley honey a distinctive flavor and a light, clear color that made it well known throughout central and southern Utah. In 1890 county apiaries produced 23,938 pounds of honey and several hundred pounds of wax. By 1900 some

1,500 hives yielded 100,000 pounds of honey.[127] James Jeffs of Castle Dale reportedly operated "the largest apiary in Utah" in 1897. Skilled apiarists such as Christian Otteson and J. Fleming Wakefield of Huntington and Andrew Nelson of Ferron won prizes for their honey at the Chicago and St. Louis world's fairs.[128]

The 1890 census found 1,107 apple, peach, apricot, cherry, pear, and plum trees in Emery County, only a few of which had come into production.[129] Many families maintained a small orchard for home use. However, the combination of cold winter temperatures, late spring frosts, and heavy saline soils made commercial fruit production impractical in most of the county. Fruit trees produced fairly reliably in a few favored locations, chiefly the canyon mouths where the soil was deep and well drained and the air currents provided some protection against frost. Ferron added to these conditions a southern exposure that lengthened the growing season and made it the most productive fruit-growing area in Castle Valley.

John C. Lemon was apparently among the first to recognize these advantages, planting extensive apple and peach orchards. When the trees began to bear, Lemon became a self-appointed ambassador promoting Ferron fruit. The *Eastern Utah Telegram* reported in November 1891 that he was "showing off his apple crop" in Price. He was still at it in 1900, turning up in Castle Dale with "as fine fruit as can be produced anywhere in Utah this season"—a claim verified by a first prize at the state fair.[130] The editor of the *Emery County Progress* portrayed John and Emma Lemon as prime examples of the success available in the county to enterprising and hard-working residents:

> After selecting a quarter section of the public domain under the timber act, Mr. and Mrs. Lemon, domiciled in a dugout, started to subdue the wild land surrounding it. Today they are living in a fine 8 room brick dwelling house, the largest in Emery County. All the rooms are very large and the house is of a pretty style of architecture. The glory of the farm is its fine orchards of well selected varieties of fruit.[131]

Others who developed commercial orchards included Andrew and Sophus Nelson, Chris Peterson, David Killpack, Kay Funk, and Mosiah Behunin.[132]

By 1900 Emery County had more than 30,000 fruit trees, 18,491 of them apples.[133] However, a comparable expansion was taking place elsewhere in the state as well. Between 1890 and 1900, the number of fruit trees in Utah increased from 223,840 to 1,747,703, far beyond the demands of local markets.[134] The Ferron fruit industry was at a disadvantage because of its remoteness from markets. The Carbon County coal camps provided a receptive outlet, and several Emery County residents made a living as peddlers hauling fruit, eggs, and other products to the camps. This market, however, could not absorb the entire output of the Ferron orchards as they came into full production. Unlike hay and grain, fruit is a highly perishable commodity. It was difficult to maintain quality during the long haul over rough roads to the railroad at Price, and once there high freight rates and the competition from orchards in western Colorado and central Utah made profitable sales even more difficult.

Green River was more favorably situated to transport its harvest to market. The ill-fated "peach boom" was still in the future, but some orchards were established before the turn of the century. An 1897 report indicated that J. T. Farrer had shipped 1,000 pounds of peaches to the Rio Grande Western boarding house at Helper. But Green River growers, too, experienced difficulty in finding buyers, a state of affairs summed up succinctly by a correspondent for the *Eastern Utah Advocate:* "Fruit is in abundance. No market."[135]

While tree fruits met with mixed success at Green River, it was obvious from an early period that the soil and climate were exceptionally well adapted to growing melons. The father of the Green River melon industry was John F. ("Melon") Brown. At his farm on the east bank of the river during the 1890s he experimented with various varieties and either developed or discovered the "now famous Eden musk melons" and a "winter melon" that would keep for several months in storage. By 1900 Brown was shipping several carloads of melons each year and selling seed as far away as France.[136]

Other crops such as potatoes and vegetables were grown chiefly for home consumption or were peddled to the coal camps. Emery County produced 12,371 bushels of potatoes on 171 acres in 1890, and 23,304 bushels on 206 acres in 1900. Small fruits provided a cash crop for a few growers, with 14,230 quarts of currants being harvested from ten acres in 1900. Four acres of gooseberries produced 5,420 quarts.[137] Sorghum cane was grown on a small scale for molasses. Beginning in the 1890s there were periodic efforts to promote a beet sugar industry in Emery county, but while some beets were grown they never became a significant commercial crop.

Domestic livestock including milk cows, hogs, and chickens contributed importantly to family diets, and butter and eggs were often bartered at the store for other goods. In 1890 the county produced a reported 32,219 pounds of butter, 800 pounds of cheese, and 13,229 dozen eggs. The corresponding figures in 1900 were 80,659 pounds of butter (of which 32,029 were marketed), 899 pounds of cheese (191 marketed), and 132,000 dozen eggs. Of the county's 458 farms, 406 had dairy products.[138] Poultry were in all likelihood equally widely distributed.

Range Livestock. The last two decades of the nineteenth century saw a rapid expansion in the livestock industry in Utah. According to census reports, nondairy cattle in the state increased from 62,648 in 1880 to 277,785 in 1900. Horse numbers grew from 38,131 in 1880 to 115,884 in 1900. The growth in sheep was even more dramatic, from 233,121 in 1880 to 2,553,134 in 1900, an increase of more than 1,000 percent in twenty years.[139] In Emery County the 1890 census found 2,908 cattle (not counting dairy cows or working oxen), 1,834 horses, and 40,161 sheep. The corresponding figures for 1900 were 5,804 cattle, 2,737 horses, and 52,895 sheep.[140]

These figures indicate the livestock *owned* by Emery County residents but do not provide a complete picture of livestock numbers in the county. The region's largest ranching operations had their headquarters in neighboring counties but made extensive use of Emery County grazing lands. The Miller ranch dominated the Castle Valley range from Gordon Creek to Cedar Mountain, running 30,000 sheep and branding more than 1,000 calves each year.[141] The Whitmore ranch, with a headquarters on the site that later became Dragerton (East Carbon City), ranged their livestock in northeastern Emery County in the Horse Canyon and Range Creek areas. A wealthy Briton who styled himself as Lord Scott Elliott developed a ranch at the Big Springs a short distance north of the Emery County border and used the Beckwith Plateau as summer range.[142] The Frandsen family of Price wintered 10,000 sheep on the San Rafael Swell in 1899, and Victor Rambaud and Joe Nouguier had herds of comparable size in the Green River Desert.[143] Just beyond the western border of Emery County, the Ireland Cattle Company had a winter ranch headquarters at Oak Springs and grazed the southern San Rafael Swell.[144] In addition, stockmen from Sanpete, Sevier, and Utah valleys continued to use the Wasatch Plateau and the San Rafael Swell as seasonal grazing grounds. In 1900 Sanpete County woolgrowers owned 449,491 sheep, many of which spent at least part of the year on Emery County ranges.[145] Added to these already large numbers were so-called "tramp herds" owned by out-of-state stockmen. Some of these herds were driven west from Colorado in the fall to winter on the Green River Desert then moved to successively higher ranges in Castle Valley and on the Wasatch Plateau in the spring and summer. Other herds were shipped by rail to Manti from as far away as Oregon, moved gradually north on the Wasatch Plateau through the summer, then shipped from Colton in the fall. Estimates of the number of sheep grazing on the Wasatch Plateau at the turn of the century run as high as 800,000.[146]

While a majority of Emery County families engaged in farming, relatively few had extensive livestock holdings. George T. Olsen reportedly was the largest stockman in Emery at the turn of the century, with other prominent growers including John S. Lewis, George Mortenson, and Brigham J. Peacock.[147] John C. Duncan, Samuel Singleton, Ernest Wild, Nathaniel Crawford, Abram G. Conover, Peter Fjeldsted, John E. King, and Chris N. Peterson were among the important stockmen on Ferron Creek.[148] Those with significant holdings in the Cottonwood Creek area included J. W. Seely, Frederick Andersen, Lorenzo Jeffs, and James B. Crawford. Stockmen in the region of Huntington, Lawrence, and Cleveland included Leander Lemmon, Robert Gordon, Edward L. Geary, J. H. Killpack, William A. Guymon, Robert W. Hill, Alma Staker, John W. Lott, Joseph B. Meeks, and Lars P. Oveson.[149] The four Swasey brothers can hardly be linked to a particular settlement. Their true home was the range, where numerous landmarks still bear their names.

Early stockmen in the eastern portion of the county included Tom Tidwell and his sons, who grazed their animals in the Tidwell

Draw area east of the San Rafael Reef. Ink Harris and Bob Fuller reportedly brought a herd of 300 cattle to the Woodside area in June 1888 and a short time later relocated to the San Rafael Valley. At about the same time, Chris Halverson established what is now known as the Hatt Ranch on the San Rafael River.[150] The Gillies family also had a ranch on the San Rafael. In addition to the livestock owners, numerous Emery County men worked at the shearing corrals for several weeks each spring. Others found year-round employment as herders.

Mining

The first commercial mining operation in what is now Emery County, and in fact the first in the Wasatch Plateau coal field, predated the settlement era. The demand for coke by the smelters of the Salt Lake Valley led to the establishment of Connellsville in the upper reaches of Huntington Canyon by the Fairview Coal Mining and Coke Company in 1875. An 1876 report indicated that seven mines had been opened, with an aggregate of two thousand feet of tunnels, and a production of twelve-and-a-half tons of coke per day from ten ovens. The report added, "The only difficulty that is now to be overcome is to construct a railroad from Springville, on the Utah Southern, to the mines."[151] The lack of transportation facilities, added to the poor coking quality of the coal, led to the abandonment of coke manufacturing at Connellsville.[152] The miners moved over the mountain to Winter Quarters in 1878, and the Connellsville mine was worked only sporadically thereafter to supply heating coal for Sanpete Valley communities. The Connellsville site is now covered by the waters of Electric Lake.

Several small coal mines were opened in Emery County during the 1880s and 1890s. Mines in operation during the winter of 1897–98 included one developed by Casper Christensen near Emery; a mine near Ferron operated by the Fugate family; a mine in Rock Canyon operated by the Fullmer brothers of Orangeville; a mine in Cedar Creek Canyon developed by brothers Erin and William Howard; and a mine near Green River owned by J. T. Farrer.[153] Typically these mines were worked only during the fall and winter to meet local heating needs. The large commercial mines in Carbon

County had a greater impact on the Emery County economy because many families divided the year between their homes and farms in Emery County and the mines at Winter Quarters and Castle Gate.

Prospectors in search of valuable minerals roamed the San Rafael Swell and Cedar Mountain areas from the beginning of the settlement period. A mining district was established in 1883 in the area between Woodside and Cedar Mountain, where "a few small veins carrying gold, silver, copper, and lead occur."[154] By the turn of the century, the Sorrel Mule mine near the San Rafael River had reached a depth of more than a thousand feet and reported some promising signs of copper and silver. Some development had also taken place in the Copper Globe district southeast of Emery.[155] While these prospects were a source of periodic excitement, none of them proved to be commercially successful.

Building Materials

The extensive construction during the period from 1880 to 1900 created a demand for lumber, most of which was supplied by small sawmills operating on the Wasatch Plateau. The sawmill installed in Rilda Canyon in 1878 by Elias Cox and Charles Hollingshead was apparently the first such operation in Emery County. Also in 1878 Abraham Day and sons set up a sawmill near the site of Huntington Reservoir, later moving it to Day Canyon. The Days were residents of Mount Pleasant at the time but continued to operate the mill after they had relocated to Lawrence.[156] Samuel Jewkes had operated both a sawmill and a gristmill from the same water-power supply while living at Fountain Green. He established a similar arrangement on Cottonwood Creek in late 1879, choosing a site two miles west of Orangeville. The saw was operated by horse power until a mill race could be constructed.[157] The Jewkes family continued in the sawmill business through several generations. Amasa Scovill and Will Reynolds of Mount Pleasant built a mill near the mouth of Potter's Canyon in 1880. Scovill moved his family to Orangeville shortly thereafter.[158] With the possible exception of the Day mill, these early operations were vertical mills with a reciprocating saw powered by a simple water wheel. Such mills were slow and inefficient and were soon replaced by circular saws powered by turbine water wheels or steam engines. Among others operating lumber or shingle mills during this period were Charles Pulsipher, Andrew J. Allen, William Marshall, Alma Staker, and James W. Bradley in the Huntington Canyon area; Henning Olsen (Ungerman) and sons, Azariah Tuttle, Carl Wilberg, and Andrew Van Buren in the Cottonwood Creek drainage; Brigham H. Higgs, James Henrie, and George Petty and sons in Ferron Canyon; and Rasmus Jacobsen, Ed Torgenson, and Chris Jensen near Emery.[159]

Apparently the first bricks manufactured in Emery County were burned by Mike Molen and Hyrum Nelson at Ferron in 1882. Later brickmakers at Ferron included Chris Jensen and J. P. Horsley.[160] Adobes were made from an early date on Orange Seely's farm east of Castle Dale. The first brick kiln was burned there in 1890 under the supervision of Samuel H. Larsen. The bricks were used to construct the Castle Dale social hall. The 1892 Emery County Court House was built of bricks burned at the Seely farm by Joe Green from Springville. In 1897 Elisha Allen Jones established a brickyard west of town and supplied materials for numerous buildings. His son, Elisha Allen, Jr., continued in the trade until the 1940s.[161] William Green and sons of Huntington began making bricks about 1896 for the construction of the Huntington meetinghouse.[162] They continued as the chief suppliers to the community for some two decades. As was the case with locally produced timber products, brick sales were almost entirely confined to Emery County markets, although Hyrum Nelson reportedly shipped some bricks to Salt Lake City for use in constructing the ZCMI store.[163]

Anders Rasmussen and his son Erastus manufactured quicklime for many years. They gathered limestone from the Cottonwood Creek bed, crushed it with hand tools, and burned it in a round kiln some sixteen to eighteen feet high. The product was marketed at Price and Helper as well as in Emery County communities.[164]

Other Industries

Harvesting and processing agricultural products were important industries in early Emery County. The first grain crops were harvested and threshed with hand tools. Samuel Jewkes brought the first threshing machine to Castle Valley in 1880 and threshed on both

Cottonwood and Huntington creeks that fall.[165] Within a short time, each community had one or more threshing machines. During the early years, power for threshing was supplied by several teams of horses or oxen hitched to wooden poles arranged like extended spokes around a central pulley that drove the threshing machine by means of a long belt. This power source was replaced during the 1890s by steam engines mounted on wagons. Self-propelled steam engines were introduced to the area around the turn of the century.

During the early settlement period, most of the grain was harvested by horse-drawn reapers that deposited the stalks in loose bundles to be tied by hand. Noah T. Guymon reportedly brought the first grain binder to Emery County. However, it was not satisfactory as it tied the bundles with wire that clogged the threshing machines. By the mid-1880s David H. Leonard, John L. Brasher, and others had acquired binders that used twine.[166]

Flour mills were an essential community industry during a period when bread made up a large portion of a typical diet. The Jewkes grist mill began operations on 17 June 1882, relieving the settlers of the necessity of hauling their entire supply of flour across the Wasatch Plateau. A mill built by Orange and J. W. Seely in the southeastern part of Castle Dale began operating in 1893 and continued, with several changes in management, until about 1940. Also in 1893 Rasmus Jacobson erected a grist mill at the mouth of Muddy Creek Canyon to serve the residents of Emery. The Huntington Roller Mill and Manufacturing Company began operations in 1896, powered first by steam, then by water, then steam again, by a diesel engine for a brief period, and ultimately by electricity. This was the longest-surviving of Emery County's flour mills, continuing into the 1980s.[167] Its building, one of the few remaining nineteenth-century commercial structures in the county, is on the National Historic Buildings Register.

The original burr-type Jewkes mill at Orangeville was replaced by the New State Roller Mill, which began operating at a site closer to town sometime between 1895 and 1897. The New Castle Mill west of Ferron was completed in early 1897. It ceased operations and was dismantled in the mid-1930s, but its former importance to the community is memorialized in the dam and reservoir built near its site and in the name of a Ferron street. Most of the output of these mills was consumed in the local communities. However, products were also marketed in Carbon County, and some flour was shipped from Ferron to Moab.[168]

Some sugar cane or sorghum was raised in Emery County during the early years. Along with his other milling machinery, Samuel Jewkes also brought a molasses mill to the valley. Frank Earl, Jens Madsen, Chris Johnson, and Hyrum Burgess operated molasses mills at various times at Huntington, and Peter Hansen made molasses at Ferron. Boyd "Cooper" Peterson of Castle Dale and James Woodward of Huntington made barrels to store the molasses in.[169]

The blacksmith was an indispensable figure in any community. Orange Seely, Joseph Boulden, P. C. Borreson, Lewis Larsen, Sampson Potter, David H. Leonard, William Howard, Hyrum Burgess, and Orson Robbins all plied this trade in early Emery County.

Transportation and communication remained rather rudimentary throughout the period. "Freighters" drove heavy wagons over almost impassable roads to haul the county's produce to market and bring back goods for local stores. Several Emery County men contracted to haul freight from the Price railhead to the federal installations in the Uinta Basin. They typically carried loads of gilsonite on the return trip. The mail was delivered from Price to Castle Valley communities at first by packhorse and later by "white top stages" that also carried passengers. Stables at Huntington and Ferron provided for a change of horses on the long daily journey from Price to Emery. Among those who held the mail contract at various times during the period from 1881 to 1900 were Samuel Grange and sons, Elisha and Joseph Jones, and Thomas Miles of Huntington; G. T. Olsen of Emery; Nephi Williams of Castle Dale; and Erastus Curtis of Orangeville.[170]

The Emery-Carbon Telephone Company was organized in Price during the mid-1890s by former Emery County residents Levi N. and Oliver Harmon. Lines were extended to Huntington, Castle Dale, and Orangeville in 1896. There was a single telephone station in each town, typically located at a store or hotel. There was no trunk line connection, but messages received at Price by telegraph could be sent to Emery County towns by telephone. Calls could also be made from one Emery County town to another, but the rates were rather steep. In 1901 a telephone call from Castle Dale to Orangeville cost fifty cents, equal to half a day's wages for a farm worker.[171]

Women's Work

The only occupation listed for women in the first census of Emery County was "keeping house." In a pioneer subsistence economy, however, housekeeping included a wide range of important responsibilities. In addition to preparing the day's meals from basic farm and garden commodities, women typically had the main responsibility for the vegetable garden and for gathering, preserving, and storing supplies during the harvest season for later use. In the early years, women and children would go to the canyons and river-bottoms to pick chokecherries for preserves and bullberries that were dried for use in pies and puddings during the winter. As fruit trees came into production, their harvest was dried, bottled, or preserved. Lowry Nelson remembered the prune orchard at his home in Ferron:

> The harvesting required the labor of the whole family in an otherwise busy season on the farm. I do not recall that there was much of the crop sold, but bushels were split by Mother and her helpers and laid out to dry on the roof of the house. Stewed fresh prunes also became a staple in the diet for weeks, and prunes were "put up" fresh and made into preserves.[172]

Apples, pears, potatoes, and squash were stored in cellars. Potatoes still remaining by the following summer were grated and made into starch. Starch cake was a specialty of some Emery County cooks. Vegetables were dried or bottled. Fall-killed hogs were cured in brine and smoked for winter use, and head cheese stored in earthenware crocks. Several women, including Ellen Anderson Miller and Mary Adams Jewkes, were expert brewers of malt beer.[173]

Most clothing was made at home, from heavy work clothes to fancy dresses and delicate baby outfits with intricate lace work and embroidery. Fabrics for the most part were "store-bought," but some cloth manufacture did take place in early Emery County. Several women spun and dyed yarn for knitting. Emma Lawton Higbee and her daughters, who lived at Wilsonville, reportedly gathered wool for spinning from greasewood thorns or pulled it from the carcasses of dead sheep. Emma Higbee also tanned buckskin and made it into clothes and gloves. Ellen Miller brought a loom when she came to Cottonwood Creek in 1878 and did considerable weaving for several years. Mary Pead Howard and Eliza Cheshire Brasher of Huntington had learned straw braiding during their childhood in England. They made fine braided straw hats for women and girls. Many women braided coarser straw hats for everyday use. Anna Johanson Anderson of Castle Dale and Sarah Ann Stevenson Fullmer of Orangeville tailored men's suits.[174] Clothing worn beyond mending was routinely recycled in the form of quilts and rag carpets.

In most families the poultry and the dairy were primarily women's responsibilities. They set the hens, cared for baby chicks, and gathered and marketed the eggs. Frank Carroll of Orangeville composed an ode to "the Emery hen" that included the following lines:

> Does the dear young girl who wishes a bonnet,
> Go keeping books or write a sonnet?
> Not much; she harnesses the mare and to town she goes,
> And the Emery hen product she exchanges for clothes.[175]

When a rooster was killed for Sunday dinner, or old hens slaughtered and bottled to be used later for chicken soup, women washed and dried the feathers for use in pillows and comforters. Women did not usually milk the cows (this was typically a job for young boys), but they skimmed the cream, churned butter, made cottage cheese and in some instances hard cheeses. In addition to forming a staple portion of the family diet, these commodities provided a significant part of many families' cash income.

Heavy field work and work with range livestock were generally regarded as male responsibilities, but necessity sometimes took precedence over socially defined gender roles. Mary Ann Rowbury Brown not only harvested a crop of wheat by hand but also "tied a rope around my waist and helped drag the logs" to construct a dugout. Millie Biddlecome, holding her infant daughter on her saddle, helped her husband drive a herd of cattle to the Robbers Roost country.[176]

In addition to their home management responsibilities, some

women were employed outside their homes. Midwives provided an essential service to the community. Mary Davis Biddlecome, who served as midwife for an estimated 450 to 500 births, sometimes traveled more than ten miles to assist at a delivery. Her usual fee for delivering a baby and caring for mother and child for ten days was $2.50. If she also did the housework during that period, the fee was $5, if the family was able to pay.[177] Annie Catherine Peterson Rasmussen, who delivered 464 babies during a career that occupied a good portion of her 102 years, did her knitting as she walked from house to house. "Often she would remove her own clothing to wrap around a new born baby and many are the times she took food and clothing from her own home to help the needy."[178] Most of the early midwives were self-taught. Some were called and "set apart" by LDS church officials. Perhaps the first midwife in Emery County with formal training was Mrs. S. J. Shipp, who came to Castle Dale from Beaver County in 1893. In addition to her work as a midwife, she also served as the Castle Dale postmistress from 1893 to 1898.[179] Anna Eliza Reynolds Seely of Castle Dale was a sister to Ellis Reynolds Shipp, one of the first women in Utah to receive an M.D. degree. Dr. Shipp traveled to Castle Dale to deliver Anna's last three babies, and while in the county visited several communities under the auspices of the LDS Relief Society to provide training in nursing and midwifery to local women.[180]

It was a common practice for the LDS church to call married men on proselyting missions sometimes lasting several years. During their absence, their wives and children shouldered not only the burden of maintaining themselves but also sent whatever funds they could to support their husband and father in the mission field. When Abinadi (Nad) Olsen of Castle Dale was called on a mission to Samoa in 1895, he left his wife with four children under the age of seven. The Utah economy, along with that of the nation, was in an economic depression that had lowered agricultural prices, and the family was forced to sell most of their livestock in order to equip Olsen for his mission and pay his fare to Samoa. His wife, Hannah Seely Olsen, took a job as janitor at the school at $5 a month to supplement what she could earn from her farm and garden and needlework and the assistance she received from her brothers and brothers-in-law. By the time of her husband's return, three-and-a-half years later, Hannah had not only provided for her family but had refurbished the house with a new rag carpet for the living room, new curtains for the windows, and a new mattress for their bed made from wool from her own sheep that she had carded and batted herself (a significant luxury at a time when most Emery County residents slept on mattresses stuffed with straw or cornhusks). The flour bin was full, and she had $25 in cash to put into Nad's hand when she met his train at Price.[181]

There were female entrepreneurs in most Emery County towns. In Huntington, for example, Ann Beers Pulsipher operated a store and hotel. Eunice Harmon also ran a store. In Castle Dale Annie Rasmussen Petersen began ordering items for herself and her neighbors that could not be found in the rudimentary stock of the first stores. She persuaded her husband James to convert a room of the house to a small store. It proved successful, and after a few years he built the large James Petersen and Sons store on Main Street, a building that later housed the Castle Dale Co-op for many years. Kathinka Wilberg Anderson managed a hotel at the corner of Main and First East Streets for more than three decades. During the early years she also had a millinery shop. In addition to her business activities, Kathinka Anderson was the first woman to hold public office in Emery County, being elected as county recorder in 1900. Orangeville's first cooperative store was started by Amelia Jewkes, Mary Fail, Mary Tuttle, and Jane R. Cox. Mary Jane Taylor, Petrea Hitchcock, and Netta Christensen all operated hotels in Ferron.[182] Many other women worked in family-owned stores, hotels, and boarding houses. A large share of the school teachers were women.

One women's industry that did not succeed was silkworm culture. In Emery County as elsewhere in Utah, LDS church leaders promoted the production of silk as a home industry during the 1880s and 1890s. Large numbers of mulberry trees were planted to provide food for the worms, and a woman was sent in to teach local women how to handle the eggs, feed the larvae, and treat the cocoons.[183] This labor-intensive project was abandoned after a few unprofitable years, leaving only the mulberry trees as a reminder of its existence.

Economic Contributions of Children

In addition to their other labors, nineteenth-century Emery County women typically bore and raised large families. However, children were regarded as economic assets for the family rather than an economic burden. Daughters constituted an important work force at a mother's disposal for cleaning, cooking, sewing, and child care, and in the process learned the skills that would later be needed to manage their own homes and families. Teenage girls would sometimes accompany their fathers or brothers to sawmills or shearing pens where they worked as cooks.

Unmarried sons were an equally important resource under the control of their fathers. A family's prosperity often depended on the effective management of sons' labor to build up the family holdings of land and livestock. Lowry Nelson drew upon his turn-of-the-century childhood in Ferron for the following summary description of child labor:

> There were almost numberless tasks which boys and girls of five years and up could perform: toting wood for the kitchen stove, bringing water from the barrel by the irrigation ditch, gathering eggs, running errands to the neighbors, and so on. A boy at six or seven years could ride a gentle horse and herd the cows away from the growing crops. By the time he was twelve he could harness a team and hitch it to a wagon. He might even mow a field of alfalfa. He could also follow a walking plow, as I did one memorable day when I plowed two acres in the upper field behind a good team, Old Pike and Roud. By age fourteen a boy was ready to do mostly what a man would ordinarily do.[184]

Teenage boys made up a large portion of the county's cowboys and sheepherders, sometimes spending weeks at a time at isolated camps. For example, Marinus and Andrew Petersen, eldest sons of Castle Dale pioneer James Marinus Petersen, were "sent out to herd sheep at an early age" and spent so much time in the wilds that they "became almost as wild as the coyotes themselves." These responsibilities prevented Marinus from attending school, and he had to be taught to read by his wife and to do arithmetic by his daughter.[185] Much of the "wild behavior" among the young men complained of by church and community leaders during this period can probably be attributed to a way of life that gave them only limited exposure to the civilizing influences of town, school, and church.

The Built Environment

The first structures in Emery County were rudimentary shelters. A "dugout" was typically constructed by excavating a hole in a south-facing hillside or riverbank and covering it with brush and dirt on a framework of poles. The front wall might be made of vertical posts planted close together, or horizontal logs, or wattle-work of posts and willows, or rarely of sawed lumber. The door was often nothing more than a piece of canvas. Some dugouts were built on level ground by digging a rectangular hole three or four feet deep then adding a low wall of rocks, logs, and dirt to provide adequate headroom—dwellings very similar to those used several centuries earlier by the Fremont people. Dugouts were intended as temporary shelters, but some continued to be occupied for extended periods. For example, Louisa Rowley Guymon and her children lived for several years at Maple Dell near the mouth of Huntington Canyon in a dugout with an attached wattle-and-daub lean-to heated by a makeshift stove made from an old washtub.[186] Charles and Mary Ann Brown lived for nine years in the dugout they built on their homestead north of Huntington Creek. Life in a dugout meant a never-ending battle with rattlesnakes at the door and scorpions in the bedding. When the Brown family at last moved into a two-room house, "The sense of exultation we experienced in making the transfer is easier left to imagination than to describe it."[187] Some Emery County families lived in dugouts well into the twentieth century. Lowry Nelson recalled visiting "a family one time with a boy my age that lived in a dugout in a bank along the creek. They had a few boughs over the top of the cave which could not possibly shed rain but which protected from the sun."[188]

Some early settlers built log cabins from the cottonwood trees that lined the waterways. With rare exceptions these structures had dirt roofs and floors of packed earth. Five or six inches of Castle Valley clay provided some insulation and protection from brief showers, but extended wet periods would saturate the roof and cause muddy water to drip onto the beds and furnishings. By the early 1880s homes and public buildings were being constructed from spruce and fir logs hauled from the canyons. These were more uniform in dimension than cottonwood logs and allowed for finer workmanship. With their sides hewn or sawed square and with neat dovetail joints, these logs made tight and durable structures, some of which are still in use after more than a century. As lumber became available, it was used for flooring, roof framing, and door and window frames. Locally produced shingles made the buildings weatherproof.

Most of these log houses were what architectural historians term "single cell" structures, which means that they had a single main room that was not subdivided. A few double cell houses were constructed, with two rooms of approximately the same size. In Emery County a single cell house was usually called a "square cabin" regardless of whether it was made from log, frame, adobe, or brick construction. In most instances a square cabin was not really square. Typical dimensions were sixteen by eighteen feet, representing the length of logs that were easily available and transportable. Some cabins had an attic bedroom reached by an exterior stair. Over time, the house might sprout one or two or three wings of frame construction and the log walls be given a "weatherboard" sheathing so that their original character was entirely concealed. In other cases the cabin might be replaced by a larger house of frame or brick and used thereafter as an outbuilding. A variation on the log house was the plank house. Heavy planks with typical dimensions of about three by twelve inches were dovetail notched at the ends and erected to form self-supporting walls. Several examples of plank construction survived into comparatively recent years. Log and plank construction was increasingly supplemented by locally produced adobes and by the lumber that became more widely available during the 1880s. Many buildings had lumber frames with adobes filling the spaces between wall studs.

House Types in the 1890s. Single cell houses continued to be built, often of frame or brick, until the turn of the century and beyond. However, growing prosperity and the move to town led to the construction of larger homes. In many cases these were variations on

Justus Wellington Seely house, Castle Dale.

what was loosely identified in Utah as "Nauvoo-style" houses. Actually an adaptation of the federal style popular in America during the late eighteenth and early nineteenth centuries, these houses were symmetrically arranged story-and-a-half or two-story structures with two rooms on each level. The ground floor plan typically took one of three forms: the hall-and-parlor with central front entry into a large square room with an adjacent smaller room at the side; the central passage plan with front entry into a stair-hall between the two rooms; and the double cell, with a front entry to each room.[189] In many cases a wing was added to the rear of the house, resulting in a T or L-shaped structure. The J. W. Seely house at First South and Center in Castle Dale is a good example of a hall-and-parlor house with T-wing. These houses were almost invariable built with the roof ridgeline parallel to the street and usually with symmetrical facades of either three or five bays. In some instances central-passage houses were two rooms deep. Similar in outward appearance to the "Nauvoo" house but different internally was the "pair house," a design brought to Utah by Scandinavian immigrants. The pair house had a large central room with a smaller room at each end. The pioneer C.

G. Larsen home (later occupied by the Paul Judd family) in Castle Dale, still standing in 1995, was a pair house.

Another house style popular in Emery County during the period from 1890 to 1910 was the cross wing. Cross wing houses typically combined a single-cell wing with ridgeline parallel to the street and a projecting double-cell wing with gable end to the street. The first brick house erected in Emery County, by Mike Molen in Ferron, was of this design, and there are surviving examples in most towns. Less common was the double cross wing, a noteworthy example of which is the well preserved Samuel Singleton home in Ferron.

Near the turn of the century, asymmetrical Victorian style houses began to appear in Emery County. The John C. and Emma Lemon house at Ferron, with its unusually long axis, was in all likelihood adapted from a Victorian pattern-book. Other Victorian houses include the mansard-roofed Jameson-Bunnell home and the nearby Frandsen-Zwahlen home (recently restored) in Castle Dale, and the Queen Anne style Lars Peter Larson home in Cleveland.

Along with larger homes came the first efforts at city conveniences. While most county residents continued to dip water from the ditches or haul it from cisterns in buckets until well into the twentieth century, E. L. Geary had by 1899 installed indoor plumbing in his Huntington home, fed by gravity from a hilltop cistern at his farm a quarter of a mile away.[190] John C. Lemon achieved a similar convenience in his Ferron home by installing a tank in the attic. Water pumped into the tank from the cistern would then flow by gravity pressure to the kitchen and bathroom faucets.[191]

Public and Commercial Buildings. In the settlement period there was little distinction made between domestic and commercial buildings; businesses were conducted in people's homes. Townsite development brought purpose-built commercial structures that were in most instances simple one-room frame buildings with perhaps a lean-to addition at the rear. While homes were usually built with roof ridgelines parallel to the street, business buildings had their gable-ends facing the street, often concealed by a false front. They typically had a central entrance flanked by two windows and a covered front porch with hitching rail.

The basic layout of commercial buildings did not change much in the 1890s, but more were constructed of brick and on a larger scale. An upper story became common, which might be used as a dance hall. Building fronts were sometimes given a more massive appearance by the use of decorative brick features or rock faced quoins and door and window trim. The building erected by Carl Wilberg on Main Street in Castle Dale is included in Carter and Goss's *Utah's Historic Architecture* as a good example of the Victorian Romanesque Revival style in commercial buildings.[192]

Probably the only architect-designed building in nineteenth-century Emery County was Green River's Palmer House, a three-story frame hotel built in French Second Empire Revival style. Other hotels in the county were simply large houses—and in some instances small houses that could offer one or two bedrooms to travelers.

Nineteenth-century Latter-day Saint meetinghouses and social halls were simple rectangular rooms designed to accommodate as many people as possible. A T-wing at the rear might provide some classroom and office space. The buildings typically had little decoration, except for the theater-social hall in Orangeville, which had large paintings on walls and ceiling. The Huntington meetinghouse erected between 1896 and 99 was the largest such building in the county, with a horseshoe-shaped second-floor gallery and decorative interior woodwork executed by local craftsman William Hunter.[193]

Most schools were makeshift structures, single rooms in the smaller communities and cross-wing buildings with three or more rooms in the larger towns. Ferron and Orangeville had fairly capacious brick buildings by the turn of the century, and the two-room Lawrence school was well designed. The major era of public school building, however, came during the early decades of the twentieth century. The first Emery Stake Academy building had four classrooms on the ground floor and a large assembly hall on the upper story. The entry and bell tower, added about 1902, provided an additional small classroom. The building was apparently used for church meetings soon after its completion, in preference to the old social hall.

Farm Buildings. Farm buildings were of a rudimentary character in nineteenth-century Emery County. Grain was typically stored in log structures—and in some instances in bins inside the home. After the extensive loss of livestock during the hard winter of 1880, the provision of some kind of shelter for farm animals became a high priority. The most typical result was a ramada-like structure with a roof of poles supported by wooden posts and covered with willows and a straw thatch. With a wall of wood slabs on two sides to provide protection from the prevailing north and west winds, such a shelter proved highly practical. These sheds continued in wide use well into the twentieth century, and their remains can still be seen throughout the county. Corrals and pigpens were made of poles at first and later of lumber slabs and "winny-edge." Chickens were largely free-ranging with sometimes rough log or adobe shelters provided as a protection from nocturnal predators. John Duncan built the first barn in Ferron, and perhaps in the county, probably during the 1890s. Barns became very prominent features of the Emery County townscape during the following decades, as did the distinctive "inside-out" granaries with exterior framing. Much hay, however, was stacked in the open, and local ingenuity developed stacking derricks in a variety of designs for this purpose.

Sickness and Health

When LDS apostle Francis M. Lyman visited Emery County in 1880, he noted with satisfaction that there had been "but three deaths, and they were of children," since the beginning of settlement.[194] If the colonists were a healthy lot, it was fortunate for them because little medical assistance was available. Charles R. Curtis rendered his memories of the pioneer era in verse including these lines:

> We never had no smallpox then and we never had no flu,
> And we never had no doctors to pay our money to.
> We lived on very common food you'll all agree no doubt
> But no one ever had to have their tonsils taken out like folks nowadays do.[195]

Bishop Orange Seely reportedly pulled teeth and set broken bones in addition to doing needed blacksmith work during his ecclesiastical visits among the settlements.[196] There were, as we have seen, capable midwives from an early date. And many colonists put their trust in the Latter-day Saint ordinance of anointing and blessing the sick or injured. For example, Joseph H. Jewkes recalled an occasion when the young son of his brother Samuel R. was seriously injured at the Jewkes sawmill:

> Sam R. ran and picked up his son whose head was mashed flat like two hands pressed together. He immediately administered to him then carried him about two hundred yards to their home. Suzannah met them and they were able to detect slight breathing. In three days, without medical attention, he was walking around completely healed through the power of the priesthood and the faith of his parents.[197]

Almost every community had at least one resident skilled at setting bones, dressing wounds, and preparing herbal remedies for various ailments. Perhaps the most noteworthy of these self-taught physicians was Wiley P. Allred, who settled on Muddy Creek in 1884. Though he was in his sixty-sixth year when he came to Emery County, he frequently traveled by horseback as far as Ferron to treat patients. So highly regarded were his skills that he was still sought out when he was in his eighties.[198]

The first licensed physician to locate in Emery County was reportedly a Dr. Moore, who came from Mount Pleasant to Orangeville in 1893. Dr. Moore died after about two years and was replaced by William P. Winters, also from Mount Pleasant. After practicing in Orangeville for two or three years, Dr. Winters moved to Castle Dale and erected a drug store on the southwest corner of Main and Center streets. Winters practiced intermittently in Emery County until sometime after 1905. He later operated a hospital in Price before moving back to his home town of Mount Pleasant where he continued to practice until the midtwentieth century.[199] In a 1919 conversation, Dr. Winters reportedly said that "he was not able to make a living in Emery County, and when he left there his patients owed him $30,000."[200] Other physicians during this period included Dr. C. E. Pearson, who was practicing medicine in Huntington in 1898 and moved to Castle Dale in 1899, where he remained until 1904. Doctor C. N. Ray located in Ferron in 1898 but stayed for only a short time.[201]

Peter Cheney practiced dentistry in Huntington for a period in the mid-1880s. A dentist reportedly located for a short time at Orangeville, operating in the Reid store. The first dentist to take up permanent residence in the county was Paul C. Christensen, who began practicing in Orangeville in 1894 and moved to Castle Dale at the turn of the century. Evidently a very handy man, he repaired watches as well as teeth, and also did occasional carpentry work.[202] Doctor Christensen had a portable dental outfit that he took on the road to other Emery County towns and to the coal camps of Carbon County.

Even if there had been more trained physicians in Emery County, nineteenth-century medicine had little to offer against the epidemic diseases that periodically ravaged the region. During a diphtheria epidemic in 1886, there were twenty-seven deaths in Huntington, thirteen of them occurring in a single week between Christmas and New Year. Thirteen children died in one week in Ferron and Molen. The Duncan family lost four children within a few hours.[203] Outbreaks of scarlet fever and smallpox also took a toll. Typhoid fever, usually contracted from polluted drinking water, was endemic in the county, claiming several lives each year. Pneumonia was also a constant threat, especially to young children. Accidental death and injury were common with the chief causes being runaway horses, work accidents, and gunshot wounds.

Burial Customs. The preparation of the dead for burial was a task carried out by committees appointed for this purpose by the local LDS wards. A sewing committee would make burial clothing from a supply of white fabric kept on hand by the Relief Society. Coffins were made by local carpenters and lined with white cloth. In the absence of embalming, fruit jars were packed with ice and placed around the corpse until time for the funeral. To prevent the discoloration of exposed skin, cloths dipped in a solution of formaldehyde were placed over the face. Both cloths and ice bottles required changing at frequent intervals, and members of the burial committee would "sit up" with the corpse until time for the funeral. Typically the meetinghouse was decorated for funerals with white draperies, and the wagon that carried the coffin to the cemetery was also draped in white.[204]

Recreation

The heavy demands of establishing a community and building an economic base still left time and energy for social and recreational activities in early Emery County. Indeed, with the isolated living conditions of the first years, social occasions were important enough to justify considerable efforts. News that a dance was to be held at some dugout or cabin would spread throughout the valley and bring people from miles away. After dancing much of the night, they would then face the long journey home, sometimes on foot. The fiddler was almost as essential a figure in a community as the blacksmith. Harrison Fugate played for early dances on Ferron Creek. Sally Wimmer, David H. Leonard, and "Bub" Burgess played the fiddle for dances on Huntington Creek, sometimes being joined by David Cheney with his accordion. On Cottonwood Creek, George Biddlecome and James Marinus Petersen were the fiddlers. On one occasion when no other music was to be had, a visiting nephew of Joseph Boulden whistled for the dancers. Often the floor space would not accommodate all who wished to participate, so the men, who were usually in the majority during the first years, were assigned numbers to determine when they could dance.[205]

The completion of a new home was typically celebrated by a "housewarming" party and dance. The dancing helped to smooth the rough planks of the floor. Weddings brought not only dancing but often multicourse dinners prepared with great labor from the settlers' limited food stores and served to dozens of guests. Nor did harsh pioneer conditions dull the desire for a bit of extravagance on special occasions. Orange Seely reportedly purchased from an early peddler who found his way to the valley two pieces of rich silk brocade, which were made into wedding dresses for his daughters Emma and Hannah.[206]

In Green River music for the dances was provided by members of the Farrer family. When a new ferryboat was brought in from Oregon in 1890, the event was celebrated with a dance on the boat. Other celebrations were more spontaneous: "Whenever a bunch of railroad workers or cowboys came into town they would give the nearest boy a nickle to go ring the school house bell long and loud.

This summoned all the village and a dance was soon in progress."[207] A social event unique to Green River was "seining parties" in which a large net was dragged across the river and the fish thus caught were divided into piles and distributed among the participants by lot.

During the diphtheria epidemics when all indoor gatherings were banned, the young people could still indulge in sleigh riding parties. J. W. Nixon recalled of his first years in Huntington in the late 1880s, "A principal feature of [the boys'] sport then was sleigh-riding and racing two and three abreast on the streets especially on moonlight nights. We made our own amusement in the way of dancing and drama and did considerable visiting with friends about town."[208] The arrival of a new horse in town was an occasion to bring out the local champion for a match race, often with sizeable wagers. Racing meets were held at Molen that attracted spectators from throughout the valley.[209]

A "woodhauler's dance" was held in many communities in the fall to reward the young men who took wagons into the hills and brought back a winter's supply of firewood for the widows and the elderly.[210] Other work parties included quilting bees, rug bees, fruit-drying, corn-husking, and starch-making parties.

Public holidays were celebrated with great enthusiasm—and endurance. The first activity held in the log meetinghouse at Huntington, on New Year's Eve 1880, included a community supper and entertainment program lasting until midnight followed by dancing until dawn. The following November a Thanksgiving party in the building began at two o'clock in the afternoon and continued through the night. The Fourth and Twenty-fourth of July were always the occasion for patriotic celebrations highlighted by games, fireworks, speeches, and brass bands. Baseball games between neighboring towns typically formed a part of these celebrations, as did horse races. In 1882 a group of Huntington men hauled a long pole from the mountains and erected it on the public square as a "liberty pole" from which the flag was flown.[211] A community flagpole was regarded as an essential item in other settlements as well.

Liquid Refreshment. The completion of the Jewkes grist mill provided another occasion for an all-night party. Some fifty years later, Charles R. Curtis recalled the event in verse:

Then the boys from Fountain Green, they came here with their
mill.
They dug their basement, built their millrace up by that big hill
And in the spring of '82 they had their building done
And of course we had to celebrate before that mill could run.
So they made a great big barrel of beer and we danced till broad
daylight
And if I should live a hundred years I'd not forget that night.[212]

According to Joseph H. Jewkes, the mill celebrants consumed "perhaps 2 or 3" forty-gallon barrels of his mother's home-brew: "anyway plenty so that everyone had all they wanted."[213] Homemade beer was a popular refreshment at many Emery County celebrations. For teetotalers, there was "lemonade" made from lemon extract and water with molasses as a sweetener.

Although the Mormon "Word of Wisdom" prohibited "wine or strong drink," this instruction was widely understood during the nineteenth century as being advice rather than commandment. Many active and devoted Latter-day Saints not only drank beer but also used tobacco, coffee, and tea. Those in particular who had come from places such as England and Denmark, where beer was a dietary staple, saw no good reason to forego a beverage they had enjoyed all their lives. Samuel Jewkes was by all accounts a pious, church-going man, but his supper of choice when he came home from work at the mill was "toast and hot beer, the hot beer being poured over the toast in a large bowl from which he always ate."[214] The wives of Huntington bishop Peter Johnson prepared home brew according to a Danish recipe and as a by-product always had a good supply of yeast to share with their neighbors. They also made rhubarb wine. Hettie Guymon McArthur Anderson remembered how the Huntington young people used to play baseball on Sunday afternoons near the bishop's home. Afterwards, "The older crowd would all go in and have a drink of Johnson's malt beer. They made about 30 gallons at a time, but I remember after the 'Manifesto' Bishop Johnson forbade them to make or drink anymore."[215] The "manifesto" referred to was not the Woodruff manifesto discontinuing the practice of plural marriage but rather stronger instructions on the Word of Wisdom that came from church leaders near the turn of the century. Bishop Johnson was reportedly rebuked by his successor, James W. Nixon, for drinking beer and ordered to make a public apology to the ward. "Peter gave a good talk and praised the new bishop, then said, 'Your good bishop thinks that I should ask for forgiveness for drinking beer on the job and I truly ask your forgiveness, but I can't promise never to do it again.'"[216]

Saloons. The tolerance extended by the community to the drinking of homemade beer did not necessarily embrace those who patronized saloons. Yet it appears that such establishments had plenty of patrons. The only licensed saloons in Emery County at the turn of the century were in Castle Dale, which boasted two of them, the Dale and the Court.[217] Other communities had similar establishments without benefit of license. Liquor was available at J. T. Farrer's store at Green River, and other saloons were opened from time to time to serve the railroad travelers and cowboys who congregated there. "Poker Pete" Olsen's saloon in Woodside was the scene of a wild brawl on Christmas Day 1901 between the local cowboys and a group of Greek railroad workers.[218] In 1897 it was reported that the women of Ferron "have threatened to cover with a coat of tar and feathers any one who attempts to start a saloon here."[219] Apparently this threat was ineffectual, however, and a liquor establishment opened a few weeks later. Bishop Jasper Robertson reportedly "threatened with trial for his fellowship" any member of the Orangeville Ward who sold or leased space for a saloon in that community.

Music and Drama

Among the early settlers of Emery County were several who had already gained recognition for their musical abilities. Perhaps most noteworthy were the talented Jewkes family. Samuel Jewkes had been director of the Fountain Green LDS Ward choir since 1862. His son Samuel R. was leader of the Fountain Green band. Both men continued to provide leadership in musical activities in their new home. The father brought the first organ to Cottonwood Creek and organized the Orangeville Ward choir, drawing heavily on members of his own family and others he had trained at Fountain Green. Samuel R. organized the Orangeville band, which was also well stocked with Jewkeses, and joined with Robert and William Johnson in forming an orchestra that played for dances throughout the valley and also provided music at community theatrical productions.[220]

Several veterans of the Fountain Green choir settled in Huntington, including brothers Milas E. and Joseph E. Johnson, their sisters Maria and Julia Wakefield, and half-brother Don C. Woodward. This family group was extensively involved in musical activities, with Joseph serving for several years as chorister of the Huntington Ward and Milas organizing the first military band in 1884.[221] Peter Johnson (also from Fountain Green but unrelated to the Johnson family mentioned above) brought the first organ to the settlement in 1881 and taught a well-attended music class during the mid-1880s. His descendants made up a large portion of Huntington's organists and choir directors for several decades.[222]

Yet another musical leader in northern Emery County was Thomas L. Hardee, who organized the Castle Valley Choir in 1895 for the purpose of competing in an eisteddfod at Scofield. Scofield, at the heart of the Pleasant Valley coal fields, was the largest town in the region, and its largely Welsh population shared the national passion for music. When the forty-plus Castle Valley singers pulled into town, they were greeted with taunts of "Hayseeds!" But in the competition, the Castle Valley Choir was awarded the prize over the Scofield Welsh Choir. Three years later Hardee took his choir to Salt Lake City where they sang at the LDS church general conference.[223]

Another talented musical family appeared on the Emery County scene in 1893 when Isaac and Catherine Evans and five sons, Harry, David, Richard, Taliesin (Tally), and Hector, made Castle Dale their home. Isaac Evans was a poet in the Welsh bardic tradition, and his wife was an accomplished singer. While the father and sons made their living as coal miners, the family was also much in demand as a vocal and instrumental performing group, both in their native Wales and throughout Emery and Carbon counties after their immigration. The parents spent the remainder of their lives at Castle Dale, but the sons divided their time between their homes in Castle Dale and the Pleasant Valley coal mines until David and Richard were killed in the Winter Quarters mine explosion on 1 May 1900. One contemporary account describes the Evans brothers as "professional musicians" who "have taken prizes at all musical events in this locality, and have the best orchestra."[224] The family of Elisha Jones also entertained the residents of Castle Dale and the entire region with vocal and instrumental performances.[225]

Drama was a companion art to music in an era of home-made entertainment. The first play produced in Emery County was *The Lost Ship,* staged in the little log school house at Orangeville during the 1880 Christmas season with a cast including John K. Reid, Jane Cox, Joe and Matilda Boulden, Samuel R. Jewkes, James C. Woodward, and Jasper Robertson. Canvas wagon covers were used for wings and front curtain. The Orangeville Dramatic Association was organized before 1885, and a theater with seating capacity for 160 was erected sometime around 1886 or 1887. In contrast to other communities where the dramatic associations used church or school facilities, in Orangeville the theater was used for several decades as a church and social hall. Although the building was constructed of logs, its decor was by no means rustic. A local resident named Gavin Jack was a talented artist and sculptor. (Among his later productions were the stone lions that guard the west door of the Utah State Capitol.) Jack painted elaborate scenery and theater decorations for the Orangeville theater, including three large ceiling panels, several panels on the walls, and a monumental rendition of the chariot race from *Ben-Hur* that spanned the entire width of the front curtain.[226]

The dominant figure in the Orangeville Dramatic Association was John K. Reid, who had been actively involved in community dramatics in Manti before moving to Emery County. Reid directed many plays and in his later years served as the association's "critic," advising other directors and coaching the actors. Other important members of the association in the early years included Andrew C. Van Buren, Brigham J. Moffitt, E. W. Fox, Alma G. Jewkes, John Taylor, Ben Luke, Maggie Snow, Emma Higgs, and Maria Killian, among others. According to Elmo G. Geary's 1953 study, based on interviews with surviving members, "Members of the dramatic company took great pride in their organization. New members were added only after they had proved their talents in tryouts, and the young men and women of the community prepared themselves diligently for these tryouts."[227]

The Orangeville Dramatic Association produced an average of

three or four plays each year during the 1880s and 1890s. The fare was mainly melodramatic "tragedies" such as *Damon and Pythias, Pizzaro, Ten Nights in a Barroom,* and *Uncle Tom's Cabin.* According to the recollections of John Taylor, performances were typically scheduled for two nights in order to accommodate all who wished to attend.

> Tickets were obtained at one of the stores in advance of the performance, and many people brought butter, eggs, grain, or other produce to exchange for theatre tickets at the store. Proceeds from plays were always devoted to some worthy civic or church project, so everyone believed it a duty as well as a pleasure to attend the show.

The Johnson-Jewkes Orchestra provided music before the show, and comic songs or recitations were presented between the acts. "The play often ended with a tableau, presenting a dramatic scene, illuminated by colored light. Sometimes a short farce or comedy followed the serious drama."[228] In addition to the performances in their own theater, the Orangeville company frequently took their shows on the road to other Castle Valley communities. Dramatic troupes from those communities, in turn, played in Orangeville. In addition, professional companies toured the county from the mid-1880s on. It would seem, then, that some form of theatrical entertainment was available almost weekly during a "season" lasting from November to April.

Locally produced plays were presented in Huntington shortly after the completion of the log meetinghouse, and the Huntington Dramatic Club was in existence by 1884 and boasted thirty-eight members by 1892.[229] Among the leaders in this organization were William Howard, Milas E. Johnson (whose papers are the main source of information on early Huntington dramatics), Joseph E. Johnson, Don C. Woodward, Job and Lizzie Whitney, Nate and Mary Stevens, Annie Johnson, Hannah Johnson, Susan Wakefield, J. K. Ingle, and William J. Green. This organization and a rival group known as the M.I.A. Dramatic Association produced several plays each year throughout the 1880s and 1890s. The repertoire and production methods were similar to those of the Orangeville company although the Huntington group never had a theater of their own but used LDS church buildings.

Other Emery County communities also produced local drama, though they did not develop the lasting dramatic organizations enjoyed by Orangeville and Huntington. The Castle Dale Dramatic Company was organized shortly after the completion of the brick social hall in 1890 and remained active for several years with a core of talented performers that included O. J. and Kathinka Anderson, David, William, and Hector Evans, Maria Anderson, Erastus and Hyrum Larsen, Frank Reynolds, and Will Lake.[230] The Ferron Dramatic Company was organized in 1884 under the leadership of John C. Duncan with members including Jim Henrie, Harrison M. Fugate, Henry Mills, and Clarabel Singleton, among others. Shortly after the brick meetinghouse was erected in 1886, a T-wing was added to its west end to provide better stage facilities, and this structure continued to be used for dramatic productions until it was destroyed by fire in 1918.[231] A dramatic association was organized under the auspices of the Emery LDS Ward in 1888, staging one or two plays each year. Among the leading performers in Emery were Joseph Evans, Eliza Miller, Lide Worthington, Hans Christensen, Isaac Allred, Alfred J. Broderick, George T. Olsen, John Olsen, Isaac A. Petty, William Petty, and Katherine Olsen.[232] While a few plays were produced by residents of Molen, Lawrence, and Cleveland, the first two communities never had formally organized theater companies, and the Cleveland Dramatic Company was not organized until 1901.[233]

Other cultural fare included debates, orations, and humorous readings at school celebrations and "Conjoint" meetings of the LDS Mutual Improvement Associations. There were not many literary outlets in early Emery County, but Oluf J. Anderson of Castle Dale served for several years during the 1890s as editor of *Bikkuben,* a Danish-language newspaper published at Salt Lake City for Utah's Scandinavian community. Anderson also edited the *Emery County Record,* a short-lived newspaper established in 1899 as a successor to the equally short-lived *Emery County Pioneer* established in 1897.[234]

ENDNOTES

1. F. M. Lyman, Letter to the Editor, *Deseret Evening News,* 15 September 1880, 4.

2. Seely, "Settlement Era," 34; "Irrigation on Cottonwood Creek," in *EC 1880–1980,* 83, 84.

3. *CV,* 91; Seely, "Settlement Era," 33; "Castle Dale Ward," in *EC 1880–1980,* 36.

4. Argene Olsen, "History of the Olsen-Seely Home" (1994), typescript copy in Emery County History Archives.

5. "Justus Wellington Seely," in *EC 1880–1980,* 463.

6. *Eastern Utah Advocate,* 4 August 1898.

7. *CV,* 25, 84–85; Seely, "Castle Dale Ward," 37; *Eastern Utah Advocate,* 28 September 1899.

8. Ida Snow, Owen McClenahan, and Jane McClenahan, "Early Businesses and Industries," in *EC 1880–1980,* 56–58.

9. F. M. Lyman, Letter to the Editor, *Deseret Evening News,* 15 September 1880, 4.

10. Emery County Historical Records Survey, quoted in *ECP,* 6 June 1941.

11. *CV,* 299, 312.

12. Lever, *History of Sanpete and Emery Counties,* 673.

13. *CV,* 304, 311, 312.

14. Elmo G. Geary, "Dramatics in Castle Valley, 33–35.

15. *Eastern Utah Advocate,* 15 April 1897.

16. Lever, *History of Sanpete and Emery Counties,* 674.

17. *Eastern Utah Advocate,* 26 January 1899.

18. Jones, *Settling of Huntington,* 36–37.

19. Ibid., 37–38.

20. *CV,* 204.

21. Huntington Manufacturing and Agricultural Company Record Book, Special Collections, Harold B. Lee Library, Brigham Young University, Provo, Utah.

22. *CV,* 209; Jones, *Settling of Huntington,* 38–40.

23. *CV,* 209.

24. "Joseph Ellis Johnson," and "Milas Edgar Johnson," in Jones, *Early Pioneers of Huntington,* 146, 152.

25. Huntington Ward Manuscript History (typescript copy in Emery County History Archives).

26. Edward G. Geary, Personal History, 6 (typescript copy in possession of the author).

27. Nixon, *Sketches,* 29.

28. *Eastern Utah Telegram,* 30 October 1891.

29. *CV,* 228, 246–49.

30. Ibid., 211–12; Nixon, *Sketches,* 60.

31. Kofford and Kelly, "Lawrence," 225.

32. *CV,* 274.

33. Kofford and Kelly, "Lawrence," 226.

34. *CV,* 161.

35. Ibid., 157, indicates that the site was south of the creek, but Velma Petersen, "Ferron," 105, claims that it was north of the creek.

36. *CV,* 157, 158; Petersen, "Ferron," 105.

37. *CV,* 161; Petersen, "Ferron," 116.

38. Lever, *History of Sanpete and Emery Counties,* 635.

39. *Eastern Utah Advocate,* 2 and 10 June, 16 September 1897.

40. *CV,* 285, 288.

41. Jean Christiansen and Arminta Hewitt, "Emery Town, Including the Muddy and Quitchumpah," in *EC 1880–1980,* 241.

42. *CV,* 141; Christensen and Hewitt, 241–42.

43. *CV,* 146.

44. Rhody Anderson, Reminiscence, "Emery Town Reunion, 1889–1989," photocopied typescript in Emery County History Archives, 23.

45. Arminta Hewitt, "Quitchumpah," in *EC 1880–1980,* 262.

46. *CV,* 141–42; Christiansen and Hewitt, "Emery," 243.

47. Christiansen and Hewitt, "Emery," 244; Emery County Historical Records Survey, quoted in *ECP,* 25 July 1941.

48. Lever, *History of Sanpete and Emery Counties,* 609.

49. *Eastern Utah Advocate,* 5 August 1897.

50. Christiansen and Hewitt, "Emery," 245.

51. Athearn, *Rebel of the Rockies,* 115.

52. *Salt Lake Herald,* 27 March 1881.

53. Thode and Ozment, *Dreams, Visions and Visionaries,* 51, 68.

54. *CV,* 185–86.

55. Pearl Baker and Ruth Wilcox, "History of Greenriver, Utah," Ms. 44 Box 9 Fd 2, Manuscript Division, Special Collections, University of Utah Marriott Library, Salt Lake City, 5, 6.

56. "Blake City, Emery County," *Utah Gazetteer, 1892–1893* (Salt Lake City: Stenhouse and Co., 1892).

57. *Eastern Utah Advocate,* 24 June 1897; see also quote from J. T. Farrer in *CV,* 186.

58. *CV,* 186–87; Muriel Smith, "Green River Schools," manuscript copy in Emery County History Archives.

59. Lever, *History of Sanpete and Emery Counties,* 678; *CV,* 124.

60. Nelson, *In the Direction of His Dreams,* 20–21.

61. *CV,* 204; Jones, *Early Pioneers of Huntington,* 134.

62. "Life Sketch of Esther Stevenson Grange," 2, typescript copy in Archives and Manuscripts, Lee Library.

63. Powell, *The Next Time We Strike,* 18–22.

64. "History of Samuel Nelson Alger and Ruth Elmina Pace Alger," in *EC 1880–1980,* 339. The historical account of Cleveland in this volume gives the date of arrival as 11 May 1884, but family records indicate that the Algers did not arrive in Emery County until later that year.

65. Lever, *History of Sanpete and Emery Counties,* 625.

66. Ibid., 622; *CV,* 112; Irene Allred, "Cleveland," in *EC 1880–1980,* 147.

67. Allred, "Cleveland," 147.

68. Lever, *History of Sanpete and Emery Counties,* 622.

69. *CV,* 113, 119; Allred, "Cleveland," 157.

70. Allred, "Cleveland," 150, 153; Ruth Litster, "William Lamph, a Pioneer," in *EC 1880–1980,* 401.

71. *CV,* 127–28.

72. The *Eastern Utah Telegram* reported in its edition of 7 May 1891, "William J. Powel & Co. are building a reservoir about four miles below Cleveland. . . . Why are there not more of these artificial lakes made in Emery county?"

73. *CV,* 130.

74. Ada Willson, "Desert Lake—Victor," in *EC 1880–1980,* 173; Lever, *History of Sanpete and Emery Counties,* 627.

75. An 1888 law set the compensation of members of the county court at $4 a day while actually attending to county business, plus $0.20 per mile for travel to the county seat. "An Act to Establish a Uniform System of County Governments," Section 41, *Laws of the Territory of Utah, Passed at the Twenty-eighth Session of the Legislative Assembly* (Salt Lake City: Tribune Printing and Publishing Company, 1888), 172.

76. *CV,* 25; Montell Seely, "Courthouses," in *EC 1880–1980,* 277; Lever, *History of Sanpete and Emery Counties,* 602.

77. *House Journal of the Twenty-seventh Session of the Legislative Assembly of the Territory of Utah* (Salt Lake City: Tribune Printing and Publishing Co., 1886), 180, 181, 281; "An Act Creating Grand County, Prescribing Its Boundaries and Appointing County Officers," Chapter LX; and "An Act Changing Boundary of Emery County," Chapter LXI, *Laws of the Territory of Utah, Passed at the Twenty-ninth Session of the Legislative Assembly* (Salt Lake City: Deseret News Company, 1890), 92–94.

78. *Eastern Utah Telegram,* 25 December 1891.

79. Lever, *History of Sanpete and Emery Counties,* 609.

80. *Council Journal of the Twenty-fifth Session of the Legislative Assembly of the Territory of Utah* (Salt Lake City, 1882), 236–37; *CV,* 19; Morris Peacock, "Pioneer History of Ferron" (typescript copy in Emery County History Archives), 4; Ferron Ward Manuscript History (typescript copy in Emery County History Archives); *House Journal of the Twenty-Sixth Session of the Legislative Assembly of the Territory of Utah* (Salt Lake City: Tribune Printing and Publishing Co., 1884), 153, 170; *House Journal of the Twenty-seventh Session of the Legislative Assembly of the Territory of Utah* (Salt Lake City: Tribune Printing and Publishing Co., 1886), 187–88, 209; *Eastern Utah Advocate,* 13 May 1897.

81. *Eastern Utah Telegram,* 1 January 1892; *Eastern Utah Advocate,* 22 April, 9 and 16 September, 14 October 1897.

82. Tanner, *The Far Country,* 94; Arrington, "Latter-day Saint Settlement of Eastern Utah," 117.

83. *CV,* 113, 138, 273, 285, 304; Arrington, "Latter-day Settlement of Eastern Utah," 118.

84. "History of Emery Stake Relief Society," typescript copy in Emery County History Archives.

85. *CV,* 85, 139–40, 166, 187, 227, 313.

86. Nixon, *Sketch,* 25.

87. 1880 Census Enumeration, Emery County, Utah; *Compendium of the Eleventh Census, 1890* (Washington, D.C.: Government Printing Office, 1892), 805; *Twelfth Census, 1900: Census Bulletin 97* (Washington, D.C.: Government Printing Office, 1901), 8.

88. *CV,* 166–67; Roma N. Powell, "A History of Emery County Schools," in *EC 1880–1980,* 297; Lever, *History of Sanpete and Emery Counties,* 635.

89. *CV,* 119.

90. Ibid., 227–29; Lever, *History of Sanpete and Emery Counties,* 646.

91. *CV,* 274.

92. Ibid., 288–89.

93. *ECP,* 8 December 1900.

94. Tabone, "Emery Stake Academy," 15–17.

95. *CV,* 32–33; Tabone, "Emery Stake Academy," 27.

96. *CV,* 219–21.

97. Tabone, "Emery Stake Academy," 20.

98. Ibid., 29–31, 105.

99. Tabone, "Emery Stake Academy," 21–23; Allan Kent Powell, "Castle Valley at the Beginning of the Twentieth Century," in *Emery County,* 22–25.

100. Nixon, *Sketches,* 60.

101. Lever, *History of Sanpete and Emery Counties,* 607–9.

102. *Eastern Utah Advocate,* 17 June 1897.

103. *CV,* 169.

104. *ECP,* 18 May 1901; 19 April 1902.

105. *Eastern Utah Advocate,* 12 August, 18 November, 2 December 1897; 14 June 1900; *ECP,* 24 August 1901.

106. Nelson, *In the Direction of His Dreams,* 127–28.

107. *Eastern Utah Telegram,* 11 September 1891. The coroner's verdict in this case was self-defense.

108. Boyd Blain, "Law and Order," in *Life Under the Horseshoe: A History of Spring City,* ed. Kaye C. Watson (Salt Lake City: Publishers Press, 1987), 101–3.

109. *ECP,* 24 August, 26 October 1901; 18 and 25 January 1902.

110. Baker, *Wild Bunch,* 13, 35–45.

111. *CV,* 308; Fae Thomas, "Orangeville," in *EC 1880–1980,* 77; Baker, *Wild Bunch,* 71–76.

112. Baker, *Wild Bunch,* 76–82. This event caused a sensation in the press because a companion of Walker named Herring, who was also killed, was believed for a time to be Butch Cassidy.

113. *Eastern Utah Advocate,* 22 April 1897.

114. Baker, *Wild Bunch,* 206–7.

115. *CV,* 50.

116. *Eastern Utah Advocate,* 19 May 1898.

117. *Deseret Evening News,* 26 June 1897.

118. Baker, *Wild Bunch,* 41–42; *Eastern Utah Advocate,* 27 May, 8 July 1897.

119. *Eastern Utah Advocate,* 10 June 1897.

120. For a summary overview of this period, see Charles S. Peterson, *Utah: A Bicentennial History* (New York: W. W. Norton, 1977), 98–105.

121. Montell Seely, "Castle Dale Ward," in *EC 1880–1980,* 37. Anderson appears in a widely reprinted photograph of Mormons in prisoner garb clustered around Apostle George Q. Cannon.

122. *Eastern Utah Telegram,* 19 February, 12 March, 26 June 1891.

123. *Report on the Productions of Agriculture as Returned at the Tenth Census (June 1, 1880)* (Washington, D.C.: Government Printing Office, 1883), 95, 136; *Report on the Statistics of Agriculture in the United States at the Eleventh Census, 1890* (Washington, D.C.: Government Printing Office, 1895), 189, 231; *Census Reports: Agriculture, Part I, Farms, Livestock, and Animal Products, Twelfth Census of the United States, 1900* (Washington, D.C.: United States Census Office, 1902), 130–31, 302.

124. *Census Bulletin No. 22, Twelfth Census, 1900* (Washington, D.C.: Office of the Census, 1902), 14.

125. *Report on the Statistics of Agriculture at the Eleventh Census,* 387; *Census Reports: Agriculture, Part II, Crops and Irrigation. Twelfth Census of the United States, 1900* (Washington, D.C.: United States Census Office, 1902), 187.

126. *Report on the Statistics of Agriculture, 1890,* 454; *Crops and Irrigation, 1900,* 263.

127. *Report on the Statistics of Agriculture, 1890,* 350; *Farms, Livestock, and Animal Products, 1900,* 668.

128. *Eastern Utah Advocate,* 12 August 1897; *CV,* 49.

129. *Report on the Statistics of Agriculture, 1890,* 533.

130. *Eastern Utah Telegram,* 13 November 1891; *ECP,* 15 September 1900.

131. *ECP,* 5 October 1901.

132. *CV,* 159.

133. *Crops and Irrigation, 1900,* 690–91.

134. *Census Bulletin 222, Twelfth Census, 1900* (Washington, D. C.: United States Census Office, 1902), 10.

135. *Eastern Utah Advocate,* 26 August 1897.

136. Ibid., 11 November 1897; *ECP,* 27 October 1900.

137. *Report on the Statistics of Agriculture, 1890,* 493; *Crops and Irrigation, 1900,* 394, 746.

138. *Report on the Productions of Agriculture as Returned at the Tenth Census,* 173, 208, 310, 318–19, 350; *Farms, Livestock, and Animal Products, 1900,* 624, 668.

139. *Census Bulletin 222, Twelfth Census, 1900* (Washington, D. C.: United States Census Office, 1902), 8.

140. *Report on Statistics of Agriculture, 1890,* 269, 310, 350; *Farms, Livestock, and Animal Products, 1900,* 486–87.

141. *CV,* 39–40; *Eastern Utah Advocate,* 22 September 1898.

142. Thursey Jessen Reynolds et al., *Centennial Echoes from Carbon County* (Price, Utah: Carbon County Daughters of Utah Pioneers, 1948), 51, 52.

143. *Eastern Utah Advocate,* 17 November, 15 December 1898; 5 January 1899.

144. *CV,* 41.

145. *Farms, Livestock, and Animal Products, 1900,* 682.

146. Antrei, *Other Forty-niners,* 207.

147. Lever, *History of Sanpete and Emery Counties,* 629–34; *CV,* 146–48.

148. Lever, *History of Sanpete and Emery Counties,* 636–43.

149. *CV,* 37–41, 146–48; Lever, *History of Sanpete and Emery Counties,* 611–21, 623–25, 636–43, 646–63; Finken, *San Rafael Swell,* 19–25.

150. Baker and Wilcox, "History of Greenriver," 4.

151. J. H. Morton, "The Coal Mines of Central Utah," *Engineering and Mining Journal,* 3 February 1877, 76–77.

152. Powell, *The Next Time We Strike,* 18–19.

153. *Eastern Utah Advocate,* 7 and 28 October, 25 November, 2 December 1897; 6 January 1898.

154. Stokes and Cohenour, "Geologic Atlas," 47; Owen McClenahan, "Mineral Deposits," in *EC 1880–1980,* 275.

155. *ECP,* 20 October 1900; "The Sorrel Mule," *Salt Lake Mining Review,* 15 November 1900.

156. Cleo M. Johnson and Thelma M. Mills, "Abraham Day III and Elmira Bulkley," in *EC 1880–1980,* 363.

157. Joseph H. Jewkes, Personal History, 2, 5–6.

158. Thelma Mills, "Timber and Sawmill Industry," in *EC 1880–1980,* 283–84.

159. *CV,* 159–60, 255–56; Mills, "Timber and Sawmill Industry," 280–86.

160. *CV,* 158, 159.

161. *Eastern Utah Advocate,* 27 May 1897; *CV,* 27, 84, 85.

162. *CV,* 211, 237–38.

163. Ibid., 158.

164. Huntsman, *That We May Understand,* 85–86.

165. *CV*, 206.

166. Ibid., 206–7.

167. *Deseret News Weekly*, 25 June 1882; *CV*, 100–101, 143, 240–42; "Huntington Flour Mills," in *EC 1880–1980*, 485.

168. *Eastern Utah Advocate*, 18 February, 10 June 1897; *CV*, 317.

169. *CV*, 90, 237.

170. Ibid., 20–21.

171. *ECP*, 3 August 1901; Reuben G. Miller papers, Special Collections, Lee Library.

172. Nelson, *In the Direction of His Dreams*, 29.

173. *CV*, 93; Joseph H. Jewkes, Personal History, 7.

174. *CV*, 81–82, 233, 306.

175. *Eastern Utah Advocate*, 9 September 1897.

176. Baker, *Robbers Roost Recollections*, 11–30.

177. *CV*, 74–76.

178. Ibid., 77; Huntsman, *That We May Understand*, 43–44.

179. *CV*, 78.

180. "Anna Eliza Reynolds Seely," in *EC 1880–1980*, 464; *Eastern Utah Advocate*, 10 June 1897.

181. Chasty Olsen Harris, "Biographical Sketch of Hannah Seely Olsen," typescript copy in Archives and Manuscripts, Lee Library.

182. *CV*, 91–92, 246–47, 315; Frona L. Johnson, "A Brief History of James and Annie Eliza Rasmussen Petersen," in *EC 1880–1980*, 422; Velma Petersen, "Ferron," 109.

183. *CV*, 235–36.

184. Nelson, *In the Direction of His Dreams*, 71.

185. "History of Marinus Peterson," typescript copy in Emery County History Archives.

186. Jones, *Early Pioneers of Huntington*, 123.

187. Mary Ann Rowbury Brown, Personal History.

188. Nelson, *In the Direction of His Dreams*, 58.

189. For a descriptive account of early Utah domestic architecture, see Thomas Carter and Peter Goss, *Utah's Historic Architecture, 1847–1940: A Guide* (Salt Lake City: University of Utah Press, 1988).

190. *Eastern Utah Advocate*, 21 December 1899.

191. Nelson, *In the Direction of His Dreams*, 67.

192. Carter and Goss, *Utah's Historic Architecture*, 123.

193. *ECP*, 15 February 1902.

194. F. M. Lyman, Letter to the Editor, *Deseret Evening News,* 28 August 1880, 2.

195. Charles R. Curtis, "Pioneers of Orangeville," in *CV,* 300.

196. Argene Olsen, "The Leader of the First Settlers of Emery County: Orange Seely I and Hanna Olsen Seely," in *EC 1880–1980,* 432.

197. Joseph H. Jewkes, Personal History, 9.

198. *CV,* 140, 146–47.

199. *Eastern Utah Advocate,* 18 and 25 May 1899; *CV,* 79.

200. Nelson, *In the Direction of His Dreams,* 90.

201. *Eastern Utah Advocate,* 1 December 1898; 15 June 1899; *ECP,* 8 September 1900; 24 August 1901.

202. *Eastern Utah Advocate,* 5 August 1897; *ECP,* 12 October 1901; *CV,* 78–79; *EC 1880–1980,* 210.

203. *CV,* 178, 223, 291.

204. Ibid., 222–23.

205. Ibid., 93, 169, 209–10.

206. Harris, "History of Hannah Seely Olsen."

207. Pearl Baker and Ruth Wilcox, "Green River," in *CV,* 195.

208. Nixon, *Sketches,* 28.

209. *Eastern Utah Advocate,* 11 March 1897.

210. *CV,* 93.

211. Ibid., 209, 260.

212. Curtis, "Pioneers of Orangeville," 299–300.

213. Joseph H. Jewkes, Personal History, 7.

214. Ibid.

215. "Autobiography of Hettie Elizabeth Guymon McArthur Anderson," in Jones, *Early Pioneers of Huntington,* 8.

216. "Peter Johnson," in Jones, *Early Pioneers of Huntington,* 161.

217. Lever, *History of Sanpete and Emery Counties,* 612–13; Owen McClenahan, "The Old Saloons," 1 (typescript copy in Emery County History Archives).

218. *ECP,* 4 January 1902.

219. *Eastern Utah Advocate,* 10 June 1897.

220. Joseph H. Jewkes, Personal History, 5, 7–9; "Samuel Jewkes," in *EC 1880–1980,* 466.

221. *CV,* 213; "Joseph Ellis Johnson" and "Milas Edgar Johnson" in Jones, *Early Pioneers of Huntington,* 137–55.

222. *CV,* 213–14; "Peter Johnson," 155–62.

223. Elizabeth J. Howard, "Eisteddfod: A Music Festival and Contest," in *CV,* 29–31.

224. J. W. Dilley, *History of the Scofield Mine Disaster* (Provo, Utah: Skelton Publishing Co., 1900), 99–100; Elmo G. Geary, "Dramatics in Castle Valley," 170–73.

225. *CV,* 94–95.

226. Geary, "Dramatics in Castle Valley," 31, 36–37.

227. Ibid., 39.

228. Ibid., 40.

229. Ibid., 76, 83.

230. Ibid., 139.

231. Ibid., 194, 196.

232. Ibid., 180–81.

233. Ibid., 213.

234. Bruce L. Olsen, "History of the *Emery County Progress-Leader,*" quoted in *EC 1880–1980,* 323.

5

Discovering the Limits, 1900–1920

In the first two decades of the twentieth century, the children of Emery County's large pioneer families reached maturity and assumed leading roles in public life. Their efforts contributed to a more intensive exploitation of the county's resources, a population peak that would not be exceeded for more than fifty years, and significant developments in politics, education, and transportation. Although the growth rate slowed around the turn of the century, the population increased from 4,657 in 1900 to 6,750 in 1910 and 7,411 in 1920. Most communities shared in the growth from 1900 to 1910, though in markedly differing degrees. The peach boom of 1906 and 1907 almost quadrupled the Green River population from 222 to 824. Cleveland (353 to 651), Ferron (660 to 1,022), and Huntington (944 to 1,293) experienced substantial growth, while Orangeville (623 to 762), Castle Dale (718 to 848), and Emery (572 to 632) grew at more modest rates. The population of some smaller communities, Desert Lake (127 to 125), Lawrence (160 to 161), and Molen (164 to 141), remained static or declined. Woodside grew from 114 to 132, and the Clawson precinct was created during this decade, reaching a population of 159 in 1910. The county's modest gain of 661 persons between 1910 and 1920 was less than the population of two new precincts, Mohrland (691) and Elmo (260). The leveling off of growth by 1920 meant that virtually all of Emery County's natural increase was being exported to other regions.

Out-migration was a significant factor throughout the period, even as people from other regions were moving into the county. During a single three-month period in 1902, for example, the *Emery County Progress* reported the departure of nine families for destinations in Idaho, Arizona, Alberta, Wyoming, and Salt Lake City. The opening of the Uintah Reservation to settlement in 1905 attracted many people. In 1915 several families moved to LaSal, San Juan County.[1] Others acquired farms in the new agricultural developments around Delta, Millard County. At the same time, however, new agricultural developments were going forward in Emery County.

Land Degradation and New Lands

The number of farms in the county grew from 458 in 1900 to 759 in 1920. Improved acreage increased from 25,918 in 1900 to 43,587 by 1920 as irrigation systems were extended to new areas.[2] This expansion, however, was offset to a considerable extent by the degradation of existing farm land. The predominant mancos shale formations of Castle Valley, having once been sea-bed deposits, are impregnated with salts. Furthermore, the tight soil structure and lack of organic matter result in poor drainage characteristics. Irrigation saturated the soil and dissolved the salts, which then collected on the surface in "alkali" patches. Where canals cut through shale hills, large quantities of water seeped into porous strata to rise to the surface in some instances several miles away. Runoff water from higher fields returned to the creeks and was reused downstream. The addition of salty water to salty soil only accelerated the degradation process. Within a few years, large areas of once productive cropland were transformed into alkali flats capable of supporting nothing but salt-grass and greasewood.

The first symptoms of land degradation appeared quite early. An 1891 observer declared, "The people of Huntington will have to do less irrigating or their houses are liable to lose a corner stone. There are a few lots that need draining already."[3] Eventually a large portion of the Huntington townsite turned "swampy." A U.S. Department of Agriculture report estimated that by 1904 some 30 percent of the farmland in Emery County had been abandoned.[4] In that year experts from the Agricultural College of Utah installed an experimental drainage project on a farm near Huntington. The experiment was reportedly successful, but the method, requiring deep parallel trenches at close intervals, proved too expensive for widespread adoption.[5]

There was, of course, no shortage of land in Emery County with its 2.8 million acres. At a local irrigation convention in 1902, a petition was drafted requesting government assistance under the recently adopted "Newlands Act" to reclaim 50,000 acres.[6] However, it would be several decades before federal reclamation projects came to Emery County. The county's turn-of-the-century "newlands" projects were accomplished in much the same way as the pioneer settlement a generation earlier: by local cooperative or entrepreneurial development of land and water resources. To replace agricultural land lost to alkali and provide farms for the second generation, highline canals were extended to more distant benches and flats. New lands brought into existence new communities.

Kingsville/Clawson. The Ferron North Ditch was completed in 1896, bringing water to the benchlands north of the river valley. Among the first homesteaders on what was called the North Flat were the families of Elias Blackburn, Edward Jorgensen, Guy King, Axel Andersen, William Cheshire, Dell Cloward, Thomas Cunningham, Robert King, Niels Nielsen, John Nordell, George Reid, Edward Salsberg, Amos Stevens, and Edward Wrigley.[7] Most of the settlers located on level ground some two miles east of the present Clawson townsite. They experienced the usual challenges of developing new farmland with little capital, keeping new ditches within their banks, and battling grasshopper invasions. It was impossible to keep the canal running during freezing weather, and the residents were compelled to haul their drinking water from the Ferron Creek at Paradise Ranch, three miles to the east. An 1897 news article referred to the area as Silver Dell, but a more common name was Poverty Flat.[8]

The first school in the new community was conducted in 1898 in the home of Guy King with Florence Barney as the teacher. She made the fourteen-mile daily round trip from her home in Ferron on horseback.[9] In the spring of 1901, a 125-lot townsite with the name of Kingsville was surveyed but apparently never officially filed. In June the county commission approved the establishment of a school district, and by August plans were reportedly under way for construction of a schoolhouse to serve the district's twenty-nine children.[10]

The introduction of irrigation on the North Flat soon led to alkali problems at Kingsville. In 1902 Emery LDS Stake president Reuben G. Miller instructed Ferron Ward bishop Hyrum Nelson to assist the settlers in selecting a new site. A traditional story holds that the singletree clip on Bishop Nelson's new buggy broke when he reached the site that was to become Clawson. He repaired the clip, but as soon as he started again the other singletree clip broke. Bishop Nelson then declared,

> "This is proof enough for me. This is the place." When the people were informed of the decision, some were dissatisfied, but Bishop Nelson told them that they had better move their houses up to the new location soon, because from observations he had made of the drainage in that locality, that by two years from then, some of the land would be so swampy that they wouldn't be able to move their houses out, and this proved to be true.[11]

As Kent Powell has remarked, this account is revealing on at least two points. It indicates that the LDS church continued to exercise quasigovernmental powers in the county into the twentieth century. It was not the county officials but the ecclesiastical leader of the region, President Miller, who took the initiative in locating a permanent townsite. And the authority of Bishop Nelson was apparently sufficient to overcome any opposition to the new site. The account of the townsite selection is further significant, as Powell points out, for "the manner in which a permanent location was selected—with a reliance on divine direction supported by a pragmatic evaluation of the situation."[12] It is interesting that the account has Bishop Nelson repeating the well known phrase attributed to Brigham Young: "This is the place." On the pragmatic side, not only was the new site on higher ground than Kingsville, and therefore presumably less susceptible to swamping, it was also situated on the established county road that later became Utah Highway 10. Kingsville had been some distance away from the main road.

Land for the new townsite was purchased from the Westingskow brothers and blocks surveyed by the fall of 1902. The schoolhouse and several homes were moved from Kingsville to the new site. Contemporary newspaper reports indicate that the new townsite was called Clawson from the beginning, refuting a local tradition that the name was bestowed two years later when Apostle Rudger Clawson organized an LDS ward.[13] Perhaps Apostle Clawson was assigned to establish the ward because the community had already taken his name. In June 1905 Bishop William H. Hitchcock began work on a large brick home, a tangible symbol of the community's permanence. A two-room school was erected in 1905, and a frame and adobe meetinghouse between 1907 and 1908.[14] The Clawson precinct had a population of 159 in 1910 and grew to 183 by 1920.

Rock Canyon Flat. The Great Western Canal was delivering water to Rock Canyon Flat by 1905, when the *Progress* reported that several Orangeville families had moved to farms there for the summer. Among the first to locate in the area were Ed Cox, George Snow, Alma Jewkes, Henry Reid, and Christian Poulsen. As many as twenty-nine families eventually had homes there, and there was some talk of establishing a town. With the coming of automobiles, however, most Rock Canyon Flat landowners chose to live in Orangeville and commute to their farms.[15]

Rochester/Moore. In late 1894 a group of forty-two men, most of them from Ferron and Emery, organized the Independent Canal and Reservoir Company with the intention of constructing a canal to carry water from Muddy Creek to Independence Flats, situated northeast of the Muddy Creek Valley.[16] W. H. Lever's 1898 *History of Sanpete and Emery Counties* declared that the canal "will be completed in '99, and a large area reclaimed. A new town to be called Freedom has been surveyed, and will be located when the canal is finished."[17] Evidently the canal did deliver some water in 1899 or shortly thereafter, but the town called Freedom was never established. By 1903 thirty families were reportedly living on Independence Flat but were struggling with an inadequate water supply.[18] The original canal followed a winding course around the hills and was subject to much water loss through seepage and broken banks. The Emery Canal Company controlled the water rights in Muddy Creek and claimed the entire available flow from midsummer onward. The Independent Canal Company sought to obtain water rights by building several reservoirs to hold the spring snowmelt but lacked resources to complete these projects.

A new phase in the history of Independence Flat began in the spring of 1904 when G. W. Laing came to do some surveying and was impressed by the region's potential. Laing and Robert Forrester organized the Gardenia Land and Water Company in August with the intention of developing Independence Flat. Their search for investors led them to M. B. Whitney, president of the Utah Implement Company, who took control of the development in November 1904, making Laing his manager. Whitney acquired enough land and water rights to be elected president of the Independent Canal Company in February 1905. In addition to purchasing land from the original settlers, he acquired several thousand acres through state land selections. A townsite was platted in December 1904 and named Rochester after Whitney's home town of Rochester, New York. Whitney attracted additional investors, apparently men in the farm equipment manufacturing industry in Minneapolis, and the Emery County Land and Water Company was incorporated in August 1906.[19]

Work on an enlarged canal and on reservoirs at Julius Flat and Spinner's Meadow went forward during 1907. In the meantime, the company acquired a steam-powered plow from the Minneapolis Threshing Machine Company (controlled by F. E. Kennaston, another investor) and planted several hundred acres to dry-land grain and alfalfa. In midsummer Laing was replaced by L. C. Moore. Moore remained in charge until 1916, when a Los Angeles promoter named Alfred F. Narver arranged to buy out the majority interest then held by Kennaston. Narver announced grandiose plans for development but apparently lacked the resources to bring them to fruition. In April 1918 he was arrested on fraud charges filed by a Salt Lake bank, and Kennaston foreclosed his mortgage. Moore then joined forces with Quince G. Crawford, D. S. Skeen, and other investors to organize the Rochester Ranch Company, which acquired much of the Kennaston holdings and also bought out some individual farmers. Crawford developed his own large farm, and some land was sold to other purchasers between 1919 and 1920. Moore managed the remaining Rochester Ranch property. On the occasion of his retirement as postmaster in 1940, the postal designation of the community was changed from Rochester to Moore.[20]

Because it was organized as a profit-making enterprise, Rochester did not have the ten- to twenty-acre subsistence farms that were found in the county's older communities. The 1930 census of agriculture listed the Rochester precinct with twenty-one farms totalling 10,140 acres, by far the largest average farm acreage in the county. By comparison, Ferron had ninety-two farms on 8,682 acres.[21] Most Rochester and Moore residents lived on their farms, and community amenities at the townsite were rather limited. L. C. Moore built a bunkhouse and a cottage for himself in 1907.[22] Several other homes were erected on the townsite during the following years. A store built by George Nelms in 1907 was operated by a succession of owners until the mid-1920s. A post office was established in 1919 and continued in operation until 1965. An LDS ward was organized in 1920, reduced to the status of a branch in 1923, and discontinued in 1946. A four-room brick school erected by the consolidated Emery County School District between 1916 and 1917 replaced a log-cabin school that had been in operation since 1913. Only two of the four classrooms were ever needed for instruction, but the building served as a general community center. The Rochester School was closed in 1925. The population in 1930, the first census in which Rochester was separately returned, was 114, declining to forty-seven in 1940.

Victor. The Desert Lake irrigation system had been extended several miles to the north by 1897, when Joseph Powell laid out a townsite near what would become Victor. In the booster tradition of nineteenth-century journalism, the *Eastern Utah Advocate* described the area as "a veritable horticultural paradise in embryo."[23] Powell was unsuccessful in attracting settlers to his proposed town, but within a few years land and water degradation had become a serious enough problem that some Desert Lake residents were looking for a new site. In October 1904 Bishop Manassa J. Blackburn of the Desert Lake

LDS Ward negotiated the purchase of about 600 acres from Powell. A townsite plat was surveyed in June 1905 and approved by the county commission in March 1906. Blackburn moved from the settlement in 1906, and the task of establishing the town fell upon his successor as bishop, Henry G. Mills. By June 1908 the *Emery County Progress* reported, "The movement to . . . the new townsite . . . is becoming quite general, and some new houses and tents begin to dot the new town."[24] The Desert Lake LDS Ward was transferred to the new site in 1908 and renamed as the Victor Ward in 1914. A post office had been established with that name in 1912. A concrete block school erected in 1910 served also as a church and social hall.[25] The precinct continued under the name of Desert Lake, and a school was maintained at the old site for several years. Residents of the old and new communities shared a cemetery located midway between the two villages. Desert Lake/Victor had 154 residents in 1920 and reached its peak population of 179 in 1930.

Elmo. In 1904 several residents of Cleveland, including Bouther H. Erickson, Samuel Richards, James A. Oviatt, Adolph Axelson, and William J. Atwood, filed on homesteads some four miles northeast of that community and constructed the Eagle Extension of the Cleveland Canal to bring water to the land. In 1907 George T. Oviatt, Lars P. Larsen, H. H. Oviatt, Sr., Hans F. Mortensen, Henry Rasmussen, and others filed on land farther out on the Washboard Flat and built another extension of the Cleveland Canal. The *Emery County Progress* reported, "The land is amongst the best in the county and it is expected quite a prosperous community will soon spring up there." These second-generation pioneers reenacted in large part the colonizing experience of their parents a generation earlier, living in tents or log shacks on their homesteads while they labored to bring their desert land into production. In 1908 Eliza Oviatt filed on eighty acres and Worth Tucker purchased eighty acres of an adjacent school section. These properties became the Elmo townsite, platted into lots that were sold to prospective residents for $10. By July 1908 the *Progress* reported the town "already has several small houses and is rapidly acquiring a population."[26]

There are differing accounts of how the community gained its name, but the prevailing local tradition holds that *Elmo* was formed from the initials of four pioneer families, Erickson, Larsen, Mortensen, and Oviatt. A post office was granted to the new community in 1912, and in the same year a branch of the Cleveland LDS Ward was organized with George H. Oviatt as presiding elder. Oviatt became the first bishop of the Elmo Ward when it was established on 11 May 1913. The community's first gathering place was a log granary. In 1911 residents purchased the old Cleveland school, sawed it in two, dragged it to the new settlement on log skids, and reassembled it in an expanded form with a new hardwood floor. A few years later a T-wing was added at the rear. This structure served as a church meetinghouse and community center until 1954. It was also used as a school until the completion of a four-room brick school in 1917.[27]

With its extensive surrounding farmland and convenient commuting distance to Price, Elmo prospered beyond the other Emery County communities established in the twentieth century, enjoying a gradual but steady growth from a precinct population of 260 in 1920 to 305 in 1930, 392 in 1940, and 432 in 1950.

Buffalo. The early development at Lawrence was on the west side of Huntington Creek with irrigation water supplied by the Avery Ditch and the Huntington Canal. Beginning in 1906, several families took up land east of the creek on Buffalo Bench and in Buffalo Hollow. Dryfarming was attempted with limited success in 1907, and the following year the Buffalo Irrigation Company was organized to build an extension of the Huntington North Ditch. The canal was finally completed in 1911, and "about 20" families farmed at Buffalo that year. The 1912 grain harvest was so heavy that three threshing crews were required.[28] A few families established year-round homes at Buffalo, while others lived there in the summers but spent the winters in town.

Cedar Mountain. Around 1905 there was a surge of interest in dryfarming in the arid West. The *Emery County Progress* reprinted numerous articles reporting the successful growing of crops without irrigation and urged Emery County farmers to adopt the practice. Senator Reed Smoot's 1909 dryland homestead bill allowed homestead entries of 320 acres on nonirrigated land and relaxed residency requirements.[29] Under the influence of these developments, dryfarming was attempted at Independence Flat, Buckhorn Flat, Buffalo Hollow, and the Salt Wash area east of Ferron. While an occasional wet summer allowed for the harvesting of dryland wheat, the prevailing climate was simply too dry for nonirrigated farming to succeed in most of Emery County.

A partial exception to this general rule was found on the higher benches of Cedar Mountain, where an elevation near seven thousand feet attracted sufficient rainfall to bring wheat to maturity in most years. In the spring of 1908, the R. W. Hill, A. N. Day, and George Kofford families took up about one thousand acres on Huff Bench. At about the same time the E. S. Day family located on Wimmer Bench. These settlers hired the steam tractor belonging to the Huntington Threshing Machine Company and planted a substantial acreage to spring wheat.[30]

Apparently this first wave of farmers on Cedar Mountain returned to their Castle Valley homes after a short period. In 1912 and subsequent years, a new group of settlers arrived and took up dryland homesteads. Joseph Curtis and his sons Guy and Dod and their families settled on Huff Bench, as did the Bill and Verl Winters families. A few years later, Clair and Pat Winters also claimed land on Huff Bench. Jim Jensen located at Bob Hill Spring. Other settlers at Huff and Wimmer benches included Joe Jensen, Fred Shrink, and John Forrester and their families. Another group of homesteaders, most of them from Castle Dale, claimed land on the mountain in 1916. Anne Curtis Allred, who was born on Wimmer Flat in 1917 and spent much of her childhood on Cedar Mountain, recalls that the homesteaders "raised lots of dry land grain" and had "big gardens and . . . good crops of potatoes." However, they also faced difficult challenges. Dry years brought crop failures. Because of the extreme remoteness, bad roads, and harsh winters, the families resided on their homesteads only during the growing season, returning to town for the winter. Cedar Mountain was extensively used for livestock grazing, making it necessary for the farmers to fence their fields with "rip-gut" fences built with heavy labor from the abundant pinyon and juniper trees. Wood gatherers from the valley would sometimes dismantle the fences in the fall as a convenient supply of firewood. Despite all difficulties, some homesteaders persevered until the 1930s, when a combination of severe drought and economic depression led to the abandonment of farming on Cedar Mountain.[31]

Buckhorn Flat. Few, if any, areas in Emery County possessed the apparent agricultural promise of Buckhorn Flat, a large expanse of gently sloping land with deep soil, a southern exposure, and the wall of Cedar Mountain to protect it from north winds. The only problem was a lack of water. Joseph W. Powell of Desert Lake constructed the first Buckhorn Reservoir impoundment at the head of the flat in 1901, hoping to capture sufficient runoff from Cedar Mountain to irrigate a portion of the area. In 1903 Powell joined forces with Joseph E. Johnson of Huntington, then the county's representative in the state legislature, in an effort to persuade the state land board to finance a large-scale reclamation project. The proposed scheme included an enlarged Buckhorn Reservoir, a canal and aquaduct from Huntington Creek, and a high-elevation reservoir at Miller Flat. The land board appropriated $1,500 for an investigation of the project by the state engineer. However, the engineer's report was unfavorable, estimating that it would cost $33 per acre to deliver water to Buckhorn Flat, a prohibitively high cost at that time.

The local promoters were disappointed but undaunted by this setback. Another investigation by the state land board in 1904 once again found the project too costly for its expected benefits. In 1905 Powell brought a party of "Eastern capitalists" to look at Buckhorn Flat but evidently failed to persuade them to invest in the project. In 1906 Robert Gordon of Huntington tried dryfarming alfalfa. The following year several families from Cleveland and Desert Lake took up land on the flat and planted crops, using what little water they could collect in Buckhorn Reservoir and depending on natural rainfall for the rest. Apparently they enjoyed some success because the following spring between forty and fifty men were reported as farming at Buckhorn. But with an average annual precipitation of less than eight inches, dryfarming was doomed to failure.

Buckhorn Flat lost one of its most ardent boosters with the death of Joseph E. Johnson in 1908. Powell continued his efforts, however, and was joined by James Petersen of Castle Dale as an enthusiastic supporter. The reservoir dam was washed out by heavy rains in the summer of 1908, but Powell rebuilt it in the fall and also undertook new surveys for a canal to see if it were possible to find a route that would not require expensive fill or pipe. In 1909 James Petersen joined with Salt Lake City promoter Henry Lund and assembled a syndicate of prominent investors including former LDS apostle John W. Taylor. The *Emery County Progress* greeted this development with a headline declaring, "Buckhorn Flat Reclamation Now a Certainty." The Salt Lake syndicate did little or nothing for three years except make periodic visits to the county to rekindle interest. In 1911 the group announced plans to offer twenty-, forty-, and one hundred-acre plots with water at $125 per acre. In 1912 the Buckhorn Fruit Lands Company was incorporated with L. A. Merrill, agriculture professor at the Agricultural College of Utah, as president and with plans for a 2,000-foot siphon to bring water to the flat. Again in 1916 there was a stirring of interest from a Los Angeles investor, and the *Progress* predicted "Big things to happen."[32]

The sticking point in all of these schemes was water delivery. The head of Buckhorn Flat is almost the same elevation as the nearest point on the Cleveland Canal, some six miles distant. Between these two points lies higher ground requiring either a massive cut or a pipeline and pumps. Both alternatives proved to be too costly for the available capital. Furthermore, it would have required a reservoir of at least 20,000 acre-foot capacity to supply sufficient water to reclaim the available land. Despite these hard realities, development schemes for Buckhorn Flat were periodically revived for many years.

Joe's Valley. The Joe's Valley region had been important as grazing and timber land from the earliest settlement period, and several herders' or squatters' cabins dotted the landscape by the turn of the century. As early as 1889, James and Sarah Reynolds filed a claim on 600 acres now covered by Joe's Valley Reservoir. In 1893 Charles E. Kofford located a homestead in Upper Joe's Valley. He was awarded water rights from Indian Creek in 1901. The substantial rock and log house built by Kofford was still standing in 1995.[33]

Upper Joe's Valley, with an elevation above eight thousand feet, was suitable only for summer grazing, but agriculture was possible in Lower Joe's Valley at elevations around seven thousand feet. In 1916 seven Castle Dale residents, William King, Marinus Petersen, Elisha Allen (Allie) Jones, Abinadi (Nad) Olsen, Fred Larsen, Frank

Fillmore, and Claiborne Elder, filed on contiguous homesteads along Lowry Water. King relinquished his claim, which was then filed on by Leo W. Peterson. Forrest Peterson has described the first year homesteaders loaded up household supplies, food, clothing, chickens, and pigs in their wagons for the annual migration to Joe's Valley, travelling together "so as to help each other if help was needed." The first day's travel took them to the Peacock ranch at the mouth of Straight Canyon. On the second day, they had to negotiate the primitive road through the narrow canyon:

> It was the time of year when the water in the river was at its highest; at one place in straight canyon the road went under a ledge right into the creek. [F]or about 100 feet, the water would be so high the wooden wagon box would float off the running gears of the wagon. [T]hen in the upper end of the canyon a rider had to be sent ahead to stop anyone from starting down the canyon until we came through because the road ran up on the mountain side and was so narrow there was no room to pass another vehicle any place.

After the canyon, there was still a hazardous crossing of Seely Creek, where "there was so much water one could hear the large boulders rolling and rumbling in the stream," and two crossings of Lowry Water before they reached the homesteads. When a threshing machine was brought to Joe's Valley to thresh the first crop of wheat, "Ropes had to be tied to the top of the machine and held by men from the mountainside above to keep the thresher from tipping over in some of the bad places on the road." In 1918 a new Straight Canyon road was constructed on the north side of the creek, "which facilitated our travels to Joes Valley immeasurably."

When the land was cleared of brush and brought under irrigation it "proved to be very productive for wheat, alfalfa, potatoes, berries, and lettuce."[34] Mixed crop farming continued on the Lowry Water ranches for more than two decades. In more recent years, the land has been used primarily for grazing and recreational purposes.

Other New Lands Projects. The Mammoth Reservoir and Canal project on the Price River was begun in 1907. After proceeding by fits and starts and passing through several different owners, what would eventually be known as the Carbon Canal began delivering water in

1912. The canal extended into Emery County north of Elmo and Victor, where a farm of more than two thousand acres was developed by the Austin brothers. "Austinville" boasted its own school for a brief period around 1916. The Austin property was sold off in smaller plots a short time after the Mammoth Reservoir dam broke in June 1917, sending a devastating flood through the Price River Valley and leading to severe late-season water shortages that recurred until the completion of the Scofield Reservoir several years later.[35]

Other developments during the period included attempts to farm at Fuller Bottom on the San Rafael River, some expansion of irrigated land in the San Rafael Valley, and expansion also at Paradise, a small valley on Ferron Creek below the Molen Reef.[36] The short-lived Enterprise Canal was constructed in an attempt to bring the flats west of Huntington under cultivation. The Carey Act, which enabled developers to obtain large expanses of the public domain, stimulated much talk of Emery County developments on a massive scale. Several promoters laid claim to huge amounts of Green River water and land in eastern Emery County, but these developments did not progress beyond the visionary stage. There were proposals also to dam the San Rafael River at the Lower Black Box, creating a large reservoir and reclaiming thousands of acres in the San Rafael Valley. Several different schemes were proposed to bring water to Poison Spring and Sagebrush benches between Huntington and Price. Don C. Robbins, a former Huntington resident, worked for several years to promote construction of a reservoir in Joe's Valley that would provide water to reclaim the western benchlands of Castle Valley and would generate power for, among other things, an electrified railroad connecting Castle Valley communities with Price. When it became apparent that the Robbins scheme was unlikely to attract sufficient capital, the new editor of the *Emery County Progress,* Jesse S. Moffitt, proposed that the county "get Uncle Sam to build the dam" in Joe's Valley—perhaps the first reference to an idea that would come to fruition half a century later.[37]

Water Development and Disputes

The opening of new agricultural lands in Castle Valley did nothing to increase the region's limited water supply. In some instances, water rights were transferred from degraded alkali land to new acreage, but total demand still increased substantially. In years of normal precipitation, the water supply was adequate for the expanded acreage until the end of the mountain snowmelt, usually about mid-June. From that point on, streamflows declined rapidly, and disputes over water rights escalated at a corresponding rate. The basic principle of western water law was first come, first served, which gave priority to the earliest developed lands. However, the newer canals had a larger capacity and were diverted higher on the creeks, making them a potential threat to the users of the older ditches.

As delivery systems grew longer and more intricate, with increased water loss through seepage and evaporation, questions arose over how and where the water should be measured. If water was measured at the diversion point, irrigators at the end of the ditch would receive less water per share of irrigation company stock than those located near the head of the system. On the other hand, if water were measured at the individual farmer's headgate (as became the prevailing practice) then those with senior rights found their water supply diminished with every extension of the canals, since transit losses were distributed throughout the system.

Conflicts were not limited to rival companies or to "upstream" versus "downstream" irrigators. Each canal company employed watermasters to insure an equitable distribution. Typically, each farm had its own headgate and measuring weir that enabled the watermaster to determine the quantity of water being received. In theory, only the watermaster was authorized to adjust the flow through the headgate, but it was a simple matter for a farmer to open his gate wider between the watermaster's visits and thereby gain more water than he was entitled to. This "midnight irrigating," as it was sometimes called, was especially common—and especially resented—during periods of low streamflow. Blood has been shed on more than one occasion in Emery County as a result of water disputes between neighbors.

Cottonwood Creek. The first major dispute over water rights arose among farmers on Cottonwood Creek during the 1890s, culminating in litigation and the Johnson Decree of 1902. Each canal on the creek had been built and operated by a separate company. The older canals, the Blue Cut, Clipper, and several smaller ditches, watered riverbottom lands and the lower benches, while the later-built and higher Mammoth and Great Western canals had the capacity to deliver water to thousands of acres of benchland from Five Mile Wash on the north to Rock Canyon Wash on the south. Montell Seely has summarized the resulting situation as follows:

> The water supply became exhausted. The upstream users, even though they came later, had first access to the creek so naturally they took what water they wanted and this often left the downstream users short changed. The waste water and seep water from the farms upstream ran back into the creek, and in the Fall the only water the downstream users had was this adulterated seep water.[38]

The disputing parties eventually chose a remedy that invoked the authority of both church and state. A "friendly" lawsuit was filed by the Blue Cut Canal Company and several individual downstream water users against the Star, Mammoth, Clipper, and Great Western companies and several individual upstream irrigators. The court appointed Emery LDS Stake president Reuben G. Miller and apostles John Henry Smith and Anthon H. Lund as referees to investigate the situation and recommend a solution to non-Mormon Judge Jacob Johnson of Spring City. Of the hearings conducted in February 1901, the *Progress* reported, "Strange to say, this water testimony is dry, the only amusement being furnished by Charley Swasey [one of the defendants], who gave expert testimony relative to the effects of alkali water on man and beast."[39]

The referees' decision, issued in May 1901 and given legal force as the Johnson Decree on 2 February 1902, favored the senior users. Water rights in Cottonwood Creek were divided into three classes, with first-class rights awarded to the lands occupied before 1884 and second-class rights given to those developed after that year. Third-class rights were granted to water users on the Great Western in recognition of the large investment required to build that canal. In effect, second- and third-class rights entitled users to flood waters only, with virtually the entire late-season streamflow belonging to those with first-class rights. Blue Cut Canal stockholders were granted a first-class right to 48.7 cubic feet of water per second. In contrast, the larger Mammoth Canal was awarded a first-class right to only 5.6 cubic feet per second, and the Great Western had no first-class rights at all.

The *Progress* reported in June 1901, "Some of the landholders under the Mammoth canal profess to feel a little bit sore by reason of the water referees' decision." In July 1902 the editor pleaded for "arbitration and consolidation" to achieve a more equitable distribution of water rights, declaring, "There is sufficient water . . . to irrigate twenty times the amount of land now cultivated, but the whole trouble is that it is unequally divided." By early August, Castle Dale town ditches, supplied from the Mammoth Canal, were dry, and farmlands under the newer canals had reached a crisis stage. At this point, the Blue Cut and Clipper stockholders agreed to allow some of their water to be turned into the Mammoth and Great Western canals in order to save the crops. This initial act of cooperation set in motion plans for a fuller consolidation, and in April 1903 the Cottonwood Creek Consolidated Irrigation Company was organized by the stockholders of all the major canals except for the Blue Cut. Blue Cut stockholders, with their excellent water rights protected by the Johnson Decree, did not join the consolidated company until 6 July 1937.[40]

Huntington Creek. Conflicts over rights to Huntington Creek began almost from the moment water started flowing in the Cleveland Canal in 1888 and continued until the eventual consolidation of irrigation companies in 1932. In an effort to secure additional water, Cleveland irrigators built a reservoir in a high valley on the Wasatch Plateau. After several successive stages of construction, the Cleveland Reservoir had a storage capacity of about 3,600 acre-feet by the early years of the twentieth century. Even though this was a small quantity compared to the creek's total flow, the few additional weeks of irrigation water it provided could mean the difference between a successful harvest and crop failure.

Huntington irrigators found themselves looking enviously at the share of the diminished late-season creek flow going into the Cleveland Canal. In 1900 the Huntington Canal and Agricultural Company selected a reservoir site at Erickson Flat, about a mile west of Cleveland Reservoir. As with the Cleveland Reservoir, construction proceeded in stages with most work being done during a two-month period in the late summer and early fall, after crops had been harvested in the valley and before snow came to the high plateau. Water storage began in 1905 and was increased in succeeding years as the dam was raised higher, reaching a capacity of 2,400 acre-feet by about 1912.

These relatively small storage facilities did not fully solve the problem of inadequate late-season water, nor did they resolve the disputes between Huntington and Cleveland irrigators. In 1912 the Huntington Canal and Agricultural Company filed suit against the Cleveland company, asking for an adjudication of water rights. The court acted two years later when Judge A. H. Christensen decreed a rather complicated formula. First-class rights to the first 150 cubic feet per second (cfs) of streamflow were divided with approximately four-fifths going to Huntington and one-fifth to Cleveland. A second-class right was awarded to Cleveland for flow between 150 and 195 cfs. A third and fourth class of rights apportioned the excess flow beyond 195 cfs among Huntington, Cleveland, and Desert Lake users, and Desert Lake was awarded storage rights to the winter flow in the amount of 13,722 acre-feet (far in excess of the actual capacity of Desert Lake).[41]

Ferron Creek. The Ferron Reservoir site was selected in 1888 by Lyman S. Beach, E. F. Bailey, and Hyrum Cook, and the first stage of construction was apparently completed within two years. Located on glacial moraine deposits in a beautiful wooded basin at an elevation of 9,250 feet, Ferron Reservoir has been a popular recreation area from the beginning. However, its maximum storage capacity was only 1,400 acre-feet, a quantity augmented in later years by other small impoundments at Willow Lake and Wrigley Springs.[42] With the extension of the North Canal to the Clawson area, conflicts arose between the older settlers and the developers of new lands. In 1905 the irrigation company attempted "to settle the water muddle without a legal battle" by appointing a committee composed of five holders of "old stock," five "new stock," and five neutral members. Apparently this group was unable to resolve the conflict, and the matter was then turned over to a committee of the Emery Stake high council.[43] Until the completion of Mill Site Reservoir in 1971, water users in Ferron, Molen, and Clawson were largely dependent on the variable natural flow of Ferron Creek, with perennial late-season shortages.

Muddy Creek. Senior rights to the water of Muddy Creek were claimed by the Emery Canal and Reservoir Company. When the Independent Canal and Reservoir Company was organized in 1894, its plan was to augment the surplus streamflow by building several reservoirs. Four sites were selected and some construction work was done at Spinner's Meadow and Julius Flat before the company ran out of funds in 1903. Apparently, completion of these two impoundments as well as the Emery Reservoir was financed in large part by the Emery County Land and Water Company after it acquired most of the property on Independence Flat. In 1906 the Emery Canal and Reservoir Company hired an attorney to fight the efforts of the rival company to acquire additional rights, claiming that "the water flow of Muddy Creek is already fully appropriated and used on land under the Emery canal."[44] Reservoir storage on Muddy Creek has never been sufficient to insure against late-season shortages with attendant conflicts over water rights, in spite of close family ties between many Emery and Rochester/Moore farmers.

Interbasin Diversions. Winter snowfall on the Wasatch Plateau is most abundant on the steep western slopes that drain into Sanpete Valley. Some of this snow, however, is carried across the skyline ridge by the prevailing winds and forms deep drifts at the head of the Emery County watersheds. Residents of Sanpete County discovered that they could collect much of the snowmelt from these drifts and divert it to their own streams through a system of ditches and tunnels. Even though the area thus diverted made up only a small portion of the Emery County drainage basins, the effect on the usable water supply was disproportionately large. These high elevation snowfields are the last to melt, thus contributing significantly to streamflows when the remainder of the watershed is bare of snow. Because the area thus exploited was in Sanpete County, and because Utah state water law was not fully codified until after the turn of the century, there was little Emery County residents could do to prevent this diversion of their water supply though there were periodic grumblings in the local press and a few instances of vandalism of collection ditches.

Green River in the New Century

Green River entered the twentieth century as a village of only 222 residents, having lost almost half of its 1890 population with the transfer of the railroad division operations to Helper. The Palmer House stood empty, its dining facilities made obsolete by the addition of dining cars to the trains. The Farrer family still controlled much of the land and commercial activity, including the general store, the saloon, and the ferry.

Navigating the Green River. The immense irrigation and power generation potential of the river stimulated frequent development schemes, most of which required more capital than was available. There were also repeated efforts to make the river into a commercial waterway. Moab had become a productive agricultural valley but was shut off from markets by bad roads. Promoters of mining claims in Labyrinth Canyon were looking for an economical way to get equipment to their workings and haul the anticipated ore to the railroad. It seemed reasonable to some people to think of regular steamboat service between Green River and Moab. Such a route would also open up a region of scenic wonders to tourism.

The first steamboat to operate out of Green River was the *Major Powell* in 1891, a thirty-five-foot launch that proved to have too deep a draft and too little power to ply the rivers on a regular basis.[45] The next attempt at commercial service came in 1901 with F. H. Summerhil's *Undine,* a shallow-draft sixty-foot stern-wheeler with a twenty-horsepower steam engine. After considerable difficulty, the *Undine* completed its maiden voyage to Moab but capsized in a riffle eight miles above Moab in May 1902 and was crushed on the rocks.[46] The most ambitious craft to attempt the Green River to Moab run was the *City of Moab,* fifty-five feet long with a ten-foot beam, two decks, a dozen staterooms, and two thirty-horsepower gasoline engines. Launched at Green River with great ceremony in May 1905, the boat never succeeded in reaching its namesake destination.

Smaller boats had better success. Edwin T. Wolverton's twenty-seven-foot gasoline-powered launch, the *Wilmont,* navigated the

Green and Grand rivers with some success from 1903 to 1908. Wolverton operated a smaller boat, the *Navajo,* until 1912, transporting prospectors and tourists and carrying supplies to his ranch at the mouth of the San Rafael. Other gasoline-powered craft included the *Marguerite,* operated by the Tom Wimmer family from 1906 to 1925, Milton Oppenheimer's fourteen-horsepower side-wheeler *Paddy Ross,* and Henry E. Blake's twenty-five-foot *Utah.*[47]

Float trips on the Green River had begun with the pioneering J. W. Powell excursion in 1869. Several trappers worked along the river around the turn of the century. Parties of explorers and adventurers embarked from Green River in 1896, 1898, 1900, and 1902. In 1907 Bert Loper, Ed Monette, and Charles Russell ran the Green and Colorado River canyons with three steel-hulled boats. Loper spent the rest of his life boating and prospecting on the rivers.[48]

The Land Boom. The oil boom of 1901 brought many prospectors and promoters to Green River, among them E. T. Merritt, who came from Portland, Oregon, but had Midwestern roots and connections. Intrigued by the region's potential for development, Merritt remained after most other oil men had departed. He began buying options on farms and ranches in 1904, at the same time promoting the region as a fruitgrower's paradise. A "peach boom" in the Grand Valley around Palisade, Colorado, had sent land prices soaring, and Merritt proclaimed that Green River was on the verge of a comparable boom. Similar views were held by Green River resident Frank Cook. Sometimes cooperating, sometimes in competition, Merritt and Cook and their associates were to be the chief influences on the coming land boom.

Both Merritt and Cook were buying land extensively from old settlers by 1905. Prominent among those who took their profits and departed were the Farrer family, most of whom moved to California between 1905 and 1906. In the spring of 1905, the Green River correspondent to the *Emery County Progress* reported, "New people are coming in almost daily" to look over the area. David S. Gillies sold his farm to a group of prospective settlers from Anita, Iowa, led by Dr. F. R. King and George Thurman. Gillies, who also had a ranch on the San Rafael, did not leave the area but used some of his profits to build "a fine 7-room house which will be the finest dwelling in town so far." By February 1906 the Cook and Merritt Land Company had acquired fifteen thousand acres and was showing land to as many as "thirty homeseekers a day." The boarded-up Palmer House was refurbished and reopened to serve the influx of visitors. The J. T. Farrer farm was platted by Cook and Merritt as the Orchard Home Subdivision, promoted as "the finest residential portion of the new Green River City." The Gamage orchard was subdivided into six one-acre lots, all purchased by families from the same town in Minnesota. A group from Palisades, Colorado, split the sixty-acre Wimmer farm into five smaller plots. The plan was to greatly expand the acreage under cultivation by pumping water to a highline canal and then to subdivide both the new land and the existing farms into smaller ten- to twenty-acre plots for intensive cultivation.[49]

Town Development. The old Blake townsite was obviously inadequate to the promoters' ambitious plans. The *Progress* correspondent wrote in December 1905, "The need for a properly laid out townsite is perfectly clear. Every day inquiries are being made about lots for residence purposes, and there is not a lot available." In February 1906 the Green River Land and Townsite Company, composed primarily of Merritt and Cook interests, purchased Joseph Gamage's desert land above the gravity canal and north of the railroad tracks for $10,000. This property had previously been occupied by stockyards and squatters' shacks. (The railroad depot and the Palmer House were on the south side of the tracks.) The Gamage land, with some additional property acquired from J. T. Farrer, was platted as the First Division with twenty-nine business and residential blocks and a tier of blocks on the west intended for schools, court house, library, and other public purposes. Each residential block was divided into thirty-two lots measuring 25 by 125 feet—a common size for town lots in the Midwest, but a marked contrast to the spacious farm-village lots in other Emery County towns. The town of Green River was incorporated in September 1906 with an area of 1,298 acres, including the Farrer (Blake) plat, the First Division, the Orchard Home subdivision, and some additional riverside land.[50]

The first structure on the new townsite was a livery stable erected by former-outlaw Matt Warner. Several other buildings soon followed, including the Merriell-Bollinger Lumber Company, the

Melrose and Metropole hotels, an ice plant, a butcher shop, a millinery, and the Wade Opera House with the W. F. Asimus hardware store and the Broadway Drug Store on the ground floor. Mrs. Eugenie B. Simonson, who arrived in 1908, was probably the first female licensed pharmacist in the region. The Green River State Bank, with R. M. Eldred as president and Frank Cook as a major stockholder, was organized in July 1906, and work began shortly thereafter on an impressive bank building. The gothic-revival Community Presbyterian Church was dedicated in October 1907. Modern Woodmen and Knights of Pythias lodges were established in 1906. In 1908 Orient Lodge 15 was established by the Masonic Order. This was to be one of Green River's most important and lasting social institutions. Apparently attracted by the prospect of a large and prosperous town, the railroad reorganized its divisional structure, once again making Green River a division point, and erected machine shops and an eight-stall engine house.

The new town was designed to be entirely up-to-date. Broadway was graded and graveled, and a sewer system was installed. Franchises for telephone and electric service were awarded early in 1907. A telephone system was in operation before the end of the year, but electric service had to wait until 1914 before a hydroelectric generator was successfully installed. A chamber of commerce was established, and the weekly *Green River Dispatch* began publication in 1907, continuing until 1920. Several blocks of concrete sidewalks were laid in 1909 and subsequent years. Early in 1911 Green River beat out Price by two weeks to become the first city of the third class in southeastern Utah.[51] Still, the new townsite was never fully occupied nor well watered. Dorothy Nethery Crawford, whose father, Thomas George Nethery, served as pastor of the Green River Presbyterian Church from 1910 to 1916, recalled that "the desert began at our back door."[52]

New arrivals soon overcrowded the small Green River school. In 1910 a two-story concrete-block building was erected on one of the plots reserved for public buildings at the west end of town. A long-sought wagon bridge across the river was completed in December 1910, funded by a state appropriation and additional funds from Emery and Grand counties. Governor William Spry made two visits to Green River to attend the dedication ceremonies for both the school and the bridge.[53]

Land and Water Development. Work on a new diversion dam began in 1905 under the supervision of O. S. Buell. Built of heavy square-sawed timbers, the dam was intended to divert water into the Gravity Canal more dependably than earlier diversion works had done and also to serve as a source of water power to generate electricity and to pump water into a high-line canal forty-two feet above the river level. By early April 1907 a dam 543 feet long and 24 feet high was completed just in time to be destroyed by spring flood waters. Despite water delivery problems, some twenty-five thousand fruit trees, mostly peaches, were planted in the spring of 1906 and an even larger number the following year. More than ten thousand crates of cantaloupes were shipped in 1906, marketed in Denver and Chicago under the "Queen of the Rockies" brand.[54]

The Mutual Irrigation Company attempted to bond to rebuild the dam in 1908 but was unable to sell its bonds in a tight credit market. The company then installed steam-powered pumps in order to deliver some water for the 1908 season. The following year George E. Thurman accepted the responsibility for reconstructing the dam. Over the next forty years, he established a dam that he claimed was "as much a part of the river bed as the ledges which hold the river up in the canyons."[55]

Waning of the Boom. The inability of promoters to deliver a dependable supply of water put a damper on the land boom. Some newcomers became disenchanted with the region and returned to their Midwestern homes. People who had purchased property on easy terms were unable or unwilling to make the payments, precipitating numerous defaults and foreclosures. The Green River State Bank, undercapitalized and heavily invested in overpriced local real estate, was declared insolvent and taken over by state banking officials in December 1907.[56]

The peach orchards that had died from lack of irrigation water were replanted and bore their first bumper crop in 1915. A combination of low prices and high freight rates, however, made it so that "the commission men were the only ones who made any money—and the growers still owed the railroad company for freight."[57] After thousands of trees were destroyed by cold winter temperatures in 1916, the peach orchards were replaced by apples, cantaloupes, and alfalfa. While the market remained strong for Green River melons, many of the small farms proved uneconomic and were consolidated into larger units. The new land under the Forty-two-Foot Canal, originally intended for subdivision into small farm-home plots, was sold for taxes and lay idle for several years. In 1917 it was acquired by Sam Wilson and sons, who developed one of the largest farming operations in the county.[58]

Ranges and Livestock

By 1900 Emery County ranges had been extensively grazed for more than a quarter of a century. Livestock numbers, especially sheep, had reached a historic high, and competition among growers was intense. Nevertheless, with open and unregulated ranges the livestock industry still provided an opportunity for an enterprising young man to begin from scratch and accumulate substantial holdings. Sheep-raising was especially appealing because the animals multiplied more rapidly than cattle and yielded a double crop of wool and meat. Many sheepmen got their start by herding on shares, building their own herds over a few years' time. It was a common practice to give children a few sheep of their own to run with the family herd, which might through cooperative effort multiply and provide a good start on a livelihood when a son came of age or a daughter was married.

A leading example of successful stockraising was Peter Johansen (better known as "Pete Joe"), who got his start as a young boy herding milk cows in the Sanpete foothills. Collecting his pay in the form of heifer calves, he had built a herd of 150 cattle by the time he reached his midtwenties. In 1889 he homesteaded a quarter section near the mouth of Huntington Canyon as a base for his ranching operations. Here he met and married Zora Cook, whose family was also engaged in stockraising. In 1903 Johansen purchased the Reynolds ranch and additional land in Joe's Valley and moved his headquarters to Castle Dale. The substantial brick house that he erected in 1912 stands, in the words of grandson Oral Eugene Johansen, "as a monument of stability and permanency to those who believe that the agricultural way of life is a permanent way of family living."[59] Several other Emery County families can boast of similar traditions.

If there were opportunities for livestock growers, there were also many risks including unpredictable markets, unpredictable weather, poisonous plants, predators, and thieves. A cold snap during lambing season could wipe out a year's profits, and deep snow on the winter range could destroy entire herds. Emery County history affords a number of examples of men like Pete Joe who began with nothing but determination, ambition, and a capacity for hard work and accumulated substantial holdings of land and livestock. But there were others, perhaps no less capable, who suffered disastrous losses and in a few instances were driven to desperate measures in an attempt to preserve their livelihood. One of the county's largest stockmen and landowners at the turn of the century was bankrupt and a convicted felon by 1910.[60]

Range and Watershed Damage. By the turn of the century, the number of sheep on the Wasatch Plateau was estimated as high as 800,000, far in excess of the range's sustainable capacity. A U.S. Forest Service grazing examiner reported in a 1911 study that "between 1888 and 1905 the Wasatch Range from Thistle to Salina was a vast dust bed, grazed, trampled, and burned."[61] Sanpete residents who were alive during that period recalled being able to count the number of sheep herds on the mountain by the dust clouds visible from the valley. As watersheds were stripped of vegetation, floods became more common and more severe, especially on the steep canyons of the western slope. Manti, Ephraim, and Mount Pleasant experienced floods that deposited mud and boulders throughout the towns. There were damaging late-summer and autumn floods also on Castle Valley streams in 1897, 1900, 1907, and 1909, washing out bridges and carrying away haystacks and farmland.[62]

Pollution of the domestic water supply by sheep herds bedded close to streams was a serious concern for Castle Valley residents. The *Progress* reported in August 1901, "The people of Huntington, as well as in other towns, are growing weary of drinking filth from the sheep and stock on the headwaters of our streams." The following month Ferron residents convened an "anti-sheep" meeting with the reported results that "Ninety-nine out of every 100 of our citizens are opposed to sheep being allowed to graze on the summer range . . . drained by Ferron creek." Several sheepherders were arrested for "befouling the waters" of Emery County streams. Convictions were rare, however, because the the law covered only pollution that occurred within seven miles of town.

Senator Thomas Kearns, defending the powerful woolgrower interests in the state, declared at the height of the debate over livestock numbers in 1904, "If it be true, and scientific men tell us it is a fact, that water purifies itself within three miles, then it occurs to me that all that is necessary . . . is to guard the streams against contamination from that distance." However, Huntington resident William Howard had anticipated and refuted that line of argument several months earlier when he wrote to the *Progress:* "when we dip up a bucket of water from our town ditches to drink or cook our food in, and find sheep droppings in it, as we often do, all the science on earth cannot make us believe it is pure water." Further supporting evidence for Howard's position, had he but known it, was to be found in the typhoid fever that was endemic in the county during this period, claiming many lives each year.[63]

In addition to health concerns, some local observers made a connection between overgrazing on the Wasatch Plateau and reduced late-season streamflows. Castle Dale residents who crossed the mountains to attend a circus in Mount Pleasant in August 1902 returned with reports that the country was "dry clear to the top of the range and on either side. The fellows that don't like sheep attribute this condition to these animals."[64]

Establishment of the Manti National Forest. In 1900 L. R. Anderson was elected mayor of Manti on a "no more floods" platform and immediately set about petitioning President Theodore Roosevelt to create a national forest reserve to protect the Manti Creek watershed.[65] In November 1901 a group of Huntington residents requested that the proposed reserve include the Huntington Creek watershed to protect it "from the abominable contamination of sheep camp and other filth." Meetings in early 1903 led to a proposal that the forest also include critical watershed in Ferron and Salina canyons but that it be "no larger than is necessary and eliminate such areas as are most suited for agriculture and grazing."[66] The Manti National Forest was created by executive order of President Roosevelt on 29 May 1903 though its exact boundaries were not established until some time later.

At the time of its extablishment, according to the first forest supervisor, A. W. Jensen, "360,000 sheep with known ownership were grazed on the forest. . . . Likely there were a great many more of unknown ownership."[67] The initial plan for 1904 divided the forest into five grazing districts and called for a limit of 100,000 sheep and 15,000 cattle and horses, with no sheep at all to be permitted on the critical Sanpete Valley watersheds. This drastic reduction brought predictable protests from the woolgrowers, who claimed that there were currently 700,000 sheep on the Wasatch Plateau and requested that 400,000 be permitted during the 1904 season.[68] An Emery County group, on the other hand, drafted a petition supporting the 100,000 limit and requesting that one-third of the sheep permits be set aside for Emery County residents. Apparently this petition had little effect. The number of sheep permits for 1904 was successively raised to 125,000, then to 175,000, and eventually to 300,000, the great majority of which were allocated to Sanpete County stockmen. The *Progress* complained,

> Through their superior organization and annual assessment of members, the sheepmen easily gained a victory over the farmers and owners of a small number of sheep, cattle, and horses. The Manti Forest reserve is now a sheepman's preserve, and the presumed objects for which it was created are . . . practically nullified. . . . Fully one-third of the area of the reserve lies in Emery county, but out of 300,000 sheep that will be allowed to overgraze it this year, less than 15,000 will be owned by residents of this county.[69]

Despite this initial appearance of capitulating to the large Sanpete sheep interests, Supervisor Jensen adopted a long range strategy that earned the respect of a majority of residents on both sides of the mountain. Sheep permits were reduced below 200,000 and cattle permits increased to 28,000 by 1907, thus placating Emery County cattlemen. Jensen invited the stockmen themselves to draw the boundaries between grazing districts. When it was necessary to reduce grazing permits during drought periods, Jensen's stated policy was "to maintain the little man in their status quo and reduce stock of big owners." Over time, grazing permits were restricted to operators who farmed land in valleys adjacent to the forest. To protect the fragile watershed along the skyline ridge, Jensen imposed the "mile limit," allowing stock to graze within one mile of the summit only at the end of the season. He also established a nursery in Upper Joe's Valley under the supervision of Ranger J. W. Humphrey to replenish and improve the timber. Some 200,000 seedlings from this nursery were transplanted to various sites on the forest.[70]

Changes in the Livestock Industry. The establishment of the Manti National Forest and attendant regulation of livestock grazing brought changes to the industry as some large operators liquidated their holdings and others sought to acquire deeded grazing land to compensate for reductions on the national forest. In 1916 Congress passed the Ferris Bill providing for 640-acre grazing homesteads. Several Emery County stockmen obtained grazing land on the Tavaputs Plateau under provisions of this act.[71]

The regulation of grazing on the national forest led in the short term to heavier use of grazing lands on Cedar Mountain, the Tavaputs Plateau, and the San Rafael Swell, with attendant conflicts between Emery County and Carbon County stockmen. In 1912 Joseph Smith of Desert Lake acquired a herd of goats, apparently the first introduction of this animal to the county's ranges. Other goat herds followed and proved destructive to vulnerable rangelands because they grazed below the surface of the ground, destroying the vital crowns of bunchgrass and other forage.[72]

Livestock Associations. Manti National Forest supervisor A. W. Jensen encouraged the formation of local livestock associations to represent the interests of the stock growers in dealings with forest officials. The Emery County Livestock Association was established in February 1906, with James B. Crawford, Peter Johansen, George Fox, and Sam Aiken as officers. This association was initially intended to represent all Castle Valley stockgrowers, but its membership was practically restricted to Orangeville and Castle Dale. A short time later, the Farmers Livestock Association was organized by a group of cattle and horse owners in Huntington. Officers included Miller E.

Black, Martin Jensen, D. H. Wood, William Marshall, William Cook, J. H. Leonard, and E. Marion Guymon. The Ferron Cattlemen's Association was established in early 1908 with Samuel Singleton, Clyde Nelson, L. A. Olsen, Joseph Nelson, and A. G. Conover as officers. These associations undertook measures to improve the quality of range cattle, which until this time had been mixed breeds. The Huntington association purchased thirty Durham bulls in 1906, and a group from Orangeville acquired fifteen purebred Hereford bulls in 1907.[73] Over time, Herefords became the standard breed. The livestock associations also provided a means for cooperative roundups and for the construction of fences and stock-watering facilities.

Associations were also organized for grazers on nonforest ranges. In 1906 a group of Cleveland stockmen banded together to develop the springs and manage the range on Cedar Mountain. This action was apparently taken in response to "newcomers" fencing off one of the springs for exclusive use. At about the same time the Sinbad Reservoir Association was formed for the purpose of developing stock-watering ponds on the San Rafael Swell.[74] Emery County livestock growers were also active in statewide organizations, with Alonzo Brinkerhoff of Emery serving as president of the Utah Cattle and Horse Growers' Association from 1919 until his death in 1923.

Dairy Farming and Creameries. Probably a majority of Castle Valley families kept one or more milk cows. In many cases these were not dairy breeds but mixed breed animals similar to those running on the range. Butter beyond that required for home consumption was bartered to local stores or marketed by peddlers to the coal camps. Butter was a relatively high-value commodity, and it was natural that those seeking ways to increase farm income would look to an expansion of dairy production and the establishment of local creameries to manufacture butter and cheese.

Cooperative creameries—most of them short-lived—were built in many small Utah communities during the early years of the twentieth century. This development was largely stimulated by equipment manufacturers, who painted glowing pictures of the large profits to be made. In most instances, however, the local milk supply was insufficient to keep the expensive equipment in profitable operation. Lowry Nelson recalls the remark of a Utah commissioner of agriculture during the 1920s to the effect that "Every community in Utah is bounded on the west by a deserted creamery."[75]

The Ideal Creamery in Ferron and a creamery in Huntington began operations in 1905. The Twin City Creamery, located between Orangeville and Castle Dale, was built in 1906. The Huntington creamery closed in 1907. The Twin City Creamery operated rather sporadically for several years. The officers of the Ideal Creamery soon realized that their operation was suffering from "a lack of good dairy cows." Samuel Singleton and William Killpack traveled to Nebraska and Iowa to purchase a carload of Jersey cows. This introduction of quality dairy stock into the county was perhaps the most lasting legacy of these early creameries.[76]

Crops

Emery County agriculture continued in a mixed farming mode, with much acreage devoted to forage crops, most importantly alfalfa, to support domestic livestock and serve as supplemental feed for range animals. Oats and wheat were still the chief grain crops.

Alfalfa Seed. Probably the most important cash crop during the first decades of the twentieth century was alfalfa seed, with some clover seed also being produced. Alfalfa flourished throughout Castle Valley except where the soil was waterlogged. Once established, the deep-rooted plants could survive without late-season irrigation. In a good year some farmers reported earning $100 or more per acre from seed crops, a very profitable return in 1910 dollars. However, alfalfa seed production was not easy. Conditions had to be just right for a good bloom, and a rainy spell during blossom time could make for poor pollinization. An early frost could destroy the entire crop, as could a hailstorm at harvest time.

Farmers in the Emery area were the first to realize the full potential of alfalfa seed as a cash crop. Being farther from markets than other growers in the county, they could appreciate the high value per pound. Emery farmers harvested seed worth $50,000 in 1906 when they shipped twelve carloads. A single grower, John S. Lewis, earned a reported $10,000 from his 1906 crops, including alfalfa seed. (To put this income into perspective, the eight-room Emery school cost

$6,500 when it was built in 1904.) The *Progress* commented, "Every man who has a little lucern patch has the same as a little gold mine."[77]

A September frost reduced the 1907 return at Emery to less than $15,000. By this time, however, other Castle Valley farmers had discovered the value of the crop. In 1909 the county's alfalfa seed harvest was valued at $150,000, and J. H. Otterstrom of Cleveland reportedly averaged $140 per acre for one twenty-acre plot. Depending on seasonal growing conditions, yields remained high for the next decade, hitting a peak of 665,000 pounds with a value of $165,000 in 1919. The first serious alfalfa weevil infestations were also reported during that year. Yields declined throughout the 1920s, and by the early 1930s the county was for all practical purposes out of the seed business.[78]

Honey. Honey and alfalfa seed were complementary crops. Alfalfa required pollinizing by bees, and the alfalfa and clover blossoms were essential to the production of the distinctive "Castle Valley white" honey. By the turn of the century, several carloads were being shipped each year to St. Louis, Chicago, and other eastern and midwestern markets, where the light colored honey was especially popular with candy manufacturers. In 1902 the Emery County Beekeepers Association had thirty-one members whose 821 colonies produced 107,262 pounds of honey. Production reached 416,000 pounds in 1910. Emery County was consistently among the top two or three counties in Utah in honey production.[79]

Fruit. The fruit boom that was largely responsible for the growth of Green River between 1900 and 1910 also had an impact in other parts of the county. Each prospective new land development was promoted as being ideal for fruit growing, and several thousand trees were planted each year. Growers soon learned by sad experience that most areas of the county were not suitable for commercial fruit production. The only fruitgrowers to make consistent profits were those whose microclimatic and soil conditions enabled them to harvest a crop when others failed and who were thus able to exploit the local market. Ferron continued to lead the west-county communities in fruit production, and some growers found moderate success on the Castle Dale north bench. Even the most successful fruitgrowers, however, tended to reduce their orchard land by the 1920s as they found the average return was insufficient to justify the intensive care required to produce quality fruit.

Booms and Busts

The opening of a new century found a mood of expectancy in Emery County. Obviously the region was rich in natural resources, and it seemed that growth and prosperity were always just around the corner. An important contributing factor to this mood was the establishment of the *Emery County Progress* in September 1900. After a short period during which the weekly newspaper was operated by the Crockett brothers of Price, publishers of the *Eastern Utah Advocate,* the *Progress* was acquired by H. T. Haines, who continued as editor until 1909. Haines was a journalist of the old school who viewed a newspaper's chief role as boosting the local community. It is likely that booms and busts would have occurred even without the influence of Haines and the *Progress,* but the newspaper was certainly an instrument for inflating the booms. About the busts it was conspicuously silent.

According to editor Haines, "Paying quantities of almost every mineral that is known to exist are found in Emery county."[80] These words expressed the hopes of many a prospector. The Summerville mining district east of Cedar Mountain continued to be the site of much activity but only limited lead, zinc, and silver production.[81] The Copper Globe claims in the southern part of the San Rafael Swell were tied up in court disputes for several years. Efforts were made in 1915 to develop an on-site reduction plant fueled by charcoal from the nearby pinyon and juniper woodlands.[82] A large quantity of wood was cut and stacked but little if any copper produced.

Elsewhere in the county, Charles Swasey, Peter Mickel, and Victor Olsen reportedly discovered copper and silver ore in the Temple Mountain area in 1901. Peter Frandsen of Castle Dale located a silver and lead deposit in the northern San Rafael Reef near Cottonwood Wash in 1906.[83] Exploration work continued intermittently at the Sorrel Mule mine. The ZCMI Mine developed by Joseph Swasey, Amos Stevens, and others in Coal Wash similarly saw sporadic work over a period of several years. There was a small gold rush in the East Mountain–Grimes Wash area in 1903 and again in 1909. Other efforts to exploit the county's mineral resources included the reported discovery of marble deposits in Lost Spring Wash and in Coal Wash; a "great ore ledge" located on the San Rafael River by James Jeffs, George Ipson, and Jerome Asay; ozokerite deposits at Mexican Bend; manganese near the point of Cedar Mountain; copper, silver, and gold ore in Keg Spring Canyon; copper at Bench Mountain near Muddy Creek; and alunite in the Sinbad region. Attempts at commercial development of the gypsum deposits south of Cedar Mountain included an effort by the Day brothers of Lawrence in 1911 to market "plaster stone." In 1914 a syndicate announced plans to build a plaster factory and a new town east of Cleveland.[84]

Uranium was reportedly discovered at Temple Mountain as early as 1898. Oscar Beebe, Ira Browning, and Seymour Olsen filed the "Orinoco" claims in 1904 at a location Beebe had discovered while herding sheep. Joseph Swasey also discovered uranium in the Temple Mountain area around the same time. The remote and rugged location delayed development, but by 1910 the interest in the "wonder" element radium was high enough to justify the long haul across the Green River Desert to the railroad. Other deposits of high grade ore, chiefly in the form of uranium-impregnated petrified wood, were discovered near Tidwell Bottoms in 1902. A similar deposit, the "Tom Boy" claim, was located east of the San Rafael bridge by Alfred Forsman of Green River and Hite Loveless and Brigham Nielson of Huntington in 1911. The *Salt Lake Mining Review* reported "some thirty or forty claims" along a three-and-a-half mile stretch of the San Rafael Reef. One carload, purchased by the American Vanadium Company of Baltimore, reportedly sold for $1.20 per pound.

The discovery of rich deposits in the Belgian Congo in 1915 brought an end to the demand for Emery County uranium. At this period the commercial value of uranium ore was chiefly in its radium content. Uranium itself had "comparatively few" uses, as the *Progress* noted in 1914: "It is employed principally for making yellow glass, for yellow glazes on pottery, and in a less degree as a chemical reagent."[85]

Oil. Oil seeps and hydrocarbon-impregnated shales near the Green River and at several places on the San Rafael Swell had attracted intermittent interest from the early days of settlement.

Major oil deposits had been discovered in anticlinal geological structures somewhat similar to the San Rafael Swell. It seemed a natural assumption that if anticlines held oil then the huge dome of the Swell might be an immense petroleum reservoir. The *Progress* of 8 December 1900 contained a brief note that a man from San Francisco had come to Green River to develop "oil mines." By the following spring, a prospecting frenzy was in full swing, the county recorder's office having processed 1,183 claims, more than had been filed in any previous complete year. A single day brought 291 claims. The *Progress* devoted a front-page column each week to the oil boom, and other news items noted the comings and goings of local residents to their claims. A July 1901 editorial proclaimed, "Good times for Emery county: plenty of coal, plenty of oil, plenty of manganese, plenty of copper and plenty of railroad inside of two years."[86]

Two wells were drilled in the Sinbad area between 1901 and 1902 by the San Rafael Oil Company with drilling equipment hauled to the site with great difficulty. Sinbad Number Two was reported as producing twenty-five barrels a day in April 1902, with a pipeline planned to transport the oil to the railroad at Desert Switch. Either the report was incorrect or the production could not be sustained. In any event, both Sinbad wells were abandoned before the end of 1902. A well near Woodside was abandoned when the drilling tools became stuck in the hole. A well some nine miles south of Green River reportedly struck oil at 1,500 feet in April 1902. By September 1903 the *Progress* remarked somewhat ruefully that there was "not much noise" about oil. The sole remaining drilling rig was sold for taxes in February 1904.[87]

Sporadic exploration activity continued over the next several years. A Philadelphia syndicate filed 654 claims in the Sinbad region in 1907. The Muddy Creek region became a center of attention in 1911 and 1912 with several hundred filings and two holes drilled east of Emery. The American Oil and Refining Company went so far as to survey a town in Sinbad, to be called Oil City. The Tasker well near Green River was drilled in 1912. Another oil boom between 1921 and 1922 brought drilling at Green River, Sinbad, Salt Wash, Woodside, and Huntington. Signs of helium in the Woodside well led to a large tract of land being set aside as a government reserve.[88]

Railroads. Castle Valley residents had never given up hope of seeing a railroad completed along the Spanish Trail route. Editor Haines fed this hope with almost weekly articles whose persistent theme was that the "Castle Valley railroad" made such good economic sense that it would have to be built sooner or later. The Denver and Rio Grande Western added periodic fuel to these rumors by sending survey crews into the county. In 1902 a route was staked out from Salina Canyon to a connection on the main line at Farnham, east of Wellington. The same year the railroad began work on twenty miles of expensive roadbed from Salina to the Ireland (Mountain) ranch. Since the road as constructed led to nowhere, it seemed inevitable that it would be extended at least as far as the D&RGW coal claims in Ivie Creek Canyon. But the unfinished roadbed lay idle, and high waters destroyed large sections in 1906.[89] One purpose of the Salina Canyon construction seemed to be to forestall the entry of other railroads into the region. Whenever another line indicated some interest in the Salina Canyon route, the D&RGW would send out a token construction crew to "repair" a portion of the roadbed, thereby reaffirming its claim to the route. These practices provoked *Progress* editor David Williams to complain in 1913 of the railroad's "blocking tactics."[90] The D&RGW finally completed a railroad to the coal mines at the head of Salina Canyon in the late 1920s, but the "Salina Cutoff" was to go no farther.

Coal

The most abundant mineral resource in Emery County is of course coal, with extensive deposits in the Wasatch and Tavaputs plateaus and in the Ferron Sandstone formation. In the early years of the century, several small mines continued to serve local markets. Among the most noteworthy operations were the Deer Creek and Bear Creek mines in the Huntington Canyon area; the Johnson Mine in Cottonwood Canyon; the Oliphant and Black Diamond mines in Straight Canyon; the Reid, Anderson, and Otteson mines in Grimes Wash; the Axel Anderson and Killpack mines in Rock Canyon; and the Casper Christensen mine in Miller Canyon southeast of Emery. In addition, the Larsen-Rigby mine and several small mines in

Valentine Gulch in upper Huntington Canyon served the Sanpete Valley market.[91]

Major firms including the Kemmerer Coal Company and the Utah Fuel Company acquired large tracts in Ivie Creek and Convulsion canyons, sometimes by questionable methods, but little actual development work occurred there during this period. In 1906 former Huntington resident Don C. Robbins acted as agent for the Freed interests of Salt Lake City in acquiring some 2,500 acres of coal land in Huntington Canyon. The government later charged that this property had been fraudulently obtained, and the Freeds did not gain clear title until 1916. In 1910 Ira Browning's San Rafael Mining Company opened a mine in the Ferron Sandstone south of Emery. The Browning mine was later operated by E. H. Duzett.[92]

Mohrland Beginnings. Sometime before 1896 brothers William and Erin A. Howard opened the first mine in Cedar Creek Canyon, eight miles north of Huntington. Apparently, however, they failed to obtain title to their 160-acre claim and discontinued their operation after a short time. In 1896 three Grange brothers, Samuel S., Ulysses W., and Ernest J., together with Albert C. Gardner, acquired ownership of this property and operated the mine for twelve years. After the turn of the century, William Howard and sons opened another mine on a forty-acre property. Like other small "wagon mines" in the county, these mines were worked primarily during the fall and winter seasons to provide fuel for home heating. The Cedar Creek coal seams were so thick that customers could drive their teams and wagons into the mine and load directly from the face.[93]

Early in 1907 a syndicate led by Salt Lake City attorney James H. Mays began buying land and water rights and conducting engineering surveys in the Cedar Creek area. (The four owners of the Grange-Gardner mine accepted a reported $500 each for their property.) By August the syndicate, incorporated as the Castle Valley Fuel Company, had surveyed a townsite called Mohrland, a name formed from the initials of four major investors: Mays, A. J. Orem, Moroni Heiner, and W. V. Rice. By December, general foreman Erin A. Howard was directing "quite a number of men" in developing "the biggest size coal veins in the state."[94]

At about the same time as the Mays group was acquiring prop-

Mohrland. (Utah State Historical Society)

erty in Cedar Creek Canyon, another syndicate, the Consolidated Fuel Company, purchased the nearby Miller ranch and began developing the Hiawatha mine in the middle fork of Miller Creek Canyon. This group also organized the Southern Utah Railroad and obtained a right of way from Price to Hiawatha. The Castle Valley Fuel Company established the Castle Valley Railway, which connected with the Southern Utah at the mouth of Miller Creek Canyon and proceeded around the point of the mountain to Mohrland following the general route of the present county road. Railroad construction as well as tipple, tram, and townsite development in both Mohrland and Hiawatha occupied the years 1908 and 1909, providing employment for many Emery County teamsters, timber workers, carpenters, and laborers. The Mohrland mine began shipping coal by rail in April 1910, although the tramway from mine to tipple was not completed until sometime later.[95]

As was common in new mining camps, the demand for labor outran the development of community amenities, and some Mohrland workers were forced to live in tents or dugouts during the

Castle Valley Coal Company Store, Mohrland, 22 February 1911. (Utah State Historical Society)

early years. The Castle Valley Fuel Company experienced financial problems in 1910 that led to a delayed payroll and default on some construction debt. Still, the building of a town went forward at a good rate. By October 1910 Mohrland could boast of "a complete water system, a fine office building and store, a number of well-built residences, a large tipple," and other improvements. Construction continued throughout 1911, and in that year Mohrland also gained another neighboring community when an Ogden syndicate opened the Black Hawk Mine in the south fork of Miller Creek Canyon and established a company town with "a large number of modern residences." The Black Hawk mine was in Emery County though the town was in Carbon County.[96] (The town known in later years as Hiawatha was originally Black Hawk. The original Hiawatha, two miles to the west, was later known as West Hiawatha and was largely dismantled during the 1920s.)

In January 1912 James H. Mays bought out the interests of the other major investors in the Castle Valley Fuel Company. In March he sold the company to the Boston-based United States Smelting, Refining, and Mining Company, which operated metal mines and smelters in the Salt Lake Valley. The USSR&M acquired the Black Hawk and Consolidated companies at about the same time. All three coal mines were absorbed into a USSR&M subsidiary named the United States Fuel Company in 1915. United States Smelting also incorporated the Utah Coal Railway and constructed a new line along the foothills from the mouth of Price Canyon to Mohrland, thereby avoiding the steep grade below Hiawatha. Little or no heavy freight traffic passed over the Castle Valley–Southern Utah Railway after the completion of the Utah Coal Railway, but passenger service continued until 1917 when the bridge across the Price River was destroyed by the Mammoth Reservoir flood.[97]

Improvements at Mohrland continued under the new ownership. By the early 1920s, there were more than two hundred houses, a large amusement hall, a small hospital, a four-room school, and a population near one thousand. Because space was limited in the narrow canyon, Mohrland grew into several distinct neighborhoods, which tended also to divide along ethnic lines. The main part of town, on a relatively level site at the mouth of the canyon, was largely populated by people of British or Scandinavian stock, many of them coming from other Emery County towns. "Silk Stocking Row," where the mine officials lived, extended from this area into a small side-canyon to the south. Another cluster of houses stood on a hill to the west known as "Gobblers Knob." "Tipple Town," at the mouth of Ben Johnson Canyon north of the tracks, was occupied mainly by residents of Italian, Slavic, or Finnish extraction. Two additional housing clusters farther up Cedar Creek Canyon toward the mine were occupied by Japanese, Greeks, and African-Americans.[98]

Much community pride in the coal camps was vested in the local baseball team, and there were always jobs available for good players. In the spring of 1915, the Mohrland team, as champions of the Carbon County league, was selected to play the Chicago White Sox in an exhibition game at Price. A crowd estimated at more than 10,000 turned out to see the game, which was won by the major league team by a score of 17 to 1.[99]

Construction and Manufacturing Industries

While agriculture, livestock, and mining were the county's economic mainstays, construction-related activities were also important during this period. New schools and other public buildings were erected in almost all communities, as were new and larger business buildings and many homes and farm structures. Locally burned brick (and unburned adobes for inner linings) continued to be used in many buildings. Most of the lumber used in the county also continued to be locally produced. The establishment of the Manti National Forest brought regulation of the lumber industry, with sawmill operators required to obtain permits to cut timber. Still, a significant number of sawmills were regularly in operation during the summer months. The Huntington Lumber Company, incorporated in 1907 by John F. Monson, LeRoy Strong, George M. Miller, and Joseph E. Johnson, operated a sawmill in Huntington Canyon and a planing mill in Huntington for several years. Ferra Young and sons, Martin Jensen and sons, and some others ran sawmills in Huntington Canyon. Carl Wilberg operated a mill near Seely Creek for several years then sold it to A. Gardner Jewkes, Frank Killian, and Clyde and Arthur A. Van Buren. This sawmill operation continued in the Van Buren family until 1950. Claiborne Elder had a mill in Reeder Canyon, and Henry Lord operated one near the Cap on Horn Mountain. George Petty and sons ran a sawmill in Ferron Canyon for many years. The original mill established in the Muddy Creek drainage by Rasmus Jacobsen, Ed Torgensen, and Chris Jensen in 1893 was acquired by Hans Jensen, G. M. Burr, and Joe Christiansen in 1912. This operation remained in the Jensen family until 1945. A sawmill also operated on Cedar Mountain for a time, harvesting the small stands of Ponderosa pine.[100]

Several inventions by county residents fostered hopes for establishment of manufacturing industries. Orangeville blacksmith Joseph S. Grange invented what was described as "a very useful & simple farm implement . . . variously known as a pulverizer, lay-off and go-devil." Short-lived foundries were established in both Orangeville and Castle Dale to manufacture the Grange implement. In 1902 B. F. Luke, manager of the Orangeville Co-op, acquired rights to Grange's invention, named it the Utah Lay-off Machine, contracted with a foundry in Logan for its manufacture, and undertook an active marketing campaign involving demonstrations at state and county fairs in Utah and surrounding states.[101] The "King Cultivator and Clod Breaker" was developed by E. M. Cox of Orangeville in 1904, and in 1911 Cox and Grange together received a patent for an "improved furrower." It is not clear whether these implements were ever marketed on a commercial scale. In 1903 Huntington resident William Howard was promoting a locking headgate of his own invention designed to prevent tampering with irrigation water settings.[102] George Ipson of Huntington invented a "station indicator," designed to display approaching stops on streetcars. Ipson died before he could put his invention on the market, but the Station Indicator Company remained in business for several years with headquarters at first in Price and later in Salt Lake City. Several county residents held stock in the company or were involved in selling stock throughout Utah and Idaho. It does not appear, however, that the company achieved its goal of having the Ipson Indicator widely adopted by streetcar companies.[103]

Making a Living

The 1900 census listed sixty-one different occupations in Emery County, including a wide range of crafts, trades, and professions.[104] The occupational range indicates a maturing of the economy, with a base in agriculture and stock raising but with probably no more than half of the families drawing their primary income from their own land and livestock. Insofar as this economic diversification provided opportunities in business, trades, and professions, it represented a positive development. However, it was apparent that the county's population was outgrowing its economic base. "Day laborers" constituted a significant occupational category, with, for example, twenty-four male heads of family so classified in Castle Dale and twenty in Orangeville. This designation was applied in most cases to men who had no regular employment and owned little or no land apart from perhaps a town lot. They might pick up work at sheep-shearing time or during harvest season on the farms and perhaps occasional building, road, or timber work, but it appears that at least one out of every five heads of household was chronically underemployed. It is also likely that some men listed as farmers possessed only small plots of land and depended on irregular day labor for a significant portion of their income.

The chief source of employment in the region was the Carbon County coal fields. Emery County men had worked in the mines of Pleasant Valley and Castle Gate from the early years of settlement. At least eleven of the 200 dead recovered in the Winter Quarters mine disaster of 1 May 1900 had homes in Emery County. Allan Kent Powell has pointed out that the toll of Emery County residents would almost certainly have been higher if the explosion had occurred during the winter. By 1 May many men had returned to their farms for the summer.[105]

The year 1899 saw the opening of a new coal mining and coke manufacturing operation at Sunnyside. The need for construction workers and miners at Sunnyside corresponded conveniently with the growing labor surplus in Emery County. The *Progress* reported in 1901 that this "flourishing coal camp" was "building up more rapidly than any other town in Eastern Utah. . . . Among the residents are many Emery county people. The camp is also a good market for the farmers of this county, and would consume many times as much produce, at good prices, than we are now supplying." From Lawrence came a report that "About one-half of our men folks have gone to Sunnyside to work on the new coke ovens." It would appear, however, that this did not represent a permanent relocation for most of them, because a few weeks later the same correspondent wrote, "Most of the men who have been working at Sunnyside the past winter have returned home for the spring work."[106]

Other jobs that took county residents away from home for extended periods included construction work, sheep shearing, and ranch work. A 1912 report from Orangeville stated, "A large number of men are leaving town, going in different directions to work." Men and teams from Orangeville and Desert Lake built railroads in Colorado and Nevada and canals in Idaho.[107]

An example of the variety of mostly short-term jobs relied on by many Emery County families can be seen in the life of George H. Westover, who came to Castle Valley in 1890 or 1891 from the

Mountain Meadow area in southern Utah. He married Alice Ann Leonard in 1898, and after a few years the couple acquired a small plot of land on the outskirts of Huntington and built a three-room log and frame home. Here they brought up six children. In order to provide for his family, George Westover ranged far and wide in search of work: shearing sheep at Colton or Scofield in the spring; doing field work in the summers with his fine team of horses on the Miller ranch some fifteen miles north of his home or at Quitchupah forty miles to the south; driving the stagecoach from Price to Fort Duchesne during the winter; serving for several years as an assistant ranger on the Manti National Forest; helping to construct the coal camp of Kenilworth; threshing, baling hay, hauling coal, peddling produce to the coal camps. In later years he rented a farm in Huntington Canyon. Never physically strong, never owning more than a few acres of land, hardly ever having what would now be regarded as a regular job, George Westover nevertheless provided a respectable living for his family and saw to it that all of the children received an education, "so that they needn't do housework for other people, or pick-and-shovel work all their lives."[108] Of course these things could not have been accomplished without the cooperative efforts of Alice Ann and the children, who kept up the house and small home acreage, raised most of their own food plus garden produce to sell, sewed their own clothing, and raised and dressed turkeys each year for the local Thanksgiving market.

Other county residents scraped a living out of relatively small farms. Albert Ferdinand Behling, who immigrated from Germany in about 1906 and settled on a forty-acre farm west of Ferron, "never worked for wages," but as his son Richard recalled, "we got along all right":

> We had a team of horses to farm with and a hand plow. . . . Mother had setting hens . . . and hatched her own chickens. We sold the eggs to the store. She would carry the eggs about 2 miles to the store and then exchange them for things we needed. We didn't buy many groceries because we raised most of what we needed. . . . It was a long time before we had a car. In fact we didn't even have a buggy, just horse and wagon. We went to church in the wagon some but most of the time we walked the 4 miles to church to go to

> Sunday School, then walked home to eat dinner then back to church for the afternoon meeting.[109]

With variations, similar stories could be told of dozens of Emery County families.

County Government

County officers served for two-year terms during the early decades of the century, which meant that local "politicking" occurred at frequent intervals. As a general rule, Emery County tended to follow the political trends of the state and nation. The county voted predominantly Democratic in 1900 and 1902 and Republican from 1904 to 1912. In 1914 the county joined in the state and national Democratic sweep, with not a single Republican winning election to a county office. In 1920 the county again followed state and national political trends with a swing to the Republicans.

The county's influence in state government was probably greater during these decades than in any period before or since. In 1908 both major party candidates for the office of state auditor were from Emery County, with the Democrats running James W. Nixon of Huntington and the Republicans Jesse D. Jewkes of Orangeville. Jewkes won the election, and after a four-year term as auditor was elected as state treasurer in 1912. William J. Seely of Castle Dale served as speaker of the state House of Representatives in 1913.[110] Mark Tuttle of Orangeville was elected state auditor in 1920. State senator Alonzo Brinkerhoff of Emery (1906–10) was a strong voice in the legislature for the prohibition of alcohol, and representative Ira R. Browning of Castle Dale (1914–16) was author of the state's first automobile licensing act. Browning later served as chief engineer of the fledgling State Road Commission until his death in 1926.[111]

An interesting sidelight on Emery County politics during this period was the presence of an active Socialist Party organization from 1904 until about 1914. The Socialists established precinct organizations in Ferron, Castle Dale, Huntington, and Cleveland, sponsored lectures, held county conventions, and ran a full slate of candidates at each election, receiving about 10 percent of the local vote in 1910 and 1912, well above the 6 percent they received nationally. While they never succeeded in capturing a county office, the Socialists did elect a justice of the peace and a constable in Cleveland in 1910. Lily Engle of Huntington contributed several articles to the state Socialist newspaper.[112]

Roads and Bridges. A large share of the attention and funds of the county government continued to be devoted to the effort to maintain the roads in a passable condition. At almost every meeting, commissioners had to deal with petitions requesting or protesting the realignment of a route, pleading for a bridge, or complaining about the condition of a particular stretch of road. New bridges were constructed between 1901 and 1907 at Ferron, Orangeville, and Lawrence, across Muddy Creek near Emery, and across the San Rafael River on the Green River-Hanksville road. Several washes were bridged on the main (Price-Emery) county road, and improvements were made to the Straight Canyon, Huntington Canyon, Huntington-Cleveland, and Castle Dale-Green River roads. The *Progress* noted in 1904 that "every cent that can be spared from the public treasury is being put into roads and bridges." This work must have seemed futile at times, however, as spring high waters and summer flash floods damaged or destroyed bridges almost annually and the unsurfaced roads deteriorated almost as soon as they were improved, becoming "a liquid mess" during wet seasons.[113]

A period of heavy rains in September 1909 destroyed every bridge between Emery and Price with the exception of the Huntington bridge. This compelled the county to resort for the first time to bonding. The $35,000 thus raised provided for steel truss bridges on Muddy Creek and at Ferron, Castle Dale, Orangeville, and Huntington. The old Huntington bridge was moved to the Cedar Creek crossing. Some of these bridges remained in use for more than fifty years. The largest project of the period was the erection of the five-span steel truss Green River bridge in 1910.[114]

The Automobile Age

The first reported automobile passed through Emery County in June 1907 on a well-publicized cross-country trip from Death Valley to Boston. Frank Cook of Green River had acquired a car by early 1908. By 1911 there were several automobiles in the county. In September of that year, Samuel Singleton and his sons-in-law

Edmund Crawford and David Seely drove Singleton's Maxwell from Castle Dale to Green River, following the old railroad grade. In 1913 the mail began to be delivered by moter vehicle, which proved to be faster but less reliable than horse-drawn mail coaches.

The first business establishment in the western part of the county to cater expressly to automobiles was the Midland Garage established in Castle Dale in 1913 by C. T. Bowen. (The garage was later converted to a feed mill by P.C. Jones and Sons and was still standing in 1995 as part of the Coast to Coast Hardware store on East Main Street.) This business was acquired by the Alger brothers in 1915, with S. N. Alger as manager. The Alger Garage obtained a Ford franchise and was reported as doing a "landoffice business" by 1916. At that time a new Ford runabout could be purchased for less that $500 (a price reduced to under $400 by the mid-1920s), which made it an appealing alternative to the horse and buggy for many county residents. George Miller erected the Huntington Garage in 1917. It was managed in its early years by Martin Black, "Shorty" Shaw, and the Mills family. (This brick building at the corner of Main and First North was still standing, much remodeled, in 1995.) The Huntington Garage had a Studebaker franchise in 1918. Edward M. Crawford of Orangeville, recently returned from an LDS mission to the center of the automobile industry in the Midwest, opened a second garage in Castle Dale in 1919 with a Buick agency. The Marshall brothers erected a garage north of the church in Huntington in 1919. Green River had two garages in 1918, the Franz Brothers Ford agency and the Green River Valley Auto Company, managed by L. H. Green. Earl V. Hills was operating a garage in Ferron the same year.[115]

With the automobile came automobile accidents. The first reported auto fatality in the county was Castle Dale attorney A. D. Dickson, whose car overturned near the Wilberg ranch in 1914. Apparently the first collision between two cars occurred just north of the Huntington bridge in August 1919 between a Price businessman and a carload of Huntington boys returning from a baseball game at Mohrland. Fortunately, no one was seriously injured.[116]

The coming of the automobile stimulated a national "good roads" movement. In Utah this movement led to the creation of the State Road Commission in 1909 and a more substantial involvement of both state and federal governments in road building and maintenance. The Price-Emery road was upgraded between 1911 and 1912 with improved drainage and several steel culverts. Improvements extended south of Emery in 1916, with steel truss bridges being erected at Quitchupah and Ivie creeks.

In 1913 one of the first transcontinental highways, the Midland Trail, was routed through Green River. The original plan was to follow the old railroad grade through Cottonwood Wash and Buckhorn Flat and continue over Wasatch (Salina) Pass. Under pressure from more populous sections of the state, the route was soon changed to cross Soldier Summit, even though the Price Canyon road was barely passable at the time. This route was improved during subsequent years by a combination of public and private efforts. O. R. Gillespie of Green River took personal responsibility for the stretch between Green River and Woodside and drew praise from motoring associations for keeping it in good condition. A ninety-foot cable-supported bridge was built at Woodside in 1915, funded by the state and county with contributions from Salt Lake City automobile clubs. Before the building of this bridge, motorists used the railroad bridge to cross the Price River during high-water periods. The Salina Canyon Route Association was organized in 1913 for the purpose of securing a national highway through Wasatch Pass. In 1921 the Pike's Peak Ocean to Ocean Highway was routed from Green River to Price to Salina.

The Orangeville-Ephraim road was designated as a state highway in 1916 after a bitter intracounty fight between the advocates of that route and those who supported the Huntington-Fairview route. The chosen plan involved building the steep White Dugway above Joe's Valley and also constructing a new road on the north side of the creek in Straight Canyon to replace the old south-bank road that was actually under water in some places during periods of high streamflow. Work on this road proceeded slowly, delayed by the war, but was finally completed in 1920. Continuing efforts by residents in the north part of the county led to the Huntington-Fairview route being added to the state highway system in 1919. The final stretch of this road, from the Forks of Huntington Creek to Connellsville, was completed in 1926.[117]

"Good roads" was something of a euphemism. Significant improvements were made in bridging streams, but the road surfaces were still nothing but Emery County "blue clay," dusty in the summer and rutted and slippery during wet weather. The county purchased several horse-drawn graders that were dragged over the roads periodically to level the ruts. A concrete road from Price to Emery was proposed in 1918, but the cost of such a project was far beyond the available resources.

Prohibition

While there had always been some local resistance to the establishment and operation of saloons, the first sustained effort to eliminate the liquor trade began in 1908 with "temperance meetings" in several towns. The first strategy adopted was to increase business license fees for saloons to prohibitive levels. Green River's four saloons closed their doors when town officials doubled the license fee from $400 to $800 per year. This closure was only temporary, however. Mass meetings in other towns demanded saloon license fees as high as $10,000. When these proposals came to the town councils, however, they ran up against the hard reality that the standard $400 liquor license fee provided a substantial portion of the operating expenses of town governments. While many citizens were eager to close down the saloons, they were less willing to raise their own taxes to compensate for the lost revenue. Nevertheless, Huntington, Ferron, Orangeville, and Castle Dale all ended up by setting their fees at $1,200, which proved sufficient to cause local saloons to shut their doors. Apparently some business continued to be conducted behind closed doors, however. In October 1909 George Brandon of Castle Dale was arrested in a "sting" by state officers who came to town pretending to be thirsty traveling salesmen.[118]

Both major political parties in Utah included a prohibition plank in their 1910 platforms, and local option prohibition was passed by the 1911 state legislature after Governor William Spry threatened to veto a bill calling for statewide prohibition. All Emery County towns with the exception of Green River voted "dry," thus bringing the liquor trade to an end in theory. In practice, however, there continued to be a market for liquor and people willing to risk the penalties of the law in order to supply that market. The Huntington correspondent to the *Progress* remarked in 1912, "We are inclined to think that whiskey is being sold here to quite an extent." The Orangeville correspondent reported a few months later that "too much of the prohibited" was showing up in that town.[119] Statewide prohibition was adopted by the 1917 legislature, and the Eighteenth Amendment to the U.S. Constitution became effective in 1920, prohibiting the manufacture, sale, or transportation of alcoholic beverages throughout the nation.

As prohibition expanded, so did the bootlegging industry. A roadblock at the Huntington bridge in the predawn hours of 4 July 1917 resulted in the arrest of thirty county residents who were bringing liquor from Carbon County to enliven the holiday celebrations. In February 1919 two Salt Lake City men attempted to cross the county in a roundabout effort to transport 1,175 bottles of whiskey from Wyoming to Salt Lake. Driving powerful Cadillacs capable of outrunning the cars of local law enforcement officers, they evaded attempts to capture them at Price. Alerted by a telephone message, Sheriff Levi Howard and Huntington town marshal Erin T. Howard set up a roadblock at the Huntington bridge. One car stopped, but the other ran the roadblock, headed south to the Wilberg ranch, then attempted to double back through Lawrence and Cleveland. Sheriff Howard commandeered the captured Cadillac and set out in pursuit with Huntington garage operator "Shorty" Shaw at the wheel. They found the fugitive stuck in the Castle Valley mud south of Cleveland.[120]

Churches

By some measures, the early decades of the twentieth century might be seen as a period of declining influence for the dominant LDS church in Emery County. Mormons were a minority in Green River and Mohrland, and virtually all towns had some residents—including prominent figures in business and the professions—who were not affiliated with the LDS church. At least eight county officers and two state representatives elected during this period were non-Mormons. Several others were nominal but inactive LDS church members. Sunday afternoon baseball games frequently attracted a larger attendance than church meetings. In contrast to the LDS church's later emphasis on wide involvement and frequent rotation of assignments, church officers at the turn of the century tended to remain in their positions for years—in some instances decades—and a small core of individuals carried the main responsibility for the operation of the ward. For example, the Cleveland Ward had only three bishops in sixty-two years. Alonzo Brinkerhoff served as bishop in Emery for twenty-six years, and even then was released only by death. Still, stake and ward leaders continued to be highly influential in public affairs, often exercising more actual power than local government officials. (In many instances, of course, church leaders also held positions in state, county, or town governments.)

Changes in LDS Leadership. The years around the turn of the century saw the passing of leadership in the Emery Stake and its wards from the pioneer generation to a younger group of leaders. In January 1899 the founding stake president, Christian G. Larsen, was succeeded by Reuben G. Miller.[121] Miller and his counselors, John H. Pace and Henry G. Mathis, were all residents of Price, making that town the real headquarters of the stake for the next decade. The latter years of President Larsen's tenure had apparently been marked by some dissension, especially in his home town of Castle Dale. An interval of almost two years followed the release of Henning Olsen as Castle Dale bishop before a successor was sustained, at least in part because of differences between the stake president and local ward members that required the intervention of church leaders from Salt Lake City to resolve. A report of a stake conference held in Castle Dale in April 1898 stated:

> The trouble of long duration which has existed at this place between the president and members was amicably settled and John Y. Jensen was chosen bishop with F. M. Reynolds and Peter Frandsen as counselors. In President Larsen's trial one charge was sustained, that of domineering. On seeing that this charge would be proven the president asked for forgiveness.[122]

Born in 1861, Reuben G. Miller was more than thirty years younger than his predecessor. President Miller served until 1910 when the Emery Stake was divided. At that time Woodside and Green

River were included in the new Carbon Stake, with G. A. Iverson of Price as president. Lars P. Oveson, who had served as bishop at Cleveland since that ward was organized in 1890, became president of Emery Stake with Alma G. Jewkes of Orangeville and Alonzo E. Wall of Castle Dale as counselors.[123]

Apparently the last months of President Miller's administration were also shrouded in controversy. In spite of the church's formal renunciation of polygamy in 1890, the period from 1900 to 1910 brought a rash of clandestine plural marriages with the tacit approval (if not the active encouragement) of some church leaders. The *Emery County Progress* of 11 June 1910 published a letter from a missionary serving in Denmark, who quoted an article from a Danish newspaper about the resurgence of polygamy in Utah. Non-Mormon editor Jesse S. Moffitt added a comment on the extent to which "the talk of polygamy is agitating the people." He continued: "If it is not true there is a way for the circulators of such stories to be punished. If it is true there is a remedy for the state and the church to apply." More than one plural marriage took place in Emery County during this period, including a union between the principal and a faculty member at the Emery Stake Academy. Lowry Nelson, who was a student at the academy during the 1911–1912 school year, claimed that Reuben G. Miller was "involved in this matter."[124] President Miller himself had secretly taken a plural wife in 1903, reportedly at the urging of apostle Mathias Cowley. (Miller was later excommunicated from the church for practicing polygamy.)[125]

In addition to the changes in the stake, most wards also experienced a transition to a new generation of leadership during this period. In some instances the transition was not easy. When David A. Killpack was proposed as the new Ferron bishop in 1904, replacing Hyrum A. Nelson, who had served for almost ten years, the action met with some resistance with "several hands" being raised "in opposition to the selection of the new bishop."[126] It is not clear whether this opposition continued, but in any event Bishop Killpack served for only two years before moving to Idaho.

Huntington's first three bishops, Elias Cox (1879–83), Charles Pulsipher (1883–91), and Peter Johnson (1891–1902), all belonged to the same generation, born during the 1830s. A younger generation came to the fore when James W. Nixon, born in 1866, was installed as bishop in 1902. Nixon was a successful businessman, but his tenure as bishop was rather stormy. His decision to close the Huntington seminary was highly controversial. His emphasis on the Word of Wisdom was not welcomed by some ward members who felt that an occasional pipe or chew or drink of Danish homebrew was not inconsistent with good standing in the church. He offended the long-established Huntington Dramatic Club by restricting their access to church buildings for performances, and then fostered the establishment of the rival Huntington Ward Dramatic Association. Matters had reached such a point by late 1905 that stake president Miller convened a special priesthood meeting to resolve the "disunity." At this meeting Bishop Nixon tendered his resignation, claiming that ward members "did not sustain him in his ideas of presiding."[127]

Ferron Presbyterian Church. In December 1905 the Reverend J. G. MacGillivray, who was in charge of Sunday schools for the Presbytery of Utah, organized a Sunday school in Ferron with William McKenzie, Thomas H. Jones, Andrew Nelson, Miss Sylva Nelson, and Mrs. John Anderson as officers. Pastor MacGillivray remained in Ferron for several weeks during which time he located a site for a combination church and school and raised $1,000 towards its construction. The 1906 minutes of the Board of Home Missions included the following account:

> In Emery County there is other virgin territory for missionary enterprise. It includes a number of towns with an aggregate population of more than four thousand. No Christian services have ever been conducted within these bounds except the gospel tent work in Ferron last summer. The communities are Mormon through and through but they are generally of a more liberal type. A petition has been signed in Ferron by fifty persons—some of them Mormons—asking that we enter permanently in that town.[128]

The Ferron Presbyterian church was organized in August 1906 with William McKenzie and Thomas Jones as elders and John Anderson, Sophus Nelson, and Wyatt Bryan as trustees. The Reverend E. J. Hanks, a Utah native and son of the founder of Hanksville, was assigned as pastor, but before he could take up his duties he received another assignment to a theological seminary in California. MacGillivray was then assigned to the Ferron church. The church met in a dance hall above Wyatt Bryan's store and had a Sunday school enrollment of fifty-four by April 1907. In 1908 "a crowded house" was reported for worship services. A well educated man who taught classics and mathematics at the Presbyterian school, Pastor MacGillivray was apparently highly regarded in the community and was invited to deliver the patriotic oration at the 1908 Fourth of July celebration. His speech provoked controversy when some in the audience understood him to be calling the patriotism of Mormons into question.[129]

Ground was broken for a church-school building early in 1908. Apparently the financial arrangements called for local residents to construct the foundation and lower floor. Funds for the construction and furnishing of the remainder of the building would be provided by the Board of Home Missions. Work on the building continued intermittently for six years with William McKenzie as construction superintendent. The completed structure was dedicated during a convention of the Southern Utah Presbytery in April 1914. Pastor MacGillivray in the meantime had moved to Twin Falls, Idaho, in 1910, apparently being replaced by the Reverend Ralph Mix.[130]

The Ferron Presbyterian church continued in operation until 1942. While there were some dedicated local members who contributed generously to its support, it was always a mission church with most of the operating budget provided by the national church organization. The impressive gothic-revival building remained a part of the Ferron townscape in 1995.

Green River Presbyterian Church. The major religious organization in Green River's first half century had its beginnings in the establishment of a Union Sunday School in March 1906 during the heady days of the land boom. A short time later a Presbyterian church was established with the Reverend McClain W. Davis as pastor. Davis was succeeded by T. G. Nethery in 1910 and W. G. McConnell in 1917. In contrast to the mission church at Ferron, the Green River Presbyterian church was a true community church with much of the financial support coming from the local membership. Adherents of some ten different Protestant denominations united to establish the church and to build a handsome frame gothic revival building on land donated by the Green River Townsite Company. Both the design of the building and the range of activities sponsored by the church were similar to those that might be found in the Midwestern small towns from which most Green River residents had come. In addition to worship services, the church was a center of community social life. Banquets were held in the church basement, and the ladies' auxiliary sponsored outdoor ice cream socials on summer Saturday evenings with music provided by the town brass band. Unlike the LDS wards in other Emery County communities that sponsored dances on every possible occasion, the Presbyterian church frowned on this form of recreation. In 1914 Pastor Nethery was assigned "to call on all dancing church members to persuade them of the error of their ways and to notify them that all who did not give up dancing would be expelled from the church."[131]

Schools

The growing school-age population, which reached 1,734 by 1901, had made most of the existing schools inadequate. The Castle Dale school could accommodate only half of the students enrolled, and the district was obliged to rent classroom space in commercial buildings. Huntington schools were spread among as many as five different locations. Among the larger communities, only the Ferron school built in the late 1890s and the Orangeville school constructed in 1901 came close to meeting local needs.[132]

The first example of a new generation of school buildings was erected in the town of Emery between 1905 and 1906. Acclaimed as "one of the finest school houses in Eastern Utah," it was a two-story brick structure with eight classrooms. This two-story rectangular block was a popular style for schools in the period from 1900 to about 1910, and buildings on the same general model were erected at Huntington (1907), Castle Dale (1908), Green River (1910), and Cleveland (1911). All were of brick construction except Green River, which was built of concrete blocks with a stucco finish.[133]

Of these buildings, only the one in Castle Dale remained standing in 1995, having been converted to city government offices. It was erected on its present site after several years of controversy and false starts. In 1901, recognizing the need for a larger building, the Castle Dale school district obtained land on the rim of the bench from Carl Wilberg, who was beginning to market lots in the Wilberg Subdivision and no doubt saw the school as an asset to his new development. District trustees invested a substantial sum in foundation work and contracted with E. A. Jones to burn a kiln of bricks. However, several prominent residents of the lower town, led by J. W. Seely, protested the building of the school so far from the center of town. Lawsuits were brought against the school board both by local groups and by the state superintendent, claiming that public funds had been expended without proper approval. After two elections in which voters rejected proposals to build on the bench site, school trustees finally obtained a more acceptable site through an exchange of property with the Castle Dale Ward Relief Society. The school was designed by the Dallin and Hedges architect firm of Salt Lake City and built by Castle Dale carpenter and contractor C. P. Anderson.[134]

Expanding Programs. Fewer than half of the county's young people at the turn of the century completed the fifth grade. Nevertheless, a growing interest in schooling beyond that level led some local districts to offer higher grades. Huntington graduated its first eighth grade class of seven members in 1903. A ninth grade was added in 1905. Ferron was providing work through the ninth grade by 1906, and both Ferron and Orangeville instituted tenth grades in 1908. Students who sought an education beyond that available at the local district schools had several options. They could attend the Emery Stake Academy or the Ferron Presbyterian Academy. Several students left the county each winter to live with relatives and attend school in Ephraim, Manti, or Mount Pleasant. Others went to Provo or Salt Lake City. When the Carbon County High School opened in 1912, the faculty actively recruited Emery County students. A small but significant number of county residents continued their education at the college level. Apparently the first native-born Emery County resident to graduate from a university was James W. Nixon III, who received an A.B. degree from the University of Utah in 1913 and an M.D. from the University of Pennsylvania in 1918. (The first county resident to earn an M.D. was Alonzo N. Leonard, who came to Huntington as a child in 1881.[135])

Emery Stake Academy. The first two decades of the twentieth century were the golden age of the Emery Stake Academy. By the time the new building on the northwest corner of the public square was dedicated in January 1903, it was already too small for the enrollment of 120. After the relatively brief terms of George Cluff (1899–1902) and Silas A. Harris (1902–04), G. F. Hickman became principal in 1904 and guided the academy for the next dozen years. Hickman began pushing for enlarged facilities almost immediately and by 1907 had won the support of President Reuben G. Miller and the Emery Stake Board of Education for a new building. The site on a terrace of the north bench was chosen in October 1907, and the construction contract awarded to M. A. Andersen of Fountain Green in May 1908. The academy was the largest building constructed in Emery County up to that time. Of the approximately $40,000 cost, $25,000 had to be paid by Emery Stake. The balance came from general church funds. Castle Dale Ward had the largest assessment of $6,000, a sum which kept the ward in debt for several years after the completion of the building. The ward purchased the old academy building in 1909 and used it for a meetinghouse until 1952.[136]

The academy held its closing exercises in the unfinished new building in May 1910 and occupied the building in the 1910–1911 school year. With sixteen classrooms and a large third-floor assembly hall, the spacious structure was well adapted to the needs of the academy, which at that time included grades seven to eleven. A twelfth grade was added by 1914 and the seventh and eighth grades were discontinued, making the academy strictly a high school. With a faculty of eight full-time teachers, augmented by several part-time teachers drawn from the local community, the Emery Stake Academy served a studentbody ranging from 100 to 140. In addition to the educational opportunities provided to local young people, the academy was an important cultural and recreational resource for the entire community, sponsoring plays, concerts, operettas, public lectures, and debates on a regular basis. At the end of the summer, some students and faculty members would make the round of the settlements in Emery and Carbon counties in what was popularly termed the "gospel wagon," giving talks and musical performances and recruiting new students. However, students from more distant towns became fewer as other educational opportunities opened up closer to home. In its later years, the Emery Stake Academy enrollment was made up almost entirely of students from Castle Dale and Orangeville. In 1920 the LDS church made a decision to close several of its academies, including the ESA. This decision was carried out in 1922. The building was then acquired by the Emery County School District and operated for the next two decades as Central High School.

Ferron Academy. A mission school began operating almost immediately after the organization of the Ferron Presbyterian church in 1906. The school started with forty-three students and two teachers, Margaret LeVenture and Ada Taylor, both from Iowa. A report to the Board of Home Missions indicated good progress during the first year:

> Ferron, Utah, fifty miles from the railroad, where we opened a school in 1906, has had a successful year. . . . The Mormons have an academy at Castle Dale, but there is no high school in the county. A teacher's home has been erected at Ferron this year, and money is now in hand to proceed with the erection of the Forsythe Memorial Chapel school house. The people have pledged a fair sum towards this building.

In 1908 the school began offering high school level work under the name of Ferron Academy. An announcement of its academic programs described the school as "Christian, but not sectarian nor theological, though funded and sustained by the Presbyterian Church." By 1910 ninety-six students were enrolled with three teachers. However, "The late entrance of many of the pupils . . . and the dropping out for the spring work decreased the average attendance." After several years in rented quarters, the school moved to the still-unfinished church-school building in 1912. A 1913 report to the Board of Home Missions stated,

> While it is generally recognized that the need for the mission day school in Utah is nearly over, yet at Ferron special conditions have made it possible for us to seize an exceptional opportunity for the extension of the Kingdom, and this we have laid hold of with much vigor and are pushing with fine results.[137]

Enrollment at the school dwindled after the establishment of Ferron High School. By 1921 the school was known as the Ferron

Branch of Wasatch Academy, offering ninth- and tenth-grade work to students who would later transfer to the Mount Pleasant institution. At this time there were sixty students and three teachers. High school programs were discontinued in 1927, but Bible school, kindergarten, and piano lessons continued to be offered until 1942, when the Ferron mission was closed.[138]

Emery County School District. The first serious proposal for consolidating the county's twelve local school districts into a single countywide district was put forward in 1910 by superintendent Don C. Woodward. Woodward's proposal met with a mostly negative public response, and the county commission refused to act on it. The objections were the same that would be voiced in response to subsequent school consolidation proposals: communities feared the loss of control of their schools; local trustees were unwilling to give up their powers; the more prosperous districts feared the loss of funds to poorer districts; smaller communities feared losing their schools altogether. On the other hand, communities in need of larger buildings were eager to draw upon the bonding resources of the entire county. By 1912 both Ferron and Huntington had outgrown their school buildings. The Ferron school, in particular, was badly outmoded, and residents felt a need for "a new building of modern style." In 1913 county superintendent M. J. Blackburn called attention to the "pitiful" equipment available in some small districts. At Blackburn's prompting, a consolidation petition drive was launched, but once again the opposition prevailed and the county commissioners rejected school consolidation. Blackburn's next move was to propose a realignment of district boundaries to achieve more equitable funding. Valuations ranged widely, from a high of $4,147 per student in Mohrland to a low of $803 per student in Ferron. The outgoing county commission redrew boundaries in the last days of 1914, provoking strong protests and threats of legal action from the two richest districts, Mohrland and Green River. The new county commissioners restored the old boundaries in March 1915, thereby arousing the ire of the poorer districts.[139]

These local disputes were rendered moot when the state legislature passed a compulsory school consolidation bill in the 1915 session. Under the terms of this law, local districts were dissolved and a single Emery County School District came into being, governed by an elected board and with a superintendent appointed by the board as the chief operating officer. The first school board, appointed by the county commission pending elections in the fall, was composed of E. E. Adams representing Green River and Woodside; M. L. Snow representing Cleveland, Elmo, Desert Lake, and Mohrland; E. G. Geary representing Huntington and Lawrence; R. O. Justesen representing Castle Dale, Orangeville, and Clawson; and B. J. Peacock, Jr., representing Ferron, Emery, Molen, and Rochester. The elected superintendent, William T. Reid, continued in that capacity.

The new school board lost little time. By July plans were under way for a new school building for Mohrland and a high school at Huntington. In 1916 voters approved $65,000 in bonds to erect buildings at Ferron, Huntington, and Elmo. The bond issue passed despite considerable opposition in Castle Dale and Orangeville, whose residents would derive no benefits from the proposed building projects and feared the effect on the Emery Stake Academy if high schools were established elsewhere in the county. The new schools were single-story, flat-roofed structures with steam heating plants installed in concrete annexes to the buildings as a safeguard against fires. The Ferron and Huntington buildings had combined auditorium-gymnasiums that were extensively used for community as well as school activities. Evidently these were among the first buildings in this style to be erected in Utah. State school inspector Mosiah Hall was reported as saying the Huntington school was "the first of that type I have visited."[140]

In 1917 the school board responded to a request from Rochester residents by erecting a four-room school there. This proved to be excess capacity for the community's needs, as only two rooms were ever used for teaching purposes. The building of the Rochester school and expansion of high school work at Huntington and Ferron led to a fiscal crisis in 1917 and 1918. The district attempted to recoup some expenses by charging high school students a $20 tuition. The "Spanish flu" epidemic of 1918 and 1919 brought another crisis as most county schools were closed down for several months. By 1920, however, the financial situation had improved to the point that the district could bond $225,000 for an ambitious construction program that included new schools in Orangeville and Clawson, new auditorium-gymnasium wings at Emery, Castle Dale, and Cleveland, and modernized heating and plumbing systems in several of the older buildings. By this time the district was operating high schools through the twelfth grade at Ferron, Huntington, and Green River, with another soon to follow with the conversion of the Emery Stake Academy to Central High.[141]

Medicine

At the turn of the century, the county was caught up in a debate over compulsory smallpox vaccination with Representative Oliver J. Harmon of Huntington speaking out in the state legislature against the practice and Judge Jacob Johnson urging residents to avail themselves of this protection. There is no indication of how many residents were vaccinated, but it was not enough to prevent recurrent outbreaks of the disease in 1903, 1907, and 1911. Diphtheria claimed several victims in Emery in 1902 and in Huntington in 1903. Whooping cough epidemics in 1906 and 1907 took a heavy toll of infants and young children with eight dying in a two-week period in the town of Emery alone. There were also frequent outbreaks of scarlet fever. The most serious public health threat, however, continued to be typhoid, which infected dozens of residents each year, bringing death or permanent disability to many. Apparently most people failed to associate typhoid with the polluted water supply from open ditches. However, a report from Ferron in July 1912 remarked of an outbreak there, "This is very uncommon for this time of the year. Something is wrong in our sanitary conditions, sadly wrong."[142]

Castle Dale began the new century with two doctors, William P. Winters and C. E. Pearson. Pearson left for Arizona in 1904, and Winters moved to Mount Pleasant in 1905. No fewer than twelve physicians came and went during the next fifteen years. The longest service during that period came from Dr. C. J. Ferguson, who arrived in 1906 and remained until 1910, when he went to Mohrland as the first company doctor there. As county physician in 1908, Ferguson persuaded the county commission to acquire a supply of diphtheria antitoxin, the use of which probably saved several lives. He also published notices in the *Progress* urging people to boil their drinking water to prevent typhoid. Despite the long parade of practitioners, Castle Dale found itself without a doctor when the Spanish Flu epidemic arrived in 1918. Walter E. Henzi came to the community in October of that year and stayed until his death in 1936. In 1920 James W. Nixon III located in Castle Dale, remaining there until 1938.[143]

Bruce Easley set up practice in Ferron in 1904 and a year later married Ferron native Clyda Conover. He moved to the new coal camp of Kenilworth in 1909 and went from there to Hiawatha and then to Moab before returning to Ferron permanently in 1916. Dr. Easley practiced in Emery County longer than any other physician, continuing to see patients almost to the time of his death in 1955. Dr. T. C. Hill came to Huntington in 1908. Except for military service in 1918 and periods of travel for his wife's health between 1916 and 1917 and again from 1926 to 1928, he remained in the community until his death in 1947.[144]

As was usual in coal camps, Mohrland always had a resident physician and a small hospital maintained by a combination of company contributions and monthly fees paid by the miners. Practice in the camps was attractive, especially to newly qualified physicians, because basic medical equipment was provided and doctors were paid a regular salary. Among the physicians who practiced in Mohrland were C. J. Ferguson, Alfred Sorensen, a Dr. Raley, and Dr. H. W. Bernard.[145]

Midwives continued to assist at many births though their activities were sometimes resented by physicians. In 1904 Drs. Pearson and Winters published a notice in the *Progress* threatening to prosecute midwives for practicing medicine without a license. Perhaps in response to this threat, Castle Dale nurse and midwife Nathalia Wilberg Anderson completed a course offered by the state board of medical examiners and passed a licensing examination in obstetrics with the highest score in the state in 1906. She continued to deliver babies long after the complaining doctors had left the county.[146]

Paul Christensen was the only dentist who practiced throughout the period. In addition to the chambers he maintained, first at his home at Center and First North and later on Main Street in Castle Dale, he traveled to other towns in the county as well as to the

Carbon County coal camps. Dentists based in Price also visited Emery County towns.

The epidemic of influenza that claimed thousands of lives throughout the nation made its appearance in Emery County in mid-October 1918, when the *Progress* carried one article calling for precautions against the disease and another reporting that two deaths had occurred in Price. By the end of the month the disease had claimed three people at Lawrence, two at Ferron, and three at Emery. School, church, and other public gatherings were suspended in all communities except Green River and Desert Lake, which were relatively free from the disease. In place of funerals for the dead, only brief graveside services were permitted. Quarantine restrictions had little effect, however, against the highly contagious disease. By the time the epidemic began to wane in the spring of 1919, at least thirty deaths had occurred in the county. An additional four servicemen from the county died of the disease in army camps. A second visitation of influenza in early 1920 claimed an additional seven reported victims.[147] The so-called Spanish strain of influenza was not too different from other varieties of flu in its immediate effects. In most cases, the symptoms continued for about a week and the sufferers recovered with no lasting ill effects. However, pneumonia was a frequent complication, and the great majority of "flu deaths" were actually the result of pneumonia.

The flu epidemic hit the county at a time when it was short of physicians, with only Dr. Easley then residing in the Castle Valley towns. To help alleviate the crisis, Dr. Walter E. Henzi was sent to Castle Dale in October 1918 by the state medical authorities, and Dr. A. N. Leonard, a former county resident, came from Salt Lake City to help out in Huntington while Dr. Hill was serving in the military. Swiss-born Dr. Henzi had received medical training at the University of Bern and at St. Louis University and reportedly had been "for several years company physician for the Union Pacific railroad and the Utah Construction company." Like Dr. Easley at Ferron, he gave his services unsparingly throughout the epidemic, visiting patients day and night assisted by his wife, Emily, who was a trained nurse. The Henzis' dedicated labors soon earned the gratitude of county residents. Apparently, however, Dr. Henzi had for some reason had his license revoked by the state medical board. He was allowed to practice during the crisis, but when he continued to treat patients after the flu epidemic he was charged with practicing medicine without a license.

The arrival in Castle Dale of an officer of the state medical board to levy those charges with the local justice court in February 1920 caused a considerable stir. A group of leading citizens took a petition to Salt Lake City in support of Henzi, stating in part, "we understood that he was practicing with consent of the medical examiners, and at a time when his services meant so much to us in the saving of lives of our fellow citizens, whom he has practically snatched back from death." Evidently the local efforts were unavailing, and Dr. Henzi's license was not restored. However, many people continued to call on him for medical assistance, and he provided services though he was unable to charge for them.[148]

Town Growth and Development

Several towns added new subdivisions during the early years of the century, including the Wilberg Subdivision at Castle Dale, the Oviatt Addition and the Cramer Subdivision at Cleveland, the Bryan Subdivision in Ferron and the Carrol Subdivision in Orangeville. Castle Valley townscapes took on an appearance that would change relatively little for the next half century, with wide, tree-lined streets, large barns, corrals, granaries, and chicken coops in the interior of the blocks, and comfortable homes in expansive, shaded yards. Nineteenth-century house types including the square cabin, hall and parlor, and cross wing forms remained popular, but there was increased stylistic variety and local builders drew more extensively on national styles available through magazines and pattern books. One of the most interesting houses built during this period was the Edmund and Thurnelda Crawford home on Center Street in Castle Dale. This two-story brick with its pyramidal roof and wide eaves and porches was actually a "catalog" house, purchased precut from the Montgomery Ward mail-order house. This allowed for rapid construction, with the foundation being poured in late July 1910 and the house almost completed by October. Adjacent to the Crawford home was a brick apartment terrace built by A. N. Leonard in 1905 to accommodate Emery Stake Academy teachers. This distinctive structure (known as "the incubator" because many young couples had their first children while living there) is Emery County's sole example of a common urban dwelling type of the period. The T. W. Dyches home on the Castle Dale bench was the first house to be referred to as a "bungalow" in the pages of the *Emery County Progress.* The bungalow became a popular house type during the period between 1910 and 1930, with numerous examples in the county.

Town Governments. During the early years of their existence, Emery County communities had no town governments. Election precincts, justices of the peace, and school districts were under the supervision of the county commission. Other aspects of civic life were largely managed by the local LDS ward organizations. The first town to be incorporated was Huntington, in 1891. Castle Dale and Ferron followed in 1900, Orangeville and Emery in 1901, Green River in 1906, and Cleveland in 1916. Green River was the first town in the county—and indeed in all of eastern Utah—to become a third-class city, receiving its charter in January 1911. Huntington gained a city charter in January 1920, and Orangeville and Castle Dale followed later the same year.[149]

Town governments operated on very limited resources. In addition to a small property tax levy, they collected money for business and dog licenses. Saloon licenses typically yielded more revenue than all other license fees combined, which meant that prohibition brought serious budgetary problems. There were frequent complaints about the poor condition of town streets, ditches, and public squares. Domestic livestock were allowed to roam at large, grazing the roadsides and frequently getting into residents' yards and gardens. Fires were a frequent and costly hazard, whether in the form of haystacks and farm buildings destroyed by children playing with matches, homes burned as a result of overheated chimneys during winter or canning season, or larger structures whose loss was felt by the entire community. With no equipment for fighting fires, the only recourse once a blaze was under way was to rescue as much as possible of a building's furnishings. Neighbors would quickly congregate at the site of a fire for this purpose, sometimes even removing doors and windows. Among the larger fire losses during this period were the

Winters building in Castle Dale in 1906; the Ferron-Molen Coop and Wyatt Bryan stores in Ferron in 1912; the Sheya building and several adjacent business structures in Green River in August 1915; the old Huntington log church in December 1918; the newly completed E. H. Duzett store-garage-dance hall in Emery in 1919; the Nixon building containing the Bonita Theater and the Pritchett Drug Store together with the adjacent McKee building containing the Palm Hotel and Cafe in Huntington on New Year's Day 1920; and the Ferron LDS church in March 1920.[150]

Water Systems. In 1900 virtually all county residents still obtained their culinary water by "ditch dipping," typically carrying water from the ditches in buckets and storing it in wooden barrels, sometimes adding alum or prickly pear juice to settle out the mud. Ditch water was muddy during spring high waters or summer stormy periods. It was difficult and sometimes impossible to keep water running in the town ditches during the winter, compelling people to haul water from creeks that were in some instances several miles away.

Around the turn of the century, some residents attempted to improve the quality and accessibility of water by constructing concrete cisterns near their homes. These were filled with water from the town ditches, and the cisterns served as both settling ponds and storage containers. In 1909 Edmund Crawford, David Seely, and A. D. Dickson jointly built a cistern on Dickson's bench property to supply their homes on Center Street in Castle Dale with piped-in water under gravity pressure.[151]

Apparently a water system was installed at Green River when the new townsite was developed between 1906 and 1907. Cleveland was the first community in the western part of the county to have a public water system, beginning work on a town cistern in 1909. Molen had a system in limited operation by early 1911. Both of these systems were cooperatively built by local contributions and labor. Mohrland enjoyed piped-in water from the beginning of its existence, provided by the coal company. Huntington bonded for a town reservoir and water lines in 1912 and had the system in operation by early 1913. After a failed attempt in 1908, Castle Dale approved bonding in 1913 and had a water system by the end of 1914. In Orangeville at least two cooperative groups, the North Side Cistern Company and the Central Cistern Company, were at work in 1915. These companies later merged into a single system. Ferron installed a cooperative system on the Orangeville model in 1916 and 1917. Elmo and Clawson built cooperative systems between 1918 and 1919, and Emery issued waterworks bonds in 1919.[152] While these systems made culinary water much more convenient, they did nothing to eliminate disease-causing organisms in the water.

Telephones. Lines of the Emery-Carbon Telephone Company were extended to Ferron by 1905, shortly before the line was acquired by the Eastern Utah Telephone Company, managed by Reuben G. Miller. Miller's company added connections to Emery in 1906, to Molen in 1911, Elmo in 1917, and Victor in 1918. This remained a long-distance toll line with only a single station in each community. Green River had a local telephone system by 1907 but did not gain long-distance connections until several years later. Eastern Utah Telephone installed a local exchange at Castle Dale in 1907 but apparently found this service unprofitable and discontinued it in 1913. Under the leadership of C. E. Larsen, the Castle Dale Telephone Company, organized in 1914, took over the system, installed new switching equipment, extended local service to Orangeville, and also arranged a connection with the Forest Service telephones. Local exchanges were put in operation in Ferron, Cleveland, and Emery between 1909 and 1913, but only the Castle Dale-Orangeville system remained in operation for more than a few years.[153]

Electricity. A proposal was made as early as 1903 for a water-powered electric generating plant at the Orangeville roller mill to serve Orangeville and Castle Dale. J. W. Seely reportedly installed a small generator in 1904 powered by the same waterwheel that ran the Eagle Roller Mill equipment in Castle Dale. In 1905 Seely and C. L. Allen moved a steam engine from the Castle Dale foundry to the Eagle mill to power a generator that began service to Castle Dale in January 1906 and to Orangeville in March. The lines were strung on cedar poles imported from Oregon and installed in the middle of the streets. The power plant operated only during evening hours, and service was billed according to the number of lights installed. It soon became apparent that the steam plant was not only unreliable but too expensive to operate. Seely and Allen joined with the owners of the

Orangeville mill to form the Electric Power and Milling Company and install a water-powered generator at the Orangeville site between 1907 and 1908. Under the management of Allen and B. F. Luke, the company began to provide daylight service one day each week in 1909. This was for the primary purpose of providing power for "wash day." Service continued to be erratic. The plant was sometimes out of commission for days or even weeks at a time while waiting for parts to be shipped in or for the feeder ditch to be repaired after flood damage. Chief engineer Allen had ambitious plans for a large hydroelectric plant on Cottonwood Creek to serve the entire western portion of the county, but he was unable to obtain financing. In 1911 Allen and Luke sold out to John H. Taylor and sons and moved to Salt Lake City. The Taylors operated the generating plant until 1926 and the distribution system until 1930.[154]

The new convenience of electric power brought new hazards. In 1911 Frank Petty, full-time barber and part-time electrician of Castle Dale, was killed while installing a telephone connection in the new home of Lars P. Oveson. At that time electric and telephone lines were strung on the same poles, and Petty apparently misjudged the time when power would begin to flow through the lines.[155]

Other communities in the county were several years behind Castle Dale and Orangeville in entering the age of electricity. Green River installed a generating plant at its irrigation diversion dam in 1915. In March 1915 the Huntington Electric Light and Telephone Company was organized by a group of local investors with more than one hundred subscribers. This company obtained power rights on Huntington Creek and was well along in planning for a hydroelectric plant when in July 1915 Utah Power and Light Company announced plans to extend its lines to Carbon and Emery counties. Utah Power reimbursed the Huntington investors for the money they had expended and acquired the Huntington franchise, beginning service in late October. Power was initially supplied from a coal-fired generating plant at Black Hawk, Carbon County.[156]

Utah Power's original plan was to serve all of western Emery County, but negotiations for the purchase of the Castle Dale-Orangeville company broke down. As time went on, Utah Power apparently found its Huntington service unprofitable and lost interest in extending its lines to other parts of the county. In 1919 the south county communities united to request service from Utah Power. The company agreed on the condition that it be paid an installation fee of $100 per customer. Unable to raise this sum, the communities proposed in 1920 to organize their own distribution company and buy electricity at wholesale from Utah Power. This plan also failed to materialize, and areas south of Castle Dale did not receive electric power until the mid to late 1920s.[157]

Retailing. These were good years for retail merchants in the county as population, income, and demand for goods increased, while distance and bad roads kept most of the business at home. Some merchants also operated as commission houses, marketing the alfalfa and clover seed and honey produced in the county as well as such commodities as grain, butter, and eggs that were often used in lieu of cash in making purchases at the store. Still, operating a retail business in the Emery County market was not easy, and the failure rate was high. Most customers charged their purchases, and many were slow to pay. Merchants' advertisements in the *Progress* were marked by frequent pleas and occasional threats to customers to settle their accounts. Almost inevitably over a period of a few years, a merchant would accumulate thousands of dollars in uncollectable accounts. In addition to general stores, the Emery County business scene included a number of specialized operations such as farm implement dealers, drug stores, millinery shops, butcher shops, and confectionaries. Innkeeping was not a large business (except perhaps in Green River during the land boom), but almost every town had its "hotel," even if it was only one or two spare bedrooms rented out to commercial travelers.

The largest of the five general stores in Ferron at the turn of the century was the Ferron and Molen Co-op, which had its origin when a group of local investors sent Samuel Singleton to Salt Lake City with $250 to buy a stock of goods. When he got to the wholesale houses, Singleton realized that this money was entirely inadequate for the purpose and added $1,600 of his own that he had just received from the sale of cattle. Thus he became the largest stockholder in the business from the beginning and increased his ownership share over the years by buying up the stock of other investors. The original building on West Main Street was destroyed by fire in January 1912, and Singleton built a forty-by-sixty-foot two-story brick building with a glass front on the same site. Under the name S. Singleton and Company (except for a period around 1920 when the store was known as Singleton and Conover), this business continued in operation through three generations.[158] Another long-lasting retail business began in 1915 when Lewis W. Petersen acquired a small store at the corner of Main and State streets and named it Ferron Mercantile Company. He erected a larger brick building around the original frame structure and added a drug store on the west side. The store burned in 1923 but was rebuilt. Lew Petersen, with the assistance of other family members, remained active in the management of the Ferron Merc into his eighties.[159]

Castle Dale had no fewer than thirteen general stores between 1900 and 1920, but no more than four at any one time. If the businesses themselves lacked permanancy, certain business locations formed lasting centers of the town's retail trade. The two-story building erected by Dr. William P. Winters on the southwest corner of Main and Center streets (rebuilt as a single story structure after a fire in 1906) was home to at least four different retail operations before it was acquired by Leonard Huntington and sons in 1928. This business continued for many years under the name of Huntington Brothers. The large two-story building erected on the south side of Main Street by James C. Petersen in 1906 was acquired by the Castle Dale Cooperative Company in 1910. The Co-op continued in business at this location under a succession of owners until the early 1980s. Probably the most successful operator was Albert D. Keller, who managed the store from 1916 to 1941. Samuel P. Snow, Jr., erected a drug store at the corner of Main and First East in 1910. This business was acquired by A. R. Coe in 1917 and then by Lorin T. and Claire Hunter in 1923. The Hunters operated the drug store for fifty-two years. Other important businesses in Castle Dale included the Anderson Hotel, which operated for more than sixty years on the northeast corner of Main and First East, the branch of the Consolidated Wagon and Machine Company managed by C. E. Larsen on West Main Street, and the Richard C. Miller lumber yard on East Main Street.[160]

Huntington had four general stores at the turn of the century, the largest of which was the Huntington Co-op located in an adobe-and-frame building on the west side of Main Street between Center and First North. In 1900 James W. Nixon purchased a small store operated by Ann Pulsipher on the northeast corner of Main and First North streets and expanded both the premises and the business into a full-line grocery-clothing-hardware-building supply-farm equipment store. In 1903 the Co-op moved into a new two-story brick building (the lower floor was still standing in 1995). In 1900 a group of local investors organized the Huntington Mercantile Company and began operations in what had been the Elias Cox store on the northwest corner of Main and First North. In 1908 this company was reorganized as Miller Mercantile Company, managed by George M. and Mina Johansen Miller. These three general merchandise operations dominated the scene until 1914 when the Co-op discontinued operations. The same year Miller Mercantile moved into a large new brick building (still standing in 1995). In 1916 Miller Mercantile sold out to Ross C. Bowen, who continued in business as Bowen Mercantile until 1923. In 1919 J. W. Nixon sold his store to Edward G. Geary, who operated Geary Mercantile until 1937. The main hotel was operated by Ruben and Ivy Brasher next door to the Nixon store on Main Street.[161]

Green River had the county's largest and most varied business community during the land boom and its aftermath—and also the highest turnover rate as many businesses were established in hope of growth that fell short of expectations. Firms in operation in 1918 included three general stores, William F. Asimus, Beebe and Sons, and E. E. Adams's Square Deal Store; a men's clothier, Eben E. Johnston, and the Misses Vandlings' women's store; two garages; two livery stables; two theaters, two billiard parlors; a butcher shop; the Broadway Drug Store; the Bonneville Lumber Company; and a weekly newspaper, the *Dispatch.* However, with the exception of the *Dispatch* and Rufus A. Wood's meat market, not a single business listed in the 1908 directory was still in operation a decade later. The growing importance of Green River as a tourist service center was evident in the town's three hotels, the Midland (named for the Midland Trail, the first transcontinental highway to pass through Green River), the Metropole, and the Melrose House.[162]

Emery had three general stores in 1908 plus two hotels, a millinery shop, a confectionery, and a saloon. Ten years later there were still three stores but only one hotel, still a confectioner but no milliner, and Prohibition had closed the saloon. The most permanent businesses were those operated by E. H. Duzett and Brigham J. Peacock.[163] Orangeville had six general stores in 1900 but only two by 1908, pioneer merchant John K. Reid and the Orangeville Cooperative Mercantile Institution. By 1920 Reid had gone out of business, the Co-op had become Crawford, Luke, and Company, and the Peacock Cash Store had been established.[164] Cleveland had two stores that remained in business throughout this period, the Cleveland Co-op and the Litster Cash Store.[165] The smaller communities typically had a single general store and sometimes not even that. Woodside, as a railroad stop, also boasted a livery stable and a saloon. Mohrland was home to almost seven hundred residents by 1920 but as a company town was restricted to a single company store supplemented by numerous peddlers.[166]

Banking. The year 1906 saw the establishment of the county's first banks. The Emery County Bank opened in Castle Dale in August with James Crawford, Jr., of Manti as president and several prominent Emery and Sanpete County men as officers and directors. Crawford, who also controlled the Manti City Savings Bank, had lived in Orangeville for periods during the 1880s and early 1890s and had run livestock on Emery County ranges. His son Edmund was made cashier, a position he held throughout the bank's independent existence. Young Edmund moved to Castle Dale and, in a manner of speaking, consolidated interests in the bank by marrying Thurnelda Singleton, whose father, Samuel, was vice president. After the death of James Crawford, Jr., in 1911, Singleton became president and James B. Crawford of Orangeville (a cousin of James Crawford, Jr.) vice president. The bank was located in the former Ottosen furniture store building on East Main Street.[167]

The Green River State Bank, established during the 1906 land boom with R. E. Eldred as president, G. M. Stevenson as cashier, and Frank Cook and associates as major stockholders, survived for less than a year and a half before being declared insolvent and closed by state banking officials. A successor institution, the Fruit Growers State Bank, was organized in 1909 with "Doc" Bricker, C. C. Jones, George Thurman, John Byers, and E. E. Adams as officers and directors. This bank conducted its business from the substantial concrete block building at the northwest corner of Broadway and State Street. It too fell victim to speculative loans on overvalued real estate and was forced to close in 1917. The Commercial and Savings Bank, organized during the 1920–21 oil boom, was later renamed the Commonwealth Bank and survived until the 1933 "bank holiday."[168]

The Castle Valley Banking Company opened its doors in October 1913 in specially designed quarters in the new Miller Mercantile building in Huntington, with officers and directors including Peter Nielson, George and Mina Miller, W. A. Guymon, Jr., Edward G. Geary, and Mount Pleasant banker Rasmus Anderson. The bank was never able to attract sufficient deposits to make it a viable financial institution and requested a cancellation of its charter after only four years of operation. It did, however, manage to pay all depositors in full before closing.[169]

The First World War

The entry of the United States into the European conflict in April 1917 was to have a significant effect on life in the county. All men between the ages of twenty-one and thirty were required to register for the draft in June, and the first group of thirteen were inducted into the army in August (some had volunteered earlier). Before the end of the war, several dozen Emery County men enlisted or were drafted, and eleven lost their lives, three dying from combat injuries and the remainder from disease and accidents.

On the home front, the declaration of war brought the organization of a county Council of Defense and several committees to encourage production and reduce waste, the motto being "Produce and Conserve." New food crops were planted, including a substantial acreage of pinto beans. Local LDS Relief Societies sold their stored wheat that had been accumulated by gleaning. A local chapter of the American Red Cross was organized and enlisted county women in making bandages. Another chapter at Green River produced 4,442 articles of clothing, with one woman, Mrs. C. O. Moons, contributing 2,417 hours. There were "Soldiers Day" celebrations and send-off parties for inductees, and the *Progress* filled its columns with letters from servicemen. Wartime labor shortages brought higher wages at the coal mines and led to difficulties in securing harvest hands. Stockmen benefitted from higher prices, while at the same time the rising prices for consumer goods brought hardship to those whose incomes did not match the inflation rate. Nevertheless, the patriotic spirit was high in the county. Emery County was the first county in the state to go "over the top" in the first Liberty Bond drive and eventually doubled its quota. The miners at Mohrland were especially generous, leading the county in bond purchases. After the war's end, many county women helped knit shawls and other warm clothing for Belgian relief efforts.[170]

Recreation

The large population of young people made the first decades of the twentieth century a period of extensive social and recreational activities in the county. Dances were frequent and heavily attended. The fiddlers and accordian players who had provided music for dancing in the pioneer period were replaced by dance bands playing popular music. The Johnson-Jewkes orchestra based in Orangeville and the Mohrland orchestra were in demand throughout Emery and Carbon counties. Community theater groups continued to provide local entertainment. The Emery Stake Academy was an important cultural and recreational resource, providing not only plays, operettas, and concerts, but also public lectures and debates. W. King Driggs, father of the King Sisters who would later make a name in popular music, taught at the Academy in 1911 and 1912 and staged his original opera *The Navajo Princess.*

Wedding parties were a prominent social activity. In most instances, these were rather informal affairs centered on dancing. Perhaps the most elaborate wedding of the period was that of Delis Lemon and Joseph A. Peterson of Ferron in September 1902. The marriage ceremony performed by Bishop Hyrum Nelson in the large Lemon home was followed by a great feast. The *Progress* reported,

> About 100 were seated at the first tables, and before the food was touched Hon. Orange Seely invoked divine blessing upon it and the assembled multitude. Under the direction of Mr. Seely the onslaught upon the generous bounty of the hosts began and continued for an hour, although Mr. Seely had everyone beaten before the third course was served.

After dinner, guests strolled through the orchards or toured the house with its newly installed plumbing: "Hot and cold water, issuing from the prettiest and most sanitary conceits of modern plumbing, were found in almost every one of the large airy rooms of this fine home." In the evening there was a dance at Killpack Hall at which Orange Seely, then in his sixtieth year, put on a vigorous demonstration of "step dancing."[171]

Other social events included community celebrations of the Fourth and Twenty-fourth of July, old folks' parties, the annual dinner and program commemorating the organization of the LDS Relief Society, and encampments of the Indian war veterans. The inaugural Peach Days celebration at Ferron in 1901 drew a disappointing attendance, but by the middle of the next decade it had become a popular attraction. The first Melon Day at Green River was celebrated in 1908. This community observance was apparently somewhat irregular for some years thereafter, but by its peak of popularity in the 1920s it drew special trains from Grand Junction and Salt Lake City. The first Emery County Fair was held at Castle Dale in 1916, after joint Emery-Carbon fairs at Price during previous years. Boxing and wrestling matches, with both local and imported athletes, and horse races were regular features of these celebrations.

Each community had its favorite outdoor recreation sites such as "The Breaks" or "The Cedars." The hilltop grove planted by Carl Wilberg on his farm north of Castle Dale was a popular recreation destination as early as 1905. A few years later, C. H. Winder developed a resort at Desert Lake featuring Saturday night dances and moonlight boat rides. Ferron residents traveled *en masse* to spend a week or so in the high elevations of Ferron Reservoir each summer, while residents of Orangeville and Castle Dale made similar pilgrimages to Joe's Valley. In some years massive Emery-Sanpete "reunions" attracted five thousand people or more to Horseshoe Flats on the divide between the two valleys. "Eastering" in the San Rafael desert was a well-established Emery County tradition by 1910.

Multipurpose recreation buildings erected during the period included the Huntington Relief Society Hall, Davis Hall in Cleveland, and the Green River Opera House. Fraternal lodges, including Masons, Modern Woodmen, and Knights of Pythias, played an important role in the cultural and recreational life of Green River but attracted little interest in the western towns of the county, though short-lived Modern Woodmen chapters were established at Ferron and Orangeville.

Commercial entertainment included frequent visits to the county by touring professional theater companies, most prominently the Walters Stock Company. In 1901 the Edison Moving Picture Company toured the county with a "Projectoscope" exhibition of the Corbett-Fitzsimmons prize fight. In 1902 Lars Christensen and Hector Evans of Castle Dale purchased an "Edison Concert Phonograph" and gave recorded concerts in several communities. In 1910 James W. Johnson obtained a projector and showed motion pictures in the upper floor of the Wall-Miller building in Castle Dale. In 1914 R. C. Miller fitted up that space as the Castle Dale Electric Theater, apparently the first motion picture theater in the county. Greenhalgh Hall in Ferron began showing movies later the same year, and in early 1915 J. W. Nixon opened the Bonita Theater in Huntington. Among the most popular attractions were the silent Westerns featuring Art Acord, who had grown up in Castle Dale.[172]

Baseball was being played by pick-up town teams by the turn of the century. Mohrland, like other coal camps, had a well equipped team with some players of semipro caliber and wide community support. The Mohrland team had two different sets of rivalries, one with the Carbon County coal camps and Helper and Price, and the other with its Emery County neighbors. Several different leagues were organized during the period, with games played on Sunday afternoons throughout the summer.

The Emery Stake Academy fielded its first basketball team in 1911 when it defeated a Ferron town team by a score of twelve to six. Basketball became the most popular sport at the new high schools, with vigorous competition among the county teams and between them and Carbon High.[173]

Fish and Game

In September 1900, through the efforts of a local fish and game association, thirty-five thousand trout were planted in Huntington, Cottonwood, and Ferron creeks. The report in the *Emery County Progress* commented, "Strange to say that these beautiful mountain streams had never had trout in them."[174] This claim is somewhat surprising as other Utah streams in the Green and Colorado drainage are known to have had native populations of cutthroat trout. Perhaps an original population had been depleted by the silting of the streams as a result of overgrazing on the Wasatch Plateau until few if any trout remained, giving rise to a local impression that there had never been any. In any event, the subsequent development of Emery County trout streams can be traced to that initial planting in 1900, which was followed by regular plants in subsequent years.

There were no bag limits on deer in the early years of the century. Reports from the fall of 1900 indicate that some hunters brought home as many as twelve carcasses. The next few years saw a dramatic decline in deer populations, however, which was blamed on bears and cougars but which might also have been the result of overhunting and competition from domestic livestock. The Manti National Forest's large elk herd had its beginning in 1916 when the Emery County commission contributed $300 to help transplant twenty-five animals from Jackson Hole, Wyoming. The elk spent the first winter on the Peacock and Miles ranches near the mouth of Straight Canyon and were somewhat reluctantly pushed onto East Mountain the following spring.[175]

ENDNOTES

1. *ECP*, 26 August 1905; 20 March, 23 October 1915.

2. *Fourteenth Census of the United States, Taken in the Year 1920,* Vol. VI, Part 3, Agriculture (Washington, D.C.: Government Printing Office, 1923), 252.

3. *Eastern Utah Telegram,* 26 March 1891.

4. United States Department of Agriculture, *Farmers' Bulletin,* no. 371, 2 October 1909.

5. *ECP,* 5 December 1903; 16 January, 2 and 9 July 1904; 5 August, 11 November 1905.

6. Ibid., 8 March, 5 April 1902.

7. Keith Wright, "Clawson," in *EC 1880–1980,* 90.

8. *Eastern Utah Advocate,* 20 May 1897; *ECP,* 25 May, 8 June 1901.

9. Wright, "Clawson," 91.

10. *ECP,* 8 June, 17 and 31 August, 9 November 1901.

11. Bessie Wright and Theo Cox, "Clawson," in *CV,* 106–7.

12. Powell, "Castle Valley at the Beginning of the Twentieth Century," 16–17.

13. Bessie Wright and Theo Cox, "Clawson," 107.

14. *ECP,* 24 June 1905; 30 March 1907; Wright and Cox, "Clawson," 107–10.

15. *ECP,* 24 June 1905; Mark Humphrey, "Life on Rock Canyon Flat" (1991), typescript copy in Emery County History Archives.

16. Except as otherwise indicated, general information on Moore is taken from Homer Edwards and Calvin L. Moore, "Moore," in *CV,* 295–98; Faye C. Curtis, "History of Moore," in *EC 1880–1980,* 263–74; and Velma C. Petersen, Oral History, typescript copy in Emery County History Archives.

17. Lever, *History of Sanpete and Emery Counties,* 628.

18. *ECP,* 11 July 1903.

19. Ibid., 26 March, 9 July, 20 August, 3 December 1904; 11 February, 23 December 1905; 17 March, 4 August 1906.

20. Ibid., 12 January, 1 and 19 June, 20 July 1907; 31 March 1917; 6 April 1918; 5 and 12 April 1919; Curtis, "History of Moore," 264, 270–71.

21. *Fifteenth Census of the United States: 1930,* Agriculture, Volume 1 (Washington, D.C.: Government Printing Office, 1932), 633.

22. *ECP,* 18 May, 24 August 1907.

23. *Eastern Utah Advocate,* 2 September 1897.

24. *ECP,* 7 November 1903; 21 May, 22 October 1904; 2 June 1905; 3 March 1906; 6 June 1908.

25. Thomas Wells, "Desert Lake and Victor," in *CV,* 127–31; Ada Willson, "Desert Lake—Victor," in *EC 1880–1980,* 171–74.

26. *ECP,* 9 November 1907; 18 July 1908.

27. George H. Oviatt, B. H. Erickson, and Florence Hall, "Elmo," in

CV, 132–36; Charles and Maude Jones, "History of Elmo," in *EC 1880–1980*, 176–80.

28. *ECP*, 4 July 1908; 30 January 1909; 1 April 1911; 2 November 1912.

29. Ibid., 7 March 1908; 27 February 1909.

30. Ibid., 28 March 1908.

31. Ibid., 6 May 1916; Anne Curtis Allred, "History of Cedar Mountain," typescript copy in Emery County History Archives.

32. *ECP*, 3 August 1901; 28 June 28 1902; 4 April, 2 May, 11 July, 5 September, 5 and 19 December 1903; 6 August, 10 December 1904; 22 July 1905; 10 and 31 March 1906; 23 February 1907; 14 March, 4 April, 21 November 1908; 30 January, 20 February 1909; 2 September 1911; 10 August 1912; 15 April 1916.

33. Ibid., 1 and 8 June 1901; 21 November 1903; LaVora H. Kofford, "An Early Pioneer Lawyer, Charles E. Kofford," 438; Forrest Peterson, "History of Joe's Valley," 313–14, in *EC 1880–1980.*

34. Forrest Peterson, "Our Joe's Valley Home," typescript copy in Emery County History Archives.

35. *ECP*, 26 March 1910; 1 June 1912; 2 September 1916; 30 June 1917.

36. Ibid., 17 January, 20 April, 18 May 1907; 18 April, 2 May, 25 July 1908.

37. Ibid., 4 April 1903; 11 March 1905; 17 January, 11 May, 20 July, 17 August, 5 October 1907; 18 January, 8 February, 2 May 1908; 16 January, 13 February, 5 June 1909; 29 January 1910.

38. Seely, "Irrigation on Cottonwood Creek," in *EC 1880–1980*, 78.

39. *ECP*, 2 March 1901.

40. Ibid., 23 February, 2 March, 25 May, 1 June, 26 October 1901; 26 July, 2 August, 15 November 1902; 10 and 17 January, 11 April 1903. Seely, "Irrigation on Cottonwood Creek," 78–89; personal communication from Montell Seely, November 1994.

41. *ECP*, 12 October 1912; 18 July 1914.

42. Velma Petersen, "Ferron," 111.

43. *ECP*, 25 March 1905; 9 June 1906.

44. Ibid., 16 January 1904; 10 February 1906.

45. Roy Webb, "A Foolhardy Undertaking: Utah's Pioneer Steamboaters," *Canyon Legacy: A Journal of the Dan O'Laurie Museum*, 5 (1990): 15–16.

46. Ibid., 16; *ECP*, 21 September, 12 October 1901; 1 March, 24 May 1902.

47. Webb, "Foolhardy Undertaking," 17, 18–19.

48. *ECP,* August 31, 1907; Baker and Wilcox, "Greenriver," 189–90; Baker, typescript account of river travel, Emery County History Archives.

49. *ECP,* 25 February, 11 and 25 March, 15 and 22 April, 3 June, 15 July, 2 September, 28 October 1905; 17 and 24 February, 17 and 31 March, 26 May, 9 June, 1 December 1906.

50. Ibid., 9 December 1905; 24 February, 17 March, 5 May, 8 September 1906.

51. Ibid., 31 March, 21 and 28 April, 19 May, 23 June, 7 and 21 July, 29 September, 3 November, 1 and 22 December 1906; 19 January, 9 and 23 February, 29 June, 16 November 1907; 8 February 1908; 3 April 1909; 7 January, 11 March 1911; 5 September 1941; Baker and Wilcox, "Greenriver," 192–93; James G. Chronopoulos, "Masonry in Southeastern Utah," typescript copy in Emery County History Archives.

52. Dorothy Nethery Crawford to Mrs. Dunham, 4 December 1991, typescript copy in Emery County History Archives.

53. *ECP,* 2 June 1906; 21 November 1908; 20 March, 18 September 1909; 5 November, 3 December 1910; Muriel Smith, "Green River Schools."

54. *ECP,* 22 April, 17 June, 2 September 1905; 5 and 26 May, 11 and 25 August, 1 September 1906; 2 and 23 February, 20 April 1907; Baker and Wilcox, "Greenriver," 184; Montell and Kathrine Seely, "Green River," 134–35.

55. *ECP,* 4 January, 29 February 1908; 30 January 1909; Baker and Wilcox, "Greenriver," 184.

56. *ECP,* 23 November, 21 December 1907; 21 November 1908.

57. Howland, "Planting of the Seed," 4.

58. *ECP,* 3 and 24 June 1916; Baker and Wilcox, "Greenriver," 191; Seely and Seely, "Green River," 134; Laura L. Acerson, "Green River Melon Days," typescript copy in Emery County History Archives.

59. Oral Eugene Johansen, "Peter Johansen II Family," in *EC 1880–1980,* 459.

60. *ECP,* 22 October 1910.

61. R.V.R. Reynolds, "Grazing and Floods: A Study of Conditions in the Manti National Forest, Utah," U.S.F.S. Bulletin 91, quoted in Antrei, *The Other Forty-niners,* 197.

62. *Eastern Utah Advocate,* 16 September 1897; *ECP,* 15 September 1900; 7 September 1907; 4 September 1909.

63. *ECP,* 9 and 16 March, 27 April, 10 August, 28 September, 9 November 1901; 5 September, 24 October, 14 November 1903; 20 February, 27 August 1904.

64. Ibid., 9 August 1902.

65. Antrei, *The Other Forty-niners,* 193.

66. *ECP,* 9 November 1901; 21 March 1903.

67. Adolf W. Jensen, Reminiscences (1953), quoted in Antrei, *The Other Forty-niners,* 205, 206.

68. *ECP,* 26 September 1903.

69. Ibid., 13 February 1904.

70. A. W. Jensen, Recollections, 206–7; J. W. Humphrey, "Recollections," (1953), in Antrei, *The Other Forty-niners,* 209; *ECP,* 3 August 1912.

71. *ECP,* 28 May, 26 November 1904; 19 May 1906; 19 October 1907; 7 March 1908; 13 January 1917.

72. Ibid., 5 October 1912; 10 May 1919.

73. Ibid., 24 February, 16 June, 22 December 1906; 6 July 1907; 25 January 1908.

74. Ibid., 3 and 24 March 1906.

75. Nelson, *In the Direction of His Dreams,* 37.

76. *ECP,* 3 September 1904; 18 March, 18 November, 23 December 1905; 10 March, 9 June, 17 November 1906; 1 and 20 June, 14 December 1907; 17 June 1911.

77. Ibid., 21 October 1905; 1 September, 10 November, 22 December 1906; 10 March, 9 June, 17 November 1906; 1 and 20 June, 14 December 1907; 17 June 1911.

78. Ibid., 28 September, 16 November 1907; 25 December 1909; 1 January 1910; 2 August, 20 December 1919.

79. Ibid., 31 January 1903; 19 October 1907; 27 August 1910.

80. Ibid., 5 January 1901.

81. *Salt Lake Mining Review,* 28 February, 15 July, 30 December 1902; *ECP,* 9 February 1901; 18 January, 1 March, 13 September 1902; 4 December 1915.

82. *ECP,* 9 February 1901; 25 January 1902; 16 January 1909; 19 June 1915.

83. *Salt Lake Mining Review,* 15 December 1911; *ECP,* 14 June 1902; 30 April, 28 May 1904; 23 December 1905; 9 June 1906; 5 January 1907; 14 November 1908; 27 April 1912.

84. *Salt Lake Mining Review,* 15 November 1900; *ECP,* 16 and 30 March 1901; 15 February, 2 August, 20 September 1902; 8 August 1903; 15 April, 6 May 1905; 10 March, 23 June 1906; 23 February, 13 June 1907; 17 April 1909; 11 March 1911; 22 August 1914; 14 August 1915; 25 March 1916.

85. *Salt Lake Mining Review,* 30 September 1911; 15 May 1912; *ECP,* 23 March 1901; 16 January, 18 June 1904; 17 June 1911; 24 January, 28 March,

6 June 1914; Stokes and Cohenour, "Geologic Atlas of Utah: Emery County," 47; Daniel K. Newsome and Betsy L. Tipps, "Cultural Resource Reconaissance and Evaluation in the Temple Mountain and Tomsich Butte Mining Areas, Emery County, Utah," Cultural Resources Report 5011–01–9311 (Bureau of Land Management, Moab District Office, 1993), 8.

86. *ECP,* 23 February, 9 March, 25 May, 22 and 29 June, 27 July 1901.

87. Ibid., 13 July, 10 and 24 August, 7 September, 9 November 1901; 4, 18, and 25 January, 1 and 15 March, 5, 19, and 26 April 1902; 3 January, 7 February, 14 March, 19 September 1903; 13 February 1904.

88. Ibid., 9 February 1907; 23 April, 14 May, 12 and 19 November 1910; 14 January, 8 April, 3 and 24 June 1911; 16 March 1912; 2, 9, and 23 July 1921; 14 April 1922; 17 November 1923; 26 January, 5 April 1924.

89. Ibid., 1 March, 19 April, 3, 10, and 24 May, 6 September, 4 October 1902; 16 May 1903; 11 March 1905; 19 May, 1 September 1906.

90. Ibid., 29 July 1911; 13 and 27 December 1913.

91. Ibid., 18 and 25 August, 8 and 15 September 1950; Thelma Mills, "Coal Industry," in *EC 1880–1980,* 286–92.

92. *ECP,* 4 May, 15 June 1901; 29 March, 30 August 1902; 20 January, 1 December 1906; 22 October 1910; 25 May 1912; 18 March 1916.

93. *Eastern Utah Advocate,* 28 October 1897; "Albert Clifton Gardner," in Jones, *Early Pioneers of Huntington,* 97–98; *CV,* 276.

94. *ECP,* 3, 10, and 17 August, 7 December 1907; 25 July 1908.

95. Ibid., 19 October 1907; 17 October, 7 November 1908; 7 and 21 August, 4 December 1909; 12 March, 9 April, 28 May 1910; *CV,* 20.

96. *ECP,* 9 April, 28 May, 17 September, 1 October 1910; 13 January 1912.

97. Ibid., 4 November 1911; 13 January, 2 March, 8 June 1912; 7 June 1913; 20 March 1915; Thode and Ozment, "In the Mountains of Utah," 84.

98. *ECP,* 17 January 1914; 3 July 1915; Irene C. O'Driscoll, "Reminiscences," typescript copy in Emery County History Archives; Luella McMullin Allen and Irene Allred, "Mohrland," in *EC 1880–1980,* 235–39; Soren and Ruth Hanson Nielson, interview, August 1994.

99. *Deseret News,* 1 April 1914.

100. Mills, "Timber and Sawmill Industry," 280–86.

101. *ECP,* 2 February 1901; 22 February, 27 September 1902; 17 January 1903; 28 November 1908; 4 May 1912.

102. Ibid., 16 May 1903; 31 December 1904; 25 February 1911.

103. Ibid., 5 and 12 March 1910.

104. Powell, "Castle Valley at the Beginning of the Twentieth Century," 5–6.

105. Ibid, 12.

106. *ECP,* 2 February, 23 March, 28 September, 26 October 1901; 15 February, 22 March 1902.

107. Ibid., 18 July 1903; 27 February, 23 April 1904; 14 December 1912.

108. Conover, *George Henry Westover,* 56–66.

109. Richard E. Behling, Oral History, typescript transcript in Emery County History Archives.

110. Drucilla Seely Bott, "William John Seely Family," in *EC 1880–1980,* 435.

111. *ECP,* 4 December 1926.

112. Ibid., 8 October, 19 November, 10 December 1904; 27 October 1906; 12 November 1910; 16 November 1912.

113. Ibid., 23 March 1901; 21 March, 9 May 1903; 27 February, 9 and 23 July, 6 and 20 August, 3 and 17 September, 3 December 1904; 26 May 1906; 2 February, 9 and 30 March, 29 June, 7 September 1907.

114. Ibid., 16 March 1907; 4 and 18 September 1909; 29 January, 16 July, 13 August, 3 December 1910.

115. Ibid., 15 June 1907; 4 April, 25 July 1908; 16 September 1911; 29 March, 17 May 1913; 14 August 1915; 11 November 1916; 13 October 1917; 1 June 1918; 3 May, 9 August 1919; *Utah State Gazetteer* (1918–19), 60, 69, 70.

116. *ECP,* 28 November 1914; 30 August 1919.

117. Ibid., 4 December 1909; 26 August 1911; 6 January 1912; 15 March, 16 August 1913; 25 July 1914; 5 June, 10 July, 11 September 1915; 1 and 15 January, 4 March, 15 July, 19 August, 9 September 1916; 13 January, 31 August, 5 October 1917; 22 March 1918; 12 April, 23 August 1919; 27 March, 22 May, 31 July 1920; 6 August 1921.

118. Ibid., 8 February, 12 September, 24 and 31 October, 14 and 28 November, 12 December, 1908; 9 January, 3 April, 29 March, 23 October 1909.

119. Ibid., 30 January 1909; 24 September, 5 November 1910; 1 July 1911; 24 February, 7 September 1912.

120. Ibid., 7 July 1917; 15 February 1919.

121. *Eastern Utah Advocate,* 12 January 1899. Both *CV* and *EC 1880–1980* erroneously report this leadership transfer as having occurred almost ten years earlier, on 20 October 1889.

122. *Eastern Utah Advocate,* 21 April 1898.

123. *ECP,* 14 May 1910.

124. Nelson, *In the Direction of His Dreams,* 167–69.

125. Reuben G. Miller, letters to Alonzo Brinkerhoff, 7 February 1914, and to President Heber J. Grant, J. Reuben Clark, and David O. McKay, 23 February 1944, Reuben Gardner Miller papers, Special Collections, Harold B. Lee Library, Brigham Young University.

126. *ECP,* 23 April 1904; see also Nelson, *In the Direction of His Dreams,* 118.

127. *ECP,* 2 August 1902; 23 April 1904; 25 November 1905; 20 January 1906; Elmo Geary, "Dramatics in Castle Valley," 91–96.

128. Quoted in letter from Gerald W. Gillette, research historian, Presbyterian Historical Society, to Sam Singleton, 30 October 1968, copy in Emery County History Archives.

129. *ECP,* 30 December 1905; 20 January, 18 August, 1 and 22 September 1906; 20 April, 16 November 1907; 23 May, 18 July 1908.

130. Ibid., 22 February, 25 July 1908; 17 September 1910; 21 March, 11 April 1914.

131. Ibid., 2 April, 18 June 1904; 31 March, 21 April, 1 December 1906; Baker and Wilcox, "Greenriver," in *CV,* 194; Green River Presbyterian Church records, photocopy in Utah State Historical Society Library, Salt Lake City; Dorothy Nethery Crawford, letter to Mrs. Dunham, 4 December 1991.

132. *ECP,* 4 May, 31 August 1901; 26 September 1903; 27 August 1904; 10 February 1906.

133. Ibid., 2 July, 13 October 1904; 9 December 1905; 13 January, 10 March, 12 May 1906; 20 March, 24 August, 21 September 1907; 5 November 1910; 11 March 1911.

134. Ibid., 1, 8, and 15 June 1901; 3 May, 28 June 1902; 17 January 1903; 8 October 1904; 10 March 1906; 1 June, 26 October 1907; 20 June 1908; 9 January 1909.

135. Ibid., 5 May 1906; 25 April 1908; 24 May, 21 June 1913; *CV,* 229–30; "In Memory of James William Nixon III and Margaret Lea Nixon," in *EC 1880–1908,* 417.

136. Tabone, "Emery Stake Academy," 35–38, 70; *ECP,* 17 January 1903; 6 August 1904; 26 January, 16 and 23 March, 13 and 27 April, 13 July, 26 October 1907; 23 May, 13 and 20 June 1908; 2 October 1909.

137. Leslie H. Correal, Board of National Missions of the United Presbyterian Church in the United States of America, to Sam Singleton, 5 December 1967, typescript copy in Emery County History Archives; *ECP,* 30 December 1905; 20 January, 10 March, 18 August, 8 and 13 September 1906; 7 September 1907; 8 February, 25 July, 5 September 1908; 11 April 1914.

138. Velma Petersen, "Ferron," 109; *ECP,* 4 October 1921.

139. *ECP,* 7 and 28 May 1910; 12 October 1912; 20 September 1913; 28 March, 11 July, 12 September 1914; 2 January, 6 February, 6 March 1915.

140. Ibid., 15 and 22 May, 3 July 1915; 15 January, 12 February, 2 and 16 December 1916; 24 March, 11 August 1917.

141. Ibid., 7 April, 21 July, 8 December 1917; 9 and 16 February, 8 June 1918; 28 February 1920.

142. Ibid., 2 and 23 February 1901; 4 January 1902; 31 January, 7 March 1903; 13 September 1906; 12 January, 2 February, 18 May 1907; 1 July 1911; 20 July 1912; 20 January 1917.

143. Ibid., 3 May 1902; 7 July, 17 September, 8 October 1904; 8 July, 26 August 1905; 7 July 1906; 8 February, 11 July, 5 September, 10 October 1908; 9 April, 25 June, 19 November, 10 December 1910; 27 January, 24 August 1912; 26 April, 2 August, 29 November 1913; 5 December 1914; 26 May 1917; 5 January, 12 October 1918; 6 September 1919; 20 March, 22 May 1920; "Emery County's Early Doctor and Nurse, Dr. Walter E. Henzi and Wife Emily Harris Henzi," "In Memory of Dr. James William Nixon III and Margaret Lea Nixon," in *EC 1880–1980,* 379, 417.

144. *ECP,* 10 September 1904; 8 April 1905; 10 March, 27 October 1906; 14 August, 25 September 1909; 5 February 1910; 10 January 1914; 1 August 1914; 25 December 1915; 16 December 1916; 29 September 1917; 7 December 1918; "Horace P. Easley," in *EC 1880–1980,* 570–71.

145. *ECP,* 9 April 1910; 20 April 1918; 12 April 1919; Allen and Allred, "Mohrland," 237–38.

146. *ECP,* 9 July 1904; 13 January 1906.

147. Ibid., 12 October, 2 and 16 November, 7, 21, and 28 December 1918; 4 and 18 January, 8 February, 8 March, 12 April, 3 May 1919; 7 and 14 February 1920.

148. Ibid., 12 October, 9 November 1918; 21 February 1920; "Emery County's Early Doctor and Nurse, Dr. Walter E. Henzi and Wife Emily Harris Henzi," 379.

149. *Eastern Utah Advocate,* 15 March 1900; *ECP,* 8 June 1901; 8 September 1906; 7 January 1911; 3 January, 20 Marcy, 22 May 1920; Irene Allred, "Cleveland, Utah," in *EC 1880–1980,* 157.

150. *ECP,* 17 February 1906; 27 January, 7 September 1912; 21 August 1915; 28 December 1918; 22 November 1919; 3 January, 6 March 1920.

151. Nelson, *In the Direction of His Dreams,* 67; *ECP,* 14 August 1909.

152. *ECP,* 1 February, 7 March 1908; 2 October, 18 December 1909; 8 April 1911; 6 April 1912; 11 January, 7 June 1913; 30 May, 5 December

1914; 13 March 1915; 24 June, 23 September 1916; 8 December 1917; 9 February 1918; 22 February, 12 April 1919.

153. Ibid., 19 August, 16 September 1905; 23 June 1906; 9 and 16 November 1907; 7 August, 20 November 1909; 14 January, 25 March 1911; 4 January, 6 and 13 September 1913; 7 and 28 March 1914; Ida Snow, "Telephone Systems," in *EC 1880–1980,* 52–53; Reuben G. Miller papers.

154. *ECP,* 5 September 1903; 9 January, 24 December 1904; 14 and 28 October, 11 November, 30 December 1905; 20 January, 31 March 1906; 9 February, 18 May, 13 June 1907; 23 January, 3 April, 21 August, 18 December 1909; 7 May 1910; 15 July 1911; *CV,* 98–99; John Taylor, personal history, quoted in *EC 1880–1980,* 69–70; "Utah Power and Light Company," in *EC 1880–1980,* 490.

155. *ECP,* 7 October 1911.

156. Ibid., 6 March, 24 July, 11 September, 30 October 1915.

157. Ibid., 13 December 1919; 17 January, 17 July 1920; John Taylor, personal history, 70.

158. Velma Petersen, "Ferron," 106; *ECP,* 27 January, 24 February, 6 July 1912; *Utah State Gazetteer and Business Directory* (Salt Lake City: R. L. Polk), 1:99 (1900), 7:60 (1918).

159. *Utah State Gazetteer,* 7:59–60 (1918); "Ferron Merc and Drug," in *EC 1880–1980,* 481; Irma Petersen Snow, Oral History, transcript in Emery County History Archives.

160. *ECP,* 17 January 1903; 4 March, 22 April 1905; 17 November 1906; 9 February 1907; 13 February, 22 May 1909; 1 January, 7 May, 6 August, 10 September 1910; 17 May 1913; 5 May 1917; *Utah State Gazetteer and Business Directory,* 7:35–36 (1918); Frona L. Johnson, "Portrait of a Family" (James and Annie Petersen), typescript copy, Lee Library; "Castle Dale Cooperative Company," and Faye H. Johnson, "Lorin T. Hunter," in *EC 1880–1980,* 495, 605–6.

161. *ECP,* 23 February 1901; 24 January, 19 December 1903; 29 April, 16 September 1905; 6 and 27 September, 11 October 1913; 7 March 1914; 21 July 1923; *Utah State Gazetteer,* 1:114–15 (1900), 3:152 (1908), 7:78 (1918); *CV,* 37, 246–51.

162. *Utah State Gazetteer,* 3:141–42 (1908), 7:69–70 (1918).

163. *ECP,* 4 March, 12 August 1905; 9 November 1907; 15 and 29 May 1909; *Utah State Gazetteer,* 1:92 (1900), 3:120 (1908), 7:53 (1918); Isaac Allred, "Emery," in *CV,* 147–48.

164. *Utah State Gazetteer,* 1:197(1900), 3:253 (1908), 7:154 (1918); *ECP,* 12 February 1916.

165. *Utah State Gazetteer,* 1:81 (1900), 7:43 (1918).

166. Ibid., 1:197(1900), 3:253 (1908), 7:154 (1918).

167. *ECP,* 11 and 18 August 1906; 3 June, 22 July 1911; Albert D. Keller, "Emery County Bank," in *CV,* 35–36.

168. *ECP,* 23 June, 7 July 1906; 23 November, 21 December 1907; 4 July 1908; Pearl Baker, "The Greenriver State Bank," in *CV,* 36–37; *Utah State Gazetteer,* 7:69 (1918).

169. *ECP,* 6 and 27 September, 11 October 1913; Albert D. Keller, "Castle Valley Banking Company of Huntington, Utah," in *CV,* 37.

170. *ECP,* 12 May, 25 August, 1 September, 20 and 27 October 1917; 26 January, 20 April, 1 June, 12 October 1918; "A Brief Summary of [Ferron] Relief Society History," typescript copy in Emery County History Archives; Baker and Wilcox, "Greenriver," 194.

171. *ECP,* 6 September 1902.

172. Ibid., 9 and 23 February, 31 August, 14 September 1901; 2 August 1902; 20 May, 5 August 1905; 12 January, 4 May, 15 June, 13 July 1907; 5 and 26 September, 3 October 1908; 2 April, 31 December 1910; 21 February, 5 September, 7 November, 19 December 1914; 9 January 1915; 15 April 1916; Baker and Wilcox, "Greenriver," 194.

173. *ECP,* 18 January 1908; 30 July 1910; 16 December 1911; 20 February 1915; 3 May, 7 June 1919; 13 March 1920.

174. Ibid., 15 September 1900.

175. Ibid., 3 November 1900; 8 January 1916.

6

Hard Times, Good Times, 1920–1945

In common with much of the rural West, Emery County experienced difficult economic and social challenges during the quarter-century from 1920 to 1945. The prices of agricultural products and livestock fell dramatically after the conclusion of the First World War and remained low during most of the 1920s. The later years of the decade brought partial recovery followed by a more drastic collapse with the onset of the Great Depression that dominated the 1930s. The general economic distress was intensified by severe drought and crop failures in 1931 and 1934. Coal miners experienced wage cuts, short weeks, and layoffs in the early 1920s and far greater cutbacks during the 1930s. The Second World War stimulated the economy but also brought scarcity, rationing, and rises in the cost of living, in addition to taking numerous residents out of the county for military service or jobs in defense industries. Individuals and families responded to hard times with resiliency and ingenuity. Communities retained their vitality and accomplished significant renewal and modernization in housing, education, transportation, and public facilities.

Overall population numbers remained static with the county's 7,411 residents in 1920 decreasing to 7,042 in 1930 and increasing slightly to 7,072 in 1940. Two communities, Mohrland and Victor, passed out of existence during this period. Woodside's population fell from 124 in 1920 to only thirty in 1940, and Rochester/Moore fell from 114 residents in 1930 to forty-seven in 1940. Other communities held their own or saw modest growth. The population was still relatively young. In 1920 almost half of the county's residents, 49.8 percent, were under the age of eighteen. In 1940 56.8 percent were under twenty-five, and only 4.8 percent were over the age of sixty-five. With no growth in the total population, it is obvious that Emery County was exporting all of its large natural increase.

For those who remained in the county, farming, livestock raising, and mining continued to be the economic mainstays. Of the 1,921 males with listed occupations in the 1930 census, 1,294 (67.4 percent) were employed in agriculture, 730 as owners and the remainder as wage workers or unpaid family workers. Coal mining employed 236 men (12.3 percent). Fifty-one men (most of them in Green River) worked for the railroad, and thirty-two were in the building trades. Business, professional, and clerical occupations employed 104 men and sixty-seven women.[1]

The 1920s

Agriculture and Stock Raising. Total land in farms increased by 10,000 acres between 1920 and 1930, from 105,268 to 115,067. However, crop land decreased by almost 30 percent from 43,587 acres to 30,762. Part of this decrease can be attributed to the development of improved pastures to replace crop land, but much of the decline reflects the continuing degradation of agricultural land as once-productive fields turned to saltgrass and alkali. The 1930 census identified 405 general, grain, or specialty crop farming operations, 127 stock ranches and animal specialty farms, twenty-four dairy farms, fourteen poultry farms, eleven fruit farms, and four truck farms. Sixty-one farms were listed as "self-sufficiency" operations, and an additional ninety-one were listed as part time. Most of the produce of these latter categories would have been consumed by the farm family.

Alfalfa, wheat, and oats were still the dominant crops. Alfalfa seed production gradually declined (it would cease altogether by the mid 1930s). Melons became an increasingly important cash crop for Green River farmers after Wilson Produce Company began shipping to eastern markets on a large scale. In 1929 seventy-five acres on eleven farms were planted to cantaloupes and twenty-eight acres on seventeen farms to watermelons. Another cash crop developed during the decade was sugar beets. Ninety-nine acres were planted at Green River in 1929 under contract with the Holly Sugar Company. Green River farmers successfully grew and marketed a large tomato crop in 1930, but for some reason this experiment was not repeated in later years. The number of apple trees in the county decreased by 38 percent from 28,293 in 1920 to 17,541 in 1930. The Castle Valley honey industry declined from 2,702 hives and 135,237 pounds in 1919 to 1,774 hives and 89,938 pounds in 1929. Egg production grew substantially from 190,839 dozen to 321,332 dozen. This reflected a shift to more commercially oriented poultry operations under the influence of the Utah Poultry Producers' Cooperative marketing organization. Home butter production fell from 123,039 pounds to 105,186, but cream sales rose from nothing in 1919 to 221,468 pounds in 1929.

Several livestock operators apparently switched from cattle to sheep during the decade, probably motivated by low beef prices. The 1920 census counted 21,381 cattle and 35,349 sheep. By 1930 cattle had decreased to 16,451 while sheep had increased to 58,345. Automobiles, trucks, and a few primitive tractors apparently had an impact on horse numbers, which decreased from 4,869 in 1920 to 3,012 in 1930.[2]

While these numbers would suggest a fairly stable farm economy, in fact farmers and stockraisers were struggling during much of the decade. The end of the wartime demand brought a sharp decline in agricultural commodity prices without a corresponding decrease in prices for items farmers had to purchase. Farm land values in the county fell significantly between 1920 and 1925. The *Emery County Progress* declared in 1925 that local memory could recall "no depression comparable" to that being suffered by the cattle industry.[3] The full appropriation (and overappropriation) of water and grazing resources made it difficult to expand operations to a more profitable scale. However, the completion of Scofield Reservoir in 1926 did provide an irrigation supply for some additional Emery County land under the Carbon Canal.[4] Competition for grazing land brought concentrated efforts to eliminate wild horses and burros from the San Rafael Swell and the Green River Desert.[5]

Several livestock operators acquired grazing homesteads in the Tavaputs Plateau (Book Cliffs) region, which they used in conjunction with their farm land in the county. The quest for range land took some families entirely out of the county, notable examples being David and Elva Singleton Seely of Castle Dale and Gilbert Wild of Ferron, who acquired large ranch properties on Hill Creek in Uintah County. Other large growers made substantial adjustments to their livestock holdings. Joe and Millie Biddlecome, who had developed one of the largest cattle and horse operations in the state in the Robbers Roost region, sold off one thousand head of cattle in 1925, fearing the effects of a possible drought.[6]

Mining. The coal industry suffered from the same postwar slump that afflicted agriculture. Utah coal production fell from 5.3 million tons in 1920 to 3.6 million in 1921.[7] Wage cuts and short weeks were commonplace. On 1 April 1922 Carbon-Emery coal operators imposed a general wage reduction from $7.95 to $5.25 per day and from seventy-nine cents to fifty-five cents per ton of coal mined. A national strike called on the same day by the United Mine Workers of America brought determined efforts by the union to organize workers in Utah's mostly nonunion mines. The strike continued until August with most of the local conflict concentrated in the Spring Canyon and Scofield-Winter Quarters districts. As had been the practice during previous strikes, coal operators recruited replacement workers from Emery County. For its part, the union held meetings at Huntington and Castle Dale to explain its point of view and discourage local men from accepting employment at the mines. On 14 May a Huntington man serving as a Carbon County deputy sheriff shot and killed a striker on the outskirts of Helper in the strike's only fatality. In the agreement that ended the strike, wages were restored to their former level. However, miners were forced to accept a series of reductions in 1925, 1928, and 1931.[8]

Emery County's own coal camp, Mohrland, reached its peak in the early 1920s when it consisted of "about two hundred modern dwelling houses, a store, post office, hospital, church, hotel, theater, and amusement hall, all of which were modern and well built."[9] By the middle of the decade, however, the U.S. Fuel Company was unable to find a market for the output of its four mines, of which Mohrland was the most productive. In February 1925 Mohrland operations were suddenly discontinued. Irene O'Driscoll recalled the impact on residents in these terms:

> If the town had been swept by fire it would not have had a more disastrous effect upon the inhabitants living there. All those people with the security that a good home and a good job brings, were given no notice. The whistle just blew, and they had no home, no job, and no place to go. The store would not give credit to anyone, and many were left without money or food.

Mohrland remained as a kind of ghost town until September 1926 when the company just as abruptly decided to reopen Mohrland operations and shut down West Hiawatha.[10]

The county's small mines found wider markets with the coming of better roads and motor trucks. The *Progress* reported in 1929 that "many tons of coal" were being shipped from the Browning-Duzett mine near Emery to Salina and other points in the Sevier Valley.[11]

A picture of the working life of coal miners during this period emerges from the reminiscences of Charles F. Jones, who joined his father at the Latuda mine in Spring Canyon in 1922 at the age of sixteen while other members of the family remained on the farm at Elmo. Mechanization had come to the mines in the form of electric-powered cutting machines to undercut the coal before blasting. Coal was still loaded by hand and hauled from the mine in horse-drawn cars. Miners worked ten-hour shifts and were paid fifty-five cents a ton. Once a month they received additional pay for "yardage," work done in the entries. This represented an improvement over earlier years when such "dead work" was uncompensated.

Young Charlie Jones was fascinated by the cutting machine and enrolled in a correspondence course on electric motors. When the cutting machine operator quit the mine, Jones was given the job, which paid fifteen cents a ton. He recalled,

> We had sixteen men in the entry, you would cut the coal for sixteen men with the cutting machine. Then we were working about three days a week in the mine, so if you worked it right, I could load coal when the mine worked, then I could cut coal on the idle days, so I got double shifts.

Jones remembered one paycheck, including his double shifts and yardage, that enabled him to buy a new 1924 Ford:

> I put everything on that coupe I could at that time, even a speedometer, that was a great thing for back then. That car cost me $721. I took the one paycheck and paid for that car and I had $10 left over. So see, we made pretty good money at that time.

Jones's situation was unusual in that he could add earnings from the skilled job of cutting machine operator to the regular pick-and-shovel work of a typical miner. Still, the mines paid well compared to other jobs available in the region. But it was hard and dangerous work. Jones described how miners would hold their carbide lights above their heads to ignite any pockets of methane that might have accumulated in the mine over a weekend:

> When we'd hit the gas, the fire would shoot back over the top of us. Sometimes we got a haircut, but then it was burned out and nobody thought about carbon monoxide being in there to work in. . . . Those machines, when you'd cut with those machines, it was dry, no water on them, no rock dust. I've wondered as the years went by, and I've seen these mines blow up, I've wondered why we didn't blow the top off of some of these mountains the way we mined coal back then.

On one occasion Jones suffered a broken foot when the cutting machine rebounded from a rock spore:

> When I had my broken leg, I laid off about three hours. I went to the doctor that night with a broken foot. He put a cast on and said you better stay off from that for a week. Well, I reported to the boss that I had this broken foot and the next morning at 10:00 he came and got me and said we've got to have you in there to cut

> coal; those men have got to have coal. So, I wrapped a burlap sack on my foot and went in the mine and cut coal.[12]

If coal mining provided a vital economic contribution to the region, it also exacted a toll. Twelve of the 173 victims of the March 1924 Castle Gate explosion were from Emery County. At least five additional victims had close relatives in the county. At least thirteen Emery County men died in other mine accidents during the decade.[13] Many more suffered serious injuries or permanent impairment to their health.

Transportation. By 1930 there were 878 motor vehicles for the county's 1,480 families.[14] This meant that many people still depended on horse-drawn transportation. Still, the rapid growth in numbers of automobiles and attendant travel stimulated a demand for better roads. The major national highway through the county was the Midland Trail, which made a growing economic contribution to Green River and which was improved during the period by route realignments, a gravel surface, and a new steel bridge at Woodside. In 1921 the Pikes Peak Ocean to Ocean Highway was routed through the county, following the Midland Trail route from Green River to Price then turning south through Castle Valley to Wasatch (Salina) Pass. While tourist traffic over this route could not be called heavy, several adventurous motorists passed through the county each week during the summers. Commercial clubs in Emery County and in Salina and Richfield boosted Wasatch Pass as the only all-season route across the mountains, but in places it was scarcely a road at all. The route used the railroad grade and tunnels in the narrow confines of the Salina Creek gorge, despite the threat of legal action by the Denver and Rio Grande, until the company finally took steps to complete the railroad to mines in Salina Canyon. A separate auto road was then built, but as originally laid out it crossed the railroad tracks seventeen times in twenty miles, and the railroad refused to run trains on the track until the numerous grade crossings were eliminated.[15]

State Highway 29, the Orangeville-Ephraim road, was finally completed after long delays in 1921. Its opening was celebrated with a "reunion" at Horseshoe Flat in mid-August, attended by three thousand people including Governor Charles R. Mabey. The Huntington Canyon road, Highway 31, was completed as far as the Forks in 1923. It was extended in 1926 to connect with the Fairview-Connellsville road, and another large celebration was staged with Governor George Dern in attendance. In 1922 a passable road was built over Hogan Summit, providing a direct connection for the first time between Emery County and western Wayne County.[16]

Highway 10, the main transportation artery for the western part of the county, received a gravel surface from Price to Ferron by 1929. In 1930 a new dugway was constructed on the blue hill south of Ferron and an all-weather gravel surface extended to Emery. Before this time Lareda Christiansen Olsen remembered riding the school bus from Emery "when the road ran around every little gully of the mountain south of Ferron. We got stuck several times trying to get up that hill, and the kids would have to get out and try to push the bus up that slick, clay hill."[17]

Retailing. Improved roads and wider access to automobiles made it easier for residents to shop outside of the county. Velma Cox Petersen remembered,

> It was an exciting time in my life when we no longer had to ride horses and the automobile became an every day occurrence in our lives. We could go to Salt Lake City to shop and see the wonders of the city. It was like a fairy land to me. I was so excited to go to ZCMI and helped pick out some special clothes for myself when I was a senior.[18]

At the same time, however, local stores continued to operate much as they had in earlier times. Iola Broderick Waxman remembered working in the Farmers Co-op in Emery, managed by her father Alfred J. Broderick:

> When I was 12 years old, "Pa" handed me a pencil and paper and said, "now write the numbers from 1 to 9 as well as you can." After he looked them over, I was told that I could start clerking the next day. It did not take me long to grasp the significance of the "numbers"—for almost all of the business was on "tick." Those who did not charge, came in with their eggs, wheat and/or oats to buy what was needed. I remember my very largest cash sale was made by Mr.

> McBroom who had just come into town and left his family outside waiting in their covered wagon. The price of eggs that day was 20 cents a dozen. Mr. McBroom said "why that's like eating nickles and dimes, 'cause where I come from eggs are 10 cents a dozen." After filling his order of bacon, lard, flour, sugar, etc., the total price was $15.[19]

A larger operation than the Farmers Co-op was the Duzett store and hotel. Bessie Anderson Jumper recalled,

> To me it seemed huge, to the west and on the ground floor was the department store where they sold everything and I mean everything. There was also the big diningroom where the hotel patrons and the "drummers" (the salesmen) could eat. On the bottom floor was a large kitchen and pantry and a barbershop at the front, also a hotel lobby. The upstairs had 20 rooms and a bathroom and toilets. In the year 1942 it burned to the ground.[20]

Utilities. The 1920s saw an extension and improvement in electric service. The Electric Power and Milling Company tied into the Utah Power and Light lines in 1925, making twenty-four-hour service available for the first time to customers in Orangeville and Castle Dale. Utah Power acquired the Electric Power and Milling franchise and distribution system in 1929 and undertook substantial improvements, among other things moving power poles from the middle to the side of the roads. In the meantime, Utah Power had extended electric service to Ferron in 1927, to Rochester, Emery, and Lawrence in 1929, Cleveland in 1930, and Elmo in 1931. Utah Power entered the Green River market when it bought the local hydroelectric plant in 1925. The company's transmission lines reached Green River in 1928.[21] Many farm homes in the county, even some located quite close to town, remained without electricity for several more years.

Richard Behling recalled the arrival of electricity in Ferron: "To turn on a switch and have light was wonderful. We celebrated for quite a time. We used to just have coal oil lamps. You had to get real close so you could see to read."[22] While electric service was a great convenience, it was still less than reliable. In fact, Irma Petersen Snow recalled that the lights went out during the dance celebrating the turning on of the lights in Ferron.[23] Some boys reportedly discovered

Electricity comes to Huntington. (Courtesy Lucinda B. Wild)

that they could create their own fireworks display by tossing a wet cord over the power lines—not realizing that by so doing they shorted out the mainline breakers at Hiawatha and plunged the entire western part of the county into darkness.[24]

The Eastern Utah Telephone Company that had provided long-distance service to the Castle Valley communities was absorbed into Mountain States Telephone in 1924. Mountain States completed a line between Price and Grand Junction in 1926 thereby providing Green River with telephone connections to the outside.[25] Local service in the county, however, deteriorated as the systems in Ferron and Emery could not generate sufficient revenue to replace worn-out equipment. Only the Castle Dale-Orangeville system continued in operation.

The town water systems made life more convenient, but apart from settling out the mud they did little to improve the quality or safety of the culinary supply. The state sanitary engineer issued a report in 1927 critical of unprotected water sources, noting, "Contrary to the popular idea, water does not purify itself by running such and such a distance."[26]

Most residents continued to depend on outhouses, but the

period brought a gradual advance in indoor plumbing. Irma Petersen Snow has described how her father, Lew Petersen, encouraged the purchase of plumbing supplies at his Ferron Mercantile:

> He could see the people had nothing. If they had no bathroom he would call them aside and say, "Now you've got a big family and you need a bathroom. What could you pay me each month?" Maybe they could give just 25 cents a month, but Dad would buy the bathroom set.[27]

With the development of indoor plumbing, sewage disposal became a necessity. For most homes, this meant a septic tank or perhaps merely a drain pipe to a nearby wash. However, Huntington, Castle Dale, and Green River installed sewer lines in their central areas. These were simple collection systems that discharged raw sewage directly into the streams.[28]

Civic Organizations. An important postwar development was the organization of the American Legion. Emery County veterans established the Blackburn-Axelson post in 1928, naming it for two of the three county residents who lost their lives in actual combat during World War I. A separate post was established in Ferron in 1930. With a large number of young veterans in the county, the American Legion and its women's auxiliary became active social and service organizations. The Masonic Lodge and associated Order of Eastern Star continued to play an important role in Green River. Women's clubs were established in most communities during the period, providing yet other social outlets and service resources. Daughters of Utah Pioneers chapters were organized in the county beginning in 1930.[29]

Schools. The construction program begun with the establishment of the Emery County School District continued into the 1920s with completion of a high school building in Ferron in 1923, a four-room school at Clawson in 1924, and auditorium-gymnasiums, central heating plants, and restroom facilities added to older buildings at Green River, Cleveland, Castle Dale, Orangeville, and Emery.

A potential disaster was narrowly averted in April 1922 when the Huntington Central School caught fire while school was in session. The two-story building had been designed with the furnace room directly under the only stairway. At the instigation of principal Leon

Leonard and sixth grade teacher William P. Jarvis, an exterior fire escape had only recently been added to the building. The fire began in the furnace room, sending smoke and flames directly up the stairway. Quick action by the staff and the discipline of the children, who had been prepared by regular fire drills, resulted in a safe evacuation of the building, but all of the furnishings and school supplies and even the children's coats and personal items were lost. School was dismissed for the remainder of the 1921–22 year and resumed the next fall in several different locations. A modern replacement building with fourteen classrooms and fire-resistant construction was completed in 1925 at the corner of Main and Center streets.[30]

The most important educational development of the decade was the growth of the high schools. Huntington High graduated its first class of ten students in 1921. Ferron and Green River high schools achieved a full senior level at about the same time. The Emery Stake Academy graduated a class of seven in 1921 and a record-large class of twenty-nine at its final commencement in 1922. After the closure of the academy, the building was acquired by the Emery County School District and operated as Central High School, raising the number of public high schools in the county to four. In addition, both Cleveland and Emery schools included the tenth grade and were referred to as high schools. The Ferron Presbyterian school, by this time known as Ferron-Wasatch Academy, offered coursework through the tenth grade in 1921 and had an enrollment of sixty. Some Ferron-Wasatch students transferred to Wasatch Academy in Mount Pleasant to complete their high school work.[31]

The distribution of the county's population among so many different communities made it difficult to satisfy the educational aspirations of all. The citizens of Emery, with a population larger than Green River and only slightly smaller than Ferron or Castle Dale, felt especially neglected because their young people could not complete a high school education at home. Alonzo Brinkerhoff was a vigorous spokesman for Emery interests, arguing in a series of letters to the editor of the *Progress* that if the county could not make a high school education available to all residents, it should close the high schools and devote its resources to improving elementary schools. He pointed out that at the beginning of the 1920s decade, only 17 percent of the total school enrollment was at the senior high school level, and that fewer than half of those students actually graduated. Brinkerhoff also carried his complaints to the state school superintendent. It is hard to tell what the outcome of his campaign might have been if he had not died in the midst of it in July 1922, at the age of fifty-eight, from complications of an infected tooth.

The number of students completing high school increased substantially during the decade of the 1920s, especially after the cancellation of tuition charges in 1926. For example, only five students graduated from Central High in 1924 and eight in 1925, compared to twenty in 1930 and thirty in 1931. In 1931 Huntington High School had an enrollment of 224, Central High and Ferron High 175 each, Green River High School forty-six, Emery High School (grades 7–10) seventy-six, and Cleveland High (grades 7–10) thirty-eight. The growth in high school enrollments led to exchanges of buildings at Huntington and Ferron with the high schools moving into more spacious elementary school buildings.[32]

In response to a new request from Emery residents in 1927 for a full high school, state school officials appointed a committee to study educational opportunities and costs in Emery County. The committee reported that, far from being capable of supporting an additional high school, the county's resources were already spread too thin. They recognized that Green River's isolation made it necessary for that community to have its own high school. They concluded, however, that three high schools were not needed in the western part of the county, and recommended as a preferred option the establishment of a single high school to be located in Castle Dale or Orangeville, with housing to be provided for students from more distant communities. This was the model that had been adopted in Carbon County. If the first option were politically impossible, the committee recommended as a second option consolidation into two high schools, one to be located at Huntington and the other at either Ferron or Castle Dale. As always, any hint of school consolidation raised a storm of opposition. The only actions actually undertaken as a direct result of the report were the closure of small schools at Victor and Lawrence.[33]

As the high schools developed, they took an increasingly prominent role in providing community sports, social, and cultural activities. School dances, plays, concerts, and athletic events attracted audiences of all ages. Basketball was the most popular school sport, with the west-county schools competing in a league with Carbon High School, and Green River High School competing against Grand and San Juan county schools. In the 1930s Green River joined the Emery-Carbon league. Green River fielded a football team for two years in the mid-1920s but gave up the sport because of a shortage of players and the difficulty of scheduling opponents. The first football game in the western part of the county was played in 1925, with Central High defeating Ferron by a score of fifty-four to nothing. Huntington High took up the sport the following year, and all three schools fielded football teams through the 1933 season when tight budgets and concern about injuries (there had been a fatal injury in 1930) led the school district to discontinue the sport.[34]

Churches. Declining population led to the dissolution of the Molen Ward in 1922, with members becoming part of the Ferron Ward. The Lawrence Ward was dissolved in 1921 but reconstituted as a branch in 1922. Its status shifted back and forth from branch to ward several times before it was finally closed in 1943. The Rochester Ward was reduced to branch status in 1923 and dissolved in 1946 with its membership transferred to Ferron.

The Orangeville Ward chapel, completed in 1929 under the leadership of Bishop John H. Taylor, was the first LDS building in the county to be designed on the "new" model that had become a standard in the church, with chapel, classrooms, and cultural hall. Only the western portion of the building was built initially. The cultural hall wing was completed in 1952, at which time the old log social hall adjacent to the church was demolished. The second "new design" LDS chapel was built in Ferron. The old meeting house and all its contents were destroyed by fire in 1920, originating in a newly installed central heating system. The ward met in the Ferron school until 1930 when a new chapel was completed on an attractive hilltop site north of the old meeting house site.[35]

After a period of several years without an LDS organization in Green River, a branch was established in 1923 under the auspices of Carbon Stake, with Wallace Curtis as presiding elder. In 1928 the branch was made into a ward with Henry Thompson as bishop. The

Green River Ward first leased and then purchased the old school building on Long Street, remodeling and expanding it in 1941. Small Seventh Day Adventist and Christian Science groups were active during part of this period, but the Community Presbyterian church continued to hold a central place in the town's religious life.[36]

Little information is available about church activity in Mohrland. The company made the large recreation hall available for worship services, and an LDS branch was in operation as early as 1913, apparently becoming a ward in the 1930s. In 1930 Latter-day Saints numbered 155 in the town's population of 620.[37] Residents of Greek and Italian extraction observed traditional religious feast days in their homes and neighborhoods, but it is not clear whether formal worship services of other faiths were conducted in Mohrland.

Entertainment and Recreation. The growth of music and drama programs in the schools and the increasing availability of commercial entertainment led to a decline in community-based arts activities. The dramatic associations that had long been active in Orangeville and Huntington ceased to exist. On the other hand, what began as a high school program developed into the county's oldest continuing community arts organization. The Huntington Male Glee Club, which was still active in 1995, traces its origins to a male chorus organized at Huntington High School in 1921 by music teacher A. E. Johnson. Directors of the glee club, in addition to Johnson, have included Perry P. Wakefield, who served for thirty-seven years, Errol T. Litster, and Bryce Wilson. The more than 127 men who have belonged to the ensemble span three generations.[38]

Baseball continued to be a popular sport with interest centered in the town teams, which played on Sunday afternoons throughout the summer. For a time, the Eastern Utah Basketball League provided organized competition for town basketball teams from Twin Cities (Castle Dale and Orangeville), Huntington, Mohrland, Hiawatha, Price, and Sunnyside. The LDS church-sponsored M-Men basketball program also took hold in the county during this decade.[39]

Movies grew in popularity throughout the period. The Star Theatre in Ferron, the Rex Theater in Castle Dale, the Bonita Theater in Huntington, and the Gem Theater in Green River all drew good audiences. In Mohrland movies were shown in the multipurpose recreation hall.[40] The 1920s and 1930s were the golden age of radio, with extensive live drama and music programs and the beginnings of news and sports programming. The first radio receivers were expensive. Castle Dale banker Edmund Crawford reportedly paid $500 for his first radio with a loudspeaker. This was more than the price of a new Ford car.[41] Townspeople without radios were invited to the *Emery County Progress* office to listen to broadcasts of the World Series.

Community Celebrations. Green River's Melon Days resumed in 1925 after a hiatus of several years, attracting a reported 700 visitors. By 1928 special trains were running for the event and organizers promised forty tons of free melons to visitors. No celebration was held in 1930 because a bumper harvest of melons and tomatoes left the community with no leisure for a holiday.[42] Peach Days also drew good crowds including political officeholders or candidates. The Emery County Fair was discontinued in the early 1920s but was replaced a few years later by the Emery County Vocational Roundup, a two-day event sponsored by the Castle Dale Commercial Club and featuring educational sessions on economic development as well as entertainment including horse pulling contests, races, games, and dances.[43]

Fishing, Hunting, Wildlife. The Carbon-Emery Fish and Game Association undertook regular plantings of trout in the county's streams. Deer populations, which had been at a low point a few years earlier, made a strong recovery during the 1920s, and the annual deer hunt became a county institution with hundreds of residents heading for the hills each fall. Pheasants were planted in 1924, joining the quail that had been imported several years earlier. The elk herd had grown sufficiently to allow limited hunting beginning in 1925. Fred E. Larsen was installed as the first fish and game warden in the region. Over a long career, Larsen seemed to develop a sixth sense that directed him to where illegal hunting or fishing was occurring in the wide district he supervised. Among other contributions, Larsen proposed the first bow hunt in Utah in 1953.[44]

The Great Depression

Because the Emery County economy was only indirectly connected to national financial markets, the stock market crash in

October 1929 did not have an immediate impact. On 4 July 1930 the *Progress* editorialized optimistically that "business is scraping bottom" and would soon begin to recover: "now is not the time to turn pessimist; the worst is over." In fact, the worst was still to come.

The effects of the Depression began to be felt in 1930, and by 1931 there could be no doubt that the county, like the nation, was in for hard times. Indeed, Emery County was one of the hardest hit regions in one of the hardest hit states because prices for the products of basic industries such as agriculture and mining declined more drastically than prices of manufactured goods. Agricultural prices fell by an average of 40 percent between 1929 and 1933 while industrial prices fell by only 15 percent. Coal production in Utah dropped from 4.6 million tons in 1930 to a low of 2.1 million tons in 1934. The county's economy suffered an additional blow when the Denver and Rio Grande Western Railway realigned its divisions in 1930, consolidating at Helper operations formerly carried on at Green River and Soldier Summit. At the depth of the Depression, almost four out of ten Emery County families were receiving public assistance.[45]

The Banking Crisis. The national financial crisis hit close to home in July 1931 when one of Mount Pleasant's two banks failed and the other experienced a "run" that forced it to close its doors as well.[46] The Emery County Bank was in relatively good financial condition, but its officers became increasingly apprehensive about its capacity to withstand a heavy run of withdrawals. These concerns were crystalized when cashier Edmund Crawford and director A. D. Keller went to Salt Lake City to deposit excess coins. At the city bank, they found a long line of depositors waiting to withdraw their money. At the request of bank management, they carried their bags of coins to the front of the line as a way of demonstrating that they had confidence in the institution's soundness. On their return from the city, they entered into negotiations with the Carbon County Bank in Price that culminated in a merger of the two institutions in February 1932. At the time of the merger, the Emery County Bank had deposits of $178,254 and total resources of $219,716 while the Carbon County Bank had deposits of $495,874 and resources of $631,018. With the merger, the county not only lost a local banking facility but also one of its leading citizens as Edmund Crawford moved to Price as assistant cashier of the new institution.

The Commonwealth Bank at Green River was forced in 1930 to levy an assessment on stockholders to strengthen its capital position. In 1932 it claimed deposits of $38,600 and resources of $67,354. However, it did not reopen after the "bank holiday" of 1933. It would be some three decades before banking services again became available in Emery County.[47]

County Revenue Crisis. With low agricultural prices and growing unemployment, county tax collections also declined. Property tax collected in 1931 came to only 75 percent of the amount assessed. Collections fell to 73 percent in 1933 before recovering slightly to 77 percent in 1934. County government expenditures were cut from $67,552 in 1929 to $40,900 in 1931. The Emery County School District reduced its operating expenditures from $173,750 in fiscal 1932 to $136,301 in 1934. While local taxes decreased, state taxes were increasing to fund various recovery programs. The resulting tax protests were often aimed at local government. A Tax Reform League had chapters in several Emery County towns by 1934. The main thrust of the league's campaign was to reduce property taxes, which imposed a disproportionate burden on farmers and stockmen, and to rely more on income taxes to finance government programs.[48]

Anger over taxes combined with dissatisfaction at the lack of representation on the county commission led the Taxpayers' Protective League of Green River to petition in 1933 that the portion of Emery County south of Price River and east of the San Rafael Reef be transferred to Grand County. The petitioners protested against "taxation without representation" and pointed out that not only was their community divided by the county line but that the Emery County seat was twice as far by highway as Moab, and the trip required them to pass through the seat of another county on the way. The Utah constitution makes changes in county boundaries difficult, requiring majority approval from the voters of both counties affected, so the chances of the Green River petitioners achieving their goal were slight. Nevertheless, the petition caught the attention of county leaders and resulted in several "fence-mending" trips to Green River.

A further territorial issue arose in 1938. The 1890 act creating

Grand County had established the Green River as the boundary line. A 1917 legislative act sought to clarify the boundary by defining it as the *center* of the main channel. However, between 1890 and 1917 the main channel had shifted about half a mile to the east in the area adjacent to Green River City. There was some uncertainty as to whether the area known as "the island" and comprising some 400 acres should belong to Emery County or Grand County. The state attorney general resolved the dispute in favor of Grand County, ruling that the 1917 act was not intended to change the 1890 boundary but merely to define it more precisely.[49] The area in question has since become some of the most valuable commercial real estate in Green River.

Drought. The winter of 1929–30 was the coldest and wettest since 1924. It was followed by one of the warmest and driest winters in history in 1930–31 and a drought that afflicted twenty-three states. Precipitation on the Manti National Forest was the lowest recorded since its establishment. The drought perhaps hastened the merger of the Huntington Canal and Reservoir Association with the Cleveland Canal and Agricultural Company to form the Huntington-Cleveland Irrigation Company. A federal drought aid program made loans available to stockmen to purchase feed, but only one Emery County grower participated even though lack of feed on the San Rafael made it "exceptionally difficult" to carry livestock through the winter.[50]

The next two winters brought heavy snow and extreme cold, causing extensive winter losses of sheep. The winter of 1933–34 apparently began with good mountain precipitation, but the snowpack failed to accumulate in the latter part of the season. Reports in March indicated that the Muddy Creek watershed was almost bare of snow clear up to Heliotrope Mountain at the 9,500-foot level. The Orangeville-Ephraim road was passable by early May, a full month earlier than normal, and the springs on North and South Horn were already drying up. By mid-May the county's streams had dropped to the levels normally expected in August, and it was obvious that Emery County, together with much of the nation, was in for a drought, in the words of the *Emery County Progress*, "the like of which has never before been experienced."[51]

In fact, as Leonard J. Arrington has noted, "never before in

United States history had so little rain fallen over so wide a territory during an entire growing season." In Utah as a whole, available irrigation water was less than 25 percent of the normal supply.[52] In Castle Valley, irrigation streams were consolidated wherever possible to reduce losses through seepage and evaporation. Even so, little could be done to save the crops, which were almost a complete failure with the exception of some first-cutting hay. The Emery-Moore area was especially hard hit with crops estimated at only 15 percent of normal. "Practically every man of that community" was reported to be unemployed by the end of the year. The Cleveland correspondent to the *Progress* wrote, "Our farmers have found that they can raise a crop of whiskers without water, so they are making good use of their opportunity. It seems that all other crops are failing this year." The 1935 Census of Agriculture reported that of 41,725 acres of crop land in Emery County in 1934, only 16,462 acres produced any harvest at all. Crop failure was listed for 10,340 acres while 14,923 acres were left idle. Livestock growers faced not only empty barns but also seriously depleted winter ranges for animals that came from the summer range in bad condition. Some five thousand head of cattle and several thousand sheep were sold to the government in an emergency buying program.

Irrigation companies that had previously been generous in supplying water to towns now began to insist that they take no more than their stock ownership entitled them to have. As a result, the Ferron water system went entirely dry for some periods of time, and Castle Dale adopted strict rules against the use of culinary water on lawns and gardens. The culinary water supply, drawn directly from the depleted irrigation canals, was reported by the state Board of Health to be "badly contaminated" in June, and an emergency typhoid immunization program was initiated.[53]

Drought conditions were responsible for the most destructive forest fire in the county's history. The fire broke out on East Mountain in mid-July and raged out of control for more than a week, destroying several thousand acres of timber in Crandall, Blind, and Horse canyons despite the efforts of a fire-fighting force that included more than 250 Civilian Conservation Corps volunteers. Only the arrival of a spell of rainy weather made it possible to bring the fire under control.[54]

The mountain snowpack continued below average for the next two years, but water shortages were less severe than in 1934. The drought was finally broken with the exceptionally wet and cold winter of 1936–37, when CCC enrollees were pressed into service to help clear the roads and deliver feed to isolated herds of livestock. The cold winter temperatures destroyed the fruit buds in most Emery County orchards, resulting in a "Peachless Peach Day" in Ferron. The Green River district did not have heavy snow but did experience an extreme temperature range from a high of 108 degrees Fahrenheit in June 1936 to a low of minus 42 degrees in January 1937.[55]

Green River Melons. The one exception to the generally bleak condition of Emery County agriculture during the 1930s was the melon industry at Green River. Even in the driest years, the river supplied ample water to irrigate all of the land accessible to cultivation. Moreover, the hot summer temperatures made for ideal growing conditions for melons. In the drought year of 1931, Green River growers produced a bumper crop of cantaloupes that sold at premium prices in New York and Boston. A record 600 acres of melons were planted in 1932. The intensive cultivation required by the crop kept "everybody busy" and made Green River "probably the best town of its size in the state" for employment. The engine shed, abandoned when the railroad moved its division operations to Helper, was converted to a packing shed by the Wilson Produce Company for more than one hundred carloads of melons shipped to eastern markets. The Wilsons were the area's largest growers on their big farm under the "forty-two foot" canal and in addition marketed melons for other growers.

The Green River reached a historic low flow of 498 cubic feet per second by mid-July 1934, making it necessary to raise the diversion dam. With an adequate water supply and another hot, dry summer, melon growers shipped 151 carloads and earned an average of $100 per acre at a time when most farms in the region were experiencing crop failure. Good crops and good markets continued in subsequent years, with shipments peaking at 263 carloads in 1938. As many as sixty workers were employed in the packing sheds during the harvest season in addition to some two hundred pickers.[56]

Relief Programs. The first relief efforts were limited in scope. The Blackburn-Axelson American Legion Post organized a program early in 1932 in which unemployed men trimmed trees and did other community improvement work in Castle Dale in return for donated groceries. The same year the American Red Cross distributed several carloads of flour and crushed wheat in the county as emergency rations.[57]

The state and federal governments began appropriating extra funds for road projects intended to provide work for the unemployed. Contractors were required to fill a certain proportion of their jobs with local workers, each of whom was permitted to work for a limited number of days. For example, each man was allowed only six days' work on a project to gravel Highway 10 from Emery to the Sevier County line. The idea was to provide some assistance for the largest possible number rather than to give more lasting employment to a few. This public works initiative brought significant improvements to the county's roads. Highway 50 was realigned and rebuilt from Woodside to Icelander Wash in 1932, and paved from Green River to Woodside in 1934. Improvements through Green River itself were delayed by a dispute between city officials, who wished to preserve the "zig-zag course" through town, and the State Road Commission, which wanted to realign the route to eliminate no fewer than nine corners. The final six-mile route through town was not agreed upon until 1937. A paved surface on Highway 10 reached Huntington in 1932 and Castle Dale in 1934. The *Progress* commented, "The oiled road will be a great improvement over the old corrugated gravel road which we have been using so long that most of our citizens have loose teeth, if any, from the steady jolting." The pavement reached Ferron in 1938, Orangeville in 1940, and Emery in 1941.[58]

Emery County voters joined in the national Democratic sweep in the 1932 election, giving large majorities to Franklin D. Roosevelt for President, Elbert D. Thomas for the U. S. Senate, and Abe Murdock for the House of Representatives. Local offices also went Democratic that year with the sole exception of Republican J. Frank

Killian as state representative. The Roosevelt New Deal soon introduced a veritable alphabet soup of economic programs. The Civil Works Administration provided temporary employment for men in several county towns to work on streets and sidewalks. Women were hired under the same program to paint schools and prepare hot lunches for school children. Works Progress Administration sewing projects also provided employment for women. By late summer 1933, several dozen Emery County men were working on forest projects. A "wheat adjustment program" compensated farmers for reducing acreage planted to wheat in an effort to eliminate surpluses and raise prices. The Federal Relief Administration distributed food and clothing to families of the unemployed. By 1936 relief and public works programs had expended in the county $291,760 in wages, $120,788 for materials, and $274,988 in direct relief payments.[59]

In addition to road projects, other public works providing significant contributions in the county included new or improved water storage and delivery systems in Clawson, Cleveland, Castle Dale, Emery, and Orangeville, made possible by grants or loans from the Federal Recovery Administration and the Production Works Administration. The PWA also assisted with the construction of a sewer system in Castle Dale. For county residents unable to connect to sewer lines, the PWA offered "sanitary outdoor toilets" at a nominal price. The PWA provided almost half of the $50,000 cost of a 1939 project to pipe culinary water from Birch Spring to Huntington, making this the first water system in the county to draw its supply from a protected source. The federal government also provided much of the cost of manual arts buildings constructed at South Emery, Central, and North Emery high schools between 1935 and 1936.[60]

An interesting, if minor, relief project took place after the Depression had largely ended. In 1941 a large quantity of surplus cotton was shipped to the county for a self-help project to make 550 mattresses.[61] For many families, this marked the end of the straw or cornhusk mattress.

Emery County Courthouse. A major contribution of Depression-era public works programs was the construction of a new courthouse. The old building had grown seriously inadequate for the needs of county government and in addition had developed structural problems that were brought to public attention in March 1933 when the plaster ceiling fell in the recorder's office. The jail, located north of the courthouse, had become unusable, forcing the county to house its prisoners in the Carbon County jail at Price. After considering the possibility of repairing and expanding the old building, county leaders finally decided to take advantage of federal funds that would cover a large share of the cost of a new building on a more prominent site on Main Street. With the assurance of a PWA grant providing 45 percent of the building's $60,000 cost, county voters approved bonding in August 1938. Construction began later that year, and the building, of "PWA Modern" design, was occupied in August 1939. Formal dedication ceremonies were held on 12 February 1940, the sixtieth anniversary of the creation of Emery County.[62]

Self-Help Programs. The LDS church established the Church Security Program (forerunner to the Welfare Program) in 1936 in response to concerns about the large number of church members on the public relief rolls. The initial thrust of this program in Emery County was to emphasize food production and storage. Several ward Relief Societies purchased canning equipment for the use of local members, while priesthood quorums planted potatoes and vegetables expressly for use in the program. In 1938 the Church Security Program acquired coal property on East Mountain, a holding that would later make an important economic contribution to the county.[63] In another self-help enterprise, the Emery County chapter of the Civic and Relief Workers Protective Union leased the old Johnson mine in Cottonwood Canyon and operated it as the Twin Cities Cooperative from 1935 to 1937.[64]

Civilian Conservation Corps. Among the many Depression-relief plans set in motion at the beginning of the Roosevelt administration was the Civilian Conservation Corps, designed to provide job training for young men, who had an especially high unemployment rate. Enrollees were paid $30 per month of which only a small personal allowance was given directly to the men with the remainder being sent to their families. The CCC was conducted under military supervision and was intended, among other purposes, to provide a measure of military training and discipline for a potential reserve force.

The CCC came to Emery County on 29 May 1933 when five officers and twenty-five men arrived in Joe's Valley to begin constructing a "reforestation" camp. Company 959 soon reached its designated strength of two hundred men, almost all of them Utah residents with between one-fourth and one-third coming from Emery County. A branch or "spike camp" was established in Ferron Canyon. The camps operated under a dual leadership, with military officers responsible for discipline but with Forest Service representatives supervising the actual work. The Joe's Valley camp housed its men in tents and had a mess hall and a shower house built of lumber. Bishop John H. Taylor of the Orangeville LDS Ward conducted a religious service at the camp on Sunday evenings, bringing with him a chorus of young women. Company member Willard Smith recalled that "On account of all the attractive young ladies, we always had a good attendance at Sunday night church."[65]

With the coming of cold weather, Company 959 was relocated to Orderville, Kane County, a place the men reportedly found less enjoyable. In the summer of 1934, they moved to Gooseberry Valley at the head of the Price River drainage. The company spent the following winter at Mount Pleasant and returned to Gooseberry for the summer of 1935. Among other projects, they constructed the Skyline Drive between the Orangeville-Ephraim road and the Huntington-Fairview road during this period. The road was dedicated at a celebration attracting more than five thousand participants. They also constructed the fish ponds at Gooseberry and Boulger that continue to provide recreation. In the fall of 1935, Company 959 was sent to a new year-round camp at Ferron, which remained in operation until 1939. A major project of this period was construction of the Ferron Canyon road. In addition, there were "many forest trails to lay, bridges to be put in, ranger stations to be erected, rock and cement work to be done, and drift fences built."[66]

Also in the fall of 1935, a year-round camp was established at the fairgrounds in Castle Dale. This was designated as a "grazing camp," with enrollees working on projects on public lands outside the national forest. The major undertaking was the construction of the road from Castle Dale to Buckhorn Draw and the building of the suspension bridge across the San Rafael River, dedicated in April 1937 at ceremonies that attracted a crowd estimated at more than two thousand. In addition, this company completed numerous stock-watering facilities. In 1938 the Castle Dale company was transferred to a new camp at Willow Springs, south of Emery, where the men built the roads into Last Chance and Mussentuchit that are still in use.[67]

Another CCC camp assigned to the grazing division was established at Green River in 1938, occupied by Company 3556. The high proportion of Slavic names on the camp roster suggests that this camp was probably manned chiefly by enrollees from the East or Midwest. Among many range improvement projects, the Green River company helped build the Green River cutoff road that reduced the travel distance from Green River to Castle Dale by almost half.[68]

The normal strength of each CCC company was between 150 and 200 men. These numbers represented a substantial addition to the population of the communities in which they were located and made a significant impact on the county's social and recreational activities. Nyla Huntsman Mumm, whose home was near the Ferron camp, remembered that her mother sewed for the men and often invited them over for Sunday dinner. According to Mumm, "Most of the girls in Ferron married a C.C.C. boy." Another account puts the number of marriages at forty-seven. Social integration into the community was apparently more difficult for enrollees at the Castle Dale camp, most of whom came from midwestern and southern states. But some of these men also married local women. Several dozen Emery County young men were enrolled in the Civilian Conservation Corps at one time or another. The money sent to their families, most of whom were on the welfare rolls, made a significant difference in their ability to obtain the basic necessities of life. The CCC program also provided employment for some local men in supervisory and support positions.[69]

Getting Along in Depression Times. The Great Depression had a severe impact on almost all residents of the county, even those with fairly substantial assets. For example, Karl Seely, who had dropped out of school in the seventh grade to herd sheep for his brother Hyrum, had accumulated a substantial herd of his own and a large home on West Main Street in Castle Dale by the time the Depression hit. The collapse of prices for wool and lambs was sudden and drastic. According to his wife, Cora, "One day they could sell wool for forty-seven cents per pound; the next day there was no market." Nevertheless, the sheep still had to be sheared and the shearers paid. Seely kept his wool in rented boxcars at the Mounds shearing corral while he sought a buyer. He eventually found a Boston company willing to store the wool in their warehouse, but it was two years before the wool was sold, and then it brought only five cents a pound.

In order to keep his operation afloat, Seely was forced to borrow money from a Salt Lake City livestock loan company. The lender exacted stringent terms, including a pay cut from $60 to $40 per month for Seely's three herders, a prohibition against buying oats to feed the horses and pack mules, and a limit of $75 a year for the Seelys' household expenses. Seely managed to survive within these strict limits largely through the ingenious use of old ewes as a barter commodity. He traded old ewes to Clabe Elder in exchange for lumber from Elder's sawmill in Reeder Canyon. The lumber was then given as an in-kind supplement to his reduced cash wages to a herder who was building a house in Ferron. Bricks for the house were obtained through a three-way trade: old ewes to Vern Petersen in exchange for coal from his Rock Canyon mine which then went to brickmaker Pete Jensen to fuel his kiln. More ewes were traded for coal that was exchanged for seven-year-old Jane Seely's dance lessons. Seely traded old ewes to Peter Johansen for oats, part of which went to feed the horses and pack mules and part of which was deposited at Singleton's store in Ferron as a credit against which the herders' wives could purchase needed commodities. Other old ewes went to Leo Petersen in exchange for lettuce from his Joe's Valley ranch.

In an effort to reduce livestock numbers during the drought year 1934, federal grazing authorities decreed that no animal over the age of five could be put on the range. The government paid ten cents for each old animal destroyed, with the ears to be turned in as proof. The pelt was worth an additional fifty cents, but the carcass had no market value. Rather than allow the meat to go to waste, Seely gave old ewes to his neighbors free for the butchering, asking only that they return the ears and pelt to him.

While her husband exercised his ingenuity to maintain the livestock operation, Cora Seely became equally adept at managing household expenses. She kept a close eye on the electric meter. If it threatened to exceed the allowance covered by the minimum $1 a month charge, she simply turned off the power for the remainder of the month. She sold cream from her milk cow to Bill Snow, who operated a confectionery. For a pint of cream, she could buy two sheets of stationery, two envelopes, and two stamps. She would write to her husband, who spent most of the time out with the sheep, in care of the post office at Hanksville, enclosing the extra stamp and stationery so that he could write back. On one occasion she made a dress for her daughter and a pair of trousers for her young son from the heavy green wool of an army coat and trousers that Karl had purchased for $2 from a destitute man on the street in Price. On another occasion she made a slip for herself and diapers for her baby from the ticking of a straw mattress that Karl had obtained from a neighbor in exchange for mutton.[70]

Charles Jones was in the home construction business in Salt Lake City when the Depression hit. The collapse of the housing market and the loss of his working capital in a bank failure sent him home to the farm near Elmo in February 1931:

> We had a shack out there to move into and I had to fix that up, you know. Boy, I could plow. So I got me a team of horses and a plow and I planted ten acres of ground. Nobody was using the water, it was just running down the wash, so I went up the canal and took the water down and watered my grain; I started watering my alfalfa. My neighbor came up by there and here I am irrigating in February. He said, "Charlie, you're not irrigating?"

This early irrigation turned out to be vital in the drought year of 1931.

The Jones family got through the Depression as many others did, producing their own food and picking up what money they could from odd jobs. Fortunately, they found that some expenses were lower in Emery County. Their first two children, born in Salt Lake City, had cost $115 each for normal obstetric care. The children born in Elmo were delivered by Dr. Hill for only $25, including prenatal care.[71]

Despite hard times, young people continued to marry and begin family life though it often required clever management to make a start. Roxie Westover Nelson recalled that during her three-year courtship with Paul A. Nelson,

> I worked and bought a sewing machine, vacuum, silverware, pressure cooker and many other things. Momma made me seven quilts and canned many cases of fruit and vegetables and jellies for me. When Paul could get time off from the farm he cut timber off the mountain and had lumber sawn from it to use for our home.

After their 1937 marriage,

> We lived with his folks for several months while Paul made dobes. Willie Thompson, his brother-in-law, and Paul built us a little three room frame home in Ferron where I live today at 650 West Mill Road. On March 3, 1938, we moved in and were very happy even though we had very little money. We built the house for $300. Paul hauled coal for Willie for his work on the house and Uncle Frank Petty came from Emery and plastered the house for us. It was very well made.[72]

Similar stories could be told of many other "Depression houses," constructed with a minimal cash outlay and maximum ingenuity. For example, the Neal and Esther Rowley home at 333 North Main in Huntington was built in 1935 of sawed logs purchased from William "Kaibab" Frandsen and delivered from Panguitch for $600. William Green did the finish carpentry for $3 a day, and other labor was paid for in farm produce. Built in bungalow style with large windows, a generous front porch, and a stucco exterior, the house reveals no outward sign of its unusual construction.[73]

An important source of inexpensive housing was the houses made surplus by reduced employment at Sunnyside and West Hiawatha and later by the closure of Mohrland. Typically four-room cottages of lightweight frame construction, these houses could sometimes be purchased for substantially less than the cost of the materials. For a modest investment, they could be moved to a new location, placed on a new foundation, and refurbished as comfortable family homes. Numerous examples of these "camp houses" can still be found in the county.

In view of the scarcity of money, the extent of homebuilding during the Depression is surprising. The Huntington correspondent to the *Progress* claimed in 1937 that more new homes had been erected in that town during the preceding three or four years than at any other time in history.[74] For those who had some money to build with, the low prices of conventional materials and labor allowed the construction of fine residences in the period revival styles that were popular at the time. Among many examples is the Willard O. Sandberg home in Spanish colonial revival style, built by a member of the first graduating class at Huntington High School who had come back from New York to assume management of the family-owned Huntington Flour Mill. The Harry S. Nielsen home in Ferron, a pressed brick Tudor revival house with local rock specimens embedded in the brickwork, was built as a combined residence-office by a native son who had returned from dental school to establish a practice in his home town.

A different approach to getting through the Depression was adopted by another Harry Nielson, known as "the hermit of Orangeville." Nielson, who had drifted to Emery County after years of wandering, set up housekeeping in a dugout south of town where he kept a small herd of sheep and spent much of his time painting and writing poetry. For a supposed hermit, he was rather sociable and received visitors quite happily. Several issues of the *Progress* in 1939 contained poems composed by Nielson.[75]

Schools. The Emery County School District saw its revenues decline while enrollments increased as former residents returned to their homes in the county after losing jobs elsewhere and as more students remained in school until graduation because there were no employment opportunities to tempt them to drop out. Expenditures were reduced from $173,750 in fiscal 1932 to $136,301 in 1934. Financial pressures made it necessary for school officials to pursue further consolidation. Grades four through eight at Clawson were transported to Ferron beginning in 1931. In 1933 the younger grades were also taken to Ferron and the Clawson school discontinued. Also in 1933 tenth grade students from Emery were transferred to Ferron and those from Cleveland to Huntington. With this move, Ferron High School adopted the name South Emery and Huntington High became North Emery. These changes were, of course, strongly protested in the affected communities. Some citizens turned to the courts in an unsuccessful effort to have the decision reversed, and many students boycotted the schools for several weeks at the beginning of the 1933–34 school year.[76]

Another Depression-related development was the school lunch program. It apparently began in Ferron when teacher Fern Young observed that some children were coming to school with little or nothing to eat. She organized a program by which parents could contribute produce and obtain credit for meals, prepared by volunteers, that were otherwise sold to the children for three cents. With the coming of government work programs, local women were hired to prepare school lunches, and the program extended throughout the county.

Superintendent James A. Nuttal guided the county's schools through the most critical period of the Depression. In 1936 Nuttal was made president of Snow College. His successor as superintendent was W. O. Bickmore, who had been coach and principal at Green River for several years. By 1937 school operating budgets and teacher salaries had generally been restored to pre-Depression levels, though there was a ripple of apprehension through all taxing entities that year when the bankrupt Denver and Rio Grande Western Railroad paid only one-fourth of its taxes by the normal deadline and demanded a reduction of 15 percent in its assessment.[77]

Consolidation continued to be promoted by the school board as a way to reduce expenses and provide wider opportunities to students but resisted by the communities threatened with loss of their schools. In 1939 seventh, eighth, and ninth graders from Emery, Orangeville, and Cleveland were required to be bused to the high schools, but parental protests resulted in the return of seventh and eighth grades to their community schools. Another conflict erupted in the fall of 1940 when the school board closed the Elmo school. Parents refused to allow their children to board the bus and instituted court action to block the move. After a boycott lasting several weeks, the residents accepted a compromise solution keeping students in Elmo through the fifth grade and sending the sixth, seventh, and eighth grades to Cleveland. The following year the Utah Supreme

Court ruled that the school board had no authority to close schools, and the Elmo school was restored to its grades one through eight status.[78]

Churches. When Lars P. Oveson was succeeded by A. Richard Peterson of Ferron as Emery Stake president in 1929, it marked the end of the pioneer generation of LDS leadership. Peterson served until 1936 when he was called to preside over the Norwegian Mission. He directed the withdrawal of missionaries at the outbreak of war, and returned to Norway again at the war's end. Peterson's successor as stake president was J. Frank Killian of Orangeville. He was succeeded in 1944 by Eldon G. Luke, also of Orangeville. The Victor Ward was dissolved in 1935 and its membership transferred to Elmo. When the Clawson school was closed in 1933, the Clawson Ward under the direction of Bishop A. Ludene Cox acquired and remodeled the building to serve as a meeting house.[79]

The new Ferron chapel was destroyed by fire in 1934 and rebuilt in 1935 using the original foundation and walls. With some additions and remodeling, this attractive building was still serving the community in 1995. The Cleveland Ward lost its meetinghouse to fire on 14 April 1938 when a projector overheated during the showing of a movie. Plans first proposed in 1935 were set in motion in 1937 under Bishop Elmer A. Nielson to demolish the original Emery Stake Academy building that had been serving as the Castle Dale Ward meetinghouse and erect a new building on the same site. Over the next few years, timber was harvested for the new building and a large brick kiln was set up near the site, with a quarter of a million bricks formed by volunteer labor and burned under the direction of Allie Jones. The outbreak of war brought a halt to building plans, and the combined Castle Dale Ward–Emery Stake building was not completed until 1952 on a different site.[80]

The Green River Presbyterian church apparently had difficulty in keeping a pastor during this period, with at least nine different men serving between 1921 and 1941. The longest tenure was that of Rev. Marion S. Hostetler (1935–40), and there were extended periods during which the pulpit was occupied by retired ministers or others on temporary assignments. Stability was provided by the lay elders and trustees and by a very active women's group.[81] The Ferron

Presbyterian Mission continued to provide Sunday school and Christian Endeavor services and summer Bible classes until 1942 when the Ferron Presbyterian Community Center was closed.[82]

Prohibition and Repeal. Law officers spent much of their time during the 1920s and early 1930s attempting to enforce the national prohibition of alcoholic beverages. Typically a majority of cases at each court session dealt with the disposition of seized liquor. People were arrested for making wine at Mohrland and Cleveland, and stills were discovered and destroyed at several locations. Eleven barrels of apple cider were seized from a Castle Dale fruitgrower. A violent confrontation occurred in 1931 when Dempsey (Slim) Rigney of Price was shot and killed during a raid by Emery and Carbon law officers on a still near Woodside.[83]

Prohibition-enforcement efforts apparently had little impact on the availability of alcohol. Owen McClenahan reported that it was easy to make home-brew beer using malt that could be purchased in local stores. "Many people made wine" in Mohrland, hauling grapes from California by the truckload. Saki was available in the Japanese district near the mine portal. A well-known bootlegger near Cleveland avoided arrest by concealing his fermenting mash under his sheep pens. A Lawrence resident had a reputation as "the greatest bootlegger of whiskey in Utah and Western Colorado," employing several men to operate stills "hidden out in the fringe areas of the San Rafael Swell, Mud Water, Gordon Creek, Nine Mile, and the Book Cliff Mountains—any remote place with a good waterhole." Bootleg whiskey was typically sold to distributors for four dollars a gallon. By using "'12-ounce short pints,' one could fill 12 pints out of a gallon and sell them for one dollar each, making a profit of eight dollars. At that time, they would have to work eight days in the hayfield for the same money." On dance nights at Wilbergs', "You only had to walk along the road between the long rows of parked cars, and someone would come up to you and ask if you were looking for a drink. The price was a dollar a pint; it never changed."[84]

Antiprohibition sentiment increased throughout the nation in the early 1930s. The *Emery County Progress* argued editorially that prohibition did little to reduce the availability of alcohol but made the liquor trade profitable for the "criminal element." On the other side, the Emery Stake Relief Society took an active role in campaigning against repeal, with stake officers visiting the wards to give talks on the evils of drink. When Utah voted in November 1933, the statewide tally was three-to-two in favor of repeal. Emery County, however, voted heavily against repeal, with only Green River and Mohrland producing pro-repeal majorities.[85]

When the sale of beer became legal in Utah in May 1934, Huntington, Castle Dale, Emery, and Green River had ordinances in place and were ready to issue bottled beer licenses immediately. In 1935 the newly established Utah Liquor Control Commission established liquor stores in Ferron, Castle Dale, Huntington, and Green River. The Ferron and Huntington outlets were later closed.[86]

Public Safety. Burglaries became more frequent after the onset of the Great Depression. In some instances the culprits were transients; in others they were local people, often young men. Burglars usually chose small, easily transportable items such as tobacco and candy, but thieves using trucks cleaned out most of the stock of the Peacock Cash Store in Orangeville and the Nellie Vandling Dress Shop in Green River. The safe at the Huntington post office was dynamited in November 1932. The same month a Castle Dale teenager was shot in the leg by the town marshall during a burglary at Huntington Brothers store. Merchants in Castle Dale and Huntington organized to hire night watchmen to patrol the streets in an attempt to discourage breakins. In 1936 druggist L. T. Hunter surprised a burglar in the act of entering his store and put a bullet through the door of the fleeing car.[87]

The development of a state highway system led in turn to the establishment of a highway patrol to enforce traffic laws. Lawrence native Joe Arnold was apparently the first state highway patrol officer assigned to Emery County. In addition to apprehending drunk drivers, investigating accidents, and trying to keep livestock off the roads, Arnold spent much time instructing local drivers about the importance of such things as stop signs.[88]

Violent crimes were not common occurrences in Emery County though there were several assaults and at least two killings at Mohrland. A "water killing" occurred at Huntington in 1924 when one farmer struck another in the head with his shovel during a quarrel over irrigation flows.[89] County residents were shocked by three violent deaths during a single month in 1936. In late July merchant Robert L. Duzett of Emery died from head injuries received in a scuffle with two young men he was attempting to eject from the Duzett beer parlor. The jury, apparently unable to agree on the defendants' intent to cause fatal injuries, convicted them of simple assault. Less than a month later, Sheriff William L. Black and Roy Black were gunned down at a farm east of Ferron by Roy Black's brother-in-law Hugh Wayman. There had reportedly been "bad blood" for some time between Wayman and Roy Black. After a threatening encounter between Mrs. Black and her brother earlier in the day, the Blacks sought the assistance of the sheriff, while at the same time Wayman went into town to purchase bullets for his .30-40 rifle. Wayman had been an unsuccessful candidate for the Democratic nomination for sheriff won by William L. Black in 1934, and reportedly had held a grudge against the sheriff since that time. At his trial, however, Wayman maintained that he had not recognized the sheriff when he fired at him. Prosecutors sought the death penalty, but the jury convicted Wayman of second degree murder in the shooting of Sheriff Black and imposed a sentence of from ten years to life imprisonment. He was paroled in 1943 over the protests of the victims' relatives but with the support of a petition reportedly signed by some five hundred county residents.[90]

Sheriff Black was the first law enforcement officer to lose his life in the line of duty in Emery County. However, sheriffs and deputies and local town marshals put their lives at risk on many occasions in carrying out their duties. For the most part these were men with no formal training in law enforcement. As citizen-police, they sometimes accomplished their tasks in unconventional but effective ways. For example, during the term of O. W. Sitterud as sheriff from 1922 to 1926, the county jail had deteriorated to such a point that he was unwilling to keep prisoners in it. Those accused of more serious crimes were held at Price, but Sitterud sometimes took minor offenders to his own home in Orangeville where one family lived in a tent in the back yard for several months.

Recreation. The Star Theatre in Ferron was the first movie house in the county to install equipment for playing the new "talkies" in

1930. The Gem Theater in Green River was purchased and upgraded by merchant W. F. Asimus in 1931. The Castle Dale LDS Ward acquired the projection equipment of the Rex Theatre in 1930 and began showing movies in the ward meetinghouse. Local wards also provided movies at Emery, Huntington, and Cleveland.[91]

Dances continued to be an important recreational activity. The formal junior proms at the high schools and Gold and Green Balls sponsored by the LDS Mutual Improvement Association attracted large crowds including both young people and older ones. The Christmas-New Year's week would have at least one dance every night somewhere in the western part of the county, and increasing access to automobiles made it possible for more people to go dancing outside their own communities. This was the era also of the outdoor dance pavilion, including the Star View pavilion built by Ross Pettey and Ivan Jensen east of Ferron and several dance pavilions in Carbon County that were patronized by Emery County residents. The most popular dancing place in the Emery-Carbon region, however, was the Wilberg Resort.

Wilberg Resort. The opening of Wilbergs' on 3 July 1929 was a landmark event. The hilltop grove planted by Carl Wilberg at his ranch midway between Castle Dale and Huntington had been a popular destination for picnics and parties for the two previous decades. Now, however, the Wilberg family undertook a more ambitious effort to turn the grove into a commercial attraction appealing to the large population of young people in the Emery-Carbon region. They constructed the largest dance floor in the area, measuring eighty by 120 feet, booked the most popular dance bands, and drew crowds as large as a thousand on peak-season Saturday nights. In addition to the dance floor, the resort also offered refreshment stands, swings, swimming, boating, and a small zoo. Ever the opportunist, Carl Wilberg extended the season into the fall by building a warming fire at the center of the dance floor and offering free watermelon to patrons.

The resort was only one facet of an extensive family economy. Carl Wilberg had displayed a strong entrepreneurial bent from the time he arrived in Castle Dale as a young school teacher in 1885. He dealt extensively in farm land, buying, selling, and trading. At one low point in his fortunes, he was reportedly reduced to living in a borrowed range shack. However, by the early years of the twentieth century he had accumulated substantial holdings. As his sons grew up, they assumed responsibilities in the family enterprises. Evin Wilberg managed the United Meat Market, which the Wilbergs acquired from Evin's father-in-law, Peter Tolboe, in 1921 and which served the Castle Dale trade with the first refrigeration plant in the area. Cyrus Wilberg ran the slaughtering operation to provide meat for the local market and for delivery to the Carbon County coal camps. In the early 1930s, the Wilbergs acquired the Black Diamond coal mine in Straight Canyon, and Cyrus and his sons assumed management of this enterprise. Rufus and Warren took the major responsibility for the family's farming and livestock operations, including a fox farm.

The entire family participated in running the resort, staffing ticket windows and food booths, directing traffic, or helping with security or cleanup. Attendance declined in the late 1930s, and the resort did not reopen after the 1941 season, but its twelve years of operation had been memorable. As Owen McClenahan recalled, "The Wilberg Resort took the edge off the depression. Everyone had to work hard to earn just enough to eat and buy a few clothes. Dancing at Wilbergs gave the people the relaxation they needed."[92]

Wildlife and Fossils. Mountain lions, bears, coyotes, and bobcats were hunted less as a sport than as predator control intended to protect domestic livestock and deer herds. According to reports from government hunter Clayton Kofford, an average of more than five hundred predators were trapped or shot each year during the late 1930s. The Joe's Valley area gained a wide reputation for producing large mountain lions. This brought a Vermont-based guide and hunter named Bill Green to the area in the winters of 1939–40 and 1940–41. From a base at the Olsen ranch, Green, his celebrity clients, and his trained lion dogs killed numerous animals. Green's Emery County hunts were the subject of a feature article in the popular magazine *Colliers* in June 1943. On one occasion the Castle Dale Lions Club served sandwiches made with meat from animals killed by Green.[93]

Emery County was gaining increased recognition as a major source of dinosaur fossils. Fossil beds east of Molen attracted the attention of researchers from the California Institute of Technology in 1941. They termed it "one of the richest finds in the country." The University of Utah excavated several specimens from a quarry near the Red Seeps in 1932. In 1937 a party from the Smithsonian Institution made a significant discovery of dinosaur fossils on North Horn Mountain. Cleveland native William Lee Stokes took his knowledge of Emery County fossils with him when he went to Princeton University for graduate study in geology. In 1941 he was mounting specimens from the county in the natural history museum at Princeton.[94]

Recovery

The low point of the Great Depression for Emery County was the drought year of 1934 and its immediate aftermath. Livestock prices, influenced by government herd-reduction programs in 1934, rose substantially in 1935 and gradually improved in subsequent years. A service bonus to veterans of the First World War injected $111,418 into the county's economy in 1936, money that was used in some cases to pay back taxes and mortgages on farms or to enable the recipients to build homes. Utah coal production, which had bottomed out at 2.1 million tons in 1934, recovered to 3.4 million tons in 1937. Still, some five hundred families remained on the relief rolls in 1938. The county's 1938 assessed valuation of $5.39 million was 23.5 percent below the 1930 level.[95]

The tax and employment base received a heavy blow in 1938 with the closing of Mohrland. Substantial coal reserves remained in Cedar Creek Canyon, but the United States Fuel Company elected to extract the coal through the King Mine and process it at a new preparation plant at Hiawatha. When the impending closure was announced, the *Progress* lamented that "one of the prettiest little towns in the county with many good substantial buildings will become a ghost town by September 1 of this year." Upon the cessation of operations, the buildings at Mohrland were sold to a Salt Lake City salvage firm for $50 each, and few traces of the town remained. The U.S. Fuel decision to consolidate operations at Hiawatha rather than at Mohrland caused some resentment in Emery County. Some people blamed the loss of the town on the school district's failure to provide a school building comparable to the larger and newer facility at Hiawatha.[96]

While this may have played a role in the company's decision, other considerations seem obvious. Hiawatha offered a slightly shorter haul to market and a more spacious site for a preparation plant. Furthermore, Carbon County's ethnic diversity was probably more congenial to most miners than Emery County's predominant Anglo-Scandinavian Mormon population.

While the county lost its major coal operation with the closing of Mohrland, smaller mines expanded production as improved motor trucks and roads made it feasible to ship coal to market without a railroad. At least ten mines were operating in Huntington Canyon by the end of the 1930s decade. The Huntington Canyon road was realigned and rebuilt between 1939 and 1940 to accommodate the heavy coal truck traffic.[97] Elsewhere in the county, the old Ottosen mine on the slopes of East Mountain north of Orangeville was acquired by the Castle Valley Fuel Company in 1938. The Oliphant and Black Diamond mines in Straight Canyon were upgraded during the same period. The Browning/Duzett mine south of Emery supplied coal to the Salina-Richfield market even though the Salina Canyon road was sometimes almost impassable to trucks.

Water Development. The drought experience of the mid-1930s had a sobering effect on water users. The Huntington-Cleveland Irrigation Company completed the Rolfson Reservoir with assistance from the Federal Emergency Reconstruction Administration in 1935. Ferron Reservoir was also enlarged. The Blue Cut Canal Company finally agreed to merge with the Cottonwood Creek Consolidated Irrigation Company, bringing all major users on that creek into one system. At the same time, Sanpete interests were looking yet again to the Castle Valley watershed to augment their water supply. Ephraim water users obtained government funding for a 7,000-foot tunnel to divert water from the Beck's Creek drainage. Spring City interests diverted water via another tunnel from Black Canyon, and Mount Pleasant City made yet another diversion from Potter and Bacon Rind canyons.[98]

The quest for a stable water supply brought renewed interest in the Joe's Valley reservoir site. The state planning board endorsed the project in 1937, and test holes were drilled at the dam site. In 1939 the Ephraim Lions Club spearheaded an effort to have the Joe's Valley reservoir built using federal relief funds on the grounds that water storage to meet the rights of Cottonwood Creek users "would permit the bringing of all available water through the Ephraim tunnel 12 months of the year."[99] With this regional support and a Bureau of Reclamation study that recognized it as one of the most economical storage projects in Utah, the Joe's Valley project made it to the top of the state's priority list. In 1941 the Bureau of Reclamation strongly supported construction of Joe's Valley dam through the Case-Wheeler Small Reservoirs Act, which would have provided half of the cost of the project through WPA and CCC labor with water users paying the other half over an extended period at an estimated cost of only $1.50 per acre-foot.[100]

Because of the limited acreage of irrigable land on Cottonwood Creek, the Joe's Valley project to be feasible required the participation of Huntington Creek water users. The Huntington-Cleveland Irrigation Company had proposed building a reservoir at Miller Flat, but the Bureau of Reclamation decided that the Miller Flat reservoir project was not cost effective and declined to participate in its construction, urging Huntington-Cleveland water users to support the Joe's Valley project instead. The proposed allocation of Joe's Valley water included 3,920 acre-feet of supplemental irrigation water to users on Cottonwood Creek, 13,430 acre-feet to the Huntington-Cleveland system, 630 acre-feet to be diverted from the Huntington watershed to the Gooseberry project, and 750 acre-feet from the Cottonwood Creek watershed to be diverted to Ephraim and Spring City.

Stockholders in the Cottonwood Creek Consolidated Irrigation Company gave unanimous approval to the Bureau of Reclamation proposal. The Huntington-Cleveland Irrigation Company withheld its support despite the prospect of receiving almost three-fourths of the Joe's Valley water. Stated reasons for hesitation included a concern about the cost of the high-line canal, concerns about the diversion of Huntington Creek water to Gooseberry, and a desire to develop the full resources of the Huntington Creek watershed with the Miller Flat project.[101] Though not publicly stated, it is likely that the old rivalry between Huntington and Castle Dale was also a factor. However, it is far from certain that Joe's Valley would have been built at that time even if it had received enthusiastic support. The Gooseberry project was ranked ahead of Joe's Valley on the Bureau of Reclamation priority list, but construction never began because of wartime shortages of materials and labor and the discontinuance of WPA and CCC programs.

Instead of continuing serious negotiations for Joe's Valley water, the Huntington-Cleveland Irrigation Company proceeded on its own to develop the Miller Flat reservoir, acquiring the land by condemnation in June 1941 and beginning excavations for the dam in October.[102] However, the outbreak of war delayed this project as well. The reservoir was completed after the war with a smaller capacity than originally intended, storing only the waters of Miller Flat Creek rather than including adjacent streams.

Regulation and Improvement of Range Livestock. Coincidental with the drought of 1934 was the passage of the Taylor Grazing Act, which for the first time introduced grazing regulations to the public lands outside the forest. Emery and Carbon counties and some adjacent areas were included in Utah Grazing District Seven, with an elected board divided equally between cattle growers and sheep growers to develop rules and allocate grazing permits. Emery County stockmen chaired this board for forty years, including Jesse M. Conover of Ferron (1935–40), Ray Jensen of Castle Dale (1940–44, 1950–54), Seely J. Peterson of Molen (1944–50), Lawrence E. Thorderson of Cleveland (1954–58), and Ellis Wild of Ferron (1958–74). In 1936 the board took a stand in opposition to the creation of the proposed Escalante National Monument, which would have included some land in southeastern Emery County. The board also pushed for policies that favored stockmen with private lands in the area over those who relied exclusively on public grazing lands.[103] The process of adjusting livestock numbers to the range resources continued over many years. In 1941, for example, the Emery Cattlemen's Association was reported to be "ready to cooperate through the purchase and cancellation of grazing permits to reduce the stock on the Muddy range in the interest of fatter stock and better range conditions."[104]

With a general reduction in the size of livestock herds, the emphasis turned to improving the quality. Cattlemen from the Huntington area organized a Hereford Days celebration beginning in October 1937 to promote the region's breeding stock. In March 1939 the first Emery County Future Farmers of America livestock show, the predecessor of the Southeastern Utah Junior Livestock Show, was held at Ferron. These organizations competed for attention and state funding for several years before the Huntington show was discontinued in 1942.[105]

Communications. Huntington finally entered the telephone age with the installation of a modern dial system by Mountain States Telephone in 1940, one of the first such systems in the state.[106] The Castle Dale Telephone Company continued to provide services to Castle Dale and Orangeville with its old-fashioned equipment. The hand-switched "party line" system had a distinctive ringing signal for each patron, but it was not uncommon for other parties to join a conversation in progress. During its latter years, the company was operated by the Alva Wall family. Wall served as manager, lineman, and general trouble shooter, while his wife and children took turns operating the switchboard, which was located, together with the Walls' living quarters, on the upper floor of the old Emery County Bank building. In addition to local calls, the operators also handled the long distance calls that came over the Bell System lines. Bell operators used codes to facilitate the transfer of information, but independent telephone companies were not allowed access to the code books. Mozell Wall Van Buren, who spent many hours at the switchboard, recalled some of the complications that could develop:

> Although the independents soon learned most of the codes, it was always a source of some irritation when the Bell operators would begin to rattle off strange letters or numbers. One day a call came in for Mr. Wall. Mozell politely told the operator that he was not available at that time but that she would have him return the call as soon as he came in. This did not satisfy the operator who curtly demanded more information. Mozell very coolly said, "O M C." After a long silence the operator came back on the line and said, "I am sorry but I do not find 'O M C' in my code book; please tell me what it means." Mozell replied, "Out milking cow."[107]

Medicine and Public Health. Dr. Bruce Easley continued to practice in Ferron throughout this period, his standing in the community attested by the frequency with which he was invited to speak at funerals. Dr. T. C. Hill also continued to see patients in Huntington. Dr. F. R. King moved his practice from Green River to Price in 1943. Only in Castle Dale was there a succession of doctors. When Dr. J. W. Nixon moved to Provo in 1938, his Emery County practice was acquired by Dr. Alfred Sorensen, who had practiced for several years at Mohrland. Sorensen stayed for only a short time before returning to his native Iowa. He was succeeded by Dr. Sims Duggins, who remained until 1943 when he moved to Panguitch to take charge of a newly constructed hospital. Duggins was followed by Dr. Benjamin Turman, who was for several years the only resident practicing physician in the county.[108] After the retirement of Castle Dale dentist Paul Christensen in the early 1920s, the county was without a resident dentist until Dr. Harry Nielsen established a practice in Ferron in the mid-1930s.

Limited public health services were offered through the schools beginning in the 1920s. Depression-era government programs included free clinics for children. A county public health program was first established in 1938, with Maurine Nielson as director.[109]

Epidemic diseases continued to take a toll, though not on the same scale as in earlier years. A diphtheria outbreak in Molen in 1936 claimed two lives in the same family. A reported 110 cases of diphtheria occurred in the county during a 1937 outbreak, but improved treatments prevented the fatalities that would have occurred during an earlier period. Improved culinary water systems, even though well below current standards, brought a marked reduction in the incidence of typhoid. At the same time as old diseases were being conquered, a new, or at any rate newly recognized disease made its appearance. The first Emery County polio victim was apparently eight-year-old Scottie J. Swasey of Ferron, who died in March 1943.[110]

The War Years

The deteriorating conditions in Europe were reflected in the syndicated boilerplate sections of the *Emery County Progress* for some time before they made any apparent impact on daily life in the county. Beginning in 1939, some LDS missionaries from the county were given early releases or reassigned to stateside missions after being withdrawn from Europe.

Voluntary enlistments in the armed services increased during 1939 and 1940. In accordance with the Selective Service Act, a draft board was established in October 1940 with county commissioners Rosel J. Jensen of Huntington and Stewart Wilson of Green River and county clerk Hector L. Peterson of Castle Dale as its first members. It turned out that Wilson was ineligible to serve because he was still of draftable age. Draft board members who served for extended periods during the war included Ed Larsen, Clive Killpack, Russell Snow, and Guy Ware, with Caroline Westover as board secretary. By early 1941 several men were being called up for induction each month. County residents serving in the armed forces increased from eighty-nine in December 1941 to 336 by March 1943. Ferron alone had 186 men and women who served in the military during the war. Leah Johansen of Cleveland was apparently the first Emery County woman to volunteer, joining the WAVES in January 1943. She was followed by several others over the next two years.[111] Twenty-nine Emery County men died in the nation's service during the war and its immediate aftermath, twenty-three of them from combat injuries. Several others spent time as prisoners of war, and a substantial number were decorated for gallant actions under fire.

The Home Front. The war's impact on civilians escalated dramatically in the months following the attack on Pearl Harbor. Rationing of rubber tires was instituted in early January 1942, and sales of new automobiles were frozen at the same time. Sugar rationing began on 1 May. Gasoline rationing and a wartime speed limit of thirty-five miles per hour went into effect on 30 October. Shoes were added to the list of rationed items in February 1943. A Home Defense Council was established before the end of 1941. Local civic clubs sponsored scrap metal and paper drives with the slogan "Salvage for Victory." Residents were encouraged to grow "victory gardens." Three Castle Dale women organized a window display at the Castle Dale Co-op with information on food selection and preparation in support of the "Keep America Fit" campaign. A "Servicemen's Ladies Club" in Huntington produced a chatty newsletter that was mailed to local servicemen. School children collected tinfoil and participated in war stamp drives. The shortage of strategic materials impelled the Denver and Rio Grande Railroad to remove the rails and bridges from Salina Canyon. A fear of possible sabotage led to the posting of a guard at the Green River railroad bridge. A guard was also posted at the ageing highway bridge to enforce load limits.[112]

"War work" took many individuals and families out of the county for employment at Hill Field or Geneva Steel or the Remington Arms factory at Salt Lake City, or to shipyards and aircraft factories on the West Coast. Some of them returned at war's end, but most remained in their new locations. Several families moved to the coal camps. A shortage of housing forced some men to "batch" in dormitory-style quarters in the camps while their families remained in Emery County. Even though they were not far from home, the tire shortage made home visits difficult. Women were drawn into the labor force in unprecedented numbers. Some county women went to work for the State Road Commission, painting yellow dividing lines on the highways by hand.[113]

The massive relocation of people of Japanese extraction from the West Coast also had an impact on Emery County. Despite the protests of local residents at an "anti-Jap" meeting, several families were resettled at Green River where they farmed a thousand acres and also worked in the sugar beet fields. The Green River correspondent to the *Progress* wrote, "Although the majority of the people say 'no,' the law says 'yes,' and according to government rights it appears they are here to stay." Apparently the hard-working Japanese succeeded in overcoming at least some of the initial prejudice. The same correspondent lamented their departure when they were moved to northern Utah the following year.[114]

The Deer Creek and Castle Valley mines initially supplied coal to the large intern camp at Topaz, Millard County. Within a short time, however, a group of Japanese miners was sent from the camp to operate the Dog Valley mine south of Emery. Buildings from the Willow Springs CCC camp were moved to the mine to serve as housing. The CCC buildings from Ferron, Castle Dale, and Green River were dismantled and moved to Fort Douglas, Tooele, and Wendover for emergency housing.[115]

The Red Cross. The Emery County Chapter of the American Red

Cross, under the direction of chapter chairs Audrey Sandberg of Huntington and Sydonia Kofford of Castle Dale and production chair Naomi A. Jensen of Castle Dale, was active in producing handmade clothing and other items for the war effort. The initial assignment to the chapter in 1941 was to make up a full railroad carload of material into such items as operating gowns, sweaters, dresses, children's clothing, diapers, and receiving blankets. The Emery County chapter had completed its allotment by early 1943 while "many chapters throughout the state still [had] great quantities of the allotted material on hand to be made up." Mrs. William Murray of Huntington knitted thirteen sweaters in nine weeks. Production continued throughout the war including not only clothing but also utility and bedside bags for military personnel and one hundred mending kits that soldiers referred to as "housewives." Many of the clothing items were shipped to war-besieged Britain. In 1949 the chapter received a citation from Lord Halifax, British ambassador to the United States, expressing appreciation for the wartime contributions.[116]

Coal Mining in the War Years. In April 1942 the Defense Plant Corporation acquired 600 acres of coal land in Horse Canyon and began development of a mine to supply coking coal for the Geneva Steel Plant being constructed in Utah County. The mine and attendant shipping facilities were located in Emery County, but Dragerton, the town built to house the workers, was in Carbon County. Peak employment of about eight hundred and production of a million tons per year were attained in the middle to late 1940s. In 1946 the Geneva Steel Plant and the Geneva Mine at Horse Canyon were taken over by the United States Steel Corporation, which continued to operate the mine until its closure in 1982.[117]

Coal production expanded at smaller Emery County mines. In 1944 a road was constructed along the base of Gentry Mountain from Huntington Canyon to the Mohrland railhead in order to reduce truck-haul distance. Popularly called the "Burma Road" after the famous military road in southeast Asia, this road proved to be too narrow for comfortable two-way traffic, so most coal truckers adopted a circular route, with loaded vehicles using the Burma Road and empty trucks returning by way of the lower road from Mohrland to Huntington.

The fourteen operating mines in Huntington Canyon adopted an interesting cooperative arrangement during this period. Because coal contracts were often larger than any one mine could fulfill, one company would officially contract for coal delivery and the other mines would then share in filling the contract. Such an arrangement was obviously risky because it depended on trust that each mine would honestly report its delivery tonnage and that the contracting mine would share the proceeds fairly. Vernon Leamaster, who with his brothers operated the Leamaster mine in Mill Fork throughout this period, cannot remember a single dispute ever arising among the cooperating parties.

While some mines, in particular American Fuel and Deer Creek, were fairly well capitalized, most Huntington Canyon mines were shoestring operations. The Leamaster Coal Company had its inception in 1936 when five brothers pooled their limited Depression-era resources to buy forty acres of coal land in Mill Fork. They later obtained a lease on 160 acres of adjacent federal land. They built a bridge across the creek, repaired a mile-and-a-half of road, and constructed a coal chute from the mine portal. The coal was drilled by hand, blasted from the solid (without undercutting the coal seam), and hand loaded onto a horse-drawn two-wheeled cart. Heavy snowfall forced closure of the mine after a few months' operation. The Leamaster brothers tried again in 1944, at the peak of the wartime demand, with a new opening into a different coal seam. This mine remained in operation until 1963. Vernon Leamaster, who was involved with the operation throughout its existence, described the enterprise as "a financial failure." He noted, however, that the mine supported twenty-five families for several years and also made some contributions to the industry. The Leamaster and Co-op mines were apparently the first mines to obtain permission from the U.S. Bureau of Mines and the Utah State Industrial Commission to use diesel-powered equipment underground, opening the way for a wider use of diesel power.[118]

The Co-op Mining Company was organized in 1939 by C. E. Kingston and associates, who leased part of the large Freed property in Trail Canyon. The necessary access road, chutes, and loading bins were built by tedious hand labor, and the coal cars and rails were salvaged from the Freed mine. In order to prevent the more valuable lump coal from being pulverized in the chute, Kingston devised a counter-weighted cable car, built entirely from scrap material, to lower the coal. To replace the slow hand drill, Eskel Peterson made an electric drill from a Dodge starter motor, operated from batteries. Average production in the early years was twenty tons per day, selling at $1.35 per ton. The miners were paid fifty cents a ton for loading the coal. In 1947 Utah Power and Light extended its lines into Huntington Canyon. With electric-powered cutting and loading equipment, production increased to 150 tons per day, with lump coal selling for about $2.85 per ton and oiled slack bringing $2.35.[119]

Some of the smaller mines, such as the Theodore LeRoy mine and the Sea Gull mine operated by Drew Richards, were primarily family operations. Tim Richards remembered that he and his cousin LaVell King as boys of twelve or thirteen worked right alongside the small crew of men in opening and operating the mine.[120] In a sense, the model for these "family mines" was the family farm so familiar in Emery County. Whether the goal was harvesting a crop or digging coal, the expectation was that every member of the family would contribute to the full extent of his or her ability without regard to arbitrary distinctions based on age or gender.

Agriculture and Stockraising. The move to upgrade the county's breeding stock that had begun in the 1930s continued through the war years and beyond. Under the influence of vocational agriculture programs at the high schools and a series of capable county agricultural extension agents, many young people engaged in livestock breeding projects. Kemp Robinson of Emery, a product of the South Emery vo-ag program under the direction of Robert Dahle, developed a purebred Hereford breeding operation that enabled him to sell fifteen bulls at the Denver livestock show in 1942 at an average price of $700 per head. The Emery County Junior Livestock Show, which found a permanent home at Ferron in 1944, became an important regional exhibition, and county residents also competed with great success at the other shows. Ina Lee Johansen of Castle Dale and Hugh Peterson of Emery were among the top winners at the

1942 Intermountain Junior Livestock Show in North Salt Lake. In 1944 Sherald Truman of Huntington showed the grand champion fat calf at the Intermountain show, and Udell Albrechtson of Moore had the reserve champion at the Ogden Livestock Show. In 1946 Emery County residents exhibited 250 calves at the Intermountain show.[121]

The Closing of Central High School. The war years brought a significant reduction in school enrollments as families moved from the county in pursuit of abundant wartime jobs elsewhere and as young men dropped out of school before graduation to enlist in the armed forces. Declining student numbers and a shortage of qualified teachers led in early 1943 to a proposal to close Central High School, setting off the most bitterly fought consolidation battle in the county's history. The official vote of the school board came in August 1943 on a motion proposed by Soren Anderson of Huntington and seconded by Morris Singleton of Ferron. The motion passed by a vote of four to one, with Melrose Luke of Orangeville being the lone dissenter. In addition to citing declining enrollments and the teacher shortage, Anderson's motion noted that the Central building was "rapidly becoming unfit for use." The motion proposed to return Castle Dale and Orangeville seventh and eighth graders to the elementary schools in their home communities and to bus grades nine through twelve from Orangeville to North Emery and from Castle Dale to South Emery.[122]

A group of Central High patrons filed suit to block the closure. Families were divided by the consolidation issue as Morris Singleton's sister Cecil Singleton Crawford of Castle Dale was one of the leaders in the campaign to preserve Central High. The beginning of the school year brought a boycott, with students refusing to board the buses. The courts, while noting that the school board lacked the authority to close the school permanently (the same position taken earlier in the attempt to close the Elmo school), ruled that the board could temporarily discontinue Central High for the duration of the wartime emergency. A compromise was reached that called for all Central High students to be bussed to South Emery instead of dividing the closely tied communities of Castle Dale and Orangeville. This solution ended the boycott, but bitter feelings continued for many years. Perhaps because the school district headquarters were in Huntington, or because the Huntington representative had made the motion for closure, or simply because of the longstanding rivalry, some Castle Dale residents persisted in the view that Huntington was responsible for the loss of their high school. Thus was recapitulated, but in the other direction, the resentment felt by Huntington residents at the closure of the Huntington LDS seminary forty years earlier.

The End of an Era

Changing times had an impact on smaller as well as larger communities. Woodside lost its livestock shipping facilities and railroad station in the late 1920s. Much of the farm land was abandoned during the drought period of the 1930s. The 1940 population of thirty gradually dwindled away over the next two decades. The Victor precinct was absorbed into Elmo in 1940, and by the mid-1940s both Victor and nearby Desert Lake had become ghost towns. The failure of Victor and Desert Lake can be attributed in large part to continuing problems with the quantity and quality of the water supply. Lying as it does at the end of the ditch, the area suffered greatly during the devastating drought of the mid-1930s. Even in better times, it was often necessary to haul culinary water several miles. With increasing access to automobiles, it became more convenient for most landowners to live in Elmo or Cleveland and commute to the surviving farms in the area.[123]

In 1940, on the occasion of L. C. Moore's retirement as postmaster, the post office and community of Rochester took the name of Moore. Moore had been the most influential citizen of the community for the greater part of its existence. He owned the property on which the townsite was built and served as manager of the 8,000-acre Kenaston estate, the largest agriculture operation in the western part of the county. When the Kenaston land was placed on the market in 1940, Moore purchased the property that he had managed for so many years and resold it short time later to the LeRoy and Hessie Bunderson family of Emery.[124]

Another indication of the end of an era occurred in November 1944 when Helen Alfsen Larsen of Ferron, the last survivor of the three colonizing parties in the fall of 1877, died at the age of eighty-eight. She had witnessed profound changes indeed since her arrival on Ferron Creek to begin a new life in a new land.[125]

ENDNOTES

1. *Fifteenth Census of the United States, 1930: Population* (Washington, D.C.: Government Printing Office, 1933), 1:1265.

2. *Fourteenth Census of the United States, 1920: Agriculture* (Washington, D.C.: Government Printing Office, 1922) 4:252, 255, 258; 7:89, 98, 307, 310, 313; *Fifteenth Census of the United States, 1930: Agriculture* (Washington, D.C., Government Printing Office, 1932) 2, part 3:378, 381; 3, part 3:275, 287; *ECP,* 14 September 1928; 2 August 1929; 25 April 1930.

3. *ECP,* 11 April, 1 July 1925.

4. Ibid., 15 May 1926.

5. Ibid., 9 July 1927.

6. Ibid., 23 July 1921; 21 June 1946; LaVora Kofford, "Vern Kofford and Isabel Caldwell," in *EC 1880–1980,* 399; Baker, 189.

7. Floyd A. O'Neil, "Victims of Demand: The Vagaries of the Carbon County Coal Industry," in Philip F. Notarianni, *Carbon County: Eastern Utah's Industrialized Island* (Salt Lake City: Utah State Historical Society, 1981), 27.

8. Powell, *The Next Time We Strike,* 121–40.

9. Irene C. O'Driscoll, "Mohrland."

10. *The Sun* (Price), 10 September 1926.

11. *ECP,* 18 October 1929.

12. Charles Franklin Jones, Oral History recorded 8 January 1993, by Sylvia Nelson, transcript in Emery County History Archives.

13. *ECP,* 17 November 1923; 8 and 22 March, 4 October 1924; 21 March 1925; 7 and 21 August 1926; 14 April 1928; 31 January, 14 and 28 February, 25 July 1930; *The Sun* (Price), 12 February 1926.

14. *ECP,* 6 June 1930.

15. Ibid., 6 August, 4 October 1921; 20 October 1923; 20 June 1930.

16. Ibid., 6 August 1921; 24 June 1922; 20 June 1923; 21 August 1926.

17. Ibid., 7 April, 7 December 1928; 29 August, 24 October 1930; Lareda Christiansen Olsen, recollections, in "Emery Town Reunion, 1889–1989: I Remember When," 20, typescript copy in Emery County History Archives.

18. Velma Cox Petersen, Oral History, recorded by Janet Petersen, 25 April 1994, transcript in Emery County History Archives.

19. Iola Broderick Waxman, Recollections, in "Emery Town Reunion," 12–13.

20. Bessie Anderson Jumper, Recollections, in "Emery Town Reunion," 13.

21. *ECP,* 15 and 22 May, 25 July 1926; 24 August, 30 November 1928; 13 and 20 September, 25 October 1929; 9 May 1930; 27 February 1931.

22. Richard E. Behling, oral history, 3.

23. Irma Peterson Snow, oral history.

24. *ECP,* 6 December 1929.

25. Ibid., 26 April 1924; 22 May 1926.

26. Ibid., 4 June 1927.

27. Snow, Oral History.

28. *ECP,* 29 October 1921; 24 August 1928; 15 February, 3 May 1929.

29. Ibid., 8 June 1928; 17 October, 28 November 1930.

30. Ibid., 15 April 1922; "History of the Emery County School District," typescript copy in Emery County History Archives.

31. *ECP,* 30 April, 7 May, 4 October 1921; 8 April, 6 May, 14 October 1922.

32. Ibid., 26 April 1924; 25 April 1925; 14 August 1926; 9 May, 15 August 1930; 13 March, 24 April 1931.

33. Ibid., 30 July, 13 August 1927.

34. *The Sun* (Price), 22 January 1926; *ECP,* 28 January, 25 February, 4 March 1922; 10 October 1930; 10 November 1933.

35. *CV,* 227; Kofford and Kelly, "Lawrence"; Curtis, "History of Moore," in *EC 1880–1980,* 230–32, 270.

36. Baker and Wilcox, "Greenriver," 194; Montell and Kathryn Seely, "Green River (Blake)," in *EC 1880–1980,* 141; Muriel W. Smith, "The Church of Jesus Christ of Latter Day Saints at Green River, Emery County, Utah," typescript copy in Emery County History Archives; *ECP,* 4 December 1931; 28 October 1932.

37. Andrew Jenson, *Encyclopedic History of the Church of Jesus Christ of Latter-day Saints* (Salt Lake City: Deseret News Publishing Co., 1941), 523; *ECP,* 1 February, 29 November 1935.

38. *ECP,* 5 February 1921; "A History of the Huntington Glee Club" (1992), typescript copy in Emery County History Archives.

39. *ECP,* 8 January 1927; 7 February 1930.

40. Ibid., January 10, March 21, 1930; January 30, 1931.

41. James E. Crawford, "Edmund and Thurnelda Singleton Crawford," in *EC 1880–1980,* 359.

42. *ECP,* 12 September 1925; 24 August 1928; 29 August, 5 and 19 September 1930.

43. Ibid., 9 September 1932; 1 and 15 September 1933.

44. Ibid., 5 July 1924; 5 December 1925; 16 August 1973.

45. Brian Q. Cannon. "Against Great Odds: Challenges in Utah's Marginal Agricultural Areas, 1925–39," *Utah Historical Quarterly* 54 (Fall 1986):321; R. Thomas Quinn, "Out of the Depression's Depths: Henry H. Blood's First Year as Governor," *Utah Historical Quarterly* 54 (Summer 1986):217; O'Neil, "Victims of Demand," 27; *ECP,* 29 November 1929; 10 January 1930; 7 and 21 October 1938.

46. *ECP,* 24 July 1931.

47. Ibid., 26 February, 8 July 1932; 6 January 1933; James E. Crawford, "Edmund and Thurnelda Singleton Crawford," 359.

48. *ECP,* 31 January 1930; 25 December 1931; 1 January, 22 July, 9 December 1932; 2 February, 31 August 1934.

49. Ibid., 13 January 1933; 4 February 1938.

50. Ibid., 17 and 24 January 1930; 30 January, 6 and 20 February, 5 June, 17, 24, and 31 July, 14 August, 2, 16, and 30 October; 20 November, 4 December 1931.

51. Ibid., 15 April, 20 May 1932; 27 January 1933; 30 March, 4 and 18 May, 1 June 1934.

52. Leonard J. Arrington, "Utah's Great Drought of 1934," *Utah Historical Quarterly* 54 (Summer 1986):247, 253.

53. *ECP,* 29 June, 6 and 20 July, 21 September, 2 November, 7 December 1934; 1 March 1935; *United States Census of Agriculture, 1935* (Washington, D.C.: Government Printing Office, 1936), 1:891.

54. Ibid., 20 July 1934.

55. Ibid., 1, 8, 22, and 29 January, 5 February, 3 September 1937.

56. Ibid., 1 July, 16 September 1932; 20 July, 28 September, 2 November 1934; 30 August 1935; 1 October 1937; 23 October 1938.

57. Ibid., 5 February, 15 and 22 April 1932.

58. Ibid., 2 August 1935; 29 January 1937; 27 January 1939; 5 July 1940; 3 October 1941.

59. Ibid., 11 November 1932; 8 and 29 September, 1 December 1933; 12 January 1934; 7 February, 23 October 1936.

60. Ibid., 4 January, 21 June, 2 August, 4 October 1935; 2 July 1937; 30 September 1938; 7 July 1939.

61. Ibid., 29 August 1941.

62. Ibid., 3 March 1933; 24 June, 12 August 1938; 6 January, 25 August 1939.

63. Ibid., 10 July 1936; 14 May 1937; 14 October 1938.

64. Ibid., 27 September 1935; 13 August 1937; Mills, "Coal Industry," 291.

65. Willard Smith, "Memories of Bygone Days: U.S.C.C.C. Company 959" (1980), typescript copy in Emery County History Archives.

66. Ibid.

67. *ECP,* 21 February 1936; 30 April 1937; 28 March 1941.

68. "Company 3556, C.C.C. Camp Green River, G-115, Green River, Utah," photocopy of camp roster and photographs in Emery County History Archives; *ECP,* 28 June 1935; 10 June 1938; 18 July 1941.

69. *The Ferron Chatterbox,* Thanksgiving 1938; Nila Huntsman Mumm, "Ferron C.C.C. Camp" (1994), typescript copy in Emery County History Archives; Arva M. Smith, "Best of Times in Worst of Times for CCC Crews," *Deseret News,* 3 August 1983, photocopy in Emery County History Archives; *ECP,* 14 June 1935.

70. Cora G. Seely, interview recorded by Montell Seely, January 1995, typescript copy in Emery County History Archives; Cora G. Seely, "Memorial to Karl Antone Seely," in *EC 1880–1980,* 436.

71. Charles Franklin Jones, Oral History.

72. Roxie W. Nelson, Oral History interview recorded by Janet Peterson, 28 February, 1994, typescript copy in Emery County History Archives.

73. *ECP,* 5 July 1935; personal statement by Vernell Rowley, March 1995.

74. *ECP,* 1 October 1937.

75. Ibid., 24 November 1939.

76. "History of the Emery County School District," typescript copy in Emery County History Archives; *ECP,* 22 July 1932; 12 May, 14 July, 1 and 8 September 1933; 27 April, 31 August 1934.

77. *ECP,* 23 August 1935; 8 and 15 May, 28 August 1936; 29 January, 17 December 1937.

78. Ibid., 17 November 1939; 6 September, 18 October, 15 November 1940; 19 September 1941.

79. Ibid., 3 May 1929; 29 May, 17 July 1936; 28 January 1944; Oviatt, Erickson, and Hall, "Elmo," in *CV,* 136; Seely, "Emery Stake (Castle Dale Utah Stake)," 279; Ada Willson, "Desert Lake—Victor," 173; Wright, "Clawson," 98–99, in *EC 1880–1980.*

80. *ECP,* 3 May 1929; 7 December 1934; 22 April 1938; 9 and 23 June 1939; Allred, "Cleveland, Utah," 154; Montell Seely, "Castle Dale Ward," in *EC 1880–1980,* 38–39.

81. Green River Presbyterian Church Records, photocopy in Utah State Historical Society library, Salt Lake City.

82. Petersen, "Ferron," 116; *CV*, 164; *ECP*, 23 January 1931; 19 May 1939; 8 May 1942.

83. *ECP*, 3 December 1921; 13 May 1922; 12 January 1924; 12 July 1929; 21 March 1930; 23 January 1931.

84. Owen McClenahan, "Days of Prohibition," typescript copy in Emery County History Archives.

85. *ECP*, 13 October, 10 November 1933.

86. Owen McClenahan, "3.2 Beer Comes to Utah," and "Utah State Liquor Stores," typescript copy in Emery County History Archives.

87. *ECP*, 31 July 1931; 6 May, 21 and 28 October, 18 November, 2 December 1932; 25 September 1936.

88. Ibid., 25 July 1941.

89. Ibid., 30 December 1922; 5 July, 30 August, 4 October 1924; 2 September 1932.

90. Ibid., 31 July, 28 August, 16 October, 27 November 1936; 26 February 1943.

91. Ibid., 10 January, 21 March 1930; 30 January 1931.

92. McClenahan, "Days of Prohibition," 8; "The Wilberg Meat and Grocery Market," and "The Wilberg Resort," typescript copies in Emery County History Archives; "Memory of Carl Wilberg and Matilda Mariah Johnson Wilberg," in *EC 1880–1980*, 448; *ECP*, 14 June 1929.

93. *ECP*, 17 November 1939; 9 February 1940; 4 June 1943.

94. Ibid., 4 October 1929; 9 October 1931; 3 June 1932; 7 May, 18 June 1937; 18 July 1941.

95. Ibid., 9 and 30 August, 4 October 1935; 12 June 1936; 29 January 1937; 7 and 23 October 1838; O'Neil, "Victims of Demand," 27.

96. Ibid., 15 April, 23 September 1938. Eva Conover, who taught school at Mohrland during this period, reported that mine superintendent Wetzel told her that if Emery County officials had "even hinted that they would oil the road to Mohrland and erect a larger warmer school house, Mohrland would never have been closed down until very recent years." Eva W. Conover to Sylvia H. Nelson, May 1993, original letter in Emery County History Archives.

97. *ECP*, 22 September 1939.

98. Ibid., 10 August 1934; 21 June, 13 December 1935; 27 November 1936.

99. Ibid., 19 May 1939.

100. Ibid., 26 January 1940; 4 April, 18 and 25 July 1941.

101. Ibid., 18 and 25 July, 1 and 8 August 1941.

102. Ibid., 6 June, 5 September 1941.

103. Ibid., 12 June, 17 July 1936; 19 November 1937; "The Bureau of Land Management," in *EC 1880–1980,* 329.

104. *ECP,* 7 March 1941.

105. Ibid., 3 July 1936; 10 September 1937; 17 March 1939.

106. Ibid., 22 September 1939; 12 January, 8 November 1940.

107. Ware, *Emery County Farmers Union Telephone Association,* 25.

108. *ECP,* 11 June, 8 October 1943.

109. Maurine Nielson, "Public Health Program," in *EC 1880–1980,* 318.

110. *ECP,* 6 March, 10 April, 22 May 1936; 7 January 1938; 26 March, 22 October, 4 November 1943.

111. Ibid., 27 October, 3 November 1939; 4, 11, and 18 October 1940; 7 November 1941; 27 March, 26 June, 25 December 1942; 22 January, 26 February, 12 March 1943; 25 August 1944.

112. Ibid., 2 and 9 January, 27 February, 6 March, 1 and 15 May, 18 September, 3 October 1942; 12 February 1943; "Emery County Red Cross: Serving on the Home Front"; Bob Judd, "Items of Interest from World War," typescript copy in Emery County History Archives.

113. Judd, "Items of Interest."

114. *ECP,* 20 March, 3 April, 1 May, 19 June 1942; 9 April 1943.

115. Ibid., 6 November, 11 and 18 December 1942.

116. "Emery County Red Cross: Serving on the Home Front During World War II."

117. *ECP,* 10 April 1942; Paul Clark, "Geneva Mine," typescript copy in Emery County History Archives.

118. Vernon Leamaster, "Leamaster Coal Company" (February 1994), typescript copy in Emery County History Archives.

119. Gerald Hansen, "A Short History of Co-op Mine" (November 1993), typescript copy in Emery County History Archives.

120. Thomas "Tim" Richards, personal recollections, typescript copy in Emery County History Archives.

121. *ECP,* 23 January, 17 April, 5 June 1942; 7 July, 10 November 1944; 4 January, 31 May 1946.

122. Ibid., 16 April, 11 June, 13 August 1943.

123. Ibid., 28 June 1940; Mildred Johnson Cox, Oral History, recorded by Jan Petersen, 14 June 1994, transcript in Emery County History Archives.

124. *ECP,* 2 February, 16 August 1940; 24 January 1941.

125. Ibid., 17 November 1944.

7

THE GRAYING OF EMERY COUNTY, 1945–1970

In 1952 editor Ray M. Williams of the *Emery County Progress* published a series of articles titled "He Made Good" and featuring county natives who had achieved noteworthy success in a variety of fields. The series included economists, accountants, geologists, government officials, education leaders, musicians, lawyers, physicians, even an animator at the Walt Disney studios. One thing the subjects all had in common was that they had "made good" after leaving Emery County. Another series could well have been presented (though it was not) about those who had made good in the county: successful livestock breeders, mine operators, business entrepreneurs, educators, public-spirited citizens who led the way in civic improvements, individuals whose abilities were recognized by election or appointment to important state and national responsibilities. Nevertheless, it is true that most Emery County people who made good (as well as most who did not) did it somewhere else. The county had been exporting its natural population growth for many years, but in the period from 1945 to 1970 the rate of out-migration outran the birthrate, resulting in a substantial decline in the population. From the 7,072 reported in the 1940 census, the population fell to 6,304 in 1950, 5,546 in 1960, and 5,137 in 1970, a decrease of 27.4 percent in thirty years. Over the same period, the median age advanced from twenty-one to twenty-eight, and the proportion of residents over the age of sixty-five increased from 4.8 percent to 11.2 percent.

As has often happened, Green River ran counter to the dominant trend. Boosted by a steady growth in tourism and the more dramatic economic stimuli of the uranium boom in the 1950s and the missile base in the 1960s, Green River grew by 61 percent from a population of 682 in 1940 to 1,099 in 1970, making it the largest town in the county. At the other extreme, the Emery-Ferron region fell from 2,008 residents in 1940 to 1,077 in 1970, a 46 percent decline. In 1970 the median age in the Emery-Ferron census district was 33.5, and 16.4 percent of the residents were over the age of sixty-five. The town of Emery, which had a population of 705 in 1940, had only 216 residents in 1970.

The chief cause of the loss in population was a generally deteriorating local economy. Utah coal production, which had peaked at 7.1 million tons in 1944, continued relatively strong into the early 1950s but then experienced a decline that bottomed out at 2.7 million tons in 1974.[1] The uranium boom provided a temporary economic boost in the mid-1950s but had little lasting impact. Agricultural prices were good in the late 1940s but fell sharply in the early 1950s. A ten-year drought cycle from the mid-1950s to the mid-1960s brought further distress to the agricultural sector, though the decline in crop yields and in carrying capacity of the range was offset to some extent by growth in value-added farm products, in particular dairying and purebred hereford breeding. The general employment trend for Emery County's basic industries, however, was downward. The unemployment rate in 1960 was a high 14.4 percent, but even more significant was the rate of *under*employment. Only 52 percent of the work force reported having full-time employment for the full year 1959. Thirty-five percent worked less than thirty-nine weeks, and 12.5 percent worked less than thirteen weeks. The median family income of $4,229 ranked Emery County twenty-second among the state's twenty-nine counties. The smaller 1970 population fared somewhat better in terms of jobs, with 55.7 percent reporting full-time full-year employment in 1969 and only 5.3 percent unemployed. But the median family income of $6,822 was 27 percent below the state average and above only four other counties. Net out-migration during the decade of the 1960s amounted to almost 30 percent. These conditions were not unique to Emery County but reflected the general flight of jobs and population from rural to urban areas.

What set the county apart from some other depopulated rural areas was the determination of its citizens not to allow their communities to wither on the vine. In the face of declining resources, the county undertook major initiatives to modernize its infrastructure and improve public facilities. Often these improvements were conceived and promoted by small groups of individuals who through dedicated effort and sacrifice eventually won others over to their vision of what could be accomplished. Federal programs aimed at improving conditions in economically distressed areas also made a vital contribution. Probably the three most significant public works projects in the county's history took shape during the decade of the 1960s: the Emery County Project, the Ferron Watershed Project, and the construction of Interstate 70.

The Postwar Years

Returning servicemen and women streamed into the county during the latter months of 1945 and on into 1946, hoping to pick up their lives and return to something like normality. There were numerous welcome-home parties and a rash of weddings. A series of more somber homecomings began a year or so later as the county's war dead were shipped home from temporary burial places abroad. Many returning servicemen found jobs in the coal mines, which continued to operate at fairly high levels until the mid-1950s. Others seized the opportunity to attend college or obtain vocational skills with G.I. Bill education benefits. Still others took advantage of veterans' programs to get a start in farming.

The pent-up demand for consumer goods and new facilities led to a miniboom as restrictions on commodities and building supplies were eased. Even before the war's end, Maurice Jensen announced plans to build a frozen food locker plant adjacent to his market in Huntington.[2] This operation, and the Killpack locker plant that opened a short time later in Ferron, enabled county residents to have meat from their own livestock throughout the year and not only at butchering time. The county's first modern motion picture house was the Castle Theatre in Huntington, opened in mid-1946 by W. O. Sandberg and Ted R. Nielson. In 1948 Carlos, Eugene, and Glen Otterstrom opened the Rocket Theatre in Castle Dale. In an interesting symbolic transition from one era to another, some of the materials for the Rocket building came from the demolition of the 1892 courthouse. Sometime later a drive-in theater was established at Huntington by R. Zen Jensen. The Huntington Lions Club and American Legion Post joined forces to erect a meeting hall adjacent to the city park. In response to renewed tourist traffic with the end of tire and gasoline rationing, two new motels were built in Green River in 1948. A heightened postwar interest in aviation was reflected in the establishment of airports at Huntington and Green River.[3] Emery County residents joined in the national demand for new automobiles, but they were compelled for the most part to go outside the county to make their purchases. However, Jack's Motor Service in Huntington, operated by John R. Corgiat, became an important regional center for auto repair and rebuilding, acquiring the first crankshaft grinder in central and southern Utah in 1948 and doing much custom work for other garages.[4]

In late 1947 military personnel suddenly appeared in the Buckhorn Flat area, provoking widespread speculation and rumors that were further fed by the atmosphere of Cold War secrecy. Eventually it was announced that explosives were to be detonated deep underground to test the structure of the rock. The Morrison-Knudson company began tunnelling in 1948 with a sizeable crew, some of whom were housed in temporary structures on-site while others lived in Castle Dale. The project was completed after several years with the detonation of some 320,000 pounds of high explosives, but its ultimate purpose, if any, was never revealed.[5]

Church Building. The availability of building materials brought a new era of construction in the Emery LDS Stake. The long-deferred plan to replace the Castle Dale meetinghouse was resumed in 1946 with the cutting of timber. In 1947 stake officials decided to make the building a combined ward-stake facility. Actual construction began in the fall of 1948 under the direction of Bishop P. Eugene Johansen with Henry Behling as construction supervisor. Bricks formed and burned on the site were used in the inner walls with factory pressed brick for the exterior. The building was placed in service in May 1950 and dedicated by church president David O. McKay on 8 July 1951.[6]

The Huntington Ward was divided in December 1947, and plans were set in motion a short time later for erection of a new building at the corner of Main Street and Second North under the direction of bishops Kenneth J. Brasher of the First Ward and Clinton N. Wakefield of the Second Ward. Ground was broken on 20 March 1950, and the building was in use by September 1951 and dedicated on 27 April 1952 by President J. Reuben Clark, Jr. A portion of the construction funds came from the sale of the old meetinghouse to the school district. This structure was used for another decade as an assembly hall for North Emery High School.[7]

The Cleveland Ward had harvested timber for a new building in 1941, but the outbreak of war put a halt to construction plans. Work finally began in late 1949 under Bishop William F. Eden on a new chapel that was dedicated on 18 November 1951 by Elder Mark E. Petersen. Irene Allred described the building of the chapel, typical for the period, in the following terms:

> Times had changed by now; it was not nearly as simple to just build a church as it had been in 1899 [when the predecessor ward-house had been erected]. Harry Mortensen was asked to be clerk and treasurer of the building committee—to receive all material orders, keep all time records of donated and paid labor, work out time sheets, submit a monthly report to the Presiding Bishopric in Salt Lake City, and make sure that somehow things balanced out. After his death in February, 1951, the Bishop asked Harry's wife, Myrtle, to take over this responsibility. Many people helped to build the church. Sand and gravel were hauled from the lower end of Cow Flat from Cottonwood Wash. Bricks, finishing lumber, plaster, shingles, insulation, doors, windows, and other materials were hauled from Salt Lake City. The truckers were paid expenses, but they donated their time. The members, both men and women,

did the painting, staining, and varnishing of the woodwork and walls.[8]

Ground was broken for a new chapel at Emery on 22 April 1954 under the direction of Bishop Alonzo Olsen, and the building was dedicated on 24 June 1956. A cultural hall addition to the Orangeville chapel was dedicated on 9 May 1954.[9]

Schools. With the end of the wartime emergency that had been used to justify the closing of Central High School, residents of Castle Dale and Orangeville began pressing the board of education to reopen the school. The campaign for Central High continued even after the historic building was destroyed by fire in August 1947. Patrons proposed using the Castle Dale Elementary building as a high school and busing elementary students to Orangeville. Sectional conflicts arising out of the Central High issue and other disputes over school management eventually led to the resignation of one school board member and the filing of civil misconduct charges (later dismissed) against another, and probably contributed to the decision of superintendent R. S. Chipman to leave the district in 1947. After an initially appointed successor was unable to obtain a release from his current contract, the school board chose Clifford L. Frye. The first challenge to confront Superintendent Frye was a short-lived boycott by high school students from Castle Dale at the beginning of the 1947–48 school year in protest of the refusal to reopen Central High.[10]

Green River School. The Emery County School District had not built a new school since the 1920s, but a compelling need arose in 1953 when the Green River building was listed by a state committee as one of four schools in the state that were "hazardous" for further use.[11] Among other structural problems, one corner of the gymnasium had sunk sixteen inches. Bonding for a new Green River school and for needed improvements at several other schools was approved by county voters in June 1954 by a four-to-one margin.[12] The new building, located on the northern outskirts of town, was completed in 1955 at a cost of $400,000. It was featured in several architectural journals for its significant innovations in design and construction. Exterior walls were of steel frame and panelling and contained more than two hundred windows, most of them reaching from floor to ceiling. Interior walls of plywood made it possible to rearrange spaces at relatively small cost. The high school occupied the west side of the building and the elementary school the east side with administrative offices in the middle. The auditorium-gymnasium was built below ground level to preserve the building's low profile.[13]

Emery County Library. The county library system came into existence shortly after the war largely through the determined efforts of Cecil Singleton Crawford, who organized a petition campaign, lobbied the county commissioners to provide funding, undertook a book drive to gather donated volumes, and opened the first public library in the old Emery LDS Stake office building in Castle Dale in December 1945. In addition to Mrs. Crawford, the original county library board included Hessie Bunderson of Emery and Moore, Christy Humphrey of Orangeville, P. C. Jones and Ervin Wimber of Castle Dale, Jane Seely of Green River, and Harry Mortensen of Cleveland. Branches of the county library opened in Ferron and Orangeville in 1946, Green River and Huntington in 1947, and Emery and Cleveland in 1948. In each case, the initial collection was largely composed of books donated by townspeople with new acquisitions and operating expenses being funded through a small county tax levy. Cecil Crawford did not have long to enjoy her success and her status as the first county librarian. She died in June 1949 at the age of fifty-six. The libraries were kept in operation and enabled to grow by dedicated librarians in each community, who worked in some instances for wages of less than a dollar an hour.[14]

Utah Pioneer Centennial Celebration. The 1947 statewide celebration of the centennial of the entry of Mormon pioneers into the Salt Lake Valley was designed to include programs in local communities. After considering and rejecting a recommendation from state officials that Emery County join with Carbon County for the celebration, the county centennial committee, chaired by Elmo G. Geary of Huntington, and a host of subcommittees and volunteers produced a full year of activities. The Peach Day and Melon Day celebrations adopted the centennial theme as did the county fair in Castle Dale and the Southeastern Utah Junior Livestock Show in Ferron. There were plays and dances in several communities and performances of the touring statewide production of the operetta *Blossom Time*. A countywide centennial chorus was organized under the direction of Claire Hunter of Castle Dale. The crowning event was a three-day celebration in July at the newly constructed Centennial Park at Huntington that included a rodeo, horse races, boxing and wrestling, a variety program, and an original pageant written by Gladys Penny and Lamont Johnson and produced under the direction of a committee chaired by Audrey Sandberg. The pageant was noteworthy not only for its ambitious scale (the cast and orchestra numbered 115) but also for its combination of local talent with former county residents who were engaged in professional musical and theatrical careers.

Centennial queen Juanita Snow of Castle Dale was crowned by Joseph Jewkes, an Emery County pioneer of 1878. In another commemorative gesture, Anna Marie Hansen Ungerman, who at the age of nineteen had represented the county in the statewide 1897 jubilee celebration, was honored again at the centennial, attended by her granddaughters.[15]

Another ambitious enterprise associated with the centennial was the publication of the first comprehensive history of the county by the Emery County Company of the Daughters of Utah Pioneers. *Castle Valley: A History of Emery County*, written by volunteers from every community and compiled under the direction of Stella McElprang, was published in 1949. Flora Jensen was county DUP president, and Delight Harding was in charge of finances for the project.

The Korean War. The county always had a significant number of its citizens in the armed forces as many young men and some women enlisted shortly after (and sometimes before) high school graduation. After the outbreak of war in Korea in the summer of 1950, the military draft became more active. Some fourteen county men were inducted into the service during the latter months of 1950 and about twice as many during 1951. Two Emery County men were killed in action, and several others were wounded. Apart from concerns about family members and friends in the combat zone, the impact of the Korean War on the home front was limited although temporary shortages of building materials delayed construction of some LDS

Sheep crossing San Rafael River Bridge. (Courtesy Carolyn Jorgensen)

chapels being erected at the time and inflationary price increases cut into residents' real income.[16]

Several county natives made careers in the armed services, some attaining high rank. Probably the highest ranking officer from Emery County during this period was Brigadier General Bruce Easley, Jr., of Ferron, a West Point graduate who in 1954 became adjutant general of all Allied ground forces in Germany.[17]

Agriculture and Livestock

Prices for farm products continued strong in the postwar years. Emery County farmers and stockraisers earned a gross income of $1,486,000 in 1946, almost double the amount for 1940.[18] Sheep numbers on county ranges decreased from eighty-three thousand in 1930 to thirty thousand in 1950. In part, this decrease resulted from growers shifting from sheep to cattle in keeping with stronger beef prices. Part of the reduction, however, reflected an ongoing adjustment to the permanent carrying capacity of the range. Farmers enjoyed generally good water years during the late 1940s, but range livestock were threatened by heavy valley snow during the winter of 1948–49 and again in 1951–52. The record snowpack of 1952 brought flooding that damaged some agricultural lands.[19] The Green River melon industry rebounded from wartime labor shortages but never regained the prominence it had achieved during the 1930s. Several new peach orchards were planted at Ferron to meet the demands of local markets.[20]

The county made important contributions to the purebred hereford industry, with Emery County bulls garnering honors and premium prices at shows and sales throughout the West. Several local breeders served as officers in state livestock associations and in the Cowbelles organization. Among the leading purebred operations were the Sorensen brothers of Emery, Crawford Hereford Ranch and Olsen brothers of Moore, C. H. and Don Snow, Gardell Snow, Paul Nelson, Owen Barton, and the Wareham Hereford Farm of Ferron, Warren Wilberg and sons of Castle Dale, and Ralph Lundy of Cleveland.[21] The higher prices commanded by purebred stock gave added value to farming operations. Still, it was far from easy to make a living in agriculture and livestock. For example, the model purebred Hereford operation of Gardell and Irma Snow of Ferron required long hours of labor by all members of the family as well as careful control of expenditures, in keeping with Gardell's stated principle of "never buying anything that didn't make something back." Irma worked as a schoolteacher in addition to her responsibilities at home and on the farm. Nevertheless, it still required forty-four years to retire the debt on the Snow ranch, with the final payment being made only two years before Gardell's death at the age of sixty-nine.[22]

Southeastern Utah Junior Livestock Show. A small barn and loading platform were constructed with the assistance of a 1945 federal government grant at the permanent site of the Emery County Junior Livestock Show in Ferron. With improved facilities, the show took on a more expansive name, becoming the Southeastern Utah Junior Livestock Show. A large show barn was built in 1947.[23] The show has continued as a highly successful event with several hundred animals exhibited each year, providing opportunities for the county's young people in beef, hog, and lamb feeding projects as well as attracting many exhibitors from other areas.

Vocational agriculture programs at the high schools continued to promote participation in other shows as well. The North and

South Emery F.F.A. chapters exhibited 250 calves at the Intermountain Junior Livestock Show in 1946, and many Emery County residents served as officers in the state Future Farmers Association.[24] The Agricultural Extension Service also promoted 4-H Club activities for the county's young people.

Young Farmers. A Young Farmers program organized under provisions of the federal G.I. Bill provided both instruction in modern farming methods and stimulus for a new generation of farmers to acquire land and set up their own operations. Under the auspices of this program, 4,000 turkey poults were brought to the county in 1948 in an effort to establish an industry that was proving highly successful in Sanpete County. Almost 100,000 birds were contracted in 1949, but high feed costs, high mortality (a single August thunderstorm killed 2,000 turkeys at Buffalo), and weak prices dampened enthusiasm. While some turkeys continued to be raised for several more years, particularly in the Ferron area, the turkey industry never became an important contributor to the county economy.[25]

Mechanization. A few tractors made their appearance on Emery County farms in the 1930s. The relatively profitable postwar years enabled more farmers to make the transition from horse power to tractor power. The Scow family of Orangeville obtained a Ford tractor franchise and were highly successful in marketing equipment well suited to the county's small fields. Other makes of tractors and equipment were sold by the Killpack Company in Ferron, P. C. Jones and Sons in Castle Dale, and Jack's Motor Service in Huntington.

Richard Behling remembered that "there were maybe two or three" tractors in the Ferron area when he acquired a used International for $1,400 in 1934 or 1935.

> Work on a farm has changed so much. Used to pitch hay onto the wagon and use a derrick to unload it into a stack. Now we have balers and bale wagons. One man can put up as much hay in a day as a dozen could at that time. Of course we used horses to pull our mowers and rakes, plowed by hand. We would rake it into a windrow. It was quite a job. Had to use pitchforks back then. There were lots of boys knew how to work then. They were good with a shovel and pitchfork.[26]

Farmers' Organizations. The influence of cooperative marketing and political action organizations became more pronounced in the formerly highly individualistic agricultural industry. The Castle Valley Marketing and Purchasing Cooperative opened its doors in Huntington in January 1947 under the management of Russell Jensen.[27] The first chapter of the National Farmers Union in the state of Utah was organized at Elmo in April 1948. Within a short time, the organization spread throughout the county. When the Utah Farmers Union was chartered in 1954, Jesse S. Tuttle of Castle Dale was elected as the first state president.[28] The county also had a strong representation in the Farm Bureau organization with several residents active at the state level. Lawrence Thorderson of Cleveland served for several years as a vice-president of the National Association of Soil Conservation Districts.[29]

Dairying. The tradition of individual families keeping their own milk cow or buying raw milk from a neighbor began to change when state health officials started enforcing laws against the sale of unpasteurized milk in 1947. At about the same time, Kenneth J. Brasher inaugurated delivery of pasteurized milk to homes and schools throughout the western part of the county from his dairy near Huntington.[30] Several other farmers including Riddel Peacock of Emery, Neldon Olsen and Homer Edwards of Moore, George Nielson and Rulon Nelson of Ferron, Archie Edwards of Clawson, and Dee Humphrey of Orangeville also developed grade-A dairy facilities and sold their milk to Carbon County retail dairies. In 1948 the Carbon-Emery Dairymens Association contracted with Arden Dairies to market their milk. After a short time, however, they withdrew from this contract and began a long-term arrangement with Hi-Land Dairies. Bulk milk was transported by refrigerated tank truck to the processing plant in Salt Lake County. By 1951 thirty-one dairy farmers in the county were producing 250,000 pounds grade-A milk per month under this arrangement.[31]

The county's dairy industry received a jolt in August 1949 when the State Health Department withdrew the grade-A rating because the county's municipal water systems did not meet state standards. After negotiations, the health department suspended the ruling on condition that water system improvements be initiated within ninety days and completed within a year. There was much grumbling at this perceived pressure on one industry as a means of prodding municipal authorities to make water system improvements. In fact, only limited improvements were made, but they were sufficient for most dairies to continue to market grade-A milk.[32] The dairy industry continued to make a significant contribution to the county's economy for three decades, with most of the operations concentrated in the Ferron area. In 1959 fifty-five dairy operations produced 5.3 million pounds of milk and earned $286,960. As late as 1978, thirteen dairy farms earned a total of $551,000.[33]

Among the industry promotions was an annual dairy princess competition. Carol Ralphs of Ferron was chosen as Emery County Dairy Princess in 1957. She won the state contest in 1958 and then was crowned as American Dairy Princess in 1959. In this role she spent a busy year of travel and public appearances.[34]

Decline and Drought. The strong postwar market for agricultural products came to an abrupt end in 1953 when nationwide beef and grain prices collapsed. Farmers who had invested heavily in new land and equipment experienced difficulty in meeting their debt payments. To complicate the decline in prices, the county experienced drought conditions during much of the decade from 1954 to 1964. From 1954 to 1956, streamflows averaged only about 60 percent of normal. Exceptionally wet seasons in 1957 and 1958 produced runoff as much as 150 percent of normal and caused widespread damage to roads, bridges, and campgrounds. Lacking reservoirs that could store water from year to year, farmers could only watch the surplus flow run down the streams. The drought cycle resumed in 1959 with three more dry years. The entire state was declared a drought disaster area in 1961.[35]

Coal Mining

While no exact figures are available, it seems likely that the "wagon mines" of Emery County employed a peak season work force approaching two hundred men during the late 1940s. More than half of these miners worked in Huntington Canyon where the American Fuel, Deer Creek, Co-op, Paramount, Leamaster, Bear Canyon, Helco, Seagull, and Stump Flat mines were in operation. Elsewhere in the county, Earl Robertson operated the old Johnson/Twin Cities mine in Cottonwood Canyon; Cyrus Wilberg and sons opened a new mine in Grimes Wash in 1949; the Bell brothers erected loading facilities in 1951 on the bench road between Orangeville and Castle Dale to market coal from their Grimes Wash mine. The Browning, Ricci, and Davis mines near Emery had a combined work force of about forty men in 1949, with an average of fifty trucks loading at the Browning Mine each day during the peak season.[36] In addition to those employed in local mines, several dozen Emery County men commuted to Hiawatha or Wattis. Smaller numbers traveled even farther to Kenilworth, Sunnyside, or Horse Canyon.

With the exception of the U.S. Steel mine at Horse Canyon, the county's mines were nonunion operations and generally paid lower wages than the unionized Carbon County mines. The United Mine Workers undertook an unsuccessful campaign to organize the county's mines in 1948. During a 1949 strike, pickets were stationed at the mouth of Huntington Canyon for two weeks with a goal of preventing the shipment of coal. Several trucks were reportedly disabled by having air let out of their tires or distributor caps removed, and there was one near-violent confrontation between the picketers and a mine operator.[37]

Deseret Mine. The LDS church initially opened a mine in the Grimes Wash area on East Mountain in 1938 as a project of the Church Security Program (later renamed the Welfare Program). The lack of water to settle the coal dust led to closure of the mine in 1941. The end of the war brought a renewed effort to develop a fuel supply not only for the Welfare Program but also for LDS chapels, the church's hospital system, and Brigham Young University. Shirl McArthur was "set apart" in 1946 as superintendent of what was then called the Deseret Mine. With the support of church officials, McArthur solved the water problem by piping water from springs on East Mountain to a reservoir inside the mine and in other ways developed the workings into a productive mine. A major development push starting in 1948 included construction of a new tipple at the mine mouth, an improved access road, a power line, and shipping and warehouse facilities on the bench road between Orangeville and Castle Dale.

As was the case with other LDS church welfare projects, much of the work at the Deseret Mine was done by volunteers under the supervision of full-time employees who were responsible for the safety of the work environment, the quality of coal mined, and completion of outlined work. There was some initial resistance from the United Mine Workers organization to voluntary service of union miners in a nonunion mine. However, after negotiations with church officials in 1949, UMW leaders agreed to classify the Deseret Mine as neither union nor nonunion but rather as a "welfare" mine.[38] Diesel-powered equipment (at that time still rare in underground mines) made efficient access possible to all areas of the mine. Capacity reached 200 tons per day in 1949 and 500 tons by 1951. The first continuous miner was installed in 1961, increasing productive capacity still further.[39] With a captive market, the Deseret Mine, almost alone among the county's coal operations, was able to maintain its production and employment through the 1960s.

Mining Casualties. The hazards of coal mining continued to exact a heavy toll, including several multiple-fatality accidents. Two men died in an attempt to recover equipment from the burning Ricci Mine in March 1953. The mine had been sealed three years earlier after a fire in the loading chute ignited the coal seam. Recovery of the bodies required several days of hazardous work by as many as eight rescue crews from Carbon County mines.[40] Mine operator Ted Robertson and two twelve-year-old boys were killed in an explosion at the Robertson mine in Cottonwood Canyon the day after Christmas in 1956. Robertson was working alone at the time attempting to blast a connecting tunnel between the mine and the adjacent mine operated by his father. The boys, one of whom was Robertson's nephew, were hunting in the area, trying out their new guns, and apparently entered the mine a short time before the explosion.[41] A rock fall at the American Fuel mine in April 1957 claimed three lives.[42] The Deseret Mine, after many years without a fatality, was the site of three fatal accidents in 1961.[43] All told, nineteen men were killed at Emery County mines during the period, and at least seventeen county residents died in mines outside the county.

The Uranium Rush

The dawning of the atomic age brought a sharply increased demand for uranium, which had formerly been a little-regarded by-product of radium and vanadium mines. To meet the demands of Cold War weapons programs, the Atomic Energy Commission sought to develop domestic uranium supplies by instituting purchasing and bonus programs intended to stimulate exploration and development. The Temple Mountain and Tidwell Draw areas of Emery County had produced uranium ores during the radium boom early in the twentieth century. At that time, only the richest ore was worth shipping; lower grade material was simply dumped near the mine entrance. In 1948 Byron Howard of Huntington with partners from Price began a profitable enterprise hauling the old Temple Mountain dumps to the AEC mill at Monticello. For some time this operation was the mill's largest supplier. By late 1949 several old mines were being reopened at Temple Mountain, most of them eventually controlled by Consolidated Mining Company. Consolidated drilled thirty-six-inch shafts to the deeper ore beds, lowered disassembled mining equipment through the shafts, then reassembled it in the ore zone. Shipments from Temple Mountain reached 100 tons per day by early 1950.[44]

Prospecting for new deposits began to heat up in 1948 and reached "fever" pitch in 1949, with 910 claims filed with the county recorder during that year. An additional 410 claims were filed in the first three months of 1950. The traditional Easter exodus to the desert was converted that year to a "Uranium-Easter" celebration at Chimney Rock. Castle Dale pharmacist L. T. Hunter served as a one-man clearing house for much of the prospecting activity in the county. He kept ore samples on display in his drug store, provided free testing of specimens for radioactivity, and supplied the *Emery County Progress* with weekly updates on promising finds. The highly publicized Mi Vida discovery by Charles Steen near Moab stimulated a new rush of prospecting in 1954. Claims filed in the county recorder's office totalled 461 in January, 800 in February, and 1,280 in March. In all, more than fifty thousand claims were filed between 1950 and 1956.[45] Owen McClenahan of Castle Dale, who actively prospected throughout the period, has described the uranium rush in these terms:

> Men by the thousands flocked into these erosional wastelands in old jalopy automobiles and army surplus jeeps. Here they would camp, and then proceed by foot in all directions climbing steep slopes until they reached the mineralized sandstones. There the ones without Geiger counters would take samples to be checked later. Those with counters would follow the mineralized areas until they had a reading from their counters which was a loud response of amplified clicking reminding one of a rattlesnake showing its annoyance to man.
>
> As a rule one of the worst things that could happen to a prospector would be to find just enough to raise his hopes, his dreams, and encourage his irresponsibility to raise money in any devious way he could. Many men lost everything they owned, including their wife and family.[46]

Uranium was found mainly in two geologic formations in Emery County: the Salt Wash member of the Morrison formation, and the Moss Back formation. The ores in the Tidwell Draw area west of Green River were in the Salt Wash formation and were usually associated with fossil logs or dinosaur bones. Some small deposits were also discovered in outcrops of the Salt Wash formation on the west side of the San Rafael Swell. The larger Temple Mountain and Delta–Hidden Splendor deposits were in the Moss Back formation.[47] Most of the uranium deposits discovered during the prospecting rush were small, often containing only a few tons of marketable ore. Larger deposits were found in the Muddy Creek drainage in the southern part of the Swell. William Hannert of Orangeville and John Tomsic of Columbia discovered profitable ore bodies at Tomsic Butte in early 1950.[48] A group of prospectors from Ferron and Clawson including Frank Blackburn, Ervin Olsen, Elden Bryan, and Thomas Worthen located a valuable deposit in Reds Canyon and another at Green Vein Mesa. They leased the Green Vein claims but elected to develop the "Lucky Strike" claims in Reds Canyon themselves even though they had no experience in hard-rock mining. Owen McClenahan recalled a visit he made to the Lucky Strike mine in the summer of 1950:

> They had a big open pit mine with a compressor and a wheel barrow for machinery. A large truck was backed into a bank, and they loaded the truck with the wheelbarrow. The ledge at that time was 30 feet high with two black bands 24 inches thick running parallel and equally spaced. The very top had a band of yellow uranium and a band of rose-red cobalt bloom. In all my years of prospecting I never did see a prettier face of ore. They were able to ship it all, but they had to break it up so there was no rock over five or six inches.
>
> The men were over 60 years of age, and they were all doing their own mining. I was interested in the efficiency with which they were going about their work. Two men were breaking the ore with sledge hammers, one was loading the truck, and the other was doing the drilling and loading the holes. Ervin Olsen's son was trucking the ore to the mill. For a long time their ore ran over 1% at the mill. I never heard how much they made, but it wasn't long until they were riding around in Buicks and Lincolns.[49]

Other locations that produced marketable ore during the early uranium rush period included the Dexter claims on Calf Mesa and the nearby Lone Tree claims, the Wickiup claims, the Consolidated claims near Family Butte, and several claims in the Tidwell Draw area.[50]

While Temple Mountain has been the largest producer of uranium ore in the county, the most publicized single discovery was Vernon J. Pick's June 1952 location of the Delta–Hidden Splendor deposit near the point where Muddy Creek cuts through the San Rafael Reef. Pick, who knew little of the country and had no training as a geologist or miner, reportedly was directed to the site by an employee of the Atomic Energy Commission who had observed a radiation anomaly during a survey flight over the area. After working the claims profitably himself for two years, Pick sold the property to the Atlas Corporation in 1954 for $9 million. Atlas recovered only about $2 million worth of ore before abandoning the workings in 1957. A 1954 article in *Life* magazine made Pick almost as famous in uranium prospecting lore as Charlie Steen. The article was met with great skepticism, however, by those who were familiar with the region. Pick told of a four-day solo ordeal during which he was stalked by mountain lions, suffered through 120-degree heat, and was compelled to make numerous hazardous crossings of the treacherous, waist-deep waters of Muddy Creek. After locating the uranium deposit, Pick claimed to have fashioned a raft by burning a log in half and tying it together with shoelaces and belt. He then made a "harrowing trip down the raging torrent" to return to civilization.[51] Emery County stockmen who had spent much of their lives in the region without ever seeing the Muddy with enough water to float a raft were contemptuous of Pick's story. Local prospectors who had been, in some instances, within a few hundred yards of his discovery were chagrined at the outsider's luck.

The Temple Mountain district produced 261,000 tons of ore between 1948 and 1956 that contained 1,287,000 pounds of uranium oxide and 3,799,000 pounds of vanadium oxide. Consolidated Uranium sold its properties to Union Carbide Nuclear Corporation in November 1956. Union Carbide continued to work the mines for several years, but a decline in the market for uranium led to an almost complete cessation of mining by 1968 even though the reserves were not yet exhausted.[52] According to Arminta Hewitt, who lived at Temple Mountain between 1953 and 1954, facilities included a boarding house, a cook shack that also sold groceries, a bath house, laundry room, machinery repair shop, three duplex houses, several trailers, and some shacks. Water for the settlement was hauled forty miles from Green River. A smaller group of trailers and shacks called North Temple was located several miles away. Hewitt recalled, "These little settlements were enjoyable to live in as they were so quiet and peaceful and the desert scenery was so beautiful."[53]

Hidden Splendor was a similar collection of prefabricated buildings and trailers during its active operating period from 1954 to 1957. A school was provided for seventeen children in 1955. The work force at the time was some seventy men.[54] Another uranium boom settlement was Temple Junction, comprising a gas station, cafe, grocery store, and pool hall at the junction of the Temple Mountain road with Highway 24.[55]

Green River received a substantial economic boost from the uranium boom, serving as a staging and supply point for prospectors and for the Temple Mountain, Muddy Creek, and Tidwell Draw mines. Union Carbide Corporation erected an ore sampling and concentrating plant on the east side of the river, which remained in operation until 1961. A number of residents found employment in the diggings or made at least wages from their own claims. The town's population grew by an estimated 150 percent in 1954, with most of the new residents occupying mobile homes. School enrollments rose to 280 in 1955. The post office was upgraded from third class to second class status. The community's first newspaper in more than thirty years made its appearance when the *Green River Journal* began publication on 21 July 1955. Jim Hurst developed a profitable business flying prospectors and mining officials from Green River to landing strips scraped out of the sagebrush at numerous locations. With the waning of the boom, however, the prospectors, miners, and many of those who provided services to them moved on, leaving little lasting benefit to the community.[56]

Oil and Gas

Significant commercial deposits of natural gas were discovered in the Flat Canyon and Clear Creek fields in 1953 and 1954, during which time drilling crews lived in Orangeville, Castle Dale, and Huntington, and a warehouse for drilling mud and supplies was erected at Huntington. Another gas field that also produced some oil was developed near Ferron in 1957. Over a period of twenty years, the Ferron field produced 7.5 billion cubic feet of gas and 165,337 barrels of oil.[57]

Transportation and Tourism

The highway bridge across the Green River collapsed on 30 July 1946 under the load of a truck carrying heavy equipment. The loss of the bridge caused a major disruption of east-west automobile traffic and cut off access for Elgin residents to the stores and other services in Green River. As the melon harvest season came on, the situation was particularly acute for east-bank farmers who had no way to get their crop to the shipping sheds at Green River. A temporary bridge was put in service in late August, and work began in October on a permanent bridge located farther upriver. The new bridge was opened to traffic in March 1948.[58] The postwar period brought a steady increase in tourism through Green River, leading to the construction of several motels, restaurants, and service stations.

The long-awaited Salina Canyon highway was finally completed in 1954 when the last stretch of Highway 10 received a paved surface.[59] This brought some additional tourists through the western part of the county and a large increase in interstate truck traffic because the route reduced the distance between Denver and Los Angeles by almost one hundred miles. The Salina Canyon highway also facilitated the marketing of coal from mines near Emery to central and southern Utah and made the shopping and banking facilities of Salina and Richfield more easily accessible to residents of Emery and Ferron as an alternative to Price.

River Running. An important new development occurred in 1947 when Harry Aleson and Georgie White set out from Green River to run the canyons in war surplus rubber rafts.[60] These did not immediately replace the old rigid river craft, however. Bert Loper, who had probably spent more time in the Green and Colorado River canyons than any other boater, announced plans in March 1949 to celebrate his eightieth birthday by running the rivers yet again. It was to be his final excursion as he was lost in the Grand Canyon in mid-July.[61]

Public Services

Public Safety. A three-tiered law enforcement system was in operation in the county at the beginning of the period. The state highway patrol usually stationed one officer in Green River and one in the western part of the county. The county sheriff employed two or three deputies, with one of them assigned to Green River. Each incorporated community had a town marshal who typically added to his law enforcement duties responsibility for maintenance of town water systems and cemeteries and control of stray dogs and truant school children. Of these, only the highway patrol officers had formal training for their positions. Don B. Kofford, first elected in 1950, was probably the first Emery County sheriff to regard himself as a career law enforcement officer. Kofford introduced a new professionalism to the sheriff's department that included training, improved equipment, and active participation in professional associations. Kofford served until 1959 when he resigned to take a law enforcement position with the Bureau of Reclamation.[62] The initiatives introduced by Kofford were continued by his successor, John M. Leamaster, who served from 1959 to 1974. Mack V. Bunderson brought a corresponding professionalism to the office of county attorney during his long tenure from 1950 to 1974.

Before this period, firefighting equipment had been virtually nonexistent in Emery County. Any fire that progressed beyond the capacity of a garden hose to extinguish it was almost certain to continue until it had consumed all available fuel. When a fire broke out, a public alarm would typically be given by the ringing of a church bell or the blowing of a siren, and volunteers would gather at the site in an attempt to save the contents of the building. The structure itself would usually end up as a total loss. Many residents lost homes, barns, and haystacks, and almost every community had seen churches, schools, and business buildings burn to the ground. In some instances, calls were sent to the Price fire department, but the time required for the fire engines to reach the scene rendered their services of limited value.

The first serious efforts to obtain equipment and organize volunteer firefighters took place during the 1950s. Orangeville, Huntington, Green River, and Castle Dale all purchased fire engines during the period between 1950 and 1956. Ferron followed in 1963.[63] While these small engines had limited capacity, they did provide a significant additional measure of protection to their communities.

Water and Sewer Systems. Under pressure of threats from the State Board of Health to withdraw the grade-A rating from the county's dairies, several communities undertook improvements in their water systems in 1950. Little Moore, very dependent on its dairy operations, installed the first filtration system in the western part of the county, followed by Castle Dale, Emery, and Ferron. Green River placed a new water treatment plant on line in 1951, drawing water from wells near the river bank in an attempt to eliminate a bad taste in the river water. This arrangement was not satisfactory and was replaced by another and larger filtration and treatment plant in 1954. Despite these and other efforts, however, a 1957 evaluation by the state health department did not list a single water system in the county as fully approved. The Green River and Emery systems were granted provisional approval, but all other communities were on the "not approved" list.[64]

Orangeville installed a sewer system in 1951. This freed some residents of the need to maintain septic tanks but did nothing to improve overall sanitary conditions as the raw sewage was discharged directly into Cottonwood Creek.[65] The Castle Dale and Huntington sewer systems were enlarged during the period, but they too continued to dump untreated sewage into the creeks.

Emery County Farmers Union Telephone Association. Mountain States Telephone upgraded its Green River service to a modern dial system in 1947 but showed no interest in serving the remainder of the county apart from its franchises in Green River and Huntington and its long distance toll line with a single local station in each community from Elmo to Emery.[66] In 1948 a group of interested citizens organized the Castle Valley Telephone Association with the goal of bringing local service to their communities. Dennis Killian of Orangeville chaired the association with Samuel N. Alger of Elmo as vice chair, R. Merrill Allred of Emery as secretary, and J. Rulon Nelson of Ferron, Jesse S. Tuttle of Castle Dale, Duane Jensen of Cleveland, and Merrill Day of Elmo as directors.

Several of the officers of the Castle Valley Telephone Association were also active in organizing the Farmers Union in the county. The National Farmers Union was lobbying Congress at the time to amend the Depression-era Rural Electrification Act to provide financing for rural telephone service. When this legislation was enacted in October 1949, the Emery County group was the first in the nation to submit an application to the Rural Electrification Administration for telephone service. Before the application could be approved, it was necessary for the local association to be incorporated as a legal entity, recruit members who would provide the required equity funds, develop preliminary engineering plans and cost estimates, negotiate interconnection agreements with Mountain States Telephone, and secure necessary franchises, easements, and regulatory approvals. This was a major undertaking for a mostly volunteer organization, but the numerous tasks were accomplished in a remarkably short time. On 12 August 1950 the former Castle Valley Telephone Association was incorporated under the name of Emery County

Farmers Union Telephone Association. On 20 February 1951, ECFUTA received approval for the second telephone loan granted by the REA and the first to go to a cooperative organization.

The accomplishments of the Emery County Farmers Union Telephone Association were remarkable not only for the effort required but also for the high level of voluntary cooperation (in keeping with the county's pioneer tradition) and for the way the telephone project transcended local rivalries. The Castle Dale Telephone Company presented a potential obstacle to ECFUTA's plans because it held the Castle Dale and Orangeville franchises. However, rather than attempting to block the new organization or demanding a high price for its obsolete equipment, Castle Dale Telephone president and manager Alva Wall and the board of directors agreed to transfer the company's rights and property at no cost and ended up charging ECFUTA a total of only $565.89 for Wall's services.

The telephone project did not go forward entirely without opposition. The decision to adopt the Farmers Union name irritated some supporters of the rival Farm Bureau organization. Some county residents objected on principle to government-sponsored projects seen as competing with private enterprise (even though in this case no private company was interested in providing telephone service, and the government support was in the form of loans rather than outright grants). Mountain States Telephone agreed to sell its toll lines at a reasonable price and to provide extended area service between its Huntington customers and ECFUTA subscribers in the Cleveland-Elmo and Castle Dale-Orangeville exchanges, but refused to allow extended area service between Huntington and Ferron-Emery as ECFUTA had proposed.

Surmounting all obstacles, the telephone system went into operation in August 1953 with 584 subscribers, four automated local exchanges (at Cleveland, Castle Dale, Ferron, and Emery), a headquarters office at Orangeville, and four full-time employees. For a monthly rate of $4.25, subscribers could call toll-free from the Oviatt ranch north of Elmo to the Browning Mine south of Emery, probably the largest extended area service in the state. Board chair and president Dennis Killian also served as acting manager during the construction phase. After operations began, Keith N. Ware, who had been serving as office manager, was appointed as general manager, a position he would hold for thirty-nine years.[67]

The leap forward in communications represented by the Farmers Union telephone cooperative brought a significant improvement in quality of life. The telephone linked the communities of the county more closely together and was sometimes a life-saver in cases of medical emergency. A shortage of equipment made it necessary to have party lines in some parts of the ECFUTA service area at first. Sylvia H. Nelson recalls the gratitude she felt when telephone service reached her farm home outside of Huntington but also remembers that the party lines "provided much frustration through non-privacy and misuse, and [were] the source of many very funny stories and jokes that went around for years."[68] In an effort to prevent domination of the line by one party, ECFUTA at first installed a timed-disconnect feature that would cut off calls after six or nine minutes. The telephone association (which officially changed its name to Emery Telephone in 1994) has continued to play an important role in the county. It turned its first profit in 1961 and has used profits both for patronage refunds to subscribers and for modernization that has kept it near the leading edge of communications technology.

Television. As television developed from a novelty to a major entertainment and information medium in the early 1950s, there was growing interest in making it available to county residents. Because of the intervening mountains, signals from the Salt Lake City stations could not be received in Emery County except in a few locations, mainly in the Cleveland-Elmo area. An attempt was made by A. R. Van Wagoner in early 1956 to "pipe" the television via cable from one such location to subscribers in other areas. A more ambitious project was undertaken a short time later by a committee led by Bill Justesen of Orangeville and including Wilford Humphrey, C. L. Witbeck, Russell Snow, LaMar Wilberg, Phillip Nelson, J. L. Larsen, and Preston Huntington. Their plan was to install a receiver on the rim of Horn Mountain, where a good signal was available, and rebroadcast to Castle Valley residents.

The television project was similar to the telephone project in that it had its inception in the determined efforts of a few volunteers who refused to accept the possibility of failure, and was later placed on a more permanent basis through the assistance of public agencies. The committee requested every family who wanted television to contribute $30 in cash plus an equal amount in labor. The funds were used to purchase equipment, most of which was installed by volunteers. Changes in Federal Communications Commission regulations made it possible to obtain a license to "translate" the VHF signals to UHF frequencies for rebroadcast. A major hurdle was getting a power line to the translator site. The site was only five miles from Orangeville but sat atop a three thousand foot escarpment, the upper third of which was a sheer cliff. When the Utah Power and Light Company estimate for building a line proved to be far beyond the available funds, the local group undertook construction of the power line themselves, planting poles and stringing wire across almost incredibly difficult terrain. The power line was completed and two translator units installed in late 1956. The FCC license had not yet been approved, so station KSL used its own broadcasting license to provide service on a temporary basis. The first continuous television transmission from the translators took place in early February 1957. A testing permit was granted in May and an operating permit followed shortly thereafter. After the system was operational, the county commission agreed to levy a small recreation tax for its maintenance. A third translator was installed in April 1958, making all three Salt Lake City commercial stations available. Initially the translators served only the area from Huntington to Ferron. An Emery group was organized in November 1957 for the purpose of installing a relay station on a ridge east of Moore, which began operating in January 1958. In 1961 Green River City applied for a translator license. In 1964 San Juan County funded the installation of more powerful transmitters to relay the signals to that area.[69]

Medicine and Public Health

Polio was the most dreaded disease of the postwar period. Successive outbreaks in the late summer and fall of 1950 and 1951 claimed the lives of four children in the county and left several others with long-term disabilities. The county participated in the 1954 clinical tests of the Salk vaccine, which effectively ended the polio threat.[70] While this disease was devastating to those who contracted it, the overall impact in terms of lives lost was small in comparison to the diphtheria and influenza epidemics and the perennial toll of typhoid in earlier years. In a sense, the very intensity of the fear caused by polio was an indication of how far medical science had progressed in controlling communicable diseases.

This period saw the passing of the county's long-serving doctors. T. C. Hill died in 1947 at the age of sixty-three. Bruce Easley died in 1955 at the age of seventy-three. F. R. King, who had practiced in Green River for thirty-seven years, died in 1964 at the age of eighty-four. Benjamin Turman maintained an active practice in Castle Dale until his health failed. He died in 1965 at the age of sixty-two. Harry S. Nielsen of Ferron, who had practiced dentistry in the community for almost thirty years, died in 1964. An elderly physician, Lena F. Schrier, came to Huntington in 1952 and continued to see patients until shortly before her death in 1981 at the age of ninety-seven.[71]

Wildlife

Huntington Creek was maintained as a prime trout stream and saw heavy use by anglers from Emery and Carbon counties. Other mountain streams also provided recreational fishing. Ferron Reservoir offered resort facilities and attracted people from Sanpete County. Cleveland Reservoir was also a popular fishing site. The deer herds on the Wasatch Plateau and in the Book Cliffs and the Wasatch Plateau elk herd were among the most important in the state, and the annual fall deer hunt attained almost ritual significance in local communities. Antelope were reestablished in the San Rafael area by stock transplanted from Wyoming in 1949 supplemented by additional animals from Montana in 1955 and by later transplants from other areas of Utah.[72]

Predatory wildlife continued to be viewed primarily as a threat to domestic livestock and deer herds. During a forty-year career as a government trapper and hunter from 1933 to 1973, Perry Oveson of Castle Dale trapped fifty-seven cougars and served as a guide to hunters who took seventy-nine more. On the occasion of the trapping of a large cougar in Straight Canyon in February 1946, the *Progress* reported that during his career to that point Oveson had also killed 1,725 coyotes, 334 bobcats, and two bears.[73] He once trapped

148 bobcats in ninety days. Oveson was known for his ability to "talk" to coyotes, mimicking their sounds in order to determine their location and direct airborne hunters in for the kill.[74]

School and Community

County residents attached great importance to their schools, particularly the high schools. High school basketball games attracted large crowds, with an amazing number of spectators filling the tiny gyms for the annual battles for supremacy between North Emery and South Emery. Elderly people often attended school dances just to watch the young people. Although the schools were old and poorly equipped by modern standards, they were staffed for the most part by dedicated teachers and offered an education that prepared students well for the workplace or for further education. Kent Petersen remembered in particular Alan Tuft, who taught at South Emery: "He was an excellent math and science teacher and due to him there were about 15 boys near my age who went on to graduate from college in one of the engineering branches, or science or mathematics. Which is amazing considering the class sizes." No one who attended South Emery High during those years would ever forget Principal Brad Jensen and his "board of education":

> Seemed like a 2 by 6 but it was probably a 1 by 6 board, painted, with holes drilled in it and it hung on his wall. Sometimes he carried it with him. I never knew anyone he used it on but he probably did. He really didn't have to because we knew it was there and no one wanted to be bad enough to have it used on them.[75]

At North Emery Stella L. Hill was a seemingly timeless institution. Jane McClenahan was well known in the banks and offices of Price and Salt Lake City for the excellent preparation given to her business students. O. Eugene and Grace N. Johansen—"Mr. and Mrs. Jo"—shaped several generations of students in civics and speech and drama. Vocational agriculture programs under Frank L. Hall at North Emery and J. Keith Albrecht at South Emery turned out leaders in the state Future Farmers of America organization. Homemaking programs directed by Lucinda B. Wild at South Emery and later at Emery County High produced twenty-two state Future Homemakers of America officers. Sylvia H. Nelson recalls, "There were many youngsters whose first trip away from home was an FHA or FFA convention to the big city and even Washington, D.C."[76] Music teachers Orson W. Peterson at North Emery and LaVell F. Johnson at South Emery regularly had some of the largest and best drilled marching bands in the state. Green River High School gained accreditation from the Northwest Association of Secondary and Higher Schools in 1955, shortly after moving to the new building. This was the first time an Emery County school had been accredited. Lee F. Gledhill served as principal at Green River during much of this period. Blaine F. Evans, who later became superintendent of the Emery County School District, came to Green River in 1959 to revive a moribund music program.[77] It would be impossible to list the many teachers in Emery County schools who made a memorable impact on students during these years.

Lifestyle

While a lack of other options or simple inertia kept some residents in the county through this period of economic decline, a large majority remained because they were attached to a distinctive lifestyle. When Emery County people spoke of having alkali in their blood, they were thinking of the county's open spaces and wide views, the easy access to the mountains and the desert, the neighborliness of the close-knit communities, and ties to land that had in some instances belonged to the family since the settlement period. Though the young people sometimes complained that there was "nothing to do," in retrospect an Emery County childhood in the 1940s or 1950s or 1960s seemed almost idyllic. Kent R. Petersen recalls,

> Living in Ferron from around 12 to high school was great fun. We lived right next to the Ferron Creek. . . . We would go down there and play cowboys and Indians or war games. We built big elaborate forts. It's all gone now, most of the time the water doesn't even run in Ferron Creek because it's dammed at Millsite. But then there were squirrels and rabbits. I got a .22 when I was about 14. It was great sport on weekends to hunt for rabbit and squirrel and birds, whatever. No thoughts of gun control at that time![78]

Hunting and fishing were popular activities in the county. Sylvia H. Nelson comments,

> Young men waited to be old enough to go hunting and fishing with their dads and uncles. Originally, what was a father and son outing for procuring family sustenance turned into a sport that many whole families could and do participate in. During the 50's and 60's, wives and girls started to hunt and fish more with their husbands, families and boyfriends.[79]

With the development of larger bodies of water, boating assumed a more important place among recreational activities.

Much of the social life of the young still revolved around high school and church dances, but dating practices were complicated by the division of the population among so many towns. Kent Petersen remembers occasions when he drove the family car from his home in Ferron to Molen and Moore to pick up his friends, then to Emery, Castle Dale, and Orangeville to get their dates, and back to Ferron for the dance. At the end of the evening, the same roundabout journey was repeated in reverse. He comments, "We put on a lot of miles but we didn't do it that often and gasoline was 25 cents a gallon so we could almost do it on $1.00 worth of gas."[80]

The period when the population of young people was shrinking also brought increased attention to youth recreation programs. In earlier years organized youth recreation had been the province of schools and churches. Community sports teams were for adults. However, in 1959 the county began participating in the Western Boys Baseball program, with teams in several towns.[81] Baseball fields were built complete with grass, groomed basepaths, and even lights for night play—a far cry from the "cow-pasture" baseball of earlier decades. Teams from the county competed successfully in state and regional WBBA play, and the program developed skills that led Emery County High School baseball teams to prominence among schools of its size. Church-sponsored softball and basketball teams provided recreational opportunities, "especially for those who couldn't make the school teams but still loved to play the sports."[82] The 4-H program was active in the county, with summer project groups ranging from cooking and sewing to livestock feeding, highlighted by an annual countywide encampment in the mountains. Boy Scout troops, most of them sponsored by the LDS church, were also active.

Organized riding clubs were an important recreation resource for adults and young people alike. The Blue Ridge Riders of Cleveland, the Huntington Saddle Club, the Blue and Gold Club of Castle Dale, and the Riders of the Spanish Trail in Ferron were all active during this period.[83] Junior riding clubs were established in several communities under the sponsorship of the adult clubs. Regular competitions were held at both the junior and senior levels, and the riding clubs were a regular feature at the parades and rodeos that made up an important part of every community celebration in the county.

The 1960s

The persistent economic decline of the 1950s was apparent to all by the end of that decade. The 28 May 1959 issue of the *Emery County Progress* contained the following lament from editor Clarin D. Ashby:

> From Emery on the south to Elmo on the north, the trend is somewhat the same. Regardless of how much we try to kid ourselves, it is evident that the population is dwindling, businesses are finding it hard to keep their doors open, and public officials are faced with greater financial problems each year.

The total population fell by 409 between 1960 and 1970, but that figure is misleading on two counts. The excess of births over deaths during the decade amounted to 591, making the actual net out-migration an even 1,000.[84] Moreover, the period was a time of growth for Green River, meaning that the other communities in the county experienced even greater losses than might at first appear. Farm numbers declined as small operations were consolidated into larger ones. The 1969 census of agriculture found 353 farms in the county, a 28 percent decrease from the 490 farms in 1964.[85] The downhill slide seemed to affect even the county's natural features. On 1 January 1967 the "Old Woman," a well known rock formation near the mouth of Ivie Creek Canyon, fell from her pedestal and collapsed into rubble.[86] Still, despite all its problems the decade of the 1960s saw the preparation of essential groundwork for the extraordinary growth of the 1970s.

County Government. Emery County usually voted Republican in national elections during this period but maintained a long-standing tradition of voting for the candidate rather than the party in local elections. Of the nine individuals who served on the county commission during the 1960s, five were Democrats and four Republicans. In contrast to the early years when county officials seldom served longer than one or two terms, county government had become highly professionalized by midcentury, and officials who could maintain the confidence of the electorate were returned to office again and again. Probably the longest-tenured official in the county's history was A. Rex Nelson, who held the assessor's office from 1942 to 1972.

Emery County Nursing Home. The county's high unemployment rate in the 1960s made it eligible for several forms of federal assistance under accelerated public works programs. An important product of this assistance was a modern nursing home constructed at Ferron to serve an ageing population. Federal funds provided under the Hill-Burton Act paid half of the $430,000 cost. Voters approved bonds for the remainder in a July 1963 election by a margin of 605 to 276. Construction began in July 1964, and the twenty-five bed facility was dedicated in December 1965.[87]

School Consolidation

Emery County School District superintendent C. L. Frye resigned in 1957 and was replaced by Orson W. Peterson of Castle Dale, the first native son to be appointed to the position in more than thirty years. Peterson had spent almost his entire career as a teacher and principal in Emery County schools. During a record-long tenure of twenty years as superintendent, he would guide the county's schools through both their most extensive consolidation and their most rapid growth.[88]

As the school-age population declined in the western part of the county, per-student operating expenditures increased. New editor Clarin D. Ashby of the *Emery County Progress* published a series of editorials in 1959 calling for a reorganization of the county's schools. He pointed out that the cost per student of $373 was much higher than the state average of $278 and well above the national average of $324, even though the county's teacher salaries were below the state average. Ashby's proposal for a single high school in the western part of the county, conversion of South Emery and North Emery to junior highs, and consolidation of the area's seven elementary schools into four was exactly what came to pass, but only after agonized discussion.[89]

A major step toward consolidation was a study by a committee chaired by state superintendent of public instruction W. Allen Bateman. The committee report, issued in February 1960, made substantially the same recommendations as the *Progress:* creation of a single high school, to be located in the Castle Dale-Orangeville area, conversion of the two existing high schools to junior highs, and closure of the elementary schools at Emery, Castle Dale, and Elmo with those students being transported to schools at Ferron, Orangeville, and Cleveland. The committee also recommended building a new elementary school at Huntington. A study of existing buildings conducted by the school district staff rated all of the elementary schools in the western part of the county as "poor" with the exception of Orangeville, which was rated as "fair." The high school buildings were given "fair" ratings. Superintendent Peterson, in support of consolidation, noted that the Emery County School District had fifty-four classrooms with enrollments smaller than required by the state and was "receiving special help on more classrooms than any district in the state." He argued that reorganization of schools would provide substantial savings in plant maintenance and operation, educational programs more specifically adapted for junior high students, and better facilities for high school students.[90]

As was to be expected, the proposed reorganization drew strong protests from residents of Emery and Elmo, the two communities that stood to lose their only schools. Committees were organized in both towns to fight consolidation, and the letters to the editor section of the *Progress* was filled with their arguments for several weeks, accompanied by a smaller number of letters in support of consolidation. Typical of the sentiments expressed was a letter from G. L. Olsen of Emery, who argued that the closing of schools was a *cause* of depopulation and that Emery's decline had been precipitated by the busing of the older grades to Ferron. Olsen declared, "Schools are an asset to community life, to social equality, to community and individual growth and contentment. Take away the school and you have taken the heart out of any community."[91]

At an April 1960 election, voters approved bonding for the new facilities by a margin of 857 to 673. In Emery only one voter favored the proposal as against 148 who voted no. In Elmo the vote was four in favor and 104 opposed. The proposal was also rejected by substantial margins in Cleveland (21 to 95) and Huntington (115 to 157). Heavy pro-consolidation majorities in Orangeville (215 to 5) and Castle Dale (221 to 20) carried the proposal to victory. A site on the Castle Dale bench was acquired in August for the new high school. Construction began in March 1961, and the building was ready for occupancy at the beginning of the 1962–63 school year. Despite some public sentiment in favor of naming the school Castle Valley High, the school board opted for Emery County High School.[92] Within a few more months, the new Huntington Elementary and the first phase of the Cottonwood Elementary in Orangeville were in use. In the subsequent years, the Cottonwood Elementary was completed to replace the Orangeville school, and the new San Rafael Elementary replaced the old Ferron Elementary.[93]

The consolidated high school could offer both academic and activity programs beyond what had been available in its predecessor schools. A wider range of math and science classes was provided. The speech, drama, and music programs soon dominated the region in interscholastic competitions and frequently placed high in the state. With a larger enrollment, the school began a football program. The basketball teams advanced to the state Class B quarterfinals in 1964 and 1967 and to the finals in 1965. Track and baseball teams also did well in regional and state competition. Girls' athletics gained more attention with successful volleyball and basketball teams. Perhaps more than any other single influence, the popular Emery County High sports teams served to unify county residents.[94]

The Emery County Project

The long-deferred dream of a large reservoir in Joe's Valley began to move toward realization when the Emery County Project was included as a participating unit in the massive Upper Colorado Reclamation Project. Several county residents worked tirelessly, first for congressional approval and then for funding. Perhaps the most prominent voice was that of O. Eugene Johansen of Castle Dale, but there were others. In a public letter to Upper Basin officials, Wilford J. Humphrey of Orangeville emphasized Emery County's great need for water storage, noting,

> Nine years out of ten it is necessary for us to irrigate before we can do our spring plowing and then we have to water again to sprout the grain because of the cold dry winds. . . . Knowing that the water will soon be gone there is a tendency to water too much when the supply is plentiful.[95]

The Colorado River Storage Act, including the Emery County Project, was passed by Congress in 1956. Engineering studies began a short time later and included a detailed examination of the lands proposed to be served by the project. A major local hurdle was the establishment of a water conservancy district, required by the government as a contracting agency. All of the old sectional rivalries that had hindered earlier efforts to build a reservoir in Joe's Valley reappeared, accentuated by fears of losing established water rights. Perhaps fortunately, these negotiations took place during a drought period when farmers were acutely aware of the need for storage facilities that would not only provide for late-season irrigation but would also allow water to be carried over from wet years to dry ones. The Emery County Water Conservancy District was formally organized on 4 April 1961 with O. Eugene Johansen of Castle Dale as president, Mark Humphrey of Orangeville as secretary, and additional directors Ralph Lundy of Cleveland, Rosel Jensen of Huntington, Russell Justesen of Orangeville, Clyde Conover and Ellis Wild of Ferron, and Rex Bunderson of Emery. A contract to repay $2,935,000 of the project's approximately $8 million cost over a period of fifty years was approved by 96 percent of the voters in a May 1962 election. A project office with Ross D. Billings as project engineer was established in the former Rocket Theatre in Castle Dale, which had been converted into an office building. The S. S. Mullen Construction Company of Seattle was awarded the major contract for the dam.[96]

Ground was finally broken for the Joe's Valley Dam on 20 June 1963. The groundbreaking ceremony attracted a large crowd of county residents as well as a host of distinguished visitors including Governor George D. Clyde, Senator Frank E. Moss, and Floyd E. Dominy, commissioner of the Bureau of Reclamation, all of whom addressed the assembly, as did O. Eugene Johansen, president of the Emery Water Conservancy District. Johansen in his remarks reflected on three Joes of Joe's Valley who together represented a significant portion of the area's history: the legendary "Indian Joe" for whom the valley was named; Joe Swasey, who built some of the first fences in the valley; and "Pete Joe" (Peter Johansen), who acquired much of Joe's Valley as ranch land in the early years of the century. Governor Clyde, whose prepolitics career had been in water engineering, recalled his first visit to Joe's Valley in 1923, and his estimate at that time that "I have never seen a damsite which appeared to be so natural and so efficient." Senator Moss emphasized the region's need for the economic boost the project would provide, noting that the unemployment rate in Emery and Carbon counties had reached a high of 15.3 percent in 1959, that one-third of the families in Emery County had annual incomes below $3,000, and that the county's net outmigration between 1950 and 1960 was an astonishing 29.6 percent.[97]

The Emery County Project included three major components: the Joe's Valley Reservoir, with a storage capacity of 62,460 acre-feet impounded by an earthfill dam 196 feet high with a crest length of 740 feet; the Swasey Diversion Dam and the 16.7-mile Cottonwood Creek-Huntington Canal; and the Huntington North Reservoir, an off-stream impoundment with a capacity of 5,420 acre-feet. Work on the Cottonwood-Huntington canal began in early 1964, and the Huntington North Reservoir was under construction by early 1965. Joe's Valley Reservoir began storing water on 1 November 1965. All major components were substantially completed in 1966. A dedication ceremony was held in Joe's Valley on 7 July 1966, just over three years from the groundbreaking. Contracts were executed in 1969 and 1970 between the Emery Water Conservancy District and the Ephraim and Horseshoe irrigation companies in Sanpete County providing for water storage rights and transbasin diversion, thus establishing on a regular basis the long-disputed claims to runoff from the upper slopes of the Cottonwood Creek watershed. Several drainage projects were undertaken between 1971 and 1974 to correct seepage and waterlogging of farmlands. The Straight Canyon road was realigned to a higher route to clear the dam and reservoir. The road finally received a paved surface in 1969.[98]

Construction of the Emery County Project provided much-needed jobs and a general economic infusion. Sylvia H. Nelson remembers that

> so many of the young men . . . relied upon this employment as an opportunity to stay in this area, marry and make their homes. So many had their first opportunity to gain experience of running heavy equipment that served as life long careers for many who sought seasonal construction work elsewhere on other projects using heavy equipment, living at home in the winter on unemployment or odd jobs they could find.[99]

In addition to the lasting benefit of a far more dependable water supply, the project made an important addition to the area's recreational resources. The Forest Service developed boat ramps and other recreational facilities at Joe's Valley Reservoir, and vacation home developments sprouted on nearby private lands. A state park was established at Huntington North Reservoir (now better known simply as Huntington Lake) with a well developed campground and boat launching facilities.

Ferron Watershed Project

The Emery County Project provided no direct benefits for Ferron Creek irrigators, whose canal diversion points were too high to be supplied from Cottonwood Creek. The idea of a reservoir near the site of the old flour mill at the mouth of Ferron Canyon had been discussed for many years, and an unsuccessful attempt had been made to have it built as a CCC project. New efforts began in 1962 to improve the Ferron Creek water supply through existing programs of the U. S. Department of Agriculture. The Soil Conservation Service in cooperation with the Forest Service initiated planning in August 1962, and water users approved a proposed development plan in August 1963 and a more definite plan in January 1965. The watershed plan encompassed range improvements and flood control as well as a major storage project.[100]

Ground was broken for the Mill Site Dam on 16 June 1969, with the Strong Construction Company of Springville as the major contractor, and the completed project was dedicated on 11 June 1971. The reservoir was built on what had formerly been the Paul and Roxie Nelson farm. The dam, 112 feet high and with a crest length of 4,043 feet, impounds 19,000 acre-feet of water and effectively controls the entire flow of Ferron Creek except for extended periods of high runoff. Half of the $3,380,000 cost of the Mill Site Reservoir was paid by the Soil Conservation Service under provisions of the Small Watersheds Act. The Utah Water and Power Board provided a long-term loan of $750,000. The Utah Department of Fish and Game paid $266,321 for a fisheries conservation pool in the Mill Site Reservoir and for the small reservoirs high in the canyon that were no longer needed for irrigation water storage. The balance of the costs were assumed by the Ferron Reservoir and Canal Company and Ferron City.[101]

Green River Missile Base

While western Emery County communities were suffering through the economic doldrums, Green River was experiencing its greatest growth since the peach boom of 1906. The uranium rush had made a dramatic but rather superficial impact on the community that faded in the late 1950s and for all practical purposes ended with the closing of the Union Carbide ore concentrating plant in 1961. A more significant phase of the town's history began with the Army's 1963 decision to establish a launch facility for the Athena missile near Green River. The Athena was a test vehicle designed to simulate the launch and reentry characteristics of the Atlas and other military ballistic missiles at a lower cost than using actual Atlas missiles. A subsidiary of the White Sands Missile Range in New Mexico, the Utah Launch Complex, located east of the river and operated by Atlantic Research Corporation, assembled, tested, and fired Athena and some Pershing missiles that landed at White Sands, four hundred miles away.

Construction and preparatory operations on the launch complex employed 419 workers by the end of 1963. The complex included four divisions: a launch area, a radar area, a missile assembly area, and a base support area.[102] Actual launches began in early 1964. Employment peaked at 530 in 1965 and fluctuated widely from that time until 1979 when the facility was placed on caretaker status. Several hundred workers were involved during active launch periods. At other times, only a small maintenance staff was employed.

Despite the fluctuating employment and uncertainty about the program's duration, the "missile base people," as they were called, made a substantial and lasting impact on Green River. Unlike the uranium prospectors, who tended to regard the town as little more than a supply and entertainment stop on their way to and from the diggings, the missile base people, many of them well educated and family oriented, had an interest in the quality of life in the community. Some of them almost immediately got involved with schools and other civic activities. Some became so attached to the community that they remained in the area after the missile base had closed. To meet the demands of growth, the city had to enlarge its water and sewer facilities several times during the 1960s and 1970s as homes were constructed in new subdivisions near the river. A well-equipped compact medical center, built with the assistance of a grant from the Sears Foundation in 1959, had attracted the full-time services of Dr. H. T. Barton by 1964.[103]

School enrollments jumped from 270 in 1962 to 312 in 1963. By 1967 the elementary school alone had 256 students, requiring split grades and construction of an addition to the school building. With increased enrollment, Green River High fielded a football team for the first time in more than four decades, and the basketball team under coach Jared Tucker became a force to be reckoned with in interscholastic competition. Star player Larry Beebe set several scoring records at the 1964 class B tournament, including fifty-two points in a single game.[104]

The influx of population gave a new lease on life to the Green River Community Church (which had by this time apparently terminated its Presbyterian affiliation). The Reverend Arvin E. Johnson served as pastor for several years in the mid-1960s. By 1964 Episcopalian services were being held in a home under sponsorship of the Moab Episcopal Church in Moab. Saint Michael's Catholic Mission began operations in a converted home in 1968.[105] Ground was broken in 1961 for a new LDS chapel, which was occupied in March 1963 under Bishop Ellis D. Peacock and dedicated on 7 January 1968 under Bishop Vail F. Hatt.[106]

Interstate 70

In 1957 legislation sponsored by Senator Wallace F. Bennett of Utah added 1,000 additional miles to the original 40,000-mile Defense Highway System (later renamed as the Interstate system). Utah officials proposed that part of the added mileage be devoted to a new highway connecting Denver with the Wasatch Front metropolitan area, but federal highway officials decreed instead that the new road should go more directly west from Denver and connect with Interstate 15 at Cove Fort. It would thus be the first major transportation link in Utah not to funnel through the Wasatch Front area. The new addition to the Interstate system was decried by Salt Lake City newspapers as a "road to nowhere" but was eagerly hailed in Emery County as a long-overdue recognition of the natural advantages of the Salina Canyon route.

Emery County officials hoped the interstate would roughly follow the Spanish Trail route through the county, leaving the Green River-Price highway near Woodside and crossing Buckhorn Flat to join Highway 10 near Castle Dale. This would have placed several county towns directly on the interstate. Ironically, it might have been an effort to promote local scenery that led to the scuttling of this plan. In the summer of 1958, county officials invited several guests including state and federal highway representatives to participate in a two-day "safari" through the San Rafael Swell with a goal of making the region's scenic attractions more widely known. The party traveled over primitive roads from Moore to Eagle Canyon, Copper Globe, and the Head of Sinbad, and returned by way of Buckhorn Draw. It was apparently this introduction to the San Rafael that gave highway officials the idea of building Interstate 70 directly through the heart of the Swell. The result was arguably the most scenic stretch of highway on the entire interstate system, but the decision also meant that the direct economic benefits to Emery County were largely limited to Green River.[107]

The route across the Swell was surveyed in early 1963. Construction began a few months later and proceeded in eight- to ten-mile chunks until the full length of the route was opened to traffic with a dedicatory service at Ghost Rock on 5 November 1970.[108] Initially only two lanes were completed across the Swell with the other two lanes being built over the following dozen years. Interstate 70 almost exactly bisects the Swell, piercing the San Rafael Reef by way of Little Spotted Wolf Canyon, where a natural gorge only a few feet wide was enlarged to four-lane capacity at immense cost. It then climbs to the grassy valleys at the Head of Sinbad, surrounded by Wingate sandstone walls, where it passes within a mile of the historic Swasey cabin at Jackass Spring, and where the Ghost Rock rest stop provides expansive vistas across the Swell. Farther west the highway crosses Eagle Canyon on an award-winning bridge, affords other dramatic views of the San Rafael Knob region to the south and Salt Wash to the north, then drops down into the valley of Muddy Creek before continuing on to a junction with Highway 10 at the mouth of Ivie Creek Canyon.

Even though Green River got only two connections to the interstate instead of the hoped-for three, the community's status as a travelers' oasis was assured by the long distances to other service areas. The 110 miles between Green River and Salina still represent the longest stretch without services on the entire interstate system. Unfortunately for the Emery County tax base, the main tourist facilities at Green River were built on the Grand County side of the line.

Development of Natural and Historic Features

Goblin Valley. The uranium boom and the building of Interstate 70 increased public awareness of the remarkable scenery of the San Rafael Swell area. The county commission sought to capitalize upon this with measures to improve visitor access. The previously little-known Entrada sandstone formations of Goblin Valley, just outside the San Rafael Reef, were made accessible by a county road in 1962. The state acquired the area from the BLM in 1964 and designated it as a state park in 1965.[109]

Cleveland-Lloyd Dinosaur Quarry. Dinosaur fossils have been found in many different locations in Emery County, but the most productive source has been the Cleveland-Lloyd quarry located near the northwest base of Cedar Mountain. Allosaurus fossils were recovered from this site as early as the 1920s. In the late 1930s, several specimens were recovered by Cleveland native William Lee Stokes for Princeton University and other major museums. In 1960 Stokes, by this time chair of the geology department at the University of Utah, spearheaded an effort to reopen the quarry. Recovery work went forward for several consecutive seasons under the auspices of the University of Utah Cooperative Dinosaur Project. By 1980 more than fifteen thousand fossils had been recovered. The quarry is noted not only for the quantity of specimens it has yielded but for the quality of their detail.

Plans were set in motion in 1967 to build a visitors center at the quarry, with the construction work to be done be enrollees at the Castle Valley Job Corps Center located near Price. The visitors center was dedicated in September 1968 and has been open seasonally under the auspices of the Bureau of Land Management since that time.[110]

Green River State Park. A major advance in public awareness of the recreational value of the Green River came with the establishment of a boat race called the Canyon Marathon and the more leisurely Friendship Cruise that attracted numerous private boat owners. The first Canyon Marathon boat race, sponsored by the Green River and Moab chambers of commerce, was run in June 1958. The marathon continued to be held for more than a decade. The noncompetitive Friendship Cruise went on for many more years, at its peak attracting more than seven hundred boats on a two-day cruise down the Green and up the Colorado to Moab. With widespread local support, the Green River State Park was opened in 1965, and its fine facilities soon made it a center for water recreation.[111]

Emery County Museum. Several county residents had accumulated collections of prehistoric artifacts over the years, mostly from the Fremont culture, but there was no suitable place for public exhibition. In 1968 an early Fremont burial site was uncovered containing the mummified bodies of a woman and a small child. The site was excavated under the supervision of College of Eastern Utah instructor Donald Burge and the recovered items put on temporary display at the college until such time as Emery County had a suitable place to exhibit them. Dixon Peacock approached county commissioner Gardell Snow to ask if the county would help to finance a museum. Peacock, together with LeRoy Maxfield, also went to the recently organized Emery County Jaycees in search of assistance. The Jaycees agreed to take on the project, and Castle Dale City offered the upper floor of the old elementary school as a museum. A fifty-year lease was granted on 4 December 1969.

The city had acquired the building after the 1962 school consolidation. The ground floor was used for city offices, and the attached gymnasium was converted to a swimming pool in 1967. The building, and especially the unused upper floor, was in poor condition. Jaycee volunteers solicited funds and provided many hours of work in fixing the leaking roof, cleaning and repairing the rooms, planting a lawn in front of the building, and laying asphalt. Emery County dinosaurs had been displayed in major natural history museums around the world for many years, but the first local exhibit was made possible when the University of Utah Cooperative Dinosaur Project donated an allosaurus skeleton that was assembled by Castle Dale native Glen Ungerman. Parker Childs designed and built display cases for the prehistoric exhibits. Much work was also done under the auspices of the Green Thumb Project, a federal program that employed retired people to work on civic improvement projects.

The museum opened on 1 May 1970 under the supervision of a board consisting of Dixon Peacock, chair, Boyd Snow, Dora Otterstrom, W. H. Maxfield, Owen McClenahan, Carlyle Jones, and Ira Hatch. The initial exhibits included the prehistoric materials and the Pioneer Room displaying items from the early history of the county. In later years other rooms were rehabilitated and devoted to exhibits of historic farm implements, mining equipment, and a simulated co-op store. Ann Wissler was added to the museum board in 1971 because of her many years of museum experience in California. She spent hundreds of volunteer hours at the museum over the next fifteen years, and her husband, Ira, worked to restore antique furniture for display. New board members and volunteers came to the forefront in the 1980s.[112]

The Vietnam War

The first reference to Vietnam in the *Emery County Progress* occurred in April 1965 with the note that Vern D. Jenkins of Castle Dale had been sent there with the Air Force. Keith Wright of Clawson spent a period of time in Saigon in the early years of the war on a civilian assignment as a teacher. Inevitably, as the conflict escalated a significant number of Emery County servicemen became involved. Jimmy McBroom of Emery, apparently the first casualty from the county, was killed in action on 2 July 1967. James Raymond Oveson of Elmo was killed in May 1968.[113]

Services

Banking. The county had been without banking facilities since the Great Depression led to closure of the Commonwealth Bank at Green River and merger of the Emery County Bank into the Carbon-Emery Bank. The possibility of a local banking office was raised in 1960 when the Wayne State Bank of Loa announced that it was interested in establishing a branch in Emery County. This announcement brought an immediate reaction from the Carbon-Emery Bank, which emphasized its long-standing ties with the county and indicated that it was willing to establish a branch office if conditions warranted. While commercial banks were engaged in these public posturings, a group of county residents organized the Castle Valley Federal Credit Union, with services available to anyone who lived within five miles of Highway 10. The credit union opened for business in Huntington in July 1960 with Grant C. Fausett of Castle Dale as president, Lee McMullin of Cleveland as vice president, Errol T. Litster of Huntington as secretary-treasurer, and a board of directors with representatives of all towns in western Emery County. A credit union was organized in Green River in 1963.[114]

The Carbon-Emery Bank eventually did open an office in Castle Dale in a newly constructed building at the corner of Main and First East in November 1963. The following month the Helper State Bank opened a branch office in the old bank building in Green River.[115]

Natural Gas. Mountain Fuel Supply Company acquired the Ferron gas field in 1965 and made plans for building a transmission line to deliver the gas to the company's primary market area on the Wasatch Front. Because the line passed near several Castle Valley communities, MFS proposed to offer natural gas service to residents. Service to Huntington began in September 1965, with Ferron, Clawson, Orangeville, and Castle Dale following within a short period.[116] The conversion of many homes and businesses to gas heating marked an advance in convenience but also accelerated the decline in the market for locally produced coal.

Economic Development

As traditional jobs eroded, efforts were initiated to take advantage of several federal and state programs aimed at economic development of depressed areas. The Castle Valley Development Corporation was organized in 1968 with an initial goal of raising sufficient local investment to allow the conversion of the old Orangeville school to a sewing factory. Some workers were employed there intermittently by a series of operators in the late 1960s and early 1970s, but the project was up against the fact that numerous other rural communities were also trying to convert abandoned schools to sewing factories in an effort to obtain work that otherwise would have gone to third-world countries. Even at the best, such jobs did not pay enough to provide very substantial economic benefits, either to individual workers or to a community.[117]

Far more significant economic forces were quietly at work with the objective of exploiting Emery County's vast coal reserves. Even as mines were closing down for lack of markets, major corporations were continuing to acquire coal properties in the county. In July 1968 Utah Power and Light Company filed an application with the state engineer for 150,000 acre-feet of water from the San Rafael River. This was followed in early 1969 by an application for reservoir and streamflow rights in Huntington Creek. In actual fact, the waters of these streams were already overappropriated, but it was a standard legal maneuver to make such applications in order to forestall other possible applicants. In response to a rising tide of rumors, Utah Power issued a news release in February 1969 stating that it was "studying" Emery County, along with several other areas, as a possible site for a power plant. In November the company announced plans to construct a 345,000-volt transmission line between Salt Lake City and Farmington, New Mexico, that would cut through Emery County.

Finally, in December the company announced that it was seeking to acquire 27,000 acre-feet of water for a generating plant to be located near the mouth of Huntington Canyon. It was proposed that this include 15,000 acre-feet of primary water rights in Huntington Creek, 6,000 acre-feet from Cottonwood Creek, and 6,000 from Joe's Valley Reservoir. The Huntington-Cleveland and Cottonwood Creek Consolidated irrigation companies were to act as agents in securing the water rights from existing stockholders. Utah Power also announced its intention of constructing a 40,000-acre-foot reservoir in Huntington Canyon to provide storage from year to year. At the same time, the company emphasized that all plans were contingent on its ability to obtain the water rights at an acceptable price.[118]

Events moved rapidly after this public announcement. While not everyone in the county was enthusiastic about the prospect of large-scale industrial development, the prevailing sentiment was that this represented the county's best hope for securing its economic future. Numerous farmers agreed to sell a portion of their precious water stock—in some cases because the more stable supply provided by the Emery County Project had actually made it possible to cultivate their land with less primary water right, in other cases out of a spirit of sacrifice for the public good. Some farmers even tendered all of their water stock, in effect abandoning their farming operations. Cottonwood Creek Consolidated Irrigation Company had obtained options for the required 6,000 acre-feet by February 1970. Enough Huntington-Cleveland stockholders had committed shares to enable Utah Power to announce firm plans to proceed with construction of the first 430,000 kilowatt unit of the Huntington Plant in May. Emery County was poised on the brink of a new era.

ENDNOTES

1. O'Neil, "Victims of Demand," 27.
2. .*ECP*, 26 January 1945.

3. Ibid., 26 April, 18 July, 27 September 1946; 7 November 1947; 2 April, 9 July 1948; 25 March, 5 August, 9 December 1949.

4. "Jack's Motor Service," in *EC 1880–1980,* 484.

5. *ECP,* 27 February, 12 March 1948; 5 October 1951.

6. Ibid., 21 November 1947; 4 October 1948; 19 May 1950; 29 June 1951; Montell Seely, "Castle Dale Ward," in *EC 1880–1980,* 38–39.

7. *ECP,* 5 December 1947; 7 January 1948; 24 March 1950; 24 August 1951; 17 April 1952; Roma N. Powell, "The History of Huntington's Churches," in *EC 1880–1980,* 190–91.

8. Irene Allred, "Cleveland," in *EC 1880–1980,* 154–55.

9. *ECP,* 23 September 1949; 1 November 1951; 29 April, 6 May 1954; 14 June 1956.

10. Ibid., 15 February 1946; 14 and 28 March, 8 and 29 August, 5 September, 3 October 1947; 18 March, 14 May 1948.

11. Ibid., 3 September 1953.

12. Ibid., 6 August, 3 September, 19 November 1953; 25 March, 3 and 24 June 1954.

13. Muriel Smith, "Emery County Schools—Green River," 5.

14. *ECP,* 20 July, 14 December 1945; 1 March 1946; 28 February, 6 June 1947; 27 August 1948; 17 June 1949; 30 May 1974; "Edward M. Crawford and Cecil S. Crawford," *EC 1880–1980,* 362.

15. *CV,* 330–38.

16. *ECP,* 1 December 1950; 2 and 23 February, 9 March, 28 September, 1 November 1951.

17. Ibid., 7 October 1954.

18. Ibid., 20 December 1946; 4 November, 30 December 1949.

19. Ibid., 28 January 1949; 3 February 1950; 10 January, 12 June 1952.

20. Ibid., 23 April 1948.

21. Ibid., 4 January 1946; 10 October 1947; 7 January 1948; 29 November 1951; 2 March 1962.

22. Irma Petersen Snow, Oral History.

23. *ECP,* 23 February, 2 November 1945; 7 March 1947.

24. Ibid., 31 May 1946.

25. Ibid., 19 March, 10 December 1948; 18 February, 12 August, 23 December 1949; 17 February, 20 October 1950; 27 April 1951.

26. Richard E. Behling, oral history, 4.

27. *ECP,* 10 January 1947.

28. Ibid., 23 April, 1948; 29 April 1954.

29. Ibid., 20 May 1954.

30. Ibid., 27 June, 4 July 1947.

31. Ibid., 4 March 1948; 8 June 1951.

32. Ibid., 26 August, 2 September 1949.

33. *Census of Agriculture,* 1959, 1978.

34. *ECP,* 11 September, 20 November 1958; Velma Petersen, "Ferron," in *EC 1880–1980,* 112–13.

35. *ECP,* 13 January, 28 July 1955; 2 August 1956; 11 April 1957; 5 February, 12 November 1959; 4 February, 27 October 1960; 2 February, 6 April, 11 May 1961; 8 March 1962; 28 February, 1 August 1963.

36. Ibid., 26 June, 23 July, 1948; 23 and 30 September, 7 October, 18 November 1949; 2 February 1951; Thelma Mills, "Coal Industry," in *EC 1880–1980,* 286–92.

37. *ECP,* 25 June 1948; 30 September, 7 October 1949.

38. Ibid., 16 July 1948; 14 January, 12 August, 7 October 1949.

39. Ibid., 16 February 1961; Mills, "Coal Industry," 292–93; Shirl McArthur, personal comments, 14 October 1995, original in Emery County History Archives.

40. *Salt Lake Tribune,* 10–16 March 1953.

41. *ECP,* 27 December 1956; 3 January 1957; Karen Peacock, note, November 1995.

42. *ECP,* 2 May 1957.

43. Ibid., 26 January, 17 August, 12 October 1961.

44. *ECP,* 21 September 1948; 11 March, 2 December 1949; 3 February 1950; Arminta Hewitt, "Temple Mountain," in *EC 1880–1980,* 335.

45. *ECP,* 3 December 1948; 2 December 1949; 24 February, 24 and 31 March, 21 and 28 April; 12 May 1950; 8 April 1954; Stokes and Cohenour, "Geologic Atlas," 50; Owen McClenahan, "Mineral Deposits," in *EC 1880–1980,* 275.

46. Owen McClenahan, "Uranium Mining in the Colorado Plateau," 1, unpublished manuscript used by permission of the author.

47. Stokes and Cohenour, "Geologic Atlas," 48–49.

48. *ECP,* 28 April 1950; McClenahan, "Uranium Mining," 4–7.

49. McClenahan, "Uranium Mining," 12.

50. Ibid., 8, 9, 17, 29.

51. Robert Coughlan, "Vernon Pick's $10 Million Ordeal," *Life,* 1 November 1954. Pick's numerous fabrications are discussed in Raymond W. Taylor and Samuel W. Taylor, *Uranium Fever: Or No Talk Less than One Million* (New York: Macmillan, 1970).

52. Daniel K. Newsome and Betsy L. Tipps, "Cultural Resource Reconnaissance and Evaluation in the Temple Mountain and Tomisch Butte Mining Areas, Emery County, Utah," 9–11, Cultural Resources Report 5011–01–9311, Antiquities Section, Utah Division of State History, and Moab District, Bureau of Land Management, 1993.

53. "Temple Mountain," 335–36.

54. *ECP,* 13 January, 25 August 1955.

55. Ibid., 25 August 1955; Finken, *San Rafael Swell,* 34.

56. *ECP,* 8 June 1951; 10 February, 10 and 31 March, 9 June, 28 July, 8 September 1955; 19 April, 12 July 1956; 2 February 1961.

57. Ibid., 28 May, 3 September, 17 December 1953; 7 January 1954; 20 January 1977; Stokes and Cohenour, "Geologic Atlas," 70–79.

58. *ECP,* 2, 9, and 23 August, 1 November 1946; 12 March 1948.

59. Ibid., 21 October 1954.

60. Ibid., 31 October 1947.

61. Ibid., 1 April, 15 July 1949.

62. Ibid., 4 June 1959.

63. Ibid., 16 June 1950; 19 April, 26 July 1956; 12 September, 10 October 1963.

64. Ibid., 14 April, 23 June 1950; 12 January 1951; 14 October 1954; 28 February 1957.

65. Ibid., 27 April 1951.

66. Ibid., 20 June 1947.

67. Ware, *Emery County Farmers Union Telephone Association,* 1–65; *ECP,* 22 April 1949; 27 March 1958.

68. Sylvia H. Nelson to Edward Geary, 3 September 1995; original in Emery County History Archives.

69. *ECP,* 29 March, 28 June, 26 July, 9 August 1956; 17 January, 7 February, 16 May, 14 November 1957; 30 January, 17 April 1958; 16 March, 13 July 1961; 9 January 1964.

70. Ibid., 15 September, 20 October 1950; 9 February, 10 August, 4 and 24 October, 8 November 1951; 8 April 1954.

71. Ibid., 2 January 1948; 27 January, 11 August 1955; 16 January, 3 September 1964; 14 October 1965; "Doctors," in *EC 1880–1980,* 210.

72. *ECP,* 27 January 1955; LaVora H. Kofford, "Wildlife," in *EC 1880–1980,* 327.

73. *ECP,* 28 February 1946.

74. Larry W. Davis, "Long-time Trapper Enters Hall of Fame," *ECP,* 22

September 1992; Perry Oveson, personal statement, November 1995, original in Emery County History Archives.

75. Kent R. Petersen, oral history interview by Janet Petersen, 22 April 1994, 7, transcript in Emery County History Archives.

76. Sylvia H. Nelson to Edward A. Geary, 3 September 1995, 3.

77. Smith, "Emery County Schools, Green River."

78. Kent R. Petersen, oral history, 5.

79. Nelson to Geary, 4.

80. Kent Petersen, oral history, 8.

81. *ECP,* 28 May 1959.

82. Nelson to Geary, 3.

83. *ECP,* 26 September 1963.

84. *ECPL,* 17 June 1971.

85. Ibid., 2 March 1972.

86. Inez P. Forbes, "There Once Was an Old Woman" (1967), typescript copy in Emery County History Archives.

87. *ECP,* 11 July 1963; 9 July 1964; 9 December 1965.

88. Ibid., 18 April, 6 June 1957; Carolyn Peterson Luke, "Education for Emery County: Orson W. Peterson," typescript copy in Emery County History Archives.

89. *ECP,* 19 February, 5 March 1959.

90. Ibid., 18 February 1960; Orson W. Peterson, "A Survey and Evaluation of the Emery County School District," 40–65.

91. *ECP,* 17 March 1960.

92. Ibid., 21 April, 18 August 1960; 16 March 1961; 14 February, 8 March, 12 November, 13 December 1962.

93. Ibid., 12 October 1961; Luke, "Education for Emery County."

94. *ECPL,* 12 March 1964; 23 March 1967; 21 March 1968.

95. *ECP,* 28 January 1954.

96. Ibid., 12 July 1956; 25 February 1960; 20 July, 28 September, 16 November 1961; 11 and 25 January, 5 April, 10 May, 5 July 1962; 9 May 1963.

97. "Joe's Valley Dam Ground-Breaking Ceremony," typescript copy in Emery County History Archives.

98. *ECP,* 26 September, 21 November 1963; 17 September 1964; 28 January, 6 May, 21 October 1965; 21 April, 30 June, 14 July 1966; 13 February 1969; Oral E. Johansen, "Emery County Project," in *EC 1880–1980,* 316–17.

99. Nelson to Geary, 5.

100. *ECP,* 30 August 1962; 8 August 1963; 7 and 21 January, 11 November 1965.

101. *ECPL,* 16 January, 31 October 1968; 24 April, 22 May, 5 June 1969; 11 March, 3 June 1970; Velma Petersen, "Ferron," in *EC 1880–1980,* 111; Roxie W. Nelson, oral history interview.

102. *ECPL,* 21 and November 1963.

103. *ECP,* 17 December 1959; *ECPL,* 2 and 9 January, 4 February, 12 March, 9 April 1964.

104. *ECP,* 29 August 1963; *ECPL,* 12 March 1964; 23 February, 7 December 1967.

105. *ECPL,* 12 and 26 March 1964; "Mission San Rafael, Huntington, Utah," typescript copy in Emery County History Archives.

106. *ECP,* 24 August 1961; Muriel W. Smith, "The Church of Jesus Christ of Latter Day Saints at Green River, Emery County, Utah" (1988), typescript copy in Emery County History Archives.

107. *ECP,* 24 and 31 October 1957; 23 January, 6 March, 8 May, 11 September 1958; interview with Eva Westover Conover, Ferron, Utah, April 1993.

108. *ECP,* 7 February, 15 March, 6 June 1963; *ECPL,* 23 February 1964; 3 November 1966; 29 October 1970.

109. *ECP,* 26 April 1962; 19 November 1964; *ECPL,* 1 April 1965.

110. *ECP,* 2 June 1960; 19 July 1962; 20 April 1967; 5 September 1968; 9 November 1972.

111. Ibid., 12 June 1958; 25 June 1964; 1 April 1965.

112. *ECPL,* 1 June 1967; 21 August, 2 October 1969; 25 June 1970; Dixon Peacock, "History of the Emery County Museum, Known as the Pioneer Museum," typescript copy in Emery County History Archives.

113. *ECPL,* 15 April 1965; 6 July 1967; 23 May 1968.

114. *ECP,* 26 May, 21 July 1960; 11 June 1964.

115. Ibid., 22 November 1962; 13 June, 31 October, 19 December 1963.

116. Ibid., 27 May, 2 September 1965.

117. *ECPL,* 21 November 1968; 26 February 1970.

118. Ibid., 11 July 1968; 13 February, 10 April, 27 November, 25 December 1969.

8

The Boom and After, 1970–1995

The decade of the 1970s brought dramatic changes to Emery County. The international "energy crisis" and fear of the imminent depletion of world petroleum supplies stimulated exploitation of the county's coal deposits on an unprecedented scale. A decade of construction on the two largest steam-electric generating plants built in the state up to that time transformed the county from a high-unemployment area to one that attracted numerous outside workers. The population grew by 155 percent from 5,137 residents in 1970 to a peak of 13,100 in 1983. Many others commuted to jobs in the county from homes in adjacent counties. Like other energy boom towns in the West, local communities faced immense challenges in accommodating rapid growth with an infrastructure barely sufficient for the existing population. Unlike some other areas, however, in which change virtually obliterated the established lifestyle, Emery County succeeded in fashioning an industrial-rural way of life that preserved much of what long-time residents most valued while at the same time reversing, at least temporarily, the depopulation trend and restoring young families to the community mix. The median age fell from almost twenty-eight in 1970 to 22.3 in 1980, making Emery County one of the youngest counties in the nation.

The Power Plants

The main obstacles to development of Emery County's extensive coal reserves had always been the distance from markets and lack of transportation facilities. Those obstacles were overcome by the siting of steam-electric generating plants near the mines, thereby converting the coal to a more easily marketable form of energy and enabling it to be delivered by way of electrical transmission lines instead of highways or railways.

Huntington Plant. Preliminary site work on the 430,000 kilowatt first unit of the Huntington Plant began in March 1971. It was situated eight miles west of Huntington on a bluff near the mouth of Deer Creek Canyon. Coal to fuel the boilers was to be transported from the Deer Creek Mine by way of a two-mile-long conveyor belt, and water came from Huntington Creek. The Huntington Plant was located on a ranch homesteaded before the turn of the century by Owen Smith and operated in later years by Byron Howard. Utah Power also acquired an adjacent historic ranch on which A. J. Lott had developed an apple orchard. This property was converted into an experimental farm to test the effects of the used cooling water from the plant, which because of its increased salt content could not be returned to the creek. The apple orchards were uprooted, but an old cabin and its immediate surroundings were preserved.

The main construction contract for the first unit was awarded to Jacobsen-Jelco in January 1972. The workforce grew from 223 in May 1972 to a peak of about 900 during the summer of 1973. The first unit went on line in July 1974. By that time, plans were already well advanced for the second unit, which was completed in June 1977. Utah Power had originally announced an intention to build as many as four units at the Huntington Plant, but these plans were apparently scaled back after the company decided to establish a second plant in the county.[1]

Electric Lake. An essential element in the plan for the Huntington Plant was construction of a reservoir on the Right Fork of Huntington Creek some eighteen miles above the plant site, intended for long-term storage of water for use during drought periods. Gibbons and Reed Construction was awarded a contract for the Electric Lake dam in January 1972, and the 220-foot-high earthfill was substantially completed by November 1973. With a capacity of 32,000 acre-feet, Electric Lake is second in size only to Joe's Valley Reservoir among Emery County impoundments. It is an efficient storage facility by virtue of its high elevation and relatively small surface area that reduce evaporative losses. Because of a small drainage basin, Electric Lake seldom fills to capacity. Its recreational value is limited by a lack of accessible shoreline and by steep sides that provide poor habitat for fish. Still, the reservoir and its tributary streams have become the home to the state's main breeding stock of Strawberry cutthroat trout.

The waters of Electric Lake covered the remains of Connellsville, Emery County's oldest industrial site. As part of an environmental mitigation project, Utah Power funded an archaeological survey of the Connellsville area and reconstructed one of the ten coke ovens on a new site above the water line.[2]

The construction of Electric Lake necessitated rerouting Highway 31 from its original canyon-bottom location to a more circuitous loop to the south and then west to Skyline Drive. Though longer, this route offered panoramic views and improved access to Cleveland, Huntington, and Miller Flat reservoirs. The construction provided the first paved highway across the Wasatch Plateau. With more than two hundred Sanpete County residents commuting to jobs in Emery County by 1977, the State Transportation Department initiated efforts to keep Highway 31 open throughout the winter, no easy task considering the elevation of more than 9,500 feet and the stretch along the skyline ridge exposed to drifting snow.[3]

Hunter Plant. Utah Power officially acknowledged in December 1973 that it was interested in a second Emery County site. In March 1974 Ferron Creek water users agreed to a forty-year lease of 7,000 acre-feet of water, "practically guaranteeing" construction of a power plant on Rock Canyon Flat. Lease payments were to be used to help retire debt for the Mill Site Reservoir and for water-saving improvements in delivery systems. In May 1974 Utah Power announced plans to construct two 415,000 kilowatt units at what was then called the

Emery Plant. The name was later changed to the Hunter Plant in honor of longtime UP&L president E. Allan Hunter. The first unit was completed in June 1978, by which time plans had been announced to build a total of four generating units. Unit two went on line in early 1980, and unit three in 1983. Water for the Hunter Plant was drawn from both Ferron and Cottonwood creeks, and coal was supplied primarily by mines on East Mountain. A new coal-haul road was constructed from the plant to Highway 29 in order to keep heavy truck traffic from passing through Orangeville.[4]

The Mines

The decision by Utah Power to construct steam-electric generating units in the county coincided with and was influenced by the international "energy crisis" of the early 1970s. Price increases and production restrictions by petroleum exporting nations led to widespread fears of an imminent exhaustion of the world's oil reserves and a consequent scramble to develop alternative energy sources. Coal, which had been losing its traditional markets to oil and natural gas for decades, was once again in demand.

Castle Valley Mining and American Coal Company. Emery County native and experienced coal man Shirl C. McArthur foresaw a future increase in demand for coal even when the industry was at a low ebb during the early 1960s. He also realized, from his experience as superintendent of the LDS church mine, that compliance with government safety and other regulations would become increasingly difficult for small mining operations. McArthur was confident that the reserves in the county's coal fields were much larger than estimated by the United States Geological Service, and he set out to prove that they could be developed at a competitive cost.

In 1961 Shirl and Bessie McArthur mortgaged their home for capital to establish Castle Valley Mining Company. The company did some exploratory drilling followed by prospect entries in Peabody Coal Company's Wilberg property, which had been closed for lack of market. Castle Valley Mining then drove three prospect entries in Peabody's Deer Creek property. As the quantity and quality of coal were established, Utah Power shifted its attention from the Kemmerer, Wyoming, area to Emery County. Shirl McArthur played an active role in promoting the county's advantages as a site for major power generation facilities and in encouraging local officials and farmers to make the necessary water available to meet Utah Power's needs. By 1970 Castle Valley Mining had almost one hundred employees and was shipping coal from the Wilberg Mine to Nevada Power's generating plants near Las Vegas.[5] Also in 1970 McArthur established two other companies: American Kinfolk, Incorporated, to provide security and other services; and Utah-American (UT-AM), a mining equipment repair company. UT-AM was sold to the Long-Airdox Company in 1980.

In 1972 Utah Power purchased the Deseret and Beehive mines from the LDS church. McArthur organized American Coal Company and contracted with Utah Power to operate the mines. By the end of 1973, even before the local power plants went into operation, American Coal was employing 140 miners and forty-five truck drivers. At the same time, Peabody employed 130 men at its Deer Creek Mine, and the Browning Mine near Emery had thirty workers.[6] The *Emery County Progress-Leader* commented in January 1974,

> The coal is sold before it hits the ground. . . . The comeback of King Coal and modern mining methods and consideration to the miner has lured many native sons and daughters back to the field and beckoned strangers, who have taken the land and people to their hearts. Some want to remain here permanently. . . . It is a standing joke that people born in Emery County are hooked on alkali and suffer withdrawal symptoms when forced to leave for greener pastures.
>
> Now that the pastures here are greener than other places, many young couples are marrying, having a trailer or modular home moved in to some of the land their parents have been saving for them, and are rearing families supported by coal mining.[7]

Coal production increased dramatically as the power plants went on line. By mid-1976 307 miners were working at Deer Creek to supply the Huntington Plant. In December 1976 Utah Power and Light purchased the Deer Creek and Wilberg properties from Peabody and contracted with American Coal to operate them in addition to the Deseret, Beehive, and Little Dove complex (Des-Bee-Dove). By April 1977 American Coal had 709 employees. Two years later the number had increased to 1,167 at five mines. A need for office space was met when the company purchased and remodeled the old North Emery High School building in Huntington. The remodeling was celebrated with a gala open house and barbecue with movie star John Wayne in attendance. In 1978 Governor Scott M. Matheson presented Shirl and Bessie McArthur with a Distinguished Service Award for Industrial Achievement.

There were, however, some inevitable problems associated with this rapid growth. American Coal was among the most efficient underground mining operations in the country in terms of output per man-hour and cost per ton. The company also made a conscious effort to foster good employee relations, hosting social activities and sponsoring recreational sports teams. But in addition to a lengthy national miners' strike between 1977 and 1978, American Coal operations were plagued by frequent work stoppages over local issues. It is not surprising that problems should arise given the nature of a work force hastily assembled from a variety of sources, including relatively young and inexperienced local men, old-time union miners from Carbon County, and a sizeable number who had relocated from depressed mining regions in Ohio, Kentucky, and West Virginia. However, there were also complaints about "nepotism" and "poor hiring practices" on the part of management. On the other hand, many employees were staunchly loyal to the McArthurs. One former employee remarked,

> They were very kind and generous employers and made their people feel like they were part of a huge family. . . . A great "homey" feeling and learning experience for some uneducated, formerly unemployable people like me and so many in depressed Emery County. [McArthur] built us up as individuals, communities, and as a county.[8]

Growing differences over management policies and practices became public in March 1979 when Utah Power demanded that American Coal either sell its operations or face the loss of its contracts. In May American Coal sold almost all of its assets with the exception of its name to Savage Brothers, whose Western Coal

Carriers already held the Utah Power haulage contract. Savage Brothers named the company Emery Mining.[9]

Emery Mining Company. The work stoppages and other labor problems experienced by American Coal did not diminish appreciably under new management. Indeed, some employees resented what they perceived as a more rigidly hierarchical management style, sharply reduced associations between the workers and the bosses, and a less supportive attitude toward community activities.[10] Nevertheless, production and employment continued to grow. Including the mines and the trucking operation, Savage Brothers interests employed about 1,600 in the county by mid-1979. By 1980 Emery County had become the largest coal producer in the state, with 6.32 million tons to Carbon County's 5.49 million and Sevier County's 1.82 million.[11]

Consolidation Coal Company. Consolidation Coal Company assumed active management of its holdings south of Emery (formerly the Browning Mine) during the 1970s. By 1980 the underground mine was producing 400,000 tons per year, and Consol announced plans for a strip mine to recover coal deposits near the surface. These plans created renewed interest in a railroad spur into the western part of the county. In 1979 Denver and Rio Grande Western officials confidently predicted construction of the Castle Valley Spur within five or six years. A detailed route map was presented to the county commission for approval in April 1981. The line was to pass east of Cleveland, parallel Highway 10 from Wilberg Ranch to Castle Dale, then go through Molen and east of Emery, terminating at the Consol mine. In sharp contrast to railroad prospects in earlier periods, the Castle Valley Spur proposal drew a largely negative response at public hearings from residents who did not want a railroad passing close to their homes or bisecting their farms. In addition to the railroad talk, there were also proposals for a coal slurry pipeline from Emery to the West Coast, to be built by Boeing Engineering.[12]

Other Proposed Energy Projects

While the county was struggling to accommodate the social impacts of the boom in construction and mining, rumored developments of even greater magnitude were in the air. One proposal during the early 1970s called for establishment of an "energy triangle" with corners at Price, Emery, and Green River as a site for large-scale coal, oil shale, and nuclear energy developments.

Intermountain Power Plant. The giant Intermountain steam-electric complex, eventually constructed in Millard County, was first proposed for a site in Wayne County a few miles south of the Emery County border. The plan, as proposed in 1975, was to draw water from the Fremont River and the coal supply from the southern Wasatch Plateau and Emery fields. Most of the population impact—estimated at some 5,500—would have been in Emery County, but property taxes for the power plant would have gone to Wayne County, a consideration that drew strong expressions of concern from county commissioners already contending with the challenges of unprecedented growth.

The proximity of the Wayne County site to Capitol Reef National Park led to the scuttling of IPP plans there in 1977. The developers then reportedly considered three sites in Emery County—one near Mounds, another near Green River, and the third just inside the southern border of the county north of Hanksville—before finally choosing the Millard County site.[13]

Coal Gasification. One effect of the higher prices and perceived shortage of petroleum was to stimulate an interest in synthetic fuels. In 1979 Mountain Fuel Supply Company announced plans to construct a large coal gasification plant near Emery. The plant, estimated to cost $1 billion, was to obtain water from a proposed reservoir near the mouth of Muddy Creek Canyon. Construction was projected to require two thousand workers for several years, and permanent operations would provide employment for eight hundred miners and several hundred plant workers. A site between Emery and Moore was selected in March 1981, and construction was projected to begin in 1982. By this time, however, the oil embargo of the early 1970s was only a memory. World oil production was sufficient to meet demand, and consumers had adjusted to higher prices. Moreover, a national economic slump had reduced the demand for industrial energy. Mountain Fuel's partners, which included a West Coast utility and a major oil company, apparently lost interest in the synfuels project, and Mountain Fuel announced in December 1981 that plans for the gasification plant had been delayed by financial and engineering considerations.[14]

Green River Energy Center. The largest proposal of all was for a nuclear energy center near Green River, which was envisioned in 1981 as including an 11,000 megawatt generating plant (more than five times larger than the combined capacities of the Huntington and Hunter plants) and a town with 20,000 residents. A report by the Utah Energy Office in September 1982 concluded that the nuclear center was "technically feasible" but economically inadvisable. The plant was estimated to cost at least $12 billion and possibly as much as $36 billion, and operations would have made heavy demands on the river's water. Moreover, construction would have brought an estimated 37,000 people to Green River.[15] Far from experiencing a growth in the nuclear industry, Green River lost several dozen jobs when the last two uranium mines in the area ceased operations in early 1982.[16]

Community Impacts

Construction of the power plants transformed Emery County within a period of a few months from a high-unemployment, low-income area to a region of dynamic economic growth. The county's assessed valuation soared from $10 million in 1970 to $36 million in 1974. Business activity increased by 165 percent in 1972 alone. Personal income grew by 170 percent between 1970 and 1975, elevating the county from among the poorest in the state to the second wealthiest. By 1977 the average per capita income of $8,300 was the highest in the state, almost 20 percent higher than second-place Summit County.[17]

The abundant high-paying jobs were welcome after two decades of deteriorating employment conditions. Experienced miners and construction workers found their skills in high demand. Some former Emery County residents returned home. Training programs were established for young people entering the job market. Still, the local labor supply fell far short of satisfying the demand. Many workers commuted from their homes in Carbon, Sanpete, and Sevier counties. Many more came to Emery County from other areas. Some planned to establish permanent homes in the county. Others, including some of the most highly skilled and highly paid, were transient workers who came for temporary assignments, usually without their families, and who had no intention of remaining permanently.

The county's infrastructure was poorly equipped to accommodate the influx of new residents. Available rental housing was very soon occupied despite a rapid escalation of rents. Even substandard accommodations were snapped up as quickly as they became available. Several mobile home parks were developed and almost instantly filled, leaving incoming workers to park mobile homes, travel trailers, and campers on vacant lots or alongside existing homes. By late 1973 Huntington had more mobile homes than houses. Of 643 dwelling units in Huntington in 1976, only 259 were conventional single-family homes while 268 were mobile homes in parks and an additional 107 mobile homes were situated on single lots. Similar conditions prevailed in Castle Dale, with 240 conventional single-family homes, 220 mobile homes in parks, and forty-one mobile homes on single lots. Many construction workers parked campers or pitched tents in Huntington Canyon and remained there for extended periods, in some instances discharging sewage directly into the creek. In August 1976 the county commission requested the Bureau of Land Management to take action against the "canyon dwellers," leading to a ban on long-term camping. The county zoning ordinance was amended in 1978 to prohibit the use of recreational trailers as permanent homes.[18]

High prices for vacant town lots combined with a desire for a more rural lifestyle to induce many newcomers to buy farm land, raising concerns about residential sprawl. Land that had sold for less than $100 per acre in the 1960s was priced as high as $7,500 per acre in 1974. Some people began constructing homes without an assured water supply. Others, unfamiliar with the peculiar qualities of Mancos shale soil, built on wet or unstable ground.

Relations between established residents and newcomers were not always harmonious. During the early days of the construction boom, residents complained of being awakened in the middle of the night by strangers who asked to use their telephones because several communities had no public telephones in service. Rumors of a "two price" system in county stores, with established residents allegedly being charged less than newcomers, brought public protests and adverse publicity in the metropolitan press.[19]

Planning to accommodate an increased population was somewhat slow in coming, but several communities had adopted zoning ordinances and annexed land for residential subdivisions by 1974. Huntington annexed residential property on its western borders and an industrial area to the north. Castle Dale expanded onto the north bench. Orangeville added subdivisions north of the creek. Ferron annexed a large area south of the creek and another area east of town along the Molen road. In June 1979 Utah Power announced plans to build a 350-home subdivision in the county. With the early termination of plant construction, however, this development was never built. As one outgrowth of the boom, Clawson was finally incorporated in 1981 after more than three-quarters of a century as a distinct but unofficial community.[20]

The Plight of the Towns. The culinary water systems in Castle Valley communities were barely sufficient for the preboom population. Sewer systems, where they existed at all, provided little or no treatment of sewage and were out of compliance with health and environmental regulations. The influx of new residents quickly exceeded system capacities. At the same time, the immense growth in the county's assessed valuation was of little benefit to town governments because the industrial installations were in unincorporated areas. The towns' increased tax receipts from business and residential expansion fell far short of what was required to upgrade water supply and waste disposal systems. Urgent water and sewer needs left little or no money available for public safety or for roads that were also in need of repair or upgrading. The challenges of rapid growth put great pressure on town governments. Huntington, Castle Dale, and Ferron all had mayors resign in midterm amid controversy over city management.

The initial impacts were felt most severely in Huntington. The culinary water supply had been augmented during the 1960s by the inclusion of additional springs in Little Bear Canyon but was still no more than sufficient for a population that had dwindled to 857 by 1970, let alone the 2,303 people who would live in the city in 1980.

Presbyterian church/school, Ferron. (Edward A. Geary)

Many water lines were more than thirty years old and subject to breakage. Even before the boom, Huntington had recognized the need to upgrade its water delivery system and had obtained a large quantity of used oil well casing to use for a new line from the springs. State health authorities could not be persuaded that this material was safe for use, and in 1973 the mayor and city council began planning for an upgraded water and sewer system using new rather than recycled materials. A bond election in August 1975 passed with a 96 percent favorable vote, and the city obtained grants and loans from the State Water Board and the Farmers Home Administration. Before construction of a new water system could begin, however, the old system began to disintegrate under the pressure of service demands far beyond its design capacity. A series of line breaks left the town without culinary water for a five-day period in November 1975. The city's bonding capacity plus available government loans and grants fell far short of the projected cost of a new system, and city officials approached Utah Power with a request for a $500,000 grant to assist the community in meeting impacts caused by the company. Utah Power officials initially agreed to assist the town, but the plan ran into trouble when the state attorney general issued an opinion opposing the addition of the grant to the UP&L rate base. Company officials were concerned about possible stockholder lawsuits if the grant were taken from earnings. After several weeks of negotiations, state officials finally approved inclusion of the grant in the Utah Power rate base in March 1976, and work was allowed to proceed. Project costs still exceeded the available funding, and the city was forced to obtain $120,000 from the newly formed Castle Valley Special Service District to complete the project. A dry season in 1977 forced the city to place a moratorium on new water connections after the Huntington-Cleveland Irrigation Company protested that the city was using more water than its company stock entitled it to. Efforts to integrate a new supply system with parts of the old distribution system led to problems with low water pressure in some parts of town and burst pipes in other sections. A treatment plant designed to allow use of creek water to supplement the supply from the springs failed to operate properly and required frequent repairs.[21]

The Castle Dale water system also began to fail under the increased demand, with a series of outages in early 1974 leading to numerous complaints from citizens and causing Mayor Larry Lofthouse to resign after only four months in office. Bonding for water system improvements was approved by voters in November 1975, and a loan was obtained from the State Board of Water Resources.[22] Ferron sought to anticipate population growth by planning in 1973 for a new sewer system that would serve eight hundred connections, twice the capacity of the existing system. A loan for water system improvements was secured from the State Board of Water Resources in 1975, and bonding was approved in December 1975 after being rejected in an earlier election.[23]

North Emery Water Users Association. The North Emery water system had its beginning before the power plant boom but developed alongside the population influx. The project was initiated in 1966 by two Lawrence residents, Bernice Cullum and Utahna Wilson, who had grown tired of hauling their culinary water from Huntington. Marius Johnson was also active from an early stage. Their first efforts were aimed at securing an extension of the Huntington water system to Lawrence. When this proposal met an unenthusiastic response from Huntington officials, they sought the assistance of local representatives of the Farmers Home Administration and on their advice approached Cleveland and Elmo officials with a proposal to develop a modern water system for the entire area. The North Emery Water Users Association was organized in 1971 with Marius Johnson as president, Duane Jensen, vice president, Bernice Cullum, secretary, and Nelson Alger, Delray Brotherson, Lee McMullin, and James Christensen as directors. The association secured a $192,000 loan (eventually increased to $272,000) from the Farmers Home Administration to develop a rural water system to serve 265 homes in Lawrence, Cleveland, Elmo, and the surrounding farms. By this time, plans for Utah Power's Huntington Plant were under way, and the prospect of growth enabled the association to obtain $867,000 in federal economic development funds through the Economic Development Administration and the Four Corners Regional Authority. Construction began on eighty-four miles of distribution lines in mid-1972. Water was piped from springs in Rilda Canyon to storage tanks near Lawrence and Cleveland.[24]

By the time the system went on line in late 1973, it had grown to ninety-three miles of distribution lines serving 380 subscribers. The availability of culinary water encouraged many newcomers and returning natives to pursue their desire for rural living, and homes began to spring up on farms throughout the North Emery service area. By 1978 the system was serving 620 subscribers and had reached the limits of its water supply, forcing it to impose a moratorium on new hookups.[25]

County Government. In anticipation of growth impacts, the county commission adopted new zoning and subdivision ordinances in 1970 and hired a zoning administrator in 1972.[26] In an effort to control residential sprawl and confine population growth to the towns, where services could be provided more efficiently, the commission instituted a zoning requirement of a ten-acre minimum building lot in unincorporated areas, at least five acres of which had to be irrigable land. Despite these efforts, the population of incorporated areas more than doubled from 995 in 1970 to 2,048 in 1980. Among the reasons were high prices for property in town, a preference on the part of many people for a rural home where they could keep horses and other livestock, and the wider availability of culinary water. One unintended effect of the zoning regulation was the loss of hundreds of acres of prime farm land.

The county was in a better position than the towns to deal with impacts of rapid growth because the power plants paid county property taxes. Nevertheless, county resources were stretched to the limit and beyond as personnel scrambled to keep abreast of rapidly increasing workloads. On one occasion county commissioners were pressed into service to guard jail prisoners in order to give overworked sheriff's officers a few hours of rest. County commissioners during this key period included Gardell Snow (D, 1968–78), Glenn E. Jones (D, 1968–78), Kent Stilson (R, 1970–76), Rue P. Ware (D, 1976–84), John Parker (R, 1978–82), and D. Roger Curtis (R, 1978–82). In 1979 a new elective office of county auditor was established, with duties that had formerly been assigned to the county clerk. The number of county employees increased with the growth in population and services, reaching 140 by 1983. Commissioners hired a full-time administrator in 1980 (this position was later eliminated) and a personnel manager in 1983.[27] In 1985, the Emery County Economic Development Council was established with Scott Truman as executive director.

Inadequate and overcrowded facilities made necessary an extensive building program. The woefully inadequate county jail was replaced by a new public safety building and jail, put into service in 1977 on the site of the old Central High School. A 1979 bond election approved renovation and expansion of the court house, which was completed in 1981. During the reconstruction period, county offices were housed in temporary quarters, which made efficient operation yet more difficult. In addition, seven new libraries were built between 1979 and 1982.[28]

The dramatic growth in assessed valuation led to a lengthy dispute with the State Tax Commission. A Tax Commission study in the mid-1970s concluded that the county's tax assessments had not kept pace with escalating market values. County officials balked at adjustments that could have meant a doubling or even tripling of local property taxes, and negotiations continued for several years, punctuated by periodic threats of legal action, without reaching a resolution entirely satisfactory to either party. While state tax officials claimed that county-assessed properties were undervalued, county officials maintained that it was the state-assessed properties, chiefly coal mines, power plants, and gas and oil wells, that were most seriously undervalued. While county assessment of businesses, farms, and homes was based on market values, the state, in assessing large industries, tended to use depreciated values often supplied by the companies themselves and seldom subjected to independent audits. In one extreme case cited by county officials, a coal mine that had sold for $13 million had a state-assessed valuation of only $700,000. The tax collected by the county on the property was less than the cost of a single tire for the road grader that maintained the county road to the mine. A further indication of tension between the county and the state became apparent in the legislative reapportionment of 1980 when Emery County was split among three different house districts, practically insuring that no resident of the county could be elected to the legislature.[29]

One of the urgent needs facing the county was waste disposal. In earlier periods each community had its "town dump" where household refuse, dead animals, and junked vehicles were deposited at a more or less convenient open site. Some towns had developed landfill operations but were finding it increasingly difficult to satisfy federal regulations. Plans for a centrally located county landfill were begun in 1978, and a garbage collection system was put into effect in 1980.[30] The county was also actively involved in providing medical services, fire protection, and recreational facilities, including a sports complex at Huntington and the Bear Creek park in Huntington Canyon. Perhaps the most significant act of the county government during this period, however, was creation of the Castle Valley Special Service District.

Castle Valley Special Service District. With the major sources of property taxes located in the unincorporated county and the major social impacts in the towns, it became obvious that some mechanism was needed to tap the greatly increased assessed value to provide for urgent community needs. The answer was the Castle Valley Special Service District, established in 1976 by the county commission and town governments. The district boundaries were described as resembling swiss cheese and included all of the incorporated cities and towns in western Emery County plus the power plants while excluding rural areas. As a governmental agency, the CVSSD had the authority to levy property taxes and issue bonds subject to voter approval. Initial bonding in the amount of $5 million, approved in January 1977 by a vote of 1,370 to 83, was used to upgrade water systems in Emery, Ferron, and Orangeville and for sewage collection and treatment systems in Castle Dale, Orangeville, Huntington, Cleveland, and Elmo. Voters also approved a three mill tax levy for operation and maintenance. Darrel V. Leamaster of Huntington was appointed as district administrator, one of several professionally trained Emery County natives who returned home during this period. A $15 million bond issue approved in 1981 by a vote of 1,619 to 508 provided funds for further water and sewer development, street improvements, and pressurized secondary water systems in the towns. The secondary water systems, which went into service between 1983 and 1984, had the triple benefit of reducing demand on culinary water systems, enabling a more efficient use of irrigation water, and lowering water tables that had flooded basements in some areas.

In 1982 the CVSSD proposed including Cleveland and Elmo with Huntington in an enlarged culinary water system. The recently completed Huntington system had never worked satisfactorily. Most of the time, demand could be met by spring water that needed only minimal treatment. However, periods of high usage required water to be drawn from the creek and sent through a treatment plant. With only irregular use, the treatment plant often malfunctioned. Moreover, it lacked the backup system capacity required by state health regulations for full approval. If Cleveland and Elmo were added to the system, the treatment plant could be upgraded and used more continuously. Furthermore, a larger supply line would insure good pressure in the expanded system even during periods of high usage. The North Emery Water Users Association was having difficulty in meeting demands in excess of its design capacity, but it had loans to be retired that depended upon maintaining its subscriber base. Therefore, extensive negotiations were necessary before the withdrawal of the two towns from the association was approved. The eventual agreement reached in 1983 provided for the CVSSD to reimburse North Emery and the Farmers Home Administration for the Cleveland and Elmo share of construction loans in exchange for the franchise and distribution systems.[31] These arrangements left the North Emery system to serve the unincorporated areas.

Public Safety. Like most other public agencies, the sheriff's department and local town marshals were inadequately staffed to meet the influx of new people and the rising crime rate that tends to accompany an economic boom. The sheriff's case load soared from 681 in 1974 to 1,119 in 1975. By 1980 the crime rate of 38.8 per thousand residents was more than double that of Sanpete County. The sheriff's department was expanded in 1975 from three deputies to six deputies and a full-time dispatcher. The completion of a new security center in October 1977 provided much-needed office and jail space. In 1976 the sheriff offered to assume full law-enforcement responsibilities for Huntington in exchange for funding equivalent to salary and expenses for one deputy. A similar offer was extended to other towns with terms dependent on a formula that took into account population, assessed value, and the frequency of police calls. Castle Dale had its own three-man police department in 1978, but a lack of resources forced the city to contract with the sheriff's office in 1980. The sheriff's department attempted, with mixed success, to maintain contractual law enforcement arrangements with the towns until the budget crunch of 1984. Because some towns were unable to meet the cost of the services, the county decided in December 1984 to terminate local law enforcement contracts and provide the same level of service throughout the county.[32]

An expanded professional sheriff's department was needed because the county was increasingly plagued by "big city" crimes. Residents were stunned in February 1979 when two women were killed during a robbery of the Zion's First National Bank office in Huntington. The county's wide open spaces attracted drug runners looking for a place to land air shipments from suppliers. In September 1983 sheriff's officers and federal drug agents seized a DC-7 aircraft that had landed at the abandoned Temple Mountain airstrip carrying 12.7 tons of marijuana. A truck loaded with the drugs was seized near the airstrip, and eleven men, most of them from Florida, were arrested and convicted on charges arising from the incident. Interstate 70 gained a reputation as a major artery in the national transportation of illegal drugs and the money gained from their sale. Both the Utah Highway Patrol and the Emery County Sheriff's Department have made numerous drug-related arrests on I-70, including seizure of $500,000 at a UHP roadblock in 1986. The sheriff's department seized more than half a ton of cocaine in three different episodes during 1989 and 1990.[33] Nor was lawlessness confined to opportunistic outsiders passing through the county. Three sheriff's officers were injured during the Ferron Peach Days celebration in September 1983 when they were attacked by a crowd as they attempted to make a drunk-driving arrest. Marijuana patches have been discovered in several remote areas of the county, and periodic drug stings have led to the arrest of a number of county residents.[34]

The growth in population and especially the construction of costly industrial installations made it imperative to improve upon the lightly equipped local volunteer firefighting organizations. The county purchased a fire engine in February 1974 with a larger capacity than the firefighting equipment owned by individual towns. The county added four more engines in 1977, and Utah Power provided a pumper truck on more or less permanent loan with provisions that it be available for fires at the generating plants. Also in 1977 the sheriff's radio dispatch system was extended to local fire department chiefs. New fire stations were constructed in the major towns, and local volunteer firefighters were provided more systematic training with county support. Fire protection continued as a joint town-county responsibility until 1992, when a countywide fire district was created.[35]

The county purchased its first ambulance in 1975, replacing a service formerly provided by a local mortuary. By 1984 the county had ambulances and emergency medical technicians in Emery, Ferron, Orangeville, Castle Dale, Huntington, and Green River.[36]

Medical Services. In common with other rural areas, Emery County has faced a major challenge in obtaining adequate local medical services. Dr. Steven Eyre began practicing in Castle Dale in 1971 in a clinic set up by the county commission in the Castle Dale Professional Building. Eyre was well received and there was some hope that the county had at last gained a long-term physician, but he elected to leave in 1973 just at a time when burgeoning growth made it more imperative than ever for the county to have a resident physician. With Commissioner Gardell Snow as the chief moving force, the county contracted with Utah Valley Hospital and Utah Health Services for "fly-in" doctors to serve the county one or two days a week. Some assistance was provided by the Johnson and Johnson Fund for Rural Medicine. In 1973 the county purchased the Mountain Fuel Supply building in Castle Dale and remodeled it as a medical clinic staffed by a full-time nurse-practitioner with weekly visits on a rotating basis from four Utah Valley doctors. The program received a setback almost as soon as it began when one of the fly-in doctors, Eugene Davie, was killed in a plane crash in December 1973. The patient load at the clinic soon exceeded the capacity, requiring an additional nurse and more frequent visits from physicians.

Continuing their efforts to obtain a full-time physician for the clinic and also to serve the Emery County Nursing Home in Ferron, commissioners recruited Dr. Charles W. Herbert from Colorado in 1975 despite some protests from residents about the financial incentives offered to Dr. Herbert (which the commissioners defended as necessary to recruit physicians for rural practice). Herbert built up a staff that included obstetrician Raymond C. Chatfield and two other physicians, Robert McKey and Thomas LeCount, together with two physician assistants and a full-time manager. The heavy workload and continuing controversy over clinic management led, however, to these doctors leaving one by one over a period of less than three years. In 1979 Dr. Robert E. Potts of Ogden leased the clinic. Dr. Konrad Kotrady joined the clinic staff in 1981 and eventually purchased the facilities. Dr. Potts left in 1984 and was replaced by Dr. Mark Ramirez. Throughout this period, a group of nurses, nurse-practitioners, physician assistants, and laboratory technicians provided continuity in the clinic's operations even though the physician turnover was high.[37] Dr. Kotrady left the county in 1990, selling the medical center to the company that operated Castleview Hospital at Price. This move led to a reduction in hours of service at the clinic and to another series of temporary physicians until Dr. L. Joe Smith and Dr. Joseph E. Ollivier came on a more permanent basis. Other health professionals practicing in Castle Dale in 1996 included dental surgeons Dr. Kent B. McKell and Dr. Daniel Coles and chiropractic physician Dr. Ronald B. Sanders.

After Dr. H. T. Barton left Green River in 1972, the community was served by the county's "fly-in" arrangement. The Green River clinic was damaged beyond repair in early 1979 when water from broken pipes eroded the building's foundations. A newly constructed clinic was opened in December 1979 with a resident family nurse-practitioner.[38]

Schools. The power plant construction had relatively little initial impact on school enrollments because few families came with the first wave of construction workers. The graduating class at Emery County High School, which had peaked at 113 in 1969, was only eighty-nine in 1973. Overall enrollments in the district declined to 1,732 in the fall of 1973 as cessation of activity at the Green River missile base more than offset the slight growth in the western part of the county. That same year an engineer's report recommended replacement of the old high school and junior high buildings at Ferron and Huntington, and the State Office of Education proposed consolidation into a single, centrally located junior high school. As late as 1975 state school officials were calling for the closure of the Cleveland Elementary on the grounds that its enrollment of 125 was too small for efficient operation. However, the growth impacts were by this time being felt more strongly. In February 1974 the school district acquired twenty acres on the Castle Dale bench as a site for an elementary school, foreseeing that Cottonwood Elementary in Orangeville could not long accommodate students from both communities. Emery County High was now operating at near capacity and needed additional classrooms and other facilities. At the same time the two junior high buildings were being described as "fire traps" that urgently needed replacement. A $6.5 million bond election in November 1974 approved funding for new junior high schools at Ferron and Huntington, a new elementary school at Green River, and replacement of the old section of the Cleveland Elementary. The Book Cliffs Elementary (the first separate elementary school in Green River) was designed with moveable partitions to allow flexible grouping of students. The same design was used with some modifications for the Castle Dale Elementary.[39]

The new or expanded elementary schools, the San Rafael Junior High at Ferron, and the Canyon View Junior High at Huntington all opened in 1977. The expanded facilities were badly needed as enrollments had grown from 1,732 in 1973 to 2,237 in 1976. Another bond in the amount of $8.5 million was approved in 1977 to build a new high school at Green River and enlarge the Huntington, Ferron, Cleveland, and Cottonwood elementaries and Emery County High School. The new Green River High building was required not for population growth (Green River in fact was losing population at the time) but because the 1955 school had developed serious structural failures from the unstable soil on which it was built. The new building was completed in 1981 on a site west of town.[40]

The impact of rapid growth was felt in other ways besides sheer numbers. A high turnover rate and boom mentality among students made it difficult to maintain academic quality. In October 1978 almost half of Emery County High students received midterm failing notices in one or more classes. There was also a high turnover in the teaching staff as many teachers left the schools for better-paying jobs in industry. In an effort to maintain a quality faculty, residents approved a voted leeway assessment in 1979 that gave Emery County School District the highest salary scale in the state.

Superintendent Orson W. Peterson, who had seen the district through a period of unprecedented retrenchment followed by a period of rapid growth, retired in 1977 and was succeeded by A. G. Kinder, a long-time teacher and administrator in the district who had been serving as principal of Emery High. Kinder served as superintendent until his retirement in 1984. He was succeeded by another county native, Dennis E. Nelson, who was succeeded in 1987 by A. Ernest Weeks, who had no prior experience in the county.[41] Weeks was succeeded in 1993 by Blaine F. Evans, who had served for years as principal at Green River.

By 1982 school enrollments had grown to 3,589 with almost two-thirds of the students in the elementary grades, reflecting the high proportion of young families in the county. There were four hundred children in kindergarten alone. In 1981 construction began on a further expansion of Emery High School including an auditorium that would seat 1,500. Building needs placed such heavy demands on school district resources that little money was available for auxiliary purposes. After several years of complaints about the poor condition of the running track at Emery High, the Spartan Booster Club finally collected matching funds from parents and local businesses to help finance construction of a rubberized track and other facilities.[42]

Churches. Frank L. Hall, who had served as president of the Emery LDS Stake since 1957, was succeeded by Donald R. Curtis in 1969. In keeping with a new church practice, the historic name was changed to the Castle Dale Utah Stake in 1974. Structural defects in the Orangeville chapel made it necessary for it to be replaced, and the old building was demolished in 1974. Orangeville Ward members were forced to go to Castle Dale for meetings during a long period of negotiations with church leaders for a new chapel that was finally completed and dedicated in 1977. With the exception of Huntington, which had been divided between two LDS wards since 1947, Castle Valley communities had remained in the village-ward pattern that had prevailed since pioneer times. This situation changed with the building of new homes and subdivisions. The Castle Dale Ward was divided in 1976, the Ferron Ward in 1977, and the Orangeville Ward in 1978. A third ward was created in Huntington in 1977 and in Orangeville, Castle Dale, and Ferron in 1980. The Huntington Utah Stake was organized in 1977 including the wards in Huntington, Cleveland, and Elmo, with Ira W. Hatch as stake president. At the same time the Castle Dale Utah Stake was reorganized with Wesley R. Law as president. The Ferron Utah Stake was created in 1981 with Jerry Mangum as president. The Huntington chapel underwent extensive remodeling between 1979 and 1980 to accommodate multiple ward use plus stake offices. In 1980 boundaries were redrawn at Huntington to create five wards, and work began on a new chapel in the southeast part of town. The Cleveland ward was divided in 1980 and a new chapel completed in 1983. New chapels were also erected on the Castle Dale bench, in the southern part of Ferron, and in Elmo.[43] When the Moab LDS Stake was organized in 1971, the Green River Ward was transferred to the new unit. The Green River Ward was divided in May 1980.[44]

Members of the Catholic church in western Emery County were served by the Notre Dame parish in Price. Home masses were celebrated in several communities beginning about 1970. As the numbers outgrew the space available in homes, there was increased interest in securing a church building. Construction on the Mission San Rafael, located between Huntington and Castle Dale, began in late 1976 with funds from a variety of sources and with most of the labor being contributed by local members. The building was far enough advanced for a mass to be celebrated there on Easter Sunday 1977. Dedicatory services were held on 17 November 1977 under the direction of Bishop Joseph Lennox Federal of the Salt Lake City Diocese. The multiple-use building was remodeled and enlarged in 1991 and continues to serve several dozen Catholic families from Emery to Elmo. Local leadership is provided by Deacon Deane L. Foote and a mission council.[45]

The First Baptist church of Emery County had its origins in a three-day evangelistic meeting conducted in Castle Dale in August 1978 by Wallace Higgins and Milton Carr of the Northwest Baptist Mission. Pastor Carr served as the resident minister until 1984, conducting services in the Senior Citizens' Center in Castle Dale and the Legion Hall in Ferron (the former Presbyterian school). In 1984 all services were moved to Ferron. Pastor Carr was succeeded by a series of ministers including Andrew Adank, Wynn M. Terwilliger, Rick Cook, John Whitlatch, and Joseph Kuefler. The church has maintained active youth programs and Ladies Missionary Fellowship, and conducted revivals and vacation Bible schools.[46] The Full Gospel Community church operated in Ferron under the Reverend James Blalack for a time in the early 1980s. Seventh Day Adventist services were also conducted in Ferron.[47]

The Huntington Christian Center was established in 1978 under the direction of the Reverend Joseph A. Williams with labor contributed by volunteers from Assemblies of God congregations in Oregon. Pastor Williams was succeeded by Curtis Treloggen in 1979, and the church was formally affiliated with the Assemblies of God. By 1984 services were no longer being held, and the First Baptist church in Price obtained use of the building and nearby home. What began as a mission sponsored by the Price church became the

Mountain View Baptist church in 1991, with Virgil Marcum as pastor. Marcum was succeeded by Orvil Williams in 1992.[48]

Emery County Centennial

The "future shock" of the late 1970s, when the county was being transformed from an agricultural to an industrial society, coincided with the centennial of settlement. Perhaps in part because of the pressures of rapid change, the centennial was celebrated with a certain nostalgia. In the summer of 1977, the Castle Dale LDS Second Ward organized a reenactment of the settlement of Cottonwood Creek with horse-drawn wagons retracing the 1877 pioneer route across the Wasatch Plateau. Ferron organized a community centennial celebration in 1978 that featured a parade including only horse-drawn vehicles.[49]

As an important reflection of the renewed interest in local history, the Castle Valley Historical Society was organized in the settlement centennial year 1977 with Eva W. Conover of Ferron as president and Ronald D. Taylor of Green River, Virginia Sorensen of Emery, Roxie Nelson of Ferron, Roger Curtis of Orangeville, Montell Seely of Castle Dale, and Elizabeth Hansen and Maudie Moffitt of Huntington as directors. The original plan was for the Castle Valley Historical Society to be an umbrella organization with three local chapters, one in western Emery County, one in Green River, and one in Carbon County. The Emery chapter was organized in February 1978 with John Jorgensen of Castle Dale as president, Wesley Curtis of Orangeville as vice president, and May J. Arnold of Huntington as secretary-treasurer. With the encouragement and assistance of Huntington native Allan Kent Powell of the Division of State History, the CVHS and particularly the Emery chapter undertook an ambitious program that included lectures, symposia, and a volume of essays titled *Emery County: Reflections on Its Past and Future,* edited by Powell and published in 1979. Plans were set in motion in early 1978 for production of "a documented history of Castle Valley from pioneer days until now." This project reached fruition in the massive volume *Emery County, 1880–1980* (1981), compiled by Montell Seely, LaVora Kofford, Owen and Jane McClenahan, and Roma Powell, with contributions from a large group of field representatives and com-

Emery LDS meetinghouse. (Edward A. Geary)

munity historians. The Castle Valley Historical Society was dissolved in June 1980, and the Emery chapter was reorganized as the Emery County Historical Society with LaVora Kofford as president, Montell Seely vice president, and Sylvia H. Nelson secretary-treasurer.[50]

The Historical Society produced the February 1980 Emery County centennial celebration. This event, held at Emery High School, featured a huge "birthday cake" and a program representing aspects of the county's history, including Indian dances, a "mountain man" tableau, pioneer songs and skits, square dances, a narrated slide presentation, and a recitation by Clyde Kofford of a lament attributed to early stockman Bill Hambrick: "You Don't Know What Misery Is Until You've Herded Sheep." Music was provided by the historic Huntington Glee Club and the Emery High School band.[51]

Castle Valley Pageant. Montell Seely played an active part in all of these historical activities. As a counselor in the bishopric of the Castle Dale Second Ward, he had been instrumental in organizing the 1977 reenactment of the pioneering journey from Sanpete to Castle Valley. Among the "new people" who had been brought to the county by the power plant construction were Ken and Carol Ann Driggs, who were members of Seely's ward. Carol Ann Driggs was an experienced vocal performer and had participated in the pageant produced on the grounds of the Oakland, California, LDS temple. She was also the ward cultural arts specialist and in that capacity approached Seely for advice on how to fulfill her calling. According to an account written by Seely,

> Back in the "catacombs" of my mind, there had been, for years, an idea that Castle Valley needed a pageant, one that would tell the story of the pioneers who settled this desolate valley. I had two objectives in mind. (1) I wanted our people to develop an increased love for their pioneer ancestors; and (2) I wanted them to feel an increased love for this land (Castle Valley).
>
> So I said to Sister Driggs, "What we really need in this area is a pageant that tells the story of the pioneers coming into this valley." As I said that, I had in mind an outdoor production, staged in a natural setting, and one that would be a historic presentation, with horses pulling covered wagons.
>
> She said, "if someone will write the script, I can direct it." I was to learn later that, as she responded, she had in her mind a stage production like the play OKLAHOMA.[52]

After trying without success to recruit a writer, Seely eventually took on the task himself. He also located a natural amphitheater high on a bench providing a panoramic view of Castle Valley, where the pageant has been performed annually since 1978 under the sponsorship of the county's LDS stakes. It is a major production demanding a heavy investment of time from a host of volunteers each year. The script, though revised somewhat over the years since its first production, continues to focus on four couples based loosely on actual Cottonwood Creek pioneers. "Wink and Anna" are modeled on Seely's grandparents Justus Wellington and Anna Reynolds Seely, who gave birth to a baby during the journey across the mountains. "Joe and Tilda" were inspired by the experience of Joseph and Matilda Curtis Boulden, who lost a child during their journey to Castle Valley. The characters of Joe and Tilda are vehicles to commemorate the sacrifices required in the pioneering of Castle Valley, with both of them meeting an early death in the course of the pageant. (The real Joseph and Matilda Boulden lived to a ripe old age.) "Abe and Neva," who provide the pageant's romantic interest, were inspired by John Y. and Sarah Nielson Jensen, who conducted a long-distance courtship across the mountains. The fourth couple, "John and Clara," were inspired less by particular individuals than by two incidents that reflected the difficult challenge faced by women in pioneering a new country. One incident was the tearful lament reportedly uttered by Ellen Miller when her husband, Niels P., brought her to the dugout on his homestead: "Has it now come to this that I have to live under the ground?" The other incident was the angry reaction of Hanna Seely on first approaching the homestead located by her husband, Orange: "Damn the man who would bring a woman to such a God-forsaken place!" Clara in the pageant is the rebellious wife who must learn to love Castle Valley (as both Ellen Miller and Hanna Seely, according to tradition, eventually did).

These four stories are punctuated by incidents that include a flash flood, a water fight, and the perennial favorite scene titled "Slippin' and Slidin' in the Castle Valley Mud." The doctrinal content has received added emphasis as the pageant has become more institutionalized as a church production, including missionary work to the Indians, minisermons on the importance of temple marriage, a reenactment of the Book of Mormon account of Christ's visit to the American continent, and a postmortal family reunion. Much of the distinctive quality of the Castle Valley Pageant, however, is still its lively reenactment of pioneering with horses and wagons. Largely under the continuing influence of Montell Seely, pageant audiences are treated to living history demonstrations of such skills as loading a pack mule, hanging a bell, and setting an iron wagon tire. The pre-performance lamb fry in the Castle Dale city park has also become a favorite tradition, patronized by busloads of visitors from other regions of the state. Performances have increased to seven nights and run concurrently with the Emery County Fair. Audiences average about twelve thousand each year and have been as large as six thousand for a single performance.

The End of the Boom

By the late 1970s, Emery County was enjoying the highest wages and the lowest unemployment rate in the state, but there were disquieting signs that the boom was approaching its end. The energy crisis of the early part of the decade, which had been widely interpreted as signaling a permanent decline in the petroleum supply, proved instead to be only a passing phase of maladjustment between supply and demand. The national economy was plagued by high interest rates and "stagflation," a combination of price inflation and recessionary economic performance. Instead of the expected steady increase in demand for electricity, demand slowed and even declined as the recession spread. Even as Utah Power was beginning construction of the third generating unit of the Hunter Plant, there were indications that the company was reaching surplus capacity. In an effort to recover some of its capital investment, Utah Power proposed to sell almost half of Hunter Two to a group of municipal power systems. This proposal caused great concern in Emery County because it threatened to remove the plant from the property tax rolls. County officials threatened legal action to preserve the county's tax base. After a period of negotiations, the sale was consummated with provisions to maintain the property's tax status.[53]

Additional indications of retrenchment appeared in 1980. The coal gasification plant proposed for Emery and the nuclear energy center proposed for Green River both dropped from consideration when it became apparent that energy demand was too low to justify the massive investments. Consolidation Coal cancelled plans to develop a strip mine on its property south of Emery.[54] Still, it was assumed in many quarters that these set-backs represented only a temporary dip in a long-term upward trend. The Bureau of Economic and Business Research at the University of Utah predicted in 1981 that Utah coal production would rise to 25 million tons or more by 1990 compared to the 13.6 million tons mined in 1980. The Utah Energy Office projected a demand for twenty-five thousand miners and other energy workers in the state by 1990.[55]

What had been a gradual easing of the county's economic growth turned into a crunch in 1982. In March of that year, Utah Power cancelled plans to build a fourth generating unit at the Hunter Plant, citing a slowdown in projected industrial demand and escalating construction costs, which had increased from about $200 million for Huntington One to $436 million for Hunter Three. At about the same time, the Utah Consumer Services Committee and disgruntled former employees were accusing Utah Power and Emery Mining of waste and inefficiency in their operations. Among the questions Utah Power was required to answer before state regulatory agencies were whether the company could save money by purchasing coal on the open market instead of operating its own mines; whether there was widespread overstaffing in all facets of its operations; whether Emery Mining had entered into costly "sweetheart" deals with subsidiaries; and whether there had been outright corruption in some aspects of plant and mining operations, including misappropriation of materials and use of company resources for the personal benefit of some managers.[56] In its efforts to justify its operations, Utah Power undertook a determined belt-tightening program that resulted in a series of rate reductions but also the loss of numerous jobs.

At the beginning of 1982, Emery County's unemployment rate was 4.2 percent, well below the statewide average of 6.1 percent. By early 1983 it had soared to 9.7 percent, with almost one-third of coal miners out of work.[57] The coal from the Wilberg Mine that supplied the Hunter Plant was deteriorating in quality, with a high dust and ash content. In March 1982 Emery Mining suspended production at Wilberg and laid off 200 miners for an indefinite period while it relocated the longwall operation to another area of the mine with better coal. In April Utah Power instituted a hiring freeze that affected the more than 200 jobs that had been expected to open up when Hunter Three went on line. At the same time, other coal producers in the area were losing their markets. The Horse Canyon Mine, once the largest in the region, laid off 200 miners in June and ceased operations entirely in October 1982. In July Consolidation Coal laid off 100 workers at its underground mine near Emery. Another 96 miners were laid off in November, leaving only a small maintenance force. In all, more than 1,000 miners in Emery and Carbon counties lost their jobs during 1982. Emery Mining Company alone cut its work force from almost 2,000 at the beginning of the year to 1,500 at year's end.[58]

Economic conditions deteriorated further in 1983. Additional layoffs reduced the Emery Mining work force to about 1,000 by mid-February. The Hiawatha mine laid off 350 workers and suspended operations in April, citing a lack of market for coal plus a high absenteeism rate that made it impossible to operate profitably. On 14 April a massive landslide near Thistle in Spanish Fork Canyon blocked both Highway 6 and the Rio Grande Railway main line, cutting off shipment of coal to western and Pacific markets and isolating southeastern Utah from the state's population centers. As an immediate result of the landslide, the unemployment rate in Emery County jumped in one month from 9.7 percent to 11.2 percent. Rail service was restored by midsummer, but it took almost a year to reopen the highway. Largely as a consequence of the Thistle slide, Utah coal production fell from 17 million tons in 1982 to 11 million in 1983. Construction employment on Hunter Three peaked at 1,200 in November 1982, fell to 650 by April 1983, and then to only a skeleton staff by July.

The wet winter of 1983 caused additional problems in Emery County. Mudslides closed Highway 31 in Fairview Canyon for significant periods during the spring, making it necessary for travelers bound for Salt Lake City either to loop south through Salina or to take the Indian Canyon route through Duchesne. Flooding creeks washed out several roads and bridges, costing the county $703,604 for replacements and repairs.[59]

As was to be expected, the population curve trailed behind the economic curve. Emery County attained its peak population of 13,100 during the troubled year 1983. The remainder of the decade brought an average population loss of about 400 per year. County schools lost fifty-four students during the single month of October 1983.[60]

The year 1984 began with a fire in the Beehive Mine caused by a burning diesel tractor, requiring the sealing off of Beehive and temporarily idling 165 Des-Bee-Dove workers. The county's unemployment rate stood at 12 percent in January. By May coal mining employment in the county was down to 550 from a high of 2,426 only a few years earlier. An estimated 30 percent of housing units in Ferron, Orangeville, and Castle Dale were vacant, largely the result of the exodus of transient construction workers after completion of Hunter Three. However, many families who had hoped to make permanent homes in the county were also being forced to leave in search of employment. Mortgage foreclosure notices filled the legal pages of the *Emery County Progress.* Many businesses shut their doors, including the First Security Bank office in Huntington and Zion's First National Bank in Ferron.

The economy received yet another blow from a month-long United Mine Workers strike against Emery Mining Company in October and November in a dispute over pension fund contributions. Emery Mining complained that the 1950 UMW pension fund was unfair on two counts: first, no current or former Emery Mining workers would be eligible to draw benefits from the fund (they were covered by a different pension plan); and, second, the fund assessments were biased against efficient operations such as Emery Mining because contributions were based on tonnage mined rather than hours worked. The union stood fast in solidarity with the retired and soon-to-retire miners who depended on the 1950 pension fund, many of whom lived in Emery and Carbon counties. An eventual settlement was based on a reworked contribution formula that took into account both production and worker hours.[61]

With the loss of a month's income just before Christmas, miners and their families might well have felt they were experiencing hard times, though it only required a glance around the neighborhood to see other families who had no employment at all. County and town governments were also suffering from declining tax receipts. But the worst was still to come. The year that began with a mine fire would end with a mine fire, but this one would be the greatest disaster in Emery County history.

The Wilberg Disaster

Twenty-seven men and one woman were working in the Fifth Right section of the Wilberg Mine on the night of Wednesday, 19 December 1984. In addition to the regular crew operating the longwall equipment, several managers were in the section because the crew was in the final stages of an attempt to set a twenty-four-hour production record. At about nine o'clock, a parts runner discovered heavy smoke near the entrance to Fifth Right and called in an alarm to the communications center. A communications operator notified a foreman in Fifth Right of the trouble only a short time before the telephone line was cut off by the fire. The trapped miners had "self-rescuer" oxygen packs available in the work area, but some failed to put them on, apparently unaware of the toxic gasses already drifting into the area. One group, including management personnel, moved along the conveyor belt toward the fire in an effort to escape and apparently died within a short time. Another group retreated toward the end of the tunnel and were attempting to erect a rubber smoke barrier when they were overcome. Three miners followed the long-wall face in an apparent attempt to escape through the Sixth Right section, but a roof-fall two months earlier had blocked that passage. One man, carrying several self-rescuers, wandered through a maze of tunnels for hours until he apparently thought he had reached breathable air and removed his oxygen equipment. His was the last body to be found. Only one of the twenty-eight survived, escaping by a route that he was unable to describe precisely.

Efforts to fight the fire were hampered because managers who would normally have been directing the rescue operations were themselves trapped in Fifth Right. Low water pressure further impeded attempts to knock down the fire. Nevertheless, the trained rescue team quickly went into action assisted by other workers who risked their own lives in an attempt to save the trapped miners. Rescue teams from other mines arrived within a few hours. At times the fire seemed close to being controlled, only to flare up again and produce heavy smoke and heat that drove everyone from the area. It was early Friday, 21 December, before rescue teams were able to enter Fifth Right, where they found nine bodies only two hundred feet beyond the fire and four others farther in. Hope remained that some miners might have successfully barricaded themselves in a new entry, but when twelve more bodies were discovered deeper in the mine on Saturday night it became apparent that there would be no survivors. A new flare-up of the fire halted attempts to recover the bodies, and on Sunday a decision was made to seal the mine in order to cut off oxygen to the fire.[62]

The impact of the Wilberg disaster on Emery County and surrounding areas was instantaneous and profound. Many of the trapped miners had young families. Almost all of them were well known in the small communities where they lived. All were involved, not only with their co-workers at Wilberg but with miners at other mines, in the bond that unites people engaged in a hazardous occupation. The occurrence of the disaster during the Christmas season only added to the pathos as the entire community clung to the rapidly fading hope that some of the trapped miners might be found alive. The magnitude of the disaster attracted national and international attention. Major news organizations sent crews to the county, and network television news programs opened for several days in succession with scenes of smoke billowing from the Wilberg portal. Some reporters, eager for a new slant on the story, added to the pain of the victims' families by their aggressive and intrusive tactics.

The healing process for survivors and friends was long and difficult, made harder by the delay in recovering the bodies and by rumors of negligence, and perhaps even sabotage, as having caused the fire. A memorial service on 26 December, a week after the outbreak of the fire, brought an overcapacity crowd of 1,700 to the recently completed Emery County High auditorium to listen to messages of solace from Gordon B. Hinckley, then a counselor in the First Presidency of the LDS church, other general and local LDS leaders, and Ann Bell of Orangeville, whose son Philip was among the victims. The United Mine Workers conducted another memorial service in the auditorium on 5 January with President Richard L. Trumka in attendance.[63] A committee chaired by county commissioner Bevan K. Wilson raised funds for a monument to be placed on the courthouse lawn. The monument, sculpted by Gary Prazen, was dedicated in September 1985 at ceremonies attended by two thousand people. Another monument was erected by the United Mine Workers near the intersection of the Wilberg Mine road with Highway 29 and dedicated on the first anniversary of the disaster.[64]

Rescue crews were not allowed back into the Fifth Right area until November 1985. The twenty-five bodies that had been located in the days immediately after the disaster were recovered within a short time, but the last two victims were not found and brought out of the mine until mid-December.[65] Thus almost a full year had passed before the families of the dead miners could bring the experience to any kind of closure.

The economic impact of the Wilberg fire was soon felt. The 224 miners put out of work added to earlier lay-offs to raise the county's unemployment rate to 15.8 percent in January 1985. In February the Department of Labor provided a $500,000 grant to retrain the idled Wilberg workers. Also in February sixty-five workers were recalled to prepare Des-Bee-Dove for reopening. Utah Power contracted with Consolidation, Genwal, Co-op, and several Carbon County mines to supply the Hunter Plant until its own mines could resume production. The resulting heavy increase in coal trucks on Highway 10 brought a rash of complaints from local motorists about windshield and paint damage.[66]

The legal and regulatory ramifications of the Wilberg fire took several years to unravel. A preliminary report by the Mine Safety and Health Administration in September 1986 traced the origins of the fire to an overheated air compressor, the safety controls of which had allegedly been disabled. This report was disputed both by Emery Mining and Utah Power, who denied that there had been any tampering with safety devices, and by the United Mine Workers union, who insisted that the fire had started in the conveyor belt system and implied that the attempt to set a production record was a contributing factor. There were also dark rumors, never substantiated, that deliberate sabotage might have been involved. At U.S. Senate committee hearings in April 1987, Emery Mining general manager William Zeller declared that the mine was operated safely and had passed an inspection only a week before the fire. The Mine Safety and Health Administration stuck by its initial determination in subsequent reports and in 1987 cited Emery Mining and Utah Power for thirty-four violations, nine of which were alleged to have contributed directly to the loss of life in the accident. The companies were fined $111,470. A later MSHA report in 1989 recommended filing of criminal charges on the grounds that some managers knew the air compressor was unsafe. However, the United States Attorney for Utah declined to prosecute.[67] In March 1987 Utah Power and Savage Industries (the parent company of Emery Mining) settled with the families of Wilberg victims for $22 million while at the same time disclaiming any legal liability.[68] Efforts by Utah Power to recover damages from insurance companies and equipment manufacturers continued for several more years. The two-entry system, which the union claims does not provide adequate escapeways in case of fire, continues to be used, with MSHA approval.

A look at the Wilberg victims reveals much about the changes that had taken place in Emery County during the decade preceding 1984.[69] In the first place, they were relatively young, with a median age of thirty-one. Ages ranged from twenty-two to sixty, but only six were older than thirty-three and most of those were managers. Thus a majority of the victims had begun working in the mines during the boom period of the mid to late 1970s. The presence of a woman among the victims would have been unthinkable in an earlier period. For many years, women were "protected" by law from working in hazardous occupations including mining. Even after the legal barriers were removed, social barriers remained, including a widespread superstition among miners that it was unlucky to have women underground. The first women to work in an Emery County coal mine were employed in 1975.[70] A decade later there were still only a few female miners.

Eighteen of the victims had homes in Emery County. Seven lived in Carbon County. Two had families living elsewhere in Utah. It is in their points of origin, however, that the altered complexion of the county's work force becomes most apparent. Only six or possibly seven of the twenty-seven victims came from Emery County stock. Two were Carbon County natives, and seven or eight came from other parts of Utah. The remaining eleven had out-of-state origins, most of them coming from the coal mining regions of West Virginia, Ohio, Pennsylvania, and Kentucky. It should be noted, however, that the Wilberg victims did not represent a cross-section of the county's miners because of the high proportion of management personnel. The proportion of Emery and Carbon County natives was larger among the rank-and-file miners.

The Aftermath

Even before recovery of the fire victims, ninety workers were recalled in June 1985 to prepare the Wilberg Mine for resumed operation. In April 1986 Utah Power terminated its contract with Emery Mining and established its own mining division, later named Energy West. Among the reasons given for the change were Emery Mining's difficulty in obtaining adequate insurance and Utah Power's desire to "reduce the financial risks that arise from operating these mines."[71] Cost-cutting measures were intensified under continuing pressure from regulatory agencies. Seventy-two miners were laid off at Des-Bee-Dove and Deer Creek, and forty salaried employees in the mining division lost their jobs in June 1986. In early June Utah Power suspended coal production entirely for two months in order to reduce stockpiles. Some 500 workers were laid off while 350 remained on the job for construction projects designed to increase productivity and efficiency. Des-Bee-Dove was closed in February 1987, idling 110 miners, and an additional fifteen salaried workers were laid off in March. There were now only 685 employees in the mining division, and yet coal production was higher than ever. In 1987 the Wilberg-Cottonwood complex became the first mine in Utah to produce more than 3 million tons of coal in a single year. Deer Creek production that year was 2.5 million tons.[72]

In few industries have mechanization and automation brought such dramatic changes as in coal mining. Within the lifetime of some Emery County residents, mining has advanced from a hand-loading operation with horse-drawn carts to the latest generation of longwall equipment that enables a crew of eight workers to produce as much as ten thousand tons in a single shift. These advances are important in keeping the county's underground mines competitive with strip mines in Wyoming and Montana, which produce coal of lower quality but at lower cost. Modern mining requires more specialized skills and is more rewarding—both intrinsically and financially—than the pick, sledge hammer, and shovel work of an earlier generation. But the number of workers needed to maintain a given level of production grows fewer and fewer. Utah Power's Emery County mines were among the most efficient underground operations in the nation in 1980, but output per miner-day doubled between 1980 and 1988.[73] Charles Jones of Elmo remembered working at Hiawatha in 1933 when that operation (which prided itself on being at the forefront of mining technology) employed 840 miners. Jones remarked in 1993,

> When the Hiawatha mine shut down they had 165 men working there. They were still producing the same amount of coal as they

> were back when there was 840 men. Now you ask why? Modernization is what happened. The truth is right now they are producing more coal in Emery County and Carbon County than they have ever produced. Fifteen or 20 men now produce as much coal as three or four hundred used to. That's it. That's what's wrong with our economy.[74]

Utah Power was acquired by the larger PacifiCorp in 1987. This merger brought increased financial strength to the company and good profits to county residents who held Utah Power stock, but it meant that the corporate offices, located in Portland, were now even farther removed, both in miles and in interest, from the Emery County operations. It also brought Utah Power's coal-fired generating plants into more direct competition with the hydro-electric plants of the Northwest and strip mine-fed steam-electric plants in Wyoming, intensifying the pressures for higher efficiency and lower costs. The state-assessed valuation of the power plants gradually declined (even though the replacement cost and hence the true market value was increasing), meaning that the share of property taxes paid by Utah Power/PacifiCorp was less each year, while the share paid by local property owners increased. Still, Utah Power/PacifiCorp regularly protested a substantial portion of its annual property tax assessment. This created budgeting problems for the county, the school district, and the Castle Valley Special Services District because taxes paid under protest were subject to being refunded if the protest was upheld. County commissioners exacted a small measure of revenge in 1991 when they delayed action on a request for assistance in refinancing the company's revenue bonds.[75] This action brought assurances from corporate officers of their desire to work more closely with local officials, but the yearly protesting of tax assessments continued as before.

Total nonfarm employment in the county fell from 5,890 in 1982 to 3,543 in 1987.[76] Most of that decline reflected a loss of construction jobs as the power plants were completed. However, several hundred jobs were permanently lost in the mining industry as well. The county's unemployment rate was in double digits during much of this period, reaching a peak of 18.4 percent in July 1987. Where a decade earlier there had been a severe shortage of housing, Emery

County's vacancy rate had now become the highest in the state. By one admittedly incomplete count, more than seventy-five homes were for sale in August 1987 in the three communities of Castle Dale, Orangeville, and Ferron.[77]

A combination of national economic recovery, with an attendant resurgence in the demand for electric power, and adjustment of the population to the available jobs brought the unemployment rate down to a respectable 5.3 percent in August 1989.[78] Nonfarm employment rose modestly to 3,710 by the end of 1989. The Utah Power/PacifiCorp mining operations provided 750 jobs, including management and support personnel. An additional 350 were employed at the Hunter Plant and 230 at the Huntington Plant.[79] Maintenance, repair, and construction work in support of the mines and power plants provided a sizeable number of additional jobs, many of them in locally owned enterprises. And these were, for the most part, high-paying jobs, especially by comparison with average rates of pay in rural Utah. However, a sizeable number of those who worked in Emery County commuted from homes outside the county. Even those who lived in the county spent much of their income on goods and services in Price or in Wasatch Front cities, thus reducing the normal "multiplier effect" of basic industry jobs on the local economy. Emery County has consistently "exported" as much as 80 percent of its consumer buying power.[80]

Agriculture in an Industrial Economy

The impact of the boom on the county's traditional base of agriculture and stock raising took three main forms. First and most significant was the diversion of precious water resources from agriculture to industrial and municipal uses. Approximately one-third of the water rights in Huntington, Cottonwood, and Ferron creeks were acquired by Utah Power through purchase or long-term lease. The growing towns also expanded their water holdings. Even with the improved water management made possible by new and enlarged storage facilities, this reallocation meant that some land had to be retired from farming and other acreage received a reduced supply of irrigation water. Some farmers who had sold a portion of their water stock to Utah Power tried to continue farming the previously cultivated acreage. During years of above-average precipitation, this was sometimes possible. But extended drought periods in the late 1970s, the late 1980s, and early 1990s brought severe restrictions on water use. As Huntington-Cleveland Irrigation Company director Clifton Brown remarked in 1980, "People sell out their water stock to Utah Power and Light and they try to keep farming. We try to distribute the water thinner and thinner and it just runs to an end."[81]

A second major impact was the subdivision of farm land into the ten-acre residential lots required by county zoning ordinances. The intent of this requirement was to discourage residential sprawl, but the ultimate effect was the creation of numerous plots that were larger than needed for residential purposes but too small to be viable farms.

The third impact was a consequence of growth in employment. A large share of the county's farmers had traditionally combined farming with mine employment. Because of seasonal mine lay-offs or short weeks during the summer, this was a workable combination of activities. However, with the more steady year-round employment requirements of the mines and power plants, the summer days formerly devoted to farm work tended to disappear. One result was the conversion of much crop land to permanent pasture in order to reduce the time demands of the farm.

To these impacts might be added a fourth, the aging of the county's farmers and a shortage of young people willing to make the financial and personal investment necessary for successful farming beyond a hobby scale. The 718 Emery County farms reported in the 1954 census of agriculture had shrunk to 420 in 1992, only 348 of which harvested any crops. More significantly, the 400 county residents who reported a primary employment in agriculture in 1960 declined to only 126 in 1990. Irrigated acreage fell by almost one-fourth, from 41,708 acres in 1964 to 31,669 in 1992. The land devoted to grain crops decreased from 4,616 acres in 1969 to a mere 902 acres in 1992 while acreage devoted to forage crops increased slightly from 16,356 to 17,598. The number of cattle held relatively steady with 27,159 in 1959 and 25,455 in 1992. These were predominantly beef cattle as only a few dairy farms remained in operation in the Ferron area. Sheep numbers fell drastically from 24,378 in 1959 to only 8,367 in 1992. Hogs and poultry virtually disappeared as economic components of the county's agriculture, and there were only six fruit orchards in 1992 totalling thirty-six acres. The overall pattern shows a change from the mixed farming and stockraising that prevailed in earlier periods to a farm economy based primarily on cattle, hay, and pasture and providing employment to only a small fraction of the county's work force. However, while agriculture and stockraising have diminished in relative economic importance, they continue to have a cultural value for many residents, as is manifest, for example, in the widespread interest in horses and horsemanship.

The Wilderness Debate

Despite periodic mineral prospecting activity and even the extensive explorations and mining during the uranium rush, the San Rafael Swell remained little known to the outside world until recent years. The building of Interstate 70 through the center of the Swell opened its dramatic features to a vastly larger audience. A growing interest in outdoor recreation via off-highway vehicles, mountain bikes, and hiking have brought increasing numbers of people into the more remote corners of the San Rafael. The region has been the topic of several books in recent years. Owen McClenahan of Castle Dale drew upon a lifetime's experience in *Utah's Scenic San Rafael* (1986). Other books include Joseph Bauman, Jr., *Stone House Lands* (1987) and Steve Allen, *Canyoneering* (1992). As the closest desert recreation area to the populous Wasatch Front, it was inevitable that the San Rafael Swell would become better known and more extensively visited.

It was inevitable, too, that the region's remarkable natural features would attract the attention of the wilderness preservation movement in the state and nation. In 1979 the Bureau of Land Management first conducted an "extensive inventory" of potential wilderness lands in the county, identifying 352,000 acres as being worthy of special consideration. A year later the potential wilderness acreage was expanded to 397,135. The lands proposed for wilderness status made a partial circle around the center of the San Rafael Swell and also included the Green River canyons.[82] With various inclusions and exclusions, these areas have remained the focus of the wilderness debate.

In 1985 there were renewed proposals to establish a national park in the San Rafael area. This idea received some initial support in the county, but when public hearings were held in November 1985, a large majority of those attending opposed both national park and wilderness status for the Swell, preferring to retain multiple-use management under the Bureau of Land Management.[83] The opposition to more formal preservation measures was stimulated by a variety of concerns. One was the possibility that there might yet be valuable mineral resources in the area that should not be "locked up" from future development. Another concern was preserving access to areas that had in some cases been a part of local family and community traditions for several generations. In addition to concerns about the effects of wilderness or national park designation on the Swell itself, however, there were serious apprehensions about potential impacts on adjacent areas. County officials and many residents feared that wilderness air-quality requirements could effectively prevent any further industrial development in the county, and in a worst-case scenario might even require the dismantling of existing industries. There was also concern that federal reserved water rights associated with the withdrawal of public land from multiple use might adversely affect the established water rights upstream.

The debate over wilderness in Emery County was far from resolution at the end of 1995. The Bureau of Land Management by this time had pared its list to some 243,000 acres in the San Rafael area plus additional areas in Desolation and Labyrinth canyons. State officials and the Utah congressional delegation were inclined to follow the BLM recommendations or trim them slightly, while Emery County officials hoped to see larger reductions. At the other end of the spectrum, some wilderness advocates were insisting that 848,000 acres—almost one-third of the entire county—should be designated as wilderness.[84]

Paleontological Resources

Emery County's extinct wildlife has continued to attract scientific attention. The Haddon Flat area produced some important fos-

Recovery of Huntington Mammoth. (Courtesy Vernell Rowley)

sil finds during the 1980s, and the Long Walk Quarry may well become one of the most important sources of information about dinosaurs of a later period from those whose fossils have been found elsewhere in the county.

A very significant discovery dating to a much later era than the dinosaurs was the almost-intact skeleton of a Columbian mammoth uncovered during reconstruction of the Huntington Reservoir dam in August 1988. The Huntington Mammoth, as it came to be called, attracted widespread media attention and competition from several museums for the distinction of serving as a final repository. After initial stabilization and study at the Utah Museum of Natural History, the bones (which were too fragile for public exhibition except in controlled-atmosphere conditions) were deposited in the CEU Prehistoric Museum at Price. In addition to being one of the most complete mammoth skeletons ever recovered, the Huntington Mammoth had the distinction of being found at a higher elevation than any previous specimen and of representing a date more than a thousand years after Columbian mammoths were thought to have become extinct.[85]

School and Society

As the growth curve generated by the county's young families moved upward through the school grades, enrollment pressures shifted from elementary to secondary schools. The Emery High School graduating class grew from 113 in 1977 to 140 in 1983 (the year of the county's peak population), declined to 104 in 1984, and then grew to a historic high of 225 in 1994.[86]

In 1990 a remarkable 34.4 percent of the county's population, 3,556 out of 10,332, were enrolled in school. Forty-nine percent of Emery County households were composed of married-couple families with children under the age of eighteen, compared to the national average of 26.7 percent. The county ranked first in Utah and third in the entire nation among counties with populations over 10,000 in its proportion of traditional families with children.[87] This family-centered lifestyle is reflected not only in high enrollment figures but in the great interest county residents have taken in their schools. While the desire has always been strong to "keep the young people at home" by providing local employment opportunities, residents have realistically understood that a large share of the county's youth will end up seeking their fortunes in the outside world. Parents are anxious to see them well prepared for whatever the future may hold.

This relatively widespread (though not universal) public commitment to education, combined with the resources made available by an enlarged tax base and the efforts of a corps of dedicated teachers and administrators, has given Emery County schools an enviable record of achievement. Residents have been willing to tax themselves (and, of course, even more willing to tax local industries) to provide high quality facilities. The Emery County School District has been a recognized leader in incorporating computers into the education process. The science wing added to Emery High in 1990 fulfilled a long-held vision of science teacher Var Lynn Peacock. In a wide range of competitive activities, ranging from mathematics and business skills through music and drama to interscholastic sports and rodeo, the county's high schools have consistently ranked among the best in the state among schools of comparable enrollments. Graduates have gained admittance to such highly competitive institutions as the

United States Naval Academy, Harvard University, and the Massachusetts Institute of Technology and garnered numerous scholarships and awards at in-state colleges and universities.

Emery County High has won numerous regional and state championships in basketball, football, track and field, cross-country, volleyball, baseball, and wrestling. The marching band has performed at Disneyland, Disney World, and the Calgary Stampede. Nineteen eighty-seven was a banner year as the boys' track team, the band, and the football team all won state titles. Perhaps the most enviable record, however, was achieved by the boys' basketball teams of 1988–90. The team attracted national attention because of seven-foot-five-inch Shawn Bradley, probably the most-publicized high school athlete of the period. Bradley was complemented by a skilled and well balanced group of teammates who played together for several years. After a disappointing thirty-win, two-loss season in 1988 (in which they failed to win the state championship after leading the polls throughout the season, and at the conclusion of which the coach was reassigned to other duties), the team fulfilled local expectations by going undefeated in 1989 on its way to the state 2A championship. The following year Emery High was reclassified in the larger 3A category over the objections of local officials. The basketball team went on to the almost-unprecedented achievement of winning consecutive state titles in two different classifications, defeating the much larger Ogden High School in the 1989 state championship game. The team's eight seniors had lost only four games in three years. Two of those losses came against big city schools in the Raleigh, North Carolina, Holiday Festival tournament. After one year of collegiate competition followed by an LDS mission, Bradley signed a multimillion-dollar National Basketball Association contract.[88]

While the Emery High Spartans were capturing most of the attention, the Green River Pirates were experiencing a comparable domination of the small-school category, placing second in the state 1A boys' basketball tournament in 1989 and winning it in 1991, capping a 23–2 season. The team had a three-year record of sixty-seven wins and only eight losses, and star center Leon Carter went on to a successful college career at San Diego State University.[89] Another Emery County athlete to achieve a high measure of success was football lineman Craig Patterson of Castle Dale, who played for the National Football League Phoenix Cardinals after a collegiate career at Brigham Young University.

Emery County in the 1990s

The 1990 census confirmed the youthful character of the county's population. The median age of 25.6 was only slightly lower than the state median of 26.3 (itself among the lowest in the nation), but the median age alone does not tell the entire story. Forty-three percent of Emery County residents were under the age of eighteen, compared to 36.4 percent in the state. On the other hand, only 6.4 percent of the county's population fell between the ages of eighteen and twenty-four, compared to 11.6 percent statewide. This indicates a large out-migration of young people following high school graduation. For other age groups, the Emery County percentage varied only slightly from statewide averages.

The largest employment category, in the county as in the nation, was service industries (including education, public administration, health and social services, business and repair services, among others), which employed 974 in 1990. Mining employment totalled 646. Retail and wholesale trade (including food and lodging services) provided 641 jobs. Transportation, communications, and public utilities employed 626, and construction 339. The 126 people reported as working in agriculture, once the mainstay of the county's economy, made up only about 3 percent of the total labor force of 4,017.

The median household income of $30,525 was well above the state average and substantially higher than neighboring counties (which ranged from Wayne County's $20,000 to Carbon County's $25,555). However, the per capita income of $9,257 was below the state average—yet another indication of the high proportion of children in the county's population mix. Not everyone shared in the general prosperity; 242 families (9.7 percent) and 1,080 individuals (10.5 percent) had incomes below the poverty level. Nevertheless, these figures were below the state average.

In other respects the 1990 census confirmed what was apparent to any observer. The population remained, as it has always been, of predominantly Anglo-European extraction. Only 219 people out of

10,332, or slightly more than 2 percent, were reported as Hispanic, which was the largest identified minority group. In the west part of the county, the majority of the population continued to be divided among four towns of roughly equal size, Huntington (1,875), Castle Dale (1,707), Ferron (1,606), and Orangeville (1,459). Three of the four had lost population since 1980 ranging from 6.5 percent in Ferron to 19 percent in Huntington. Only Orangeville had registered a gain of 11.5 percent. Cleveland and Elmo and the surrounding unincorporated areas also lost population between 1980 and 1990.

Emery, which had once been the second most populous town in the county, participated to only a limited extent in the growth that the energy boom brought to other Castle Valley communities. The 1970 population of 216 increased to 372 in 1980 but fell to 300 in 1990. With the suspension of production at the Consolidation mine, there were few local jobs. The necessity of even young children being bussed fifteen miles to Ferron for school was a likely factor in discouraging residential growth. Despite several proposed projects over the years, Muddy Creek remains the one major Emery County stream that is not managed by a large reservoir. Nor has Emery's proximity to Interstate 70 brought much economic benefit despite the county's paving of the Miller Canyon road, providing a second access point to the Interstate. It would seem that the Muddy Creek exit would be a natural site for travellers' service facilities on the long stretch between Green River and Salina, but nothing has been developed there.

The population of Green River (including the Grand County portion of town) declined by 12.6 percent from 1,115 in 1980 to 968 in 1990. However, the night-time population becomes much larger during the tourist season as travelers bed down in the town's numerous motels. With the cessation of missile testing and the waning of the mineral industry, Green River has become increasingly dependent on tourism. Agriculture is still important, with the Thayn brothers operating the county's largest irrigated farm. Green River melons are among Utah's best known farm products.

The first half of the 1990s decade has seen a continued slow erosion of industrial employment. Consolidation Coal idled its Emery mine in June 1990, with a loss of ninety jobs. Overall jobs declined from 3,470 in 1991 to 3,310 in 1992, with most of the losses coming in the coal industry. And yet production continues at a high level. PacifiCorp (Energy West) has consolidated its coal production in two interconnected mines, Cottonwood and Deer Creek, which together constitute the largest underground operation west of the Mississippi, producing 7 million tons per year. The Genwall mine in Huntington Canyon produced 1.5 million tons in 1994. The Co-op Bear Canyon mine is probably the oldest continuously active operation in the county. The Skyline and Plateau mines, portals of which are in Carbon County, extract the greater part of their coal from Emery County (a situation that led to a lengthy dispute over the distribution of mineral lease impact funds between the road special service districts of the two counties).[90] The power plants, like the mines, have found ways to maintain high output with reduced manpower.[91] Other mineral resources in the county remain little developed, but the large gypsum deposits have attracted a mining and processing operation, Gypsum Resources Development Corporation. Locally owned construction and equipment repair businesses have prospered and provided quality jobs.

Also on a positive note, the county has taken advantage of grants from the Community Impact Fund to make substantial improvements in its infrastructure, including roads, water and sewer systems, public buildings, recreation facilities including the Mill Site Golf Course and a golf course adjacent to Green River State Park, and two fine museum facilities, the John Wesley Powell River History Museum at Green River and the Museum of the San Rafael at Castle Dale. (It should be noted, however, that the county's grants *from* the fund have amounted to only a small fraction of the contributions *to* the fund from mineral leases in Emery County.) The Castle Valley Special Service District continues to be a major asset. A $10 million bond issue approved by voters in 1994 will provide for storm drainage, street improvements, and further water and sewer improvements. Also in 1994 the town of Clawson was annexed into the CVSSD. In addition to voter approved bonds, the CVSSD had obtained through 1995 more than $13 million in grants from the Community Impact Board, the Environmental Protection Agency, and Farmers Home Administration, and the Four Corners Regional Administration.[92] Another agency, Emery County Special Service

District Number One, was established in 1988 to receive a share of mineral lease royalties for the purpose of building and maintaining roads in the unincorporated areas of the county. By 1996 ECSSD #1 had spent about $10 million to improve coal haul and school bus roads.

In 1992 and 1993 Emery Telephone (which dropped the Farmers Union name in 1994) took over the outdated Huntington and Green River telephone exchanges from U.S. West Communications and upgraded them with the same state-of-the-art digital switching systems and fiber optic cables already in use elsewhere in the county. The company moved into a large new headquarters building at Orangeville in early 1996. As a result of the initiative displayed by this local cooperative, Emery County now enjoys probably the most advanced communications facilities in all of rural Utah.[93]

The county's ties with its past have been strengthened and reaffirmed by historic preservation activities of the Emery County Historical Society under presidents Roma Powell (1982–90), Sylvia H. Nelson (1990–92), Dixie Swasey (1992–93), Vernell Rowley (1994–95), and Janet Petersen (1996–). In 1991 Vernell Rowley initiated a project to place signs along the Buckhorn road identifying geological formations. A Geologic Tour Guide was prepared by Bryant Anderson and Owen McClenahan. In 1993 a group consisting of Rowley, Montell Seely, Don Clements, Ron Jewkes, and others undertook to map and mark the route of the Old Spanish Trail through the county. Completion of the project in March 1994 was celebrated by a tour and an informational brochure compiled by Bryant Anderson. After the "swinging bridge" across the San Rafael River was rendered obsolete by new construction, Mark H. Williams of Castle Dale spearheaded a restoration project carried out in cooperation with the historical society and the county commission, which appropriated $10,000. The restoration work was done under contract in 1994 by Bruce Funk and family of Clawson. Other historic preservation projects include the restoration of the Molen cemetery by a Ferron committee, headed by JoAnn Behling, and restoration of the Woodside cemetery and marking of the Gunnison Trail, by the historical society. Several of these projects have benefitted from funds provided by the Division of State History, and community involvement has been widespread, including assistance by Boy Scout troops. Local Bureau of Land Management officials and the Emery County Road Department also provided assistance.[94]

The county committee for the Utah Statehood Centennial, with widespread public support, chose the restoration of the much-vandalized Buckhorn Draw rock art panel as the county's landmark legacy centennial project. Under the direction of an active committee headed by Reed Martin and with funding provided by the county commission, centennial license plate receipts, and numerous individual donations, professional art restorer Constance Silvers was hired to remove graffiti and restore the Fremont and Barrier Canyon-style pictographs and petroglyphs. With the cooperation of the Bureau of Land Management and the Emery County Road Department, the road was realigned and surfaced to reduce dust and a parking area created. Trails, fences, and information signs were installed to protect and interpret the prehistoric art, and additional visitor facilities were planned in 1996. This project has been recognized as one of the most distinctive and meaningful centennial activities in the state.

Prospects and Challenges

The county's current relative prosperity is founded primarily on coal, which is a finite and nonrenewable resource. The coal reserves are still extensive, but not all of them are economically recoverable under current conditions. Those that are are being consumed at a rate that would have been scarcely imaginable a few decades ago. The oldest units of the power plants are now past the midpoint of their thirty-year design life. That in itself is not highly significant. Design life is a kind of business fiction that is useful for planning purposes but has little bearing on how long an industrial installation actually continues to operate. Barring some unforeseeable breakthrough that might revolutionize the energy industry, and in view of the increasingly stringent environmental regulations and immense cost of new fossil fuel-burning installations, it seems likely that PacifiCorp or its successors will continue to operate the Emery County plants for as long as the technology and fuel supply enable them to make a profit. Since PacifiCorp controls one-third of the water in the western part of the county and provides almost 90 percent of the tax base, Emery County has many of the advantages and disadvantages of a "company town." Despite the many benefits the county has derived from the presence of the company, most residents would probably characterize PacifiCorp as a rather indifferent corporate citizen.

The author remembers a remark made some forty years ago by distinguished Emery County-native geologist William Lee Stokes in response to a question about the county's economic prospects. "You've got coal," Stokes said, "and you've got what the land will produce." He might have added at least two other resources that have been important in the county's history and will likely play an even more important role in the future: a spectacularly varied and endlessly fascinating natural landscape, and the ingenuity and determination of the county's people in using their natural resources to achieve the quality of life they desire.

Perhaps even more vital than coal among those resources is water, without which the county's coal reserves would have been much less attractive to the power industry. Nor would agriculture be possible in arid Emery County without the streams that originate in the snowbanks on the Wasatch Plateau. Eugene Johansen, who might well be regarded as the county's "elder statesman" of water affairs, has remarked laconically, "Water runs down hill and water runs toward money."[95] Johansen notes that the streamflow of the three main tributaries to the San Rafael is highly variable, ranging from less than 90,000 acre-feet in drought years to as much as 400,000 acre-feet in an exceptionally wet year such as 1984. About 40 percent of the total annual streamflow occurs during the months of May and June. Annual demand from water users is about 160,000 acre-feet. There is no way to increase the water supply, but reservoirs with a combined storage capacity of 135,000 acre-feet have made it possible to manage the supply more efficiently.

Where in early periods virtually all of the county's available water was devoted to agriculture, industrial and municipal users now control 40 percent of the water rights. The 60 percent that remains in agricultural use must absorb almost all of the losses from seepage and evaporation from an extensive and rather inefficient distribution system that includes a hundred miles of unlined canals and an additional hundred miles of lateral ditches. Johansen notes that farmers "are slowly installing pipe, sprinklers, and water saving devices," but these improvements occur only as individual farmers perceive them as being cost-effective. More efficient water delivery and use may receive a boost from the desire of federal officials to reduce the salinity entering the Colorado River system from runoff from the county's farms. On the other hand, Johansen points out that state water law provides a disincentive for large-scale conservation efforts because "the water saved must go to the next appropriator." Additional challenges facing the county's water users include disruption and pollution of the underground water flows by mining operations and increasing federal demands for wetlands preservation and natural streamflows. Johansen notes that "every stream of the San Rafael and its tributaries are overappropriated. Any change of use will have to come from the presently appropriated privately owned water."

In its water situation, as in so many other respects, Green River faces a different set of challenges and opportunities than other Emery County communities. The large unused portion of Utah's allocation of Colorado River Basin water runs past Green River City every day of the year on its course toward the Lower Basin. In theory, this water should be available for beneficial use. Only about three thousand acres are irrigated in the Green River area, an acreage that has not increased significantly in three-quarters of a century. Municipal and industrial uses are also modest. In the case of Green River, the problem is not obtaining water but rather finding an economically beneficial use for it.

The economic contributions of tourism to the county are largely confined to Green River and still come far short of their potential. In contrast to its Grand County neighbor Moab, which has become a destination resort for mountain bikers from around the world, Green River remains essentially a service area on Interstate 70. There has been some commercial development of river recreation, and the John Wesley Powell River History Museum is a valuable addition to the community. There would seem to be room for much greater development of Green River as a gateway both to the river canyons and to the San Rafael Swell. While Green River remains remote from the other communities in the county in some respects, the building of

Interstate 70 and more recently the inclusion of Green River in the countywide Emery Telephone system has strengthened the cross-county bonds to some extent. County officials have recently initiated discussions with Green River residents and Grand County officials exploring the possibility of uniting all of the Green River community in Emery County.

As a general rule, areas at a distance from major population centers are at a heavy disadvantage in economic development. However, Emery County with its strong industrial and tax base, its location on a major Interstate highway, and with communications facilities that enable full access to the electronic "information highway" is comparatively well positioned to claim a share in the state's economic growth that so far has been largely concentrated in the Wasatch Front and the St. George sunbelt. Whether the ingenuity of county residents will meet this challenge as it has met others over the county's 120-year history, and whether in the process they will preserve their cherished way of life, remains to be seen.

ENDNOTES

1. *ECPL,* 11 March 1971; 4 May 1972; 24 May 1973; 1 August 1974; "Utah Power and Light Company," in *EC 1880–1980,* 491.

2. "Archaeologists Save Historic Kiln," *BYU Today,* November 1973, 16.

3. *ECPL,* 27 January 1972; 28 June 1973; *ECP,* 2 February 1978; 25 January, 22 February 1978.

4. *ECPL,* 6 December 1973; 7 March, 30 May 1974; 11 August 1977; *ECP,* 8 June 1978; 24 January, 14 February, 26 June, 17 September, 10 December 1980.

5. *ECPL,* 9 March 1967; Thelma Mills, "Coal Industry," 292–93; personal communication from Thelma Mills and Shirl McArthur, January 1996.

6. *ECPL,* 27 January, 3 August 1972; 24 May 1973; "Shirl C. McArthur," in *EC 1880–1980,* 673.

7. *ECPL,* 3 January 1974.

8. Sylvia H. Nelson, personal communication, January 1996.

9. *ECPL,* 24 June, 16 December 1976; 14 April, 18 August 1977; *ECP,* 29 March, 3 May 1979.

10. Nelson, January 1996.

11. *ECP,* 3 May 1979; 1, 8, and 29 April 1981.

12. Ibid., 16 August 1979; 10 April, 26 June, 24 September 1980; 29 April, 29 July, 30 September 1981.

13. *ECPL,* 13 February 1975; 4 March, 10 June, 1976; 17 February, 29 September 1977.

14. *ECP,* 28 June 1979; 10 April, 22 May, 4 September 1980; 11 March, 22 April, 16 December 1981.

15. Ibid., 29 September 1982.

16. Ibid., 2 August 1979; 13 March 1980; 4 and 18 November 1981.

17. *ECPL,* 3 May, 19 July, 15 November 1973; 15 August 1974; 6 May, 24 June 1976; 16 June 1977; *ECP,* 27 April 1978.

18. *ECPL,* 15 November 1973; 10 January, 14 March 1974; 24 April 1975; 12 August, 16 December 1976; *ECP,* 26 January, 16 March 1978.

19. *ECP,* 23 February 1978.

20. *ECPL,* 14 March, 27 June 1974; 12 June 1975; 8 April, 25 November 1976; *ECP,* 7 June 1979; 4 September 1980; 9 December 1981.

21. *ECPL,* 23 August 1973; 3 July, 7 August, 27 November 1975; 1 and 22 January, 18 March 1976; 17 March, 8 December 1977; *ECP,* 1 June, 7 December 1978; 1 May 1980; Darrell Leamaster, personal note, January 1996.

22. *ECPL,* 14 March 1974; 3 July, 13 November 1975.

23. Ibid., 16 August 1973; 1 August 1974; 3 July, 13 November, 18 December 1975.

24. Ibid., 8 April 1971; 4 May, 3 August, 28 September 1972.

25. Ibid., 28 June, 30 November 1973; *ECP,* 16 February, 2 March 1978.

26. *ECPL,* 19 March, 5 November 1970; 13 January 1972.

27. *ECP,* 10 January 1980; 6 April 1983.

28. *ECPL,* 6 October 1977; *ECP,* 14 June, 8 November 1979; 13 March 1980; 21 January 1981; 13 January, 31 March 1982.

29. *ECP,* 25 February, 15 and 22 April, 25 November 1981; 20 January 1982.

30. Ibid., 24 August 1978; 11 January, 10 May 1979.

31. *ECPL,* 28 August 1975; 12 February, 18 March 1976; 6 and 20 January, 5 May 1977; *ECP,* 14 and 28 October, 4 November 1981; 14 July, 15 December 1982; 23 November 1983.

32. *ECPL,* 6 September 1973; 17 January 1974; 5 February, 29 April,

3 June 1976; 6 October 1977; *ECP,* 19 January 1978; 20 March 1980; 4 February, 5 August 1981; 4 January, 4 April, 11 July, 15 August, 14 November, 12 December 1984.

33. *ECP,* 26 November 1986; 3 October 1989; 16 January, 13 March 1990.

34. Ibid., 1 March 1979; 21 September, 26 October 1983.

35. *ECPL,* 14 February 1974; 17 February, 2 June 1977; *ECP,* 28 September, 9 November 1978; 14 June 1979; Price *Sun Advocate,* 14 January 1992.

36. *ECPL,* 26 December 1974; 13 March 1975; *ECP,* 4 April 1984.

37. *ECPL,* 24 June 1971; 3 May, 12 July, 6 September, 30 November, 6 December 1973; 1 January 1974; 20 March, 10 April, 10 July 1975; 15 January 1976; 22 July 1976; 24 March, 26 May, 14 July 1977; *ECP,* 11 May, 20 July 1978; 28 June 1979; 13 January, 10 November 1982; 30 May, 4 July 1984; Scott Truman, "Medical Center," in *EC 1880–1980,* 318–19.

38. *ECPL,* 10 October 1974; 24 November 1977; *ECP,* 8 February 1979; 13 December 1979.

39. *ECPL,* 22 May 1969; 24 May, 30 August 1973; 28 February, 5 September, 7 November 1974; 23 January 1975; 22 April 1976.

40. Ibid., 18 December 1975; 16 September 1976; 13 January, 3 March, 13 October 1977.

41. *ECP,* 12 and 19 May 1977; 8 August, 3 October 1984; 24 March, 26 May 1987

42. Ibid., 19 October 1978; 8 November 1979; 31 July, 4 September 1980; 25 February, 16 September 1981; 27 January, 25 August, 15 September 1982; 12 October 1983; 1 May 1985.

43. *ECPL,* 8 July 1976; 19 May, 2 June 1977; *ECP,* 24 August 1978; 29 May, 22 October 1980; Montell Seely, "Emery Stake (Castle Dale Utah Stake)," 279; Velma Petersen, "Ferron," 116; Irene Allred, "Cleveland," 155, in *EC 1880–1980.*

44. *ECPL,* 30 September 1971; Montell and Kathryn Seely, "Green River (Blake)," in *EC 1880–1980,* 141.

45. *ECPL,* 22 June 1972; 18 November 1976; 24 November 1977; 29 January 1991; "The Catholic Church in Huntington," in *EC 1880–1980,* 198.

46. *ECP,* 27 September 1979; 23 May 1984; 16 June 1987; 6 September 1988; 21 May 1991; Mary Thomsen and Jean Morlan, "First Baptist Church of Emery County" (1994), typescript copy in Emery County History Archives.

47. *ECP,* 6 October 1982; 3 September 1986.

48. Ibid., 15 June 1978; 3 September 1986; "Huntington," in *EC 1880–1980,* 199; Joan Smith, "Brief History of Mountain View Baptist Church of Huntington, Utah," 18 October 1995, manuscript copy in Emery County History Archives.

49. *ECPL,* 21 July 1977; *ECP,* 25 May 1978.

50. *ECPL,* 17 November 1977; *ECP,* 26 January, 2 and 30 March 1978; letter from Sylvia H. Nelson, January 1996.

51. "Emery County Centennial Program," in *EC 1880–1980,* 500–501.

52. Montell Seely, letter to descendants of John Y. and Sarah Jensen, 12 September 1995, copy in Emery County History Archives.

53. *ECP,* 27 April 1978; 24 January 1980.

54. Ibid., 24 September 1980.

55. Ibid., 7 January, 8 April, 5 August 1981.

56. Ibid., 10 and 24 March 1982; 9 March 1983.

57. Ibid., 4 January 1982; 19 January, 11 May 1983.

58. Ibid., 31 March, 14 April, 2 June, 28 July, 27 October, 15 December 1982.

59. Ibid., 16 February, 16 March, 20 July, 13 April, 11 May, 14 September 1983.

60. Ibid., 30 November 1983.

61. Ibid., 4 and 18 January, 8 February, 28 March, 10 October, 7 November 1984.

62. Ibid., 26 December 1984; 2 January 1985; Susan Lyman-Whitney, "Dangered Out: Lessons from Wilberg," *Deseret News,* 14 December 1994, C2–C3.

63. *ECP,* 2 and 9 January 1985.

64. Ibid., 26 June, 25 September, 25 December 1985.

65. Ibid., 6 and 13 November; 18 December 1985.

66. Ibid., 9 January, 6 and 13 February 1985.

67. Ibid., 1 October 1986; 31 March, 12 May 1987; 12 September 1989.

68. Ibid., 17 March 1987.

69. Wilberg Mine victims included James M. Bertuzzi, Randall P. Curry, Robert S. Christensen, Brian J. Howard, Barry Jacobs, and Nannette Saintz Wheeler of Castle Dale; Philip Earl Bell and John Dean Wilsey of Orangeville; Gordon Paul Conover, Roger Glenn Ellis, Lee Grant Johansen, Kelly Blake Riddle, Lynn Walton Robinson, and Ray Paul Snow of Ferron; Curtis A. Carter, Victor A. Cingolani, Gary K. Jennings, John F. Waldoch, and Lester Walls, Jr., of Huntington; David W. Bocock, Ricci G. Camberlango, Owen Keith Curtis, Jr., James F. Hamlin, Jr., and Alex T. Poulos of Price; Joel T. Nevitt of Wellington; LeRoy Tom Hersh of East Carbon; and Bert A. Bennett of Fillmore.

70. Ibid., 1 May 1975.

71. Ibid., 26 June 1985; 23 April 1986.

72. Ibid., 14 May, 11 and 25 June, 6 August, 3 September 1986; 10 February, 17 March 1987; 12 January 1988.

73. Ibid., 28 February 1989.

74. Charles F. Jones, oral history.

75. *ECP,* 16 April 1991.

76. Ibid., 5 July 1988.

77. Ibid., 18 and 25 August 1987.

78. Ibid., 19 September 1989.

79. Ibid., 28 February 1989; 30 January 1990.

80. Ibid., 5 July 1988; 22 June 1993.

81. Ibid., 17 December 1980.

82. Ibid., 19 July 1979; 10 April, 19 November 1980.

83. Ibid., 20 November 1985; 22 January 1986.

84. *Deseret News,* 23 February 1995, B-1.

85. *ECP,* 16 August 1988.

86. Ibid., 26 May 1977; 18 May 1983; 23 May 1984; 24 May 1994.

87. *Deseret News,* 22 August 1992, B-1.

88. *ECP,* 19 May 1982; 19 May, 17 November 1987; 17 May 1988; 28 February, 7 March, 10 October, 14 November 1989; 2 and 9 January, 27 February 1990; 19 and 26 February, 5 March 1991.

89. Ibid., 14 March 1989; 12 March 1991.

90. Ibid., 5 June 1990; 16 January 1994; Price *Sun Advocate,* 21 April 1992.

91. *Deseret News,* 7 August 1995, B-5.

92. Darrel Leamaster, personal communication, January 1996.

93. *ECP,* 10 September 1991; Price *Sun Advocate,* 28 April 1992.

94. Sylvia H. Nelson, letter, January 1996; "San Rafael Swell Geological Tour Guide"; "Old Spanish Trail Tour Guide"; Bruce C. Funk, "Restoration of the Swinging Bridge," typescript copy in Emery County History Archives.

95. Eugene Johansen, untitled article on Emery County water resources, typescript copy in Emery County History Archives.

Selected Bibliography

Antrei, Albert C. T., editor. *The Other Forty-Niners: A Topical History of Sanpete County, Utah, 1849–1983.* Salt Lake City: Western Epics, 1982.

Athearn, Robert G. *Rebel of the Rockies: A History of the Denver and Rio Grande Western Railway.* New Haven, Conn.: Yale University Press, 1962.

Baker, Pearl. *Robbers Roost Recollections.* Logan: Utah State University Press, 1976.

———. *The Wild Bunch at Robbers Roost.* Revised edition. Lincoln: University of Nebraska Press, 1989.

Bauman, Joseph M., Jr. *Stone House Lands: The San Rafael Reef.* Salt Lake City: University of Utah Press, 1987.

Beckwith, E. G. *Report of Exploration of a Route for the Pacific Railroad, Near the 38th and 39th Parallels of Latitude, from the Mouth of the Kansas to Sevier River, in the Great Basin.* Washington, D.C.: A.O.P. Nicholson, Printer, 1855.

Bennion, Glynn. "A Pioneer Cattle Venture of the Bennion Family," *Utah Historical Quarterly* 34 (1966): 312–23.

Black, Kevin D., and Michael D. Metcalf. "The Castle Valley Archaeological Project: An Inventory and Predictive Model of Selected Tracts."

Cultural Resource Series no. 19. Salt Lake City: Utah State Office, Bureau of Land Management, 1986.

Brewerton, George D. "A Ride with Kit Carson through the Great American Desert and the Rocky Mountains," *Harper's New Monthly Magazine,* August 1853, 306–34.

Brooks, George R., editor. *The Southwest Expedition of Jedediah S. Smith: His Personal Account of the Journey to California, 1826–1827.* Glendale, Calif.: Arthur H. Clark, 1977.

Carvalho, S. N. *Incidents of Travel and Adventure in the Far West; with Col. Fremont's Last Expedition Across the Rocky Mountains: Including Three Months' Residence in Utah, and a Perilous Trip Across the Great American Desert to the Pacific.* New York: Derby and Jackson, 1857.

Castleton, Kenneth B. *Petroglyphs and Pictographs of Utah. Volume 1: The East and Northeast.* Salt Lake City: Utah Museum of Natural History, 1978.

"The Chronicles of George C. Yount," *California Historical Society Quarterly* 2.1 (April 1923).

Conover, Eva W. *The History of George Henry Westover and Family.* Privately published, 1981.

Cooley, John. *The Great Unknown: The Journals of the Historic First Expedition Down the Colorado River.* Flagstaff, Ariz.: Northland, 1988.

DeCourten, Frank L. "The Long Walk Quarry: A New Horizon in Dinosaur Research," *Canyon Legacy: A Journal of the Dan O'Laurie Museum* 6 (1990): 15–22.

Dellenbaugh, Frederick S. *A Canyon Voyage: The Narrative of the Second Powell Expedition down the Green-Colorado River from Wyoming, and the Explorations on Land, in the Years 1871 and 1872.* New Haven, Conn.: Yale University Press, 1926.

Dutton, Clarence E. *Report on the Geology of the High Plateaus of Utah, with Atlas.* Washington, D.C.: Government Printing Office, 1880.

Finken, Dee Ann. *A History of the San Rafael Swell.* Price, Utah: Bureau of Land Management, San Rafael Resource Area, 1977.

Geary, Elmo G. "A Study of Dramatics in Castle Valley from 1875 to 1925." M.A. thesis, University of Utah, 1953.

Gottfredson, Peter. *History of Indian Depredations in Utah.* Salt Lake City: Published by the author, 1919.

Gunnerson, James H. "The Fremont Culture: A Study in Culture Dynamics on the Northern Anasazi Frontier." Papers of the Peabody Museum of

Archaeology and Ethnology. Cambridge, Mass.: Peabody Museum, 1969.

———. "Unusual Artifacts from Castle Valley, Central Utah." Anthropological Papers, no. 60, Department of Anthropology, University of Utah. Salt Lake City: University of Utah Press, 1962.

Hafen, LeRoy R., editor. "Colonel Loring's Expedition Across Colorado in 1858," *Colorado Magazine* 23 (1946).

———, and Ann W. Hafen. *Old Spanish Trail, Santa Fe to Los Angeles.* Glendale, Calif.: Arthur H. Clark, 1954.

Heap, Gwinn Harris. *Central Route to the Pacific, from the Valley of the Mississippi to California: Journal of the Expedition of E. F. Beale . . . and Gwin Harris Heap from Missouri to California in 1853.* Philadelphia: Lippincott, 1854.

Huntsman, Evelyn Peacock. *That We May Understand.* Privately published, 1994.

Jones, J. Albert. *A Story of the Settling of Huntington, Utah.* Privately printed, 1975.

———. *Some Early Pioneers of Huntington, Utah, and Surrounding Area.* Privately printed, 1980.

Jorgensen, John L. "A History of Castle Valley to 1890." M.A. thesis, University of Utah, 1955.

Lever, W. H. *History of Sanpete and Emery Counties.* Ogden, Utah: Published by the author, 1898.

Madsen, David B. "Three Fremont Sites in Emery County, Utah." *Antiquities Section Selected Papers,* no. 1. Salt Lake City: Division of State History, March 1975.

McClenahan, Owen. *Utah's Scenic San Rafael.* Castle Dale, Utah: Published by the author, 1986.

McElprang, Stella, compiler. *Castle Valley: A History of Emery County.* Emery County Daughters of Utah Pioneers, 1949.

Nelson, Lowry. *In the Direction of His Dreams: Memoirs.* New York: Philosophical Library, 1985.

Nixon, James W. *Sketches of the Life of James William Nixon.* Washington, D.C.: Privately published, 1937.

Olsen, Bruce L. "A History of the Emery County Progress-Leader and Its Predecessors." M.A. thesis, Brigham Young University, 1965.

Petersen, Wanda Snow. *Ferron Creek: Its Founders and Builders.* Bountiful, Utah: Horizon Publishers, 1989.

Peterson, Orson W. "A Survey and Evaluation of the Emery County School District." M.A. thesis, Brigham Young University, 1961.

Powell, Allan Kent. *Emery County: Reflections on Its Past and Future.* Salt Lake City: Utah State Historical Society, 1979.

———. *The Next Time We Strike: Labor in Utah's Coal Fields, 1900–1933.* Logan: Utah State University Press, 1985.

Powell, John Wesley. *Exploration of the Colorado River of the West and Its Tributaries.* Washington, D.C.: Government Printing Office, 1875.

———. *Report on the Lands of the Arid Region of the United States, With a More Detailed Account of the Lands of Utah* (1878). Edited by Wallace Stegner. Cambridge, Mass.: Harvard University Press, 1962.

Reynolds, R. V. R. "Grazing and Floods: A Study of Conditions in the Manti National Forest, Utah." *United States Forest Service Bulletin* 91 (1911).

Schroedl, Alan R., and Patrick F. Hogan. "Innocents Ridge and the San Rafael Fremont." *Antiquities Section Selected Papers, No. 2.* Salt Lake City: Division of State History, 1975.

Seely, Montell, LaVora Kofford, Owen and Jane McClenahan, and Roma Powell, editors. *Emery County, 1880–1980.* Emery County Historical Society, 1981.

Stokes, William Lee. *Geology of Utah.* Salt Lake City: Utah Museum of Natural History and Utah Geological and Mineralogical Survey, 1986.

———, and Robert E. Cohenour. *Geological Atlas of Utah: Emery County.* Utah Geological and Mineralogical Survey Bulletin 52. Salt Lake City: University of Utah, 1956.

Tabone, Paul Robert. "A History of the Emery Stake Academy." M.A. thesis, Brigham Young University, 1976.

Ware, Keith N. *A History of the Emery County Farmers Union Telephone Association.* Privately published, 1992.

Wilson, O. Meredith. *The Denver and Rio Grande Project, 1870–1901: A History of the First Thirty Years of the Denver and Rio Grande Railroad.* Salt Lake City: Howe Brothers, 1982.

Wright, Keith. *Greasewood Greens.* Clawson, Utah: Bessandy Publications, 1982.

Index